BARRON'S

HOW TO PREPARE FOR THE CBEST

CALIFORNIA BASIC EDUCATIONAL SKILLS TEST

Second Edition

Model Tests by
Decision Development Corporation
Concord, California

Coordinating Editor
Sharon Green

Former Member, English Department
Merritt College, California

BARRON'S EDUCATIONAL SERIES, INC.

Portions of this book from:
Barron's How to Prepare for the Graduate Record Examination by Samuel C. Brownstein and Mitchel Weiner
Barron's How to Prepare for the California High School Proficiency Examination by Sharon Green and Michael Siemon
Barron's How to Prepare for the Scholastic Aptitude Test by Samuel C. Brownstein and Mitchel Weiner
Barron's Guide to the New Law School Admission Test by Jerry Bobrow, Ph.D. and associates

Library of Congress Catalog Card No. 88-3419

International Standard Book No. 0-8120-3954-8

Library of Congress Cataloging-in-Publication Data

Barron's How to prepare for the CBEST, California basic educational skills test / model tests by Decision Development Corporation; coordinating editor, Sharon Green. — 2nd ed.
p. cm.
ISBN 0-8120-3954-8
1. California Basic Educational Skills Test—Study guides.
I. Green, Sharon. II. Decision Development Corporation.
III. Barron's Educational Series, inc. IV. Title: How to prepare for the CBEST, California basic educational skills test.
LB3060.23.C34B37 1988
370'.7'76—dc19 88-3419

PRINTED IN THE UNITED STATES OF AMERICA

890 100 987654321

CONTENTS

PREFACE

YOU CAN PREPARE YOURSELF FOR THE CBEST!

No matter how long it has been since your last algebra class, no matter how much you hate taking tests, you *can* equip yourself to handle the sorts of questions you will face on the California Basic Educational Skills Test (CBEST).

By going through the review materials and practice exercises in this book, you will refresh your memory of fundamental mathematical concepts and techniques; you will polish your reading and composition skills; and you will familiarize yourself with proven test-taking strategies that can help you on the CBEST and on tests in general.

This book is organized in four major parts:

INTRODUCTION: a brief description of the format of the examination, answers to commonly asked questions about the test, and test-taking hints.

DIAGNOSE YOUR WEAKNESSES: a brief Diagnostic Mini-Exam to give you an idea of what the CBEST covers and help you to measure your strengths and weaknesses.

CORRECT YOUR PROBLEMS: a review section to help you study for the exam and improve in those areas in which your skills are weak. It is divided into three sections:

Reading Skills Review: an analysis of the specific reading skills tested, including graph-reading techniques, with practice passages.

Mathematics Review: a concise but thorough review of the fundamentals of arithmetic, algebra, and geometry, plus basic formulas and practice exercises.

Writing Skills Review: a discussion of approaches to writing essays, plus a review of basic grammar and usage.

PRACTICE YOUR SKILLS: three full-length, complete model tests with answer keys and explanations.

Your success on the CBEST matters not only to you but also to the students you will teach. Students need professional, dedicated teachers who set high standards both for themselves and for their students. Live up to your potential. Make sure that you have mastered yesterday's skills; you will be sharing them with your students tomorrow.

CHAPTER **1**

INTRODUCTION

The California Basic Educational Skills Test (CBEST) provides an opportunity for future teachers to demonstrate their proficiency in three basic areas: reading, mathematics, and writing. Unless specifically exempted by the state legislature, applicants for a first teaching credential or a service credential must pass the CBEST.

To pass the CBEST, applicants must get passing scores in all three areas, receiving a total score of at least 123 out of 240 possible points.

BASIC FORMAT AND SCORING OF THE CBEST

The composition of the sections of the CBEST may vary slightly, but the basic format is:

SECTION	NUMBER OF QUESTIONS	MINUTES
Reading Comprehension	Approximately 50	60
Mathematics	Approximately 50	65
	(A Short Break)	
Writing	2 Essays	60

Scaled scores on each section range from 20 to 80. To pass you must have a total combined score of 123 (all three sections) and a minimum of 37 on each section.

Scores are ranked as follows:

61–80 Superior
41–60 Passing
37–40 Borderline
20–36 Needs Work

ANSWERS TO SOME COMMONLY ASKED QUESTIONS

Who should take the CBEST?

The CBEST currently is required of applicants for a first teaching credential or a service credential. It is also required of applicants for a newly issued or renewed Emergency Credential. Some applicants are exempt from this requirement: consult the Commission on Teacher Credentialing, P.O. Box 944270, Sacramento, CA 94244-2700 [(916) 445-7254].

Is a passing score on the CBEST all I need for a California credential?

No. You still must meet any requirement of subject matter knowledge, professional training, and practice teaching or field work pertaining to your credential.

Do I need to pass the CBEST for admission to a student teaching program or to upper division status?

You may. Some universities have begun to require it. Consult your county credentials office or school of education.

Do I need to pass the CBEST to be employed by a California school district?

Again, you may. If you have not taught for 39 months before new employment, passing the CBEST may be a condition of employment. Check with the school district or county department of education where you are considering employment.

How do I register for the CBEST?

Pick up a CBEST information booklet at your county credential office, your school district's personnel office, or your campus school of education. If these offices are out of information booklets, write to the CBEST Program, Box 23260, Oakland, CA 94623-2326, or the State Department of Education. Fill out the registration form on the booklet, and send the form and your fee ($32 currently) to the CBEST Program at the Educational Testing Service (ETS) in Berkeley.

When is the test given?

At present, the CBEST is given on five Saturday mornings a year. Exact dates vary; consult the CBEST Program (Box 23260, Oakland, CA 94623-2326, [415] 654-1200).

What if I cannot take the test on a Saturday?

You may ask for a special test administration. When you send in your registration form, include with it a letter from your minister or rabbi (on official stationery) that states that you belong to a recognized religious group that observes its Sabbath on Saturday. You will be notified of the date and test center separately. To qualify for special test administration, *you must get in your complete registration packet (form, letter, and fee) to ETS by the deadline for regular registration.*

Where is the test given?

Currently the CBEST is administered at approximately sixty test centers throughout the state. Center locations are listed in the information booklet. If you have a handicap that prevents you from taking the test without special arrangements, or if you would have to travel more than 150 miles within California to reach a CBEST test center, ETS may be able to help. [(415) 654-1200].

What should I bring to the test center?

Bring your admission ticket, personal identification containing both your photograph and signature (a California driver's license will do; so will a passport), several No. 2 pencils (soft lead), a good eraser, a couple of ballpoint pens, and a watch so that you can pace yourself during the exam. (No time announcements will be made during the writing section.) *Don't* bring scratch papers, calculators, books, or rulers: they are not allowed in the testing room.

What does the test cover?

The CBEST covers the three basic skills of reading, mathematics, and writing. The exam includes three separate tests: a 65-minute multiple-choice test consisting of reading and vocabulary questions; a 70-minute multiple-choice test consisting of mathematics questions; and a 60-minute essay test containing two essay topics. One topic calls for you to analyze a statement or situation; the other calls for you to discuss a personal experience. You must write on both topics.

What score must I get to pass?

The total score required for passing the CBEST (the sum of your reading, mathematics, and writing scores) is 123. No section score can be lower than 37 to pass.

To whom will my CBEST score be sent?

Your CBEST score is sent to you, and to you alone. ETS will release your scores to California colleges and universities only if you request them to do so on your registration form.

May I take the test more than once?

Yes. If you do not pass the CBEST, you may retake the exam as many times as you choose. You do not have to repeat those sections you have passed. However, you still must pay the $32 registration fee. If you are retaking the exam, you must use the special reregistration form that comes with your original score report.

Is it possible to cancel my CBEST score?

Yes, but there's not much point in doing so: you will be the only one to receive your score, whatever it is. If you do decide to cancel, however, act immediately: notify the test supervisor that you wish to cancel *before* you leave the test center.

Should I guess on the test?

Definitely! There is no guessing penalty on the CBEST, so by all means guess. Try to eliminate any answers that seem obviously wrong before you fill in your answer: you'll have a better chance of coming up with the right answer that way.

May I write on the test?

Again, yes. Use the test booklet for any scratch work and computations you have to do. Also, make marks in your test booklet to indicate questions that you want to skip for now and come back to later. Be careful, however, to keep your answer sheet free of unnecessary marks. Fill in your personal data as requested and fill in your answers; that's all.

Can I prepare for the CBEST?

Yes. Subject matter review in arithmetic, algebra, and geometry will be of inestimable help to you. So will going over basic test-taking tips. Familiarize yourself with the sorts of problems you are likely to encounter on the test. To prepare yourself thoroughly, work through this book and practice the techniques and strategies illustrated in each section.

SOME HINTS ON TAKING THE TEST

The One-Check, Two-Check System

Many people score lower than they should on the CBEST simply because they do not get to many of the easier problems. They puzzle over difficult questions and use up the time that could be spent answering easy ones. In fact, the difficult questions are worth exactly the same as the easy ones, so it makes sense not to do the hard problems until you have answered all the easy ones.

To maximize your correct answers by focusing on the easier problems, use the following system:

- Work through the whole section, answering only the easy questions (those that you are able to answer in 30–40 seconds). If you run across a problem that is too difficult or time-consuming, mark it on your answer sheet with one check (√). If you run across a problem that you can't even *begin* to solve, put two checks next to it (√√). (You may wish to take a guess now.)
- After you have answered all the easy questions in any one section, go back and try your one-check problems, solving as many of them as you can during your remaining time.
- If you finish your one-check problems and still have time remaining, go back and try the two-check problems. In many cases you will find yourself able to solve some of these problems, which looked so impossible at first.
- Finally, a few minutes before time is called, *erase the check marks from your answer sheet* and guess an answer to each unsolved question. There is no penalty for guessing on the CBEST.

You should use this system as you work through the practice tests in this book; such practice will allow you to make "one-check, two-check" judgments quickly when you actually take the CBEST. As our extensive research has shown, use of this system results in less wasted time on the CBEST.

The Elimination Strategy

Faced with four or five answer choices, you will work more efficiently and effectively if you *eliminate unreasonable or irrelevant answers immediately*. In most cases, two or three choices in every set will stand out as obviously incorrect. Many test takers don't perceive this because they painstakingly analyze every choice, even the obviously ridiculous ones.

The wise test taker, aware that most answer choices can be easily eliminated, does so without complicating the process by considering unreasonable possibilities.

To summarize the elimination strategy:

- Look for unreasonable or incorrect answer choices first. Expect to find at least two or three of these with every problem.
- When a choice seems wrong, cross it out in your test booklet *immediately*, so that you will not be tempted to reconsider it.

Eliminating choices in this fashion will lead you to correct answers more quickly, and will increase your overall confidence.

Marking in the Test Booklet

Many test takers don't take full advantage of opportunities to mark key words and draw diagrams in the test booklet. Remember that, in the reading comprehension section, *marking key words and phrases will significantly increase your comprehension and lead you to a correct answer.* Marking also helps to keep you focused and alert.

Further, more specific hints about marking are given in the introductory chapters that follow. The important general point to stress here is that active, successful test taking entails marking and drawing, and that passive, weak test takers make little use of this technique.

The "Multiple-Multiple-Choice" Item

You are sure to encounter a number of test problems that contain two sets of multiple choices. Here is an example:

According to the theory of aerodynamics, the bumblebee should be unable to fly. But it flies anyway.

Which of the following can be logically inferred from the above statement? Ⓐ Ⓑ Ⓒ Ⓓ Ⓔ

I. The bumblebee's behavior contradicts scientific theory.
II. The bumblebee is not really able to fly.
III. Some theories don't hold true in all cases.

(A) I only (B) II only (C) I and II (D) I, II, and III (E) I and III

When faced with a problem of this structure, begin by considering the Roman numeral choices. Label each as "TRUE" or "FALSE" (or "yes/no" or "correct/incorrect"), and eliminate final answer choices accordingly.

With the above problem, you should proceed as follows:

Statement I: TRUE—Eliminate (B) because it does not contain I.
Statement II: FALSE—Eliminate (C) and (D) because they do contain II.
Statement III: TRUE—Eliminate (A), and choose (E).

HOW TO USE THIS BOOK EFFECTIVELY

Take the Diagnostic Mini-Exam

In the following chapter you will find a CBEST diagnostic mini-exam. Your results on this mini-test will indicate the sorts of problems which you need to practice. Some of them you may already recognize as troublesome to you. You will become aware of others as you work through the mini-test. This book thoroughly reviews the basic educational skills covered by the CBEST. Your results on this mini-test will pinpoint which parts of the book demand the most attention from you.

Study the Appropriate Chapters

You will discover that Chapter 3 includes worthwhile advice on how to go about answering the sorts of reading questions you will find on the CBEST (literal, logical, and critical comprehension questions, including questions based on charts or graphs). Chapter 4 is devoted to a comprehensive review of the mathematical skills you need to do well on the CBEST. Chapter 5 contains a handy outline of the elements of grammar, as well as guidelines for writing the essays on the test. The remainder of the book provides you with practice answering simulated CBEST questions. Three model tests comparable to the actual CBEST in format, number of questions, level of difficulty, and time allowed are provided.

Take the Model Tests

Each model test includes 50 reading comprehension questions, 50 quantitative questions, and 2 essay topics. You will probably find that the actual CBEST follows this pattern.

Use the model tests in this book as a means of confirming your strengths and diagnosing your weaknesses. Correct answers and thorough explanations follow each model test: use them as you continue your analysis of your skills.

Follow this pattern. First, take the diagnostic mini-exam and pinpoint your weak areas. Concentrate on these weak areas during your general review (Chapters 3-5). Then take each model test in turn, being sure to analyze your results and review newly revealed weak spots before you go on to the next model test. If you follow this study plan assiduously, you will be able to face the CBEST with confidence.

ANSWER SHEET— A DIAGNOSTIC MINI-EXAM

Reading

1. Ⓐ Ⓑ Ⓒ Ⓓ Ⓔ	6. Ⓐ Ⓑ Ⓒ Ⓓ Ⓔ	11. Ⓐ Ⓑ Ⓒ Ⓓ Ⓔ
2. Ⓐ Ⓑ Ⓒ Ⓓ Ⓔ	7. Ⓐ Ⓑ Ⓒ Ⓓ Ⓔ	12. Ⓐ Ⓑ Ⓒ Ⓓ Ⓔ
3. Ⓐ Ⓑ Ⓒ Ⓓ Ⓔ	8. Ⓐ Ⓑ Ⓒ Ⓓ Ⓔ	13. Ⓐ Ⓑ Ⓒ Ⓓ Ⓔ
4. Ⓐ Ⓑ Ⓒ Ⓓ Ⓔ	9. Ⓐ Ⓑ Ⓒ Ⓓ Ⓔ	14. Ⓐ Ⓑ Ⓒ Ⓓ Ⓔ
5. Ⓐ Ⓑ Ⓒ Ⓓ Ⓔ	10. Ⓐ Ⓑ Ⓒ Ⓓ Ⓔ	15. Ⓐ Ⓑ Ⓒ Ⓓ Ⓔ

Mathematics

1. Ⓐ Ⓑ Ⓒ Ⓓ Ⓔ	6. Ⓐ Ⓑ Ⓒ Ⓓ Ⓔ	11. Ⓐ Ⓑ Ⓒ Ⓓ Ⓔ
2. Ⓐ Ⓑ Ⓒ Ⓓ Ⓔ	7. Ⓐ Ⓑ Ⓒ Ⓓ Ⓔ	12. Ⓐ Ⓑ Ⓒ Ⓓ Ⓔ
3. Ⓐ Ⓑ Ⓒ Ⓓ Ⓔ	8. Ⓐ Ⓑ Ⓒ Ⓓ Ⓔ	13. Ⓐ Ⓑ Ⓒ Ⓓ Ⓔ
4. Ⓐ Ⓑ Ⓒ Ⓓ Ⓔ	9. Ⓐ Ⓑ Ⓒ Ⓓ Ⓔ	14. Ⓐ Ⓑ Ⓒ Ⓓ Ⓔ
5. Ⓐ Ⓑ Ⓒ Ⓓ Ⓔ	10. Ⓐ Ⓑ Ⓒ Ⓓ Ⓔ	15. Ⓐ Ⓑ Ⓒ Ⓓ Ⓔ

CHAPTER 2

A DIAGNOSTIC MINI-EXAM

This chapter contains a short version of a typical CBEST. Take the test and then check your answers in the Answer Key. Give yourself one point for each correct answer. Then use the Analysis of Errors table to help you determine the areas in which you scored low and are weak so that you may concentrate your studies on this material.

THE DIAGNOSTIC TEST

This test, like the CBEST, is divided into three sections: Reading, Mathematics, and Writing. Allow yourself 100 minutes for the entire test.

Reading

In this mini-test you may spend up to 20 minutes on this section.

Directions: Each passage in this test is followed by a question or questions about its content. Select the best answer to each question from among the five choices given. Answer all questions on the basis of what is stated or implied in the passage.

Questions 1–2

The new tax law supplies some important incentives for saving. Whether you are an inveterate saver or one who has never been able to keep over $1,000 in the bank at one time, it is advisable to investigate some of these incentives for saving. One category of incentives includes tax-exempt "All-Savers" certificates; a second category consists of tax-deferred retirement accounts, the provisions for which are very generous.

1. Saving incentives are, according to the author,

(A) only appropriate for a certain class of savers.
(B) available only to someone with more than $1000 in the bank.
(C) categorized according to financial advantage.
(D) all tax-exempt.
(E) important to know about.

2. The word "inveterate," as used in this selection, means

(A) infrequent.
(B) habitual.
(C) haphazard.
(D) prominent.
(E) impoverished.

Questions 3–5

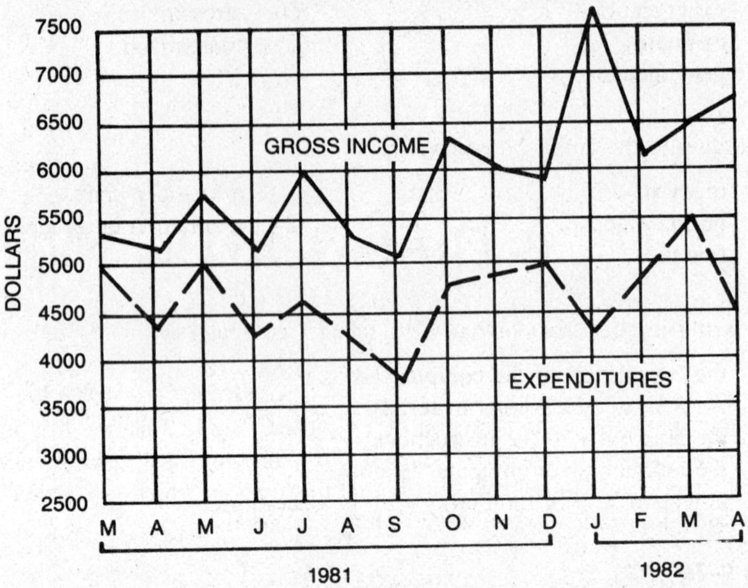

The graph represents the gross income and expenditures for a small business for each month of one year. Refer to the graph to answer the questions.

3. The graph shows that the greatest net profits for this business were in

(A) March 1981.
(B) April 1981.
(C) January 1982.
(D) August 1982.
(E) January 1981.

4. From this graph, one may conclude that

(A) there is a direct relation between income and expenditures.
(B) this business has been successful for each month shown.
(C) profits must be increased if the business is to survive.
(D) the summer months are usually best for this business.
(E) 1981 was a better year than thus far in 1982.

5. If the owner of this business used the year shown as an indication of its health, he could conclude that

(A) the "ups" are outweighed by the "downs".
(B) he is spending too much on new goods.
(C) the losses it is showing for some months must be eliminated.
(D) it is showing a healthy trend.
(E) there is little hope of the business surviving.

Questions 6–8

Fear is by no means the only obstacle to learning the language of computers. The language used by humans is replete with vagueness. Not a sentence uttered can be considered to be free from some degree of ambiguity. Computers, on the other hand, require a precision of expression or exactness that is extremely rare in ordinary language. The use of language in normal discourse assumes some shared experiences, and we take for granted that a listener has some common sense. The computer, unfortunately, has not shared our experiences, and it has absolutely no common sense.

6. The writer makes his point by use of

(A) exaggeration.
(B) examples.
(C) generalization.
(D) sarcasm.
(E) comparison.

7. According to the author, a computer has

(A) many flaws.
(B) no intelligence.
(C) few uses.
(D) a memory bank.
(E) a common language.

8. The writer implies that one barrier to using a computer is

(A) the complexity of the equipment.
(B) the lack of educational materials.
(C) the ambiguity of the instructions.
(D) the uniqueness of computer language.
(E) a general lack of familiarity with its operations.

Questions 9–10

Young children have mastered language through a complex process of trial and error. In fact, they have had to be wrong many times in order to learn the right responses. More importantly, they are not usually penalized for being wrong when learning to use oral language. This atmosphere, which was pervasive in their homes, should be carried over to the classroom. Teachers should do the following: emphasize questions that have more than one correct answer; reinforce attempts to find an answer by crediting any part that is right; solicit reasons for responses that are incorrect; allow students to see that their teacher can be wrong or that teachers don't always know the answer. Let them prove the teacher wrong or find the information needed to resolve an issue.

9. The author compares learning in the classroom to

(A) a very complex process of questioning.
(B) learning to speak.
(C) the attempt to solve problems.
(D) taking a risk in life.
(E) trying to respond to questions without answers.

10. It is possible to conclude that the author would agree that

(A) classroom teachers do not ask enough questions.
(B) children should not be taught at home.
(C) the teacher must serve as a model for students by having the content well in hand.
(D) the opportunity to make mistakes is essential to learning.
(E) the way children learn oral language cannot be adopted in the classroom.

Questions 11–13

Latin, with its fossilized beauties, unfolds a wealth of meaning that lazy, linear English, worn smooth of almost all grammatical inflections, tends to gloss over

11. One can conclude from the passage that

(A) Latin is a more difficult language than English.
(B) English is distorted by lazy writers.
(C) English has changed more than Latin.
(D) Latin has more inflections than English.
(E) more and deeper meaning is conveyed by English.

12. Latin's "fossilized beauties" are

(A) former beauty queens.
(B) archaic grammatical elements.
(C) old coins.
(D) words that are obsolete.
(E) ancient ruins.

13. The author's main point is that

(A) English has lost many grammatical features that add to the depth of meaning in Latin.
(B) Latin is no longer a spoken language anywhere in the world.
(C) many people who speak English make grammatical errors.
(D) English is linear, and Latin is indirect.
(E) if Latin were spoken today, fewer communication problems would arise.

Questions 14–15

In contrast with the country's centers of population, the Pacific slope of its isthmus to the west of the interoceanic route presents a linguistic picture with relatively few complicating factors. The population, although sparse, has been stable, and non-Hispanic influences on its speech have not been significant until recent times, when communication with the larger cities of the country has affected the dialogue.

14. The author's main point is that

(A) the geography of this part of the country isolated the inhabitants.
(B) the language of city-dwellers is subject to a wider range of influences.
(C) the language of populations which are not stable reflects a variety of influences from other languages.
(D) the language of this section of the country has not been affected by many external factors.
(E) population shifts produce drastic changes in language and produce dialects.

15. This paragraph was probably taken from

(A) a selection describing linguistic factors which inhibit communication.
(B) an essay on the influences of geography on linguistic development.
(C) a paper describing the dialects of a specific Spanish-speaking country.
(D) a report on the difficulty of carrying out improvement projects in countries where language barriers exist.
(E) an encyclopedia article detailing the geography and linguistic history of a country.

Mathematics

In this mini-test you may spend up to 20 minutes on this section.

Directions: Select the best answer to each of the following questions. Any figures provided are there as reference; they are approximations and are not drawn to scale except when stated.

You may refer to the following information during this section of the test.

$=$ is equal to	$\sqrt{\ }$ square root of
$\neq$ is unequal to	$^\circ$ degrees
$<$ is less than	$\parallel$ is parallel to
$>$ is greater than	$\perp$ is perpendicular to
$\leq$ is less than or equal to	π pi, approximately 3.14
$\geq$ is greater than or equal to	

Circle: Radius $= r$; Circumference $= 2\pi r$; Area $= \pi r^2$; a circle contains 360°

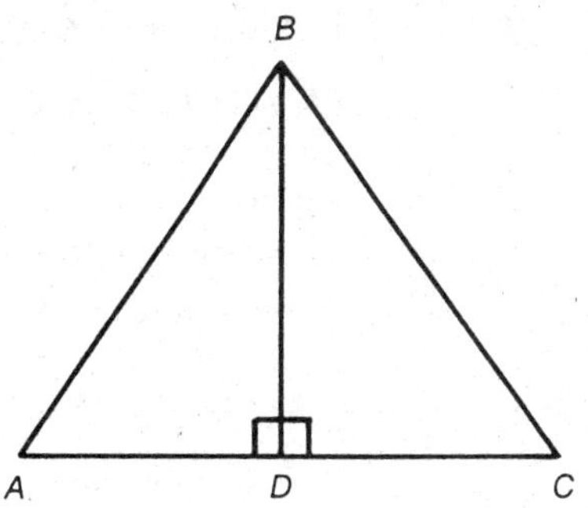

Triangle: In triangle ABC, if $\angle BDA$ is a right angle,

Area of $\triangle ABC = \dfrac{AC \times BD}{2}$;

Perimeter of $\triangle ABC = AB + BC + CA$

Sum of the measures of the degrees of the angles is 180.

Rectangle: Area $= L \times W$; Perimeter $= 2 \times (L + W)$

1. What is the value of $\dfrac{6a^2b^3}{18}$ when $a = 3$ and $b = 2$?

(A) 12
(B) 17⅓
(C) 1
(D) 24
(E) 36

2. A block of wood is 5 inches × 10 inches × 15 inches. What is the *surface area* of the block? (Refer to the diagram.)

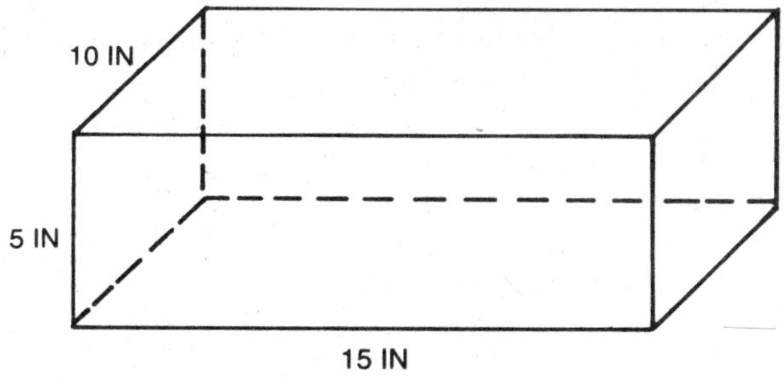

(A) 750 square inches
(B) 750 cubic inches
(C) 550 square inches
(D) 75 square inches
(E) Not enough information given

3. A recipe for 6 servings of potato soup calls for 3-cups of milk. How many cups of milk should be used to make 15 servings of soup?

(A) 7½ cups
(B) 9 cups
(C) 13 cups
(D) 14 cups
(E) 30 cups

4. Which of the following expressions is equal to $\dfrac{x}{x + 1/x}$?

(A) $\dfrac{x}{x + 1}$

(B) $1 + x^2$

(C) $\dfrac{1}{1 + x^2}$

(D) $\dfrac{x^2}{x^2 + 1}$

(E) None of the above

5. If 5 is added to the triple of a number, the result is 80. What is the number?

(A) 30
(B) 25
(C) 13
(D) 28
(E) None of the above

6. The perimeter of a square is 20 centimeters. What is the area of the square?

(A) 40 square centimeters
(B) 20 square centimeters
(C) 16 square centimeters
(D) 10 square centimeters
(E) 25 square centimeters

7. A truck can carry a load weighing $\frac{3}{4}$ of a ton. How many trips must the truck make to deliver $1\frac{15}{16}$ tons of gravel?

(A) 3
(B) 4
(C) $2\frac{7}{12}$
(D) $1\frac{3}{16}$
(E) $3\frac{7}{8}$

8. Sharon worked a total of 40 hours one week at two jobs. One job paid her $4.50 per hour and the other $5.00 per hour. She made $189.00. How many hours did Sharon work at the job with the lower hourly wage?

(A) 22 hours
(B) 20 hours
(C) 18 hours
(D) 15 hours
(E) Cannot be determined

9. Put the following numbers in order from smallest to largest:

$$.6,\ \frac{57}{100},\ .625,\ \frac{4}{7}$$

(A) $\frac{57}{100}$, .6, .625, $\frac{4}{7}$
(B) .625, .6, $\frac{57}{100}$, $\frac{4}{7}$
(C) $\frac{57}{100}$, .6, $\frac{4}{7}$, .625
(D) $\frac{57}{100}$, $\frac{4}{7}$, .6, .625
(E) $\frac{4}{7}$, $\frac{57}{100}$, .6, .625

10. Ron has 58 cents in his pocket in dimes, nickels, and pennies. If he has a total of 11 coins, how many nickels does he have?

(A) 1
(B) 3
(C) Either 1 or 3
(D) 5
(E) 10

11. How many square meters of pasture does a goat have for grazing if he is tied to a stake by a 10-meter rope?

(A) 100π square meters
(B) 100 square meters
(C) 20π square meters
(D) 50π square meters
(E) None of the above

12. In a bicycle shop the number of 10-speed bicycles is 25 more than twice the number of 3-speed bicycles. Which number sentence is a correct expression of this information? (Note: x denotes 10-speed bicycles and y denotes 3-speed bicycles.)

(A) $2x = y + 25$
(B) $2x + 25 = y$
(C) $2x - 25 = y$
(D) $x = 2y + 25$
(E) $x = 2(y + 25)$

Use the problem statement below to answer item 13.

> ***Problem:*** Robinson, Simpson, and Thornton are stamp collectors. Robinson's collection is worth $25,000, which is twice the value of Simpson's collection. Thornton's collection is worth three times the difference in the values of Robinson's and Simpson's collections. How much is Thornton's stamp collection worth? Answer: $75,000

13. Which statement best describes why the answer given for this problem is *not* reasonable?

(A) Simpson's collection is worth $50,000.
(B) $75,000 is 3 times the value of Robinson's collection, not 3 times the difference of Robinson's and Simpson's collections.
(C) $75,000 is not twice the value of Robinson's collection.
(D) Thornton's collection is worth $112,500.
(E) Because there is not enough information to answer the question.

Use the information given below to answer item 14.

> ***Statement:*** Mr. Hernandez has taught 7th grade for 9 years. His salary over these 9 years has averaged $23,400.

14. With only the information given, which of the following questions can be answered?

I. What was Mr. Hernandez's salary during his 1st year?
II. What was Mr. Hernandez's salary during his 5th year?
III. How much money has Mr. Hernandez earned during the past 9 years?

(A) I only
(B) II only
(C) III only
(D) I and II only
(E) I, II and III

Refer to graph below to answer item 15.

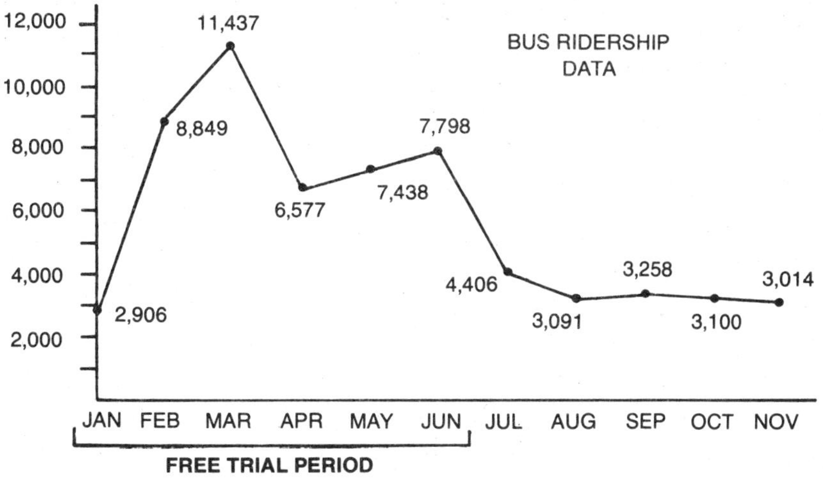

15. The graph shows the change in bus ridership in a small city during an eleven month period. The greatest percent decline in ridership in a one month period was from

(A) June to July
(B) March to April
(C) January to February
(D) July to August
(E) None of the above

Writing

Directions: You will have 60 minutes to write an essay on each of the following two topics. Try to spend approximately 30 minutes on each topic, as they are of equal value in the evaluation. While quantity is not as important as quality, the topics selected will probably require an essay rather than just a paragraph or two. Organization is an integral part of effective writing, so you may want to use some of the allotted time to plan your work. Support your ideas with clear, specific examples or explanations. Write legibly, and do not skip lines.

First Topic:

Much has been written about the effects of television on the present generation. Discuss the positive and negative effects you believe television has had on children.

Second Topic:

In a democracy, one of the greatest challenges is for people to work together to reach a decision. Describe an experience you have had, whether working on a committee, attending a town meeting, or planning a reunion, in which people were or were not able to work together to achieve their goal.

ANSWER KEY

Reading

1. E	**4.** B	**7.** B	**10.** D	**13.** A
2. B	**5.** D	**8.** D	**11.** D	**14.** D
3. C	**6.** E	**9.** B	**12.** B	**15.** C

Mathematics

1. D	**4.** D	**7.** A	**10.** D	**13.** B
2. C	**5.** B	**8.** A	**11.** A	**14.** C
3. A	**6.** E	**9.** D	**12.** D	**15.** A

ANALYSIS OF ERRORS

You now have completed your diagnostic mini-exam and checked your answers against the answer key, giving yourself one point for each correct answer. If you scored 12 or less on either the reading or the mathematics sections, you need to spend some time studying the review chapters in this book. In this diagnostic mini-exam, 11 correct answers to 15 questions approximates a *marginal* passing score; however, you want to enter the testing room knowing you can do better than just a borderline pass.

Go over the mini-exam answer explanations and correct any of your answers that are wrong.

If you scored better than 12 on both the reading and mathematics sections of the mini-test, see how you do on one of the lengthier model tests. (Remember, you *must* follow the time guidelines.)

If you scored 12 or below on either multiple-choice section, use the following chart to help you in your review. Find the question numbers that you got wrong and study the subject matter covered in those questions. Then do the sample exercises at the end of the appropriate review chapter.

SECTION	QUESTION NUMBERS	SUBJECT AREA
READING	1, 13, 14	Finding the Main Idea
	7, 9	Finding Specific Details
	8, 10, 11, 15	Finding Implications
	2, 12	Determining the Meaning of Strange Words
	6	Determining Special Techniques
	3, 4, 5	Interpreting Tables and Graphs
MATHEMATICS		
Arithmetic	9	Whole Numbers (IA)
	7, 9	Fractions (IB)
	9	Decimals (IC)
	15	Percentage (ID)
	14	Averages, Medians, Ranges and Modes (IG)
Algebra	1, 4, 8, 12	Algebraic Expressions (IIA)
	5, 12, 13	Verbal Problems (IIC)
	3	Ratio and Proportion (IIE)
Geometry	11	Circles (IIIF)
	2, 6, 11	Area, Perimeter, and Volume (IIIG)
	10	Trial and Error (see Answer Explanations)

ANSWER EXPLANATIONS

Reading

1. E The author suggests that saving incentives are worth investigating, regardless of one's financial status.

2. B In making the contrast between types of savers, the writer refers to the other type as those who are inconsistent about saving.

3. C The letters at the bottom represent the months from March 1981 to April 1982. Net profits are gross income (solid line) less expenditures (dashed line). The difference between income and expenditures was greatest for the month of January 1982.

4. B The graph shows that profits were greater than expenditures each month of the period shown.

5. D Since the business profits are good each month and generally increasing, it appears to be in good health.

6. E The writer compares computer language to the language of normal discourse or the language used by humans.

7. B The writer states that the computer has no common sense and implies that it cannot reason about vagueness or make assumptions and is, therefore, not intelligent.

8. D As the writer explains, computer language requires exactness and precision, unlike human language; as such, it is unique.

9. B The author describes the process of mastering language in the home; then, in lines 5 and 6, he relates this directly to effective teaching techniques.

10. D It is the author's main point that risk-taking behaviors are important in learning.

11. D Since the writer states that English is ''worn smooth'' of inflections, it can be concluded that Latin has more.

12. B Although the figurative expression, ''fossilized beauties,'' may be unclear in isolation, the later reference to ''grammatical inflections'' makes B the best answer.

13. A If the reader understands that Latin's ''fossilized beauties'' are grammatical elements that have been lost in English, then it will be clear that the writer means that they add to the depth of meaning in Latin. The author does not go so far as to imply, as in answer (E), that Latin would be a viable substitute as a spoken language.

14. D The author describes a geographical area where the language of the inhabitants has not been affected to any great extent by external factors.

15. C The passage is specific enough and includes references to other sections of the country so that one can conclude that it is presenting a linguistic picture of a Spanish-speaking country.

Mathematics

1. D $\frac{6a^2b^3}{18} = \frac{6 \cdot 3^2 \cdot 2^3}{18} = \frac{6 \cdot 9 \cdot 8}{18} = \frac{432}{18} = 24$

2. C *Surface area* refers to the combined areas of the 6 surfaces on the block of wood.

2 surfaces have area = 10×15 = 150 square inches
2 surfaces have area = 5×15 = 75 square inches
2 surfaces have area = 5×10 = 50 square inches
$(2 \times 150) + (2 \times 75) + (2 \times 50) = 550$ square inches

3. A $\frac{6 \text{ servings}}{3 \text{ cups milk}} = \frac{15 \text{ servings}}{x \text{ cups milk}}$

$6x = 45$
$x = 7\frac{1}{2}$ cups of milk

4. D $\dfrac{x}{x + 1/x} = \dfrac{x}{(x^2 + 1)/x}$

$\dfrac{x \cdot x}{x^2 + 1} = \dfrac{x^2}{x^2 + 1}$

5. B Let N represent the number.

$3 \cdot N + 5 = 80$

$3 \cdot N = 75$

$N = 25$

6. E Perimeter $= 4s$, so $20 = 4s$ and $s = 5$.
Area $= s^2$, so Area $= 5^2 = 25$ square centimeters.

7. A To find how many ¾ ton loads are in $1\frac{15}{16}$ tons, you divide $1\frac{15}{16}$ by ¾.
$1\frac{15}{16} \div \frac{3}{4} = \frac{31}{16} \div \frac{3}{4} = \frac{31}{16} \times \frac{4}{3} = \frac{31}{4} \times \frac{1}{3} = \frac{31}{12}$
$\frac{31}{12} = 2\frac{7}{12}$ loads. Consequently, it will require 3 trips to deliver the gravel.

8. A Let A = number of hours worked at \$4.50 per hour and
B = number of hours worked at \$5.00 per hour.

$A + B = 40$

and $\$4.50 \times A + \$5.00 \times B = \$189.00$

$B = 40 - A$

so $\$4.50A + \$5.00(40 - A) = \$189.00$

This equation simplifies to:

$\$4.50A + \$200.00 - \$5.00A = \$189.$

$\$4.50A - \$5A = \$189. - \$200.$

Thus $-\$.50A = -\$11.00$

so $A = 22$ hours

9. D The correct order is $\frac{57}{100}$, $\frac{4}{7}$, .6, .625.
(Note: $\frac{57}{100} = .570$, $\frac{4}{7}$ is approximately .571 and .6 = .600)

10. D By use of "educated" trial and error, it can be shown that there are 5 nickels, 3 dimes, and 3 pennies. Alternatively, the answer can be obtained by solving the equations:

$$D + N + P = 11$$
$$10D + 5N + P = 58$$

11. A The 10-meter rope allows the goat to graze over the area of a circle of radius 10 meters. The formula for the area of a circle is πr^2, where r is the radius. So, $\pi(10)^2 = 100\pi$ square meters is the area.

12. D Twice the number of 3-speed bicycles is $2y$. 25 more than $2y$ is $2y + 25$. So, x, the number of 10-speed bicycles, is $2y + 25$. $x = 2y + 25$.

13. B \$75,000 = 3 × \$25,000, not 3(\$25,000 − \$12,500), which is the correct expression to use.

14. C There is no way to determine Mr. Hernandez's salary for any particular year. However, since the average is the sum of each year's salary divided by the total number of years (i.e., \$23,400 = sum ÷ 9), the sum or total salary earned is found by multiplying 9 × \$23,400.

15. A The percent decline in ridership from June to July was 43.5% (7798 − 4406 = 3392 and $\frac{3392}{7798} \times 100\% = 43.5\%$).

Writing

The following essay and essay outline have been written to demonstrate a well-written answer and the planning of a well-written answer. Use these only as guidelines to evaluating your own writing and organization. Many different organization patterns and plans could work equally well for the topics given.

First Topic:

Much has been written about the effects of television on the present generation. Discuss the positive and negative effects you believe television has had on children.

Essay:

Newspapers and magazine articles, as well as professional journals, frequently report on studies which examine the effects of television on children. If we review these studies' findings, we begin to believe that we can prove whatever we wish: that television has contributed to the deterioration of students' spelling ability or that it has stimulated interest in reading or other classroom activities. Television is a medium which permits us to sit at dinner with a president and to experience visually many situations and places. At the same time, it makes only limited demands on our thinking ability. Television supplies even the laughter for situation comedies so shallow in plot that the purpose of the laugh track can only be to convince us that the program content is, in fact, humorous. A general review, then, of studies and commentaries on television's effects would demonstrate that both positive and negative effects exist.

It is, in fact, difficult to distinguish between the positive and negative effects of television viewing since any effect we identify as positive we can rather easily reinterpret as negative, or at least possessing negative side-effects. As an example, we might say that television helps to broaden experience, exposing children to situations and events to which they might not otherwise have access. By means of television, they experience the excitement of the Olympic games, as well as the horrors of the latest military confrontation in the world. They see parts of the world whose names and locations they have not yet learned in school. From television, they learn words, concepts, behaviors, and facts they wouldn't otherwise know. There is a drastic difference between what a child growing up in the 1940's knew and what the child of the 1980's knows. Certainly there is value in all of this. A child with a broader background of knowledge learns more and learns it faster. But how much of this knowledge is information we would rather children did not have? How much violence, injustice, and adult sexual behavior do children "experience" before they are ready to do so? The most common criticism of television viewing is that it does not allow children to remain children in knowledge.

Some advocates of television point out the higher-quality dramatic productions as stimuli to reading. The popular "Little House on the Prairie" series is often cited in this regard. Television producers have made some effort with certain quality productions to encourage children to "read all about it" by suggesting readings related to the topic of the program. On the other hand, some detractors suggest that these efforts are minimal, that television viewing merely absorbs time better spent in reading. They also suggest that reading which has been stimulated by a pre-digested television program is more shallow than independent reading and less open to individual thinking and interpretation.

The effects of television viewing—positive and negative—seem to revolve around one crucial problem. It is true that television allows us to see excellent productions of Shakespeare and to be present at a presidential inauguration, but television bombards us with such an array of experiences that we get little opportunity for any creative contemplation. Children move from one experience to another, often ones that they do not fully understand, without ever responding creatively or reacting to any of these experiences. It is a process of passive "viewing", not active "seeing", in which children participate. No ferment of ideas takes place. No implications are considered. No questions are posed. Children are exposed to an excess of experiences which are improperly digested.

It seems quite certain that television will remain part of our lives and that comments on television viewing and its effects will remain as well. For every positive effect that is cited, a negative value will be assigned by those who interpret it differently. Parents and teachers alike will share the responsibility of controlling the quantity of children's viewing and of helping children to assimilate what they view.

Second Topic:

In a democracy, one of the greatest challenges is for people to work together to reach a decision. Describe an experience you have had, whether working on a committee, attending a town meeting, or planning a reunion, in which people were or were not able to work together to achieve their goal.

Essay Outline:

A. Introduction
   1. Give background for the theme of the paper.
   2. Present thesis or main point of the paper.

B. Description of experience
   1. Context
   2. People involved
   3. Group goals and strategies

C. Explanation of problems or absence of problems
   1. Describe, in general, how your experience progressed.
   2. Give examples to support the description.

D. Summary and conclusions
   1. Restate your theme in brief terms.
   2. State conclusions you could draw from this experience, implications for viability of the democratic procedure, or recommendations.

CORRECT YOUR PROBLEMS

CHAPTER **3**

READING SKILLS REVIEW

The reading questions on the CBEST test your ability to

1. Find the main idea of a selection
2. Find specific details mentioned in the passage
3. Draw inferences or logical conclusions from a text
4. Determine the meaning of unfamiliar words from their context
5. Determine special techniques the author uses to achieve effects (methods of organizing a passage)
6. Interpret tables and graphs

You may have to apply ideas or information in a passage to situations that are not included in the passage or make generalizations on the basis of information in the passage.

You will have 65 minutes in which to answer 50 questions. You do not need any outside knowledge to answer these questions; you can choose the best answer simply by analyzing whatever is stated or implied in the particular passage or graph. The passages will vary in length from 200 words to just a sentence or two.

When you prepare for the test, read through the following review. Then work your way through the sample passages, taking time to study the answer explanations for approaches that might be new to you. In general, before tackling a particular passage, you may want to skim the questions to get a general sense of what is wanted. Then read the passage keeping those questions in mind. *Answer every question:* remember, the CBEST has no penalty for guessing.

REVIEW

This section provides material to study and review in preparation for the reading questions. Helpful hints and practical approaches to answering the questions are given.

Finding the Main Idea

Questions testing ability to find the main idea often take the following forms:

1. The title that best expresses the ideas of the passage is . . . .
2. The main idea of this selection may be best expressed as . . . .
3. Which of the following best states the theme of the passage?
4. This passage illustrates . . . .
5. The author's purpose in writing this passage is . . . .

Since a paragraph is defined as a group of sentences revolving about a central theme, any title that is appropriate must include the thought that each of the sentences of the paragraph is developing. It should not be too broad or too narrow in its scope; it should be specific and yet comprehensive enough to include all the essential ideas presented by the sentences.

> Note: A good title for a passage of two or more paragraphs should include the thoughts of *all* the paragraphs.

Very frequently, authors provide the reader with a sentence that expresses the main idea succinctly. Such *topic sentences* may appear anywhere in the paragraph, although we are accustomed to looking for them in the opening or closing sentences. However, in the kind of reading that you are expected to be able to handle, topic sentences are often implied rather than stated.

One Way to Identify the Main Idea

If you cannot identify a topic sentence, you can find the main idea in other ways. One way is to write a mental headline, as if to summarize the passage for the readers of a newspaper. A quick way to do this is:

1. Decide the person, place, or thing which is the subject of the reading passage. The subject can be something abstract, such as an idea. It can be a process, or something in motion, for which no single-word synonym exists. This *person, place, thing, idea,* or *process* then becomes the subject of the headline sentence.
2. Decide the most important thing that is being said about the subject. Either the subject must be *doing* something, or something is *being done* to it. This action becomes the verb of the mental headline.

Illustration I

The much-maligned profit motive may not be the only or even the most basic incitement for the development of trade in human societies. Very likely the enjoyment of variety accounts sufficiently for those early, unrecorded exchanges—one family's beans for another's squash, for instance, or a blue feather for a red one. In addition, the differences between human beings naturally caused one person to manufacture a better reed flute, another to be a superior discoverer of good scraping stones, a third to know, by an unselfconscious acuteness of observation that could almost be called instinct, where the choice berries and fruits were to be found. Trade encouraged each to become still more proficient in his or her specialty. So commerce has encouraged the development of skills and, over the long run, an ever-increasing quality of goods. Yet it may be questioned whether the human being is implicitly greedy, as might be supposed by a superficial study of economics. Many human needs have been filled by the exchange of goods we now call business.

A good title for this passage would be:

1 The Maligned Profit Motive
2 Trade—Society's Basic Need
3 Why Trade?
4 Reasons for Trade
5 Shallow Economic Theories

All of the above choices have something to do with the passage. A question which asks for a title, however, is asking you to select the *main* idea from several subsidiary ones. First, find the person, place, thing, idea, or process which is repeated throughout the passage. Are there any words in the second sentence which repeat something in the first sentence? *Exchanges* repeats the idea of *trade.* Go on to the third sentence. The idea of trade is not repeated in words. However, the three skills mentioned imply three products for trade. *Trade* occurs in the fourth sentence, *commerce* in the fifth, and *exchange of goods* and *business* in the last. The subject, then, must be something about trade, and the idea will include the most primitive forms of trade as well as modern business.

Now, look for the verb of the headline. What is trade *doing,* or what is *being done* to it? Look again for a repetition of ideas. The first sentence tells us that the causes of early trade were *more than* the profit motive, which must, then, be one cause. The second sentence gives us another cause of trade—the enjoyment of variety. Still another cause—superior products—is implied, though not stated, by the third and fourth sentences. The next sentence gives us some results of trade. Then, another possible cause—man's implicit greed—is doubted in the sixth sentence. The final sentence is a summation and a correction of a misconception—trade fills several needs.

The subject of our mental headline is *trade* and the predicate of the headline sentence is *has several causes* or *fills a variety of needs*. A number of headlines can be built on these ideas: TRADE IS PRODUCT OF HUMAN NEEDS, or SEVERAL HUMAN CHARACTERISTICS CAUSE TRADE, etc. Note that the last sentence of the passage is now clearly seen to be a topic sentence.

Which of the proposed titles fits the headline best? Choice 1 can be rejected for it is only one cause of trade. Choice 2 is not stated in the passage. Trade may be a basic need of society, but this passage does not say so. Choice 5 may be rejected for it is not part of the main idea as stated in the mental headline. We must choose between Choice 3 and Choice 4. Choice 3 can imply a decision to be made in the future or an argument against trade. Choice 4 is directed more toward the past, which accords better with the passage. The answer is Choice 4.

Another Way to Identify the Main Idea

Another way to find the main idea is mentally to order the ideas presented, deciding which are equal, which subordinate. We could also say that we weigh them, separating the heavy from the light. Using this approach with the same passage, we find: In the first two sentences, *profit motive* is equal to or possibly less than *enjoyment of variety*. *Superior products* (implied by the third sentence) are equal to the first two ideas because of the words *in addition*. Sentence 6 denies the importance of *greed*, despite appearances. It cannot be superior to the others. The final sentence refuses to place any of these motives first, so they must all be balanced in the statement of the main idea: *People have several motives for trade*. We then look for the title that most nearly reflects this balance of ideas, or ordering of importance.

Note: Some common words to indicate *equality* of elements:

again	another	first	moreover
also	as well as	furthermore	similar
and	besides	likewise	

For example:

Laxity of application is, *again*, one reason for . . .
The salubrious climate was *also* . . .
Promptness *and* neatness are requisites . . .
Another earth-renewing crop is . . .
A visit by the chief engineer *as well as* a government inspection sent shivers of apprehension . . .
Besides the delay in ratification, the committee . . .

Note: Some common words to point out elements of greater value:

above all	importance
deciding	significantly

For example:

The quick application of justice is, *above all*, the determining . . .
The *deciding* factor was to be found not in . . .
A technique of *importance* in the Impressionist movement . . .
Significantly, the bearer of this news . . .

Finding Specific Detail

In the development of ideas, a writer will make statements in support of his or her point of view or the message he or she is trying to convey. The questions most frequently found in reading tests merely require you to identify one of these statements, often expressed in different words. This kind of question may take one of these forms:

1. The author states that . . .
2. The writer mentions all of the items listed below EXCEPT . . .
3. Which of the following statements is correct, according to the reading passage?

Note: The answer to questions of specific detail must be in the passage. You must be able to find a word or sentence or group of sentences which justifies the choice. You must not call on information from other sources. You must not let yourself be hurried into making unfounded assumptions.

Example

In Illustration I above, the author states that
1 the profit motive is the cause of trade
2 differences between human beings cause envy
3 men sometimes work by instinct
4 people have generally become more skillful
5 studying economics leads to wrong ideas

Choice 1: Reject. The first sentence states that the profit motive is not the only cause of trade. This expression in the question—"is *the* cause"—does not allow for other causes. Choice 2: Reject. Differences between human beings may cause envy, but the passage does not say so. Choice 3: The passage says that one may work by a process that could *almost* be called instinct—but it is not. Reject. Choice 5: Only one kind of study—superficial—will lead to wrong ideas. "Eating leaves leads to death by poisoning"? Only a certain kind of leaf. Choice 4: The author states that "commerce has encouraged the development of skills." Skills do not develop alone, but in people, so people must be more skillful. The word *generally* allows for interruptions by war, natural disasters, etc.

Finding Implications and Drawing Inferences

This is a more difficult kind of question since you must draw forth an answer not stated in the text—a process which is open to many errors. You may not be able to find words or sentences which clearly support your choice, as is possible in questions which ask for identification of detail. Nevertheless, by grasping the author's ideas, you should be able to reject inferences which can *not* be made.

> Note: How to draw inferences:
> 1. *Reason*—If X is true, Y must also be true.
> 2. *Perceive Feelings*—If the author feels this way on one subject, he probably feels a certain way about another subject.
> 3. *Sense a Larger Structure*—This passage is part of an argument for a proposal, or part of a description, or part of a longer story.

A question which calls on the reader to make inferences could be stated in any of these ways:

1. The author probably feels that . . .
2. The passage is intended to . . .
3. It may be inferred from this passage that . . .
4. An inference which may *not* be made from this passage is . . .
5. The paragraph preceding this passage probably states that . . .

Example:

In Illustration I above, the author seems to be

1 defending business against accusations of greed
2 preparing for an indictment of business
3 skeptical of recorded history
4 proficient in his specialty
5 ashamed of his ignorance of economics

The author says that the profit motive has been *maligned.* He *questions* whether humans are greedy, which implies that someone has said that they are. This passage—a collection of various motives for business—may then be aimed at a defense against the accusation that there is only one motive for business—greed. However, we must be sure to consider all the choices. Choice 1 is possible. Choice 2 must then be wrong. There is no basis in the reading for Choices 3 and 4. Since he says that others have a superficial knowledge of economics, he must feel that he is in a position to judge. Therefore, Choice 5 is rejected. Choice 1 is the only possibility.

Illustration II

As for the great passenger trains of the United States, they ceased service and slowly, one by one, were shunted into oblivion. The Twentieth Century Limited, the Broadway Limited, and other luxury trains faded away, no longer to sing along the rails at 60 to 80 miles an hour, their whistles keening a mournful goodbye, which is now, alas, final. On the long runs that remain, passengers raise a complaint of old cars, poor service, and unwarranted expenditure of their time and money. By contrast, the long-distance traveller of today accepts without murmur ear-splitting jet noise, long, irritating hold-ups between airport and city, and, in air terminals, jostling, shoving, and seatless milling about. A roomier, more relaxed and elegant means of transit has become only a memory.

In reference to the disappearance of long-run passenger trains, this writer feels

1 regret
2 gratification
3 grief
4 joy
5 anger

The author comments *alas* on the final goodbye of luxury trains. The last sentence also praises train travel in contrast to air travel. So Choices 2 and 4 are wrong. We are left with 1, 3, and 5. There is no expression of *anger,* and *grief* is too strong. He is sorry, not stricken with grief. Choice 1 is the answer.

In perceiving feelings, pay close attention to adjectives and words that imply a metaphor—such as *great* and *sing,* which indicate approval, and *earsplitting, irritating,* and *seatless* which indicate disapproval.

The paragraph which preceded this may have

1 discussed the Twentieth Century Limited
2 described some kind of U.S. travel
3 praised air travel
4 found fault with train travel
5 compared punctuality of commuter trains.

The words *as for* indicate that the great passenger trains must be mentioned at the risk of leaving a larger subject incomplete. Choice 1 is more specific than the subject *passenger trains.* It is unlikely to be the larger, more general subject. Choice 3 and Choice 4 would contradict the passage. *As for* indicates a continuation of a subject, not a contradiction. Choice 5 is unlikely, for it is a current concern. Most writers follow chronological order unless there is good reason to forgo it. This subject, then, would usually follow this paragraph about the recent past, not precede it. Furthermore, punctuality has not been mentioned. Choice 2 is better than any other.

Determining the Meaning of Strange Words

When a question in the reading part of an examination asks for the meaning of a word, it can usually be deduced from the context. The purpose of this kind of question is to determine how well the student can extract meaning from the text, not how extensive his general vocabulary is.

> *Note:* Sometimes the unknown word is common but used in one of its special or technical meanings.

For example:

He *threw* the pot in an hour. The wheel turned busily and the shape grew quickly under his forming fingers. (*Throw* here means to shape on a potter's wheel.)

> *Note:* At other times, the unknown word may bear a deceptive resemblance to a known word.

For example:

He fell *insensible* to the ground. (He was unconscious. He did not fall foolish or without common sense to the ground.)

> *Note:* Sometimes a word may be completely new. Punctuation and surrounding words can form clues.

For example:

Japanese do not talk comfortably or freely about the *burakumin*, the social outcasts. (Burakumin = social outcasts.)

> *Note:* Do not assume that you know the meaning if you know *one* meaning of a word. The student must find the meaning of that word *as used* in that passage. He must look within the reading for clues. Often the thought is repeated in the same sentence or near it.

Illustration III

He laughed and shrugged. "I have no choice," he said. "I must bow to the *ineluctable*."

The word *ineluctable* is closest to

1 impermissible
2 unavoidable
3 unknown
4 terror
5 evil

If a person has *no choice,* he probably wants to avoid something, but it is *unavoidable.* This does not necessarily mean that he does not permit it, or does not know it. *Terror* and *evil* are not implied. The ineluctable could be an unwanted dessert thrust on a guest by an implacable hostess.

> *Note:* Sometimes the opposite of the meaning is given somewhere in the passage:

Illustration IV

Conventional Japanese artists use methods of painting on paper with stone pigments which they learned from visits to China. These are the traditional paintings Westerners often think of or refer to as drawings—though they are not drawings. Conversely, a Japanese painter who works in Western style—painting abstractions, for instance—is seldom a *draftsman.*

Drafters are

1 conventional artists
2 non-Japanese
3 abstract
4 artists who draw
5 schooled

The word *conversely* tells us that a contrast is being presented. One thing is unlike another, and we may find that they are opposites. The contrast is between Japanese artists who work in Western style and Japanese artists who work in a traditional style (in *their* tradition). Those who work in Western style are not often draftsmen, but, it is implied, those who work in traditional style are draftsmen. What, then, is characteristic of the traditional style and is not evident in the Western style? It could be the use of stone pigments, or the fact that the method was learned from the Chinese, or the fact that these works appear to be drawings. If artists can use paint to appear like drawings, they must also be able to draw with drawing materials. None of the other possibilities is among the choices given. Only Choice 4 relates to the passage.

Note: Sometimes the meaning of a word can be tracked by following pronoun referents.

Illustration V

In his strong Scottish burr, he said that he liked a room without *gewgaws* and tin-plate souvenirs from an otherwise unmemorable event. He complained that *these* things tried to appear valuable, but nevertheless were worthless.

A *gewgaw* is
1 something from Scotland
2 a World's Fair souvenir
3 a showy trifle
4 a little statue
5 pillows

Look back in the text for the meaning of *these*. We find *these things* are *gewgaws* and *souvenirs*, so both are described as worthless, but seemingly valuable. A *gewgaw*, then, must be a showy trifle. It could be any one of the other things as well, but there is no evidence of what exactly it is.

Note: Sometimes the meaning of a word is given before it is used.

Illustration VI

During the 1974 spring labor offensive, 6,000,000 members of labor unions, either local or national, worked together to organize the most efficient strikes ever reported in the nation. The consequent wage increases, ranging from 10 per cent to 50 per cent, added to inflationary pressures. Because of the uncertain economy, this year's *shunto* was timid and subdued, and the resulting wage increases much less.

The word *shunto* is closest to
1 replacement
2 wage increase
3 labor union
4 yearly push to better wages
5 inflationary pressure

The *shunto* of this year is being compared with that of a previous year. When we look at the only previous year given—1974—we find that what also resulted in wage increases was the *spring labor offensive*, which organized *strikes*. The choices do not offer *strikes*, but Choice 4 is close to a spring labor offensive.

Note: Sometimes the entire selection describes a situation which is a definition of a word:

Illustration VII

The problem of *kaso* remains serious. Some villages have disappeared completely; others struggle with continually declining job opportunities. There are, officially, some one thousand such districts. One typical *kaso* town was Ohtaki, which has lost more than half its population in the last 15 years. Its few mines ceased operation several years ago. People continue to work on small farms, with some lumbering on the side. Most young people attend high schools in other towns, and some go on to college, but few come back to work. Ohtaki is beautifully situated in mountains on the edge of a large national park, offering hope of a tourist industry someday. But this kind of development takes time, and, meanwhile, Ohtaki dwindles, like so many others of its kind.

The problem of *kaso* is one of
1 decline of population in rural areas
2 poverty
3 poor farming
4 lack of educational opportunity
5 lack of a tourist industry

Choices 2 and 3 are not mentioned, and Choice 5 could solve the problem—so it is itself not the problem. Ohtaki is an example of *kaso*; therefore, the problem of *kaso* could be Choice 4 or Choice 1. However, educational opportunity is mentioned only once, while a decline of population is mentioned or implied three times. Choice 1 is best.

Determining Special Techniques Used by the Author

An alert reader expects to find certain techniques in certain kinds of writing. For instance:

In *literature*, writers often:
—create a mood
—present a setting
—describe a character
—narrate an event

In *social studies*, authors frequently:
—use dates to arrange events in sequential order
—point out cause and effect relationships
—make comparisons
—define terms
—propagandize, or reason deceptively

In *science*, writers often
—classify things and events
—try to solve problems
—define technical terms
—discuss experiments and their results

While the purpose of writing determines many of these techniques, no class of writing excludes techniques that may also be found in some other class. Literature offers examples of cause and effect relationships, and a social studies text may try to solve problems. However, the reader who quickly identifies the kind of writing before him expects certain techniques and may recognize them more quickly.

Note: Some common words indicating *cause and effect*:

accordingly	final	in short
as a result	hence	lastly
conclusion	in conclusion	therefore
		thus

For example:

The selection of a design was, *accordingly* . . .
As a result, the vote in Congress split . . .
The decision is of crucial importance and forces us to the *conclusion* that . . .
The *final* outcome of these endeavors . . .
Hence, in future conflicts, we believe . . .
Therefore, whatever his detractors may imagine, we know . . .
Thus, the development of the town followed the route of . . .

Note: Some common words signaling a *comparison* or *contrast*:

but	nevertheless	still
however	otherwise	yet

For example:

The philosophy of my youth was progressivism, *but* . . .
The study of law fell into disrepute . . . *however,* after a lapse of a decade . . .
Most laboratories use a process . . . . *Nevertheless,* the method under discussion . . .
If this point were strengthened, the defense of the Pacific would . . . *otherwise,* the exposure of the West Coast . . .
A common means of communication between members of Congress and . . . *yet* the efficacy . . .

Note: Some common ways to indicate a *change of direction* (a new thought, but not necessarily a comparison nor an effect):

although	instead of	oddly enough
despite	notwithstanding	regardless
in spite of		

For example:

Although the passage of the bill was widely acclaimed, its executive . . .
Despite a high volume of attendance, the quality of performance . . .
Instead of a gentle decline into senescence, the octogenarian . . .
The price rise, *notwithstanding,* was indicative of . . .
Oddly enough, the product was soon . . .

Note also:

Words calling attention to important ideas:

don't overlook
notice that
of significance is

Words announcing an illustration:

for example	in such cases	namely
for instance	in the same manner	specifically
in other words	just as	

Negative and all-inclusive words:

always	never
at all times	no
entirely	none
every	not
only	under all circumstances

Superlatives:

best	worst

Interpreting Tables and Graphs

You *must* know how to interpret tables and graphs to score well on the CBEST in English *and* mathematics. (A) Make sure to look at the *entire* table or graph. (B) Figure out what *units* the table or graph is using. Make sure to express your answer in the correct units. (C) If calculations are called for, look at the possible answers before calculating. Many questions call for only an approximate answer; it may be possible to round off, saving time and effort. (D) Don't confuse decimals and percentages. If the units are percentages, then an entry of .2 means .2%, which is equal to .002. (E) In inference questions, use *only* the information given.

A. Tables

EXAMPLE: (Refer to the table on page 30.)

1. What percent of the babies born in the U.S. in 1947 died before the age of 1 year?

(A) 3.22
(B) 4.7
(C) 26.7
(D) 32.2
(E) 47

To find a percentage, use the information given in the rate columns. The rate is given *per thousand*. In 1947 the rate was 32.2 per thousand which is $\frac{32.2}{1000}$ = .0322 or 3.22%. So the correct answer is (A). If you assumed incorrectly that the rate was per hundred, you would get the incorrect answer (D); if you looked in the wrong column you might get (B) or (E) as your answer.

2. Which state had the most infant deaths in 1940?

(A) California
(B) New Mexico
(C) New York
(D) Pennsylvania
(E) Texas

INFANT DEATHS (UNDER 1 YEAR OF AGE) AND RATES PER 1,000 LIVE BIRTHS, BY STATES: 1940 TO 1950

STATE	NUMBER OF INFANT DEATHS					RATE PER 1,000 LIVE BIRTHS				
	1940	1947	1948	1949	1950	1940	1947	1948	1949	1950
United States	110,984	119,173	113,169	111,531	103,825	47.0	32.2	32.0	31.3	29.2
Alabama	3,870	3,301	3,228	3,345	3,044	61.5	37.5	37.8	39.6	36.8
Arizona	983	973	1,083	1,034	953	85.5	50.8	56.4	51.0	45.8
Arkansas	1,810	1,445	1,363	1,539	1,209	47.0	29.5	28.4	33.7	26.5
California	4,403	7,233	6,885	6,574	6,115	39.2	29.4	28.6	26.8	25.0
Colorado	1,270	1,234	1,267	1,153	1,167	60.4	37.5	38.4	35.1	34.4
Connecticut	868	1,150	1,026	943	886	34.0	25.2	24.3	23.1	21.8
Delaware	217	239	214	224	235	47.7	31.0	29.5	30.4	30.7
District of Columbia	554	691	531	576	603	49.3	31.9	25.5	29.1	30.4
Florida	1,818	2,285	2,103	2,088	2,078	53.8	38.2	35.3	33.8	32.1
Georgia	3,744	3,251	3,169	3,101	3,064	57.8	34.2	34.2	33.3	33.5
Idaho	506	478	481	431	434	42.9	29.4	29.8	27.0	27.1
Illinois	4,398	5,672	5,123	5,195	4,868	35.3	28.9	27.7	27.4	25.6
Indiana	2,595	2,949	2,760	2,746	2,520	42.1	30.6	29.8	29.1	27.0
Iowa	1,636	1,817	1,610	1,591	1,555	36.5	28.5	26.6	25.7	24.8
Kansas	1,106	1,251	1,151	1,136	1,130	38.3	28.1	26.9	25.9	25.7
Kentucky	3,387	2,971	3,073	3,139	2,616	53.1	37.1	39.8	41.2	34.9
Louisiana	3,268	2,773	2,779	2,810	2,639	64.3	37.2	37.9	37.2	34.6
Maine	810	853	706	713	650	53.2	35.7	32.0	32.5	30.9
Maryland	1,590	1,794	1,537	1,636	1,465	49.1	31.6	28.8	30.5	27.0
Massachusetts	2,458	3,027	2,613	2,347	2,240	37.5	28.1	26.8	24.5	23.3
Michigan	4,032	5,080	4,639	4,545	4,230	40.7	31.5	30.0	28.9	26.3
Minnesota	1,758	2,165	1,959	1,893	1,889	33.2	28.6	26.9	25.6	25.1
Mississippi	2,869	2,448	2,474	2,631	2,385	54.4	36.8	37.9	39.6	36.7
Missouri	2,885	2,929	2,585	2,563	2,510	46.9	32.5	30.3	30.0	29.2
Montana	537	484	461	457	441	46.5	32.1	30.7	29.7	28.2
Nebraska	792	894	835	761	796	36.0	27.8	26.8	24.1	25.0
Nevada	109	134	147	118	139	51.7	33.2	39.8	32.1	37.9
New Hampshire	341	399	361	333	282	40.9	30.1	29.1	27.9	24.5
New Jersey	2,121	2,965	2,585	2,534	2,467	35.5	27.9	26.5	26.0	25.2
New Mexico	1,488	1,379	1,438	1,408	1,211	100.6	67.9	70.1	65.1	54.8
New York	7,297	9,123	8,258	7,878	7,429	37.2	28.2	27.3	26.1	24.7
North Carolina	4,631	3,938	3,858	4,113	3,674	57.6	34.9	35.3	38.1	34.5
North Dakota	593	523	487	517	453	45.1	30.6	29.4	30.7	26.6
Ohio	4,744	5,817	5,693	5,315	4,990	41.4	29.5	30.5	28.1	26.8
Oklahoma	2,238	1,733	1,731	1,531	1,514	49.9	32.3	34.4	30.8	30.2
Oregon	585	895	897	869	812	33.2	24.7	25.5	24.6	22.5
Pennsylvania	7,404	7,741	6,442	6,567	6,126	44.7	31.1	28.4	29.2	27.6
Rhode Island	410	522	444	395	450	37.9	28.2	26.3	24.0	27.8
South Carolina	3,042	2,352	2,331	2,283	2,220	68.2	39.5	40.4	39.0	38.6
South Dakota	466	511	525	448	473	38.7	30.9	32.0	26.0	26.6
Tennessee	2,954	3,144	3,098	3,331	2,961	53.5	36.3	37.7	40.2	36.4
Texas	8,675	8,161	9,131	8,628	7,630	68.3	41.1	46.2	42.7	37.4
Utah	539	545	568	535	503	40.4	25.1	27.4	25.3	23.7
Vermont	309	303	271	301	221	44.5	31.2	28.9	32.4	24.5
Virginia	3,335	3,142	3,163	3,162	2,836	58.5	36.6	38.5	38.1	34.6
Washington	992	1,643	1,537	1,530	1,522	35.2	28.1	27.5	27.1	27.3
West Virginia	2,269	2,091	2,108	2,082	1,822	53.7	38.0	40.2	39.6	36.1
Wisconsin	2,046	2,476	2,148	2,202	2,121	37.3	29.5	26.3	26.5	25.7
Wyoming	232	249	293	280	247	44.7	34.0	39.5	37.4	32.5

Source: Department of Health, Education, and Welfare, Public Health Service, National Office of Vital Statistics; annual report, *Vital Statistics of the United States.*

Source: Statistical Abstract of the U.S. 1957

Look in the numbers column under 1940. Only Texas had more than 8,000 in 1940, so the correct answer is (E). New Mexico had a *higher rate*, but the question asked for the *highest amount. Make sure you answer the question which is asked.*

3. Which of the following statements can be inferred from the table?

   I. In 1950 less than $\frac{1}{20}$ of the babies born in the U.S. died before the age of 1 year.
   II. The number of infant deaths in the U.S. decreased from 1945 to 1950.
   III. More than 5% of the infant deaths in the U.S. in 1950 occurred in California.
   IV. The number of infant deaths in North America in 1950 was less than 150,000.

   (A) I only
   (B) II only
   (C) I and III only
   (D) I, III, IV only
   (E) I, II, III, IV

Statement I can be inferred since $\frac{1}{20}$ of 1,000 = 50 which exceeds the rate per thousand of 29.2 in 1950.

Statement II can't be inferred since the table has no information about 1945. Infant deaths decreased between 1940 and 1950, but that doesn't mean they decreased between 1945 and 1950.

Statement III can be inferred from the table. The total number of infant deaths in 1950 was 103,825, and 6,115 occurred in California. A calculation of 6,115/103,825 could be made, but it is much quicker to find 5% of 103,825 which is 5,191. Since 6,115 is greater than 5,191, more than 5% of the infant deaths in the U.S. occurred in California.

Statement IV can't be inferred, because the table only gives information about the U.S. and there are other countries in North America.

So the correct answer is (C).

B. Circle Graphs

CIRCLE GRAPHS are used to show how various sectors share in the whole. Circle graphs are sometimes called pie charts. Circle graphs usually give the percentage that each sector receives.

EXAMPLE: (Refer to the graph on page 32.)

1. The amount spent on materials in 1960 was 120% of the amount spent on

   (A) research in 1960
   (B) compensation in 1960
   (C) advertising in 1970
   (D) materials in 1970
   (E) legal affairs in 1960

When using circle graphs to find ratios of various sectors, don't find the amounts each sector received and then the ratio of the amounts. Find the *ratio of the percentages,*

Expenditures of General Industries
By major categories

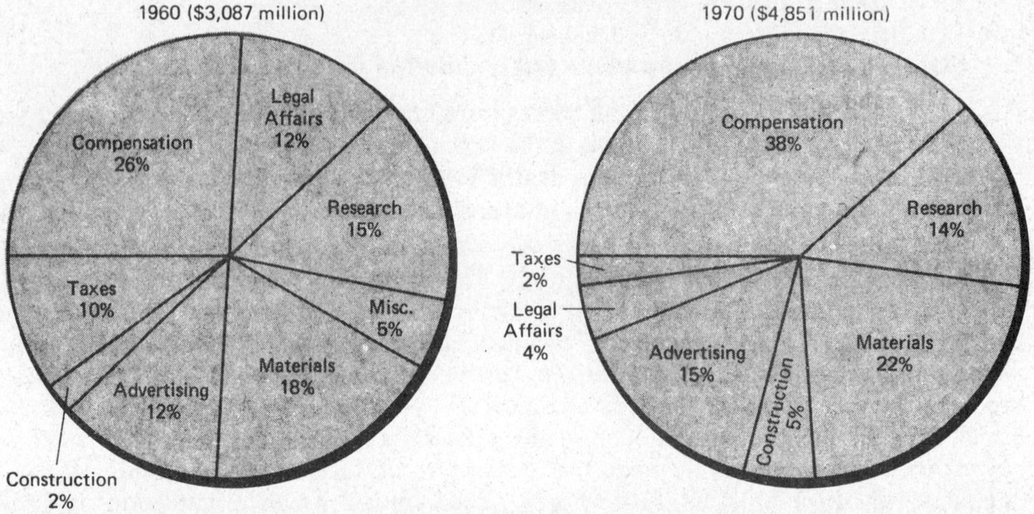

which is much quicker. In 1960, 18% of the expenditures were for materials. We want x where 120% of $x = 18\%$; so $x = 15\%$. Any category which received 15% of 1960 expenditures gives the correct answer, but only one of the five choices is correct. Here, the answer is (A) since research received 15% of the expenditure in 1960. Check the 1960 answers first since you need look only at the percentages, which can be done quickly. Notice that (C) is incorrect, since 15% of the expenditures for 1970 is different from 15% of the expenditures for 1960.

2. The fraction of the total expenditures for 1960 and 1970 spent on compensation was about

(A) $\frac{1}{5}$
(B) $\frac{1}{4}$
(C) $\frac{1}{3}$
(D) $\frac{3}{7}$
(E) $\frac{1}{2}$

In 1960, 26% of $3,087 million was spent on compensation and in 1970 compensation received 38% of $4,851 million. The total expenditures for 1960 and 1970 are $(3,087 + 4,851) million. So the exact answer is [(.26)(3,087) + (.38)(4,851)]/(3,087 + 4,851). Actually calculating the answer, you will waste a lot of time. Look at the answers and think for a second.

We are taking a weighted average of 26% and 38%. To find a weighted average, we multiply each value by a weight and divide by the total of all the weights. Here 26% is given a weight of 3,087 and 38% a weight of 4,851. The following general rule is often useful in average problems: The average or weighted average of a collection of values can *never* be:

(1) less than the smallest value in the collection, or
(2) greater than the largest value in the collection.

Therefore, the answer to the question must be greater than or equal to 26% and less than or equal to 38%.

Since $\frac{1}{5} = 20\%$ and $\frac{1}{4} = 25\%$, which are both less than 26%, neither (A) nor (B) can be the correct answer. Since $\frac{3}{7} = 42\frac{6}{7}\%$ and $\frac{1}{2} = 50\%$, which are both greater than 38%, neither (D) nor (E) can be correct. Therefore, by elimination (C) is the correct answer.

3. The amount spent in 1960 for materials, advertising, and taxes was about the same as

(A) $\frac{5}{4}$ of the amount spent for compensation in 1960
(B) the amount spent for compensation in 1970
(C) the amount spent on materials in 1970
(D) $\frac{5}{3}$ of the amount spent on advertising in 1970
(E) the amount spent on research and construction in 1970

First calculate the combined percentage for materials, advertising, and taxes in 1960. Since 18% + 12% + 10% = 40%, these three categories accounted for 40% of the expenditures in 1960. You can check the one answer which involves 1960 now. Since $\frac{5}{4}$ of 26% = 32.5%, (A) is incorrect. To check the answers which involve 1970, you must know the amount spent on the three categories above in 1960. 40% of 3,087 is 1234.8; so the amount spent on the three categories in 1960 was $1,234.8 million. You could calculate the amount spent in each of the possible answers, but there is a quicker way. Find the *approximate* percentage that 1,234.8 is of 4,851, and check this against the percentages of the answers. Since $\frac{12}{48} = \frac{1}{4}$, the amount for the 3 categories in 1960 is about 25% of the 1970 expenditures. Compensation received 38% of 1970 expenditures, so (B) is incorrect. Materials received 22%, and research and construction together received 19%; since advertising received 15%, $\frac{5}{3}$ of the amount for advertising yields 25%. So (D) is probably correct. You can check by calculating 22% of 4,851 which is 1,067.22, while 25% of 4,851 = 1,212.75. Therefore, (D) is correct.

In inference questions involving circle graphs, *do not compare different percentages.* Note in question 3 that the percentage of expenditures in 1960 for the three categories (40%) is *not equal* to 40% of the expenditures in 1970.

C. Line Graphs

LINE GRAPHS are used to show how a quantity changes continuously. Very often the quantity is measured as time changes. If the line goes up, the quantity is increasing; if the line goes down, the quantity is decreasing; if the line is horizontal, the quantity is not changing. To measure the height of a point on the graph, use your pencil or a piece of paper (for example, the edge of the test booklet) as a straight edge.

EXAMPLE: (Refer to the graph on page 34.)

1. The ratio of productivity in 1967 to productivity in 1940 was about

(A) 1:4
(B) 1:3
(C) 3:1
(D) 4:1
(E) 9:1

In 1967 productivity had an index number of 400, and the index numbers are based on 1940 = 100. So the ratio is 400:100 = 4:1. Therefore, the answer is (D). [If you used (incorrectly) output or employment (instead of productivity) you would get the wrong answer (E) or (C); if you confused the order of the ratio you would have incorrectly answered (A).]

TRENDS IN INDUSTRIAL INVESTMENT, LABOUR PRODUCTIVITY, EMPLOYMENT AND OUTPUT, 1940 TO 1967

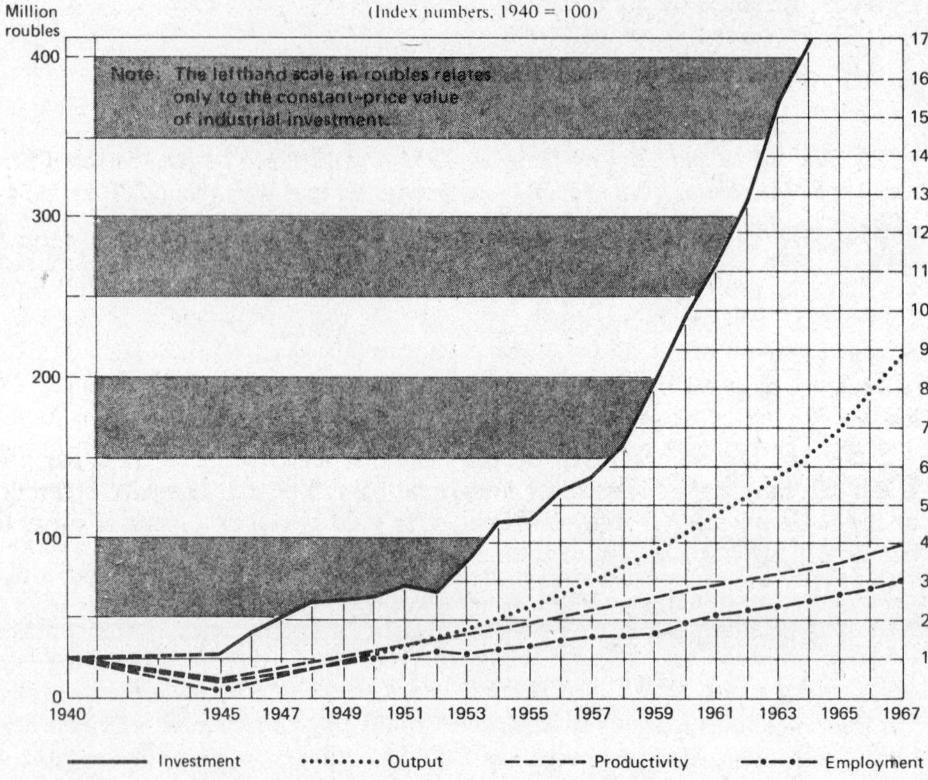

Source: United Nations Economics Bulletin for Europe

2. If 1 rouble = $3, then the constant-price value of industrial investment in 1959 was about

(A) $1.9 million
(B) $200 million
(C) $420,000,000
(D) $570,000,000
(E) $570,000 million

In 1959, the value was about 190 million roubles. (It was a little below 200 million.) The answers are all in dollars, so multiply 190 by 3 to get $570 million or $570,000,000 (D). If you are not careful about units, you may answer (B) or (E), which are incorrect.

3. Employment was at its minimum during the year

(A) 1940
(B) 1943
(C) 1945
(D) 1953
(E) 1967

The minimum of a quantity displayed on a line graph is the lowest place on the line. Thus in 1945, (C), the minimum value of employment was reached.

4. **Between 1954 and 1965, output**

(A) decreased by about 10%
(B) stayed about the same
(C) increased by about 200%
(D) increased by about 250%
(E) increased by about 500%

The line for output goes up between 1954 and 1965, so output increased between 1954 and 1965. Therefore, (A) and (B) are wrong. Output was about 200 in 1954 and about 700 in 1965, so the increase was 500. Since $\frac{500}{200} = 2.5 = 250\%$, the correct answer is (D).

D. Bar Graphs

Quantities can be compared by the height or length of a bar in a bar graph. A bar graph can have either vertical or horizontal bars. You can compare different quantities or the same quantity at different times. Use your pencil or a piece of paper to compare bars which are not adjacent to each other.

DISABILITY BENEFICIARIES REPORTED AS REHABILITATED:
Number, as percent of all rehabilitated clients
of State vocational rehabilitation agencies,
Years 1955–1971

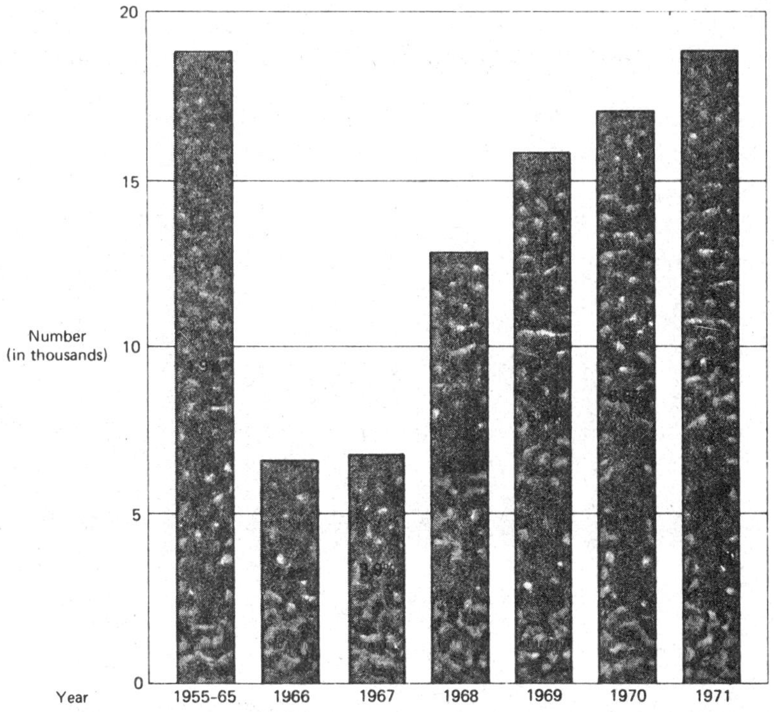

Source: Social Security Bulletin

1. Between 1967 and 1971, the largest number of disability beneficiaries was reported as rehabilitated in the year.

(A) 1967
(B) 1968
(C) 1969
(D) 1970
(E) 1971

The answer is (E) since the highest bar is the bar for 1971. The percentage of disability beneficiaries out of all rehabilitated clients was higher in 1969, but the *number* was lower.

2. Between 1955 and 1965, about how many clients were rehabilitated by State vocational rehabilitation agencies?

(A) 90,000
(B) 400,000
(C) 1,000,000
(D) 1,900,000
(E) 10,000,000

1.9% of those rehabilitated were disability beneficiaries, and there were about 19,000 disability beneficiaries rehabilitated. So if T is the total number rehabilitated, then 1.9% of $T = 19{,}000$ or $.019T = 19{,}000$. Thus, $T = 19{,}000/.019 = 1{,}000{,}000$ and the answer is (C).

E. Cumulative Graphs

You can compare several categories by a graph of the cumulative type. These are usually bar or line graphs where the height of the bar or line is divided up proportionately among different quantities.

FEDERAL PRISONERS RECEIVED FROM THE COURTS, BY MAJOR OFFENSE GROUPS: Years 1944–1952

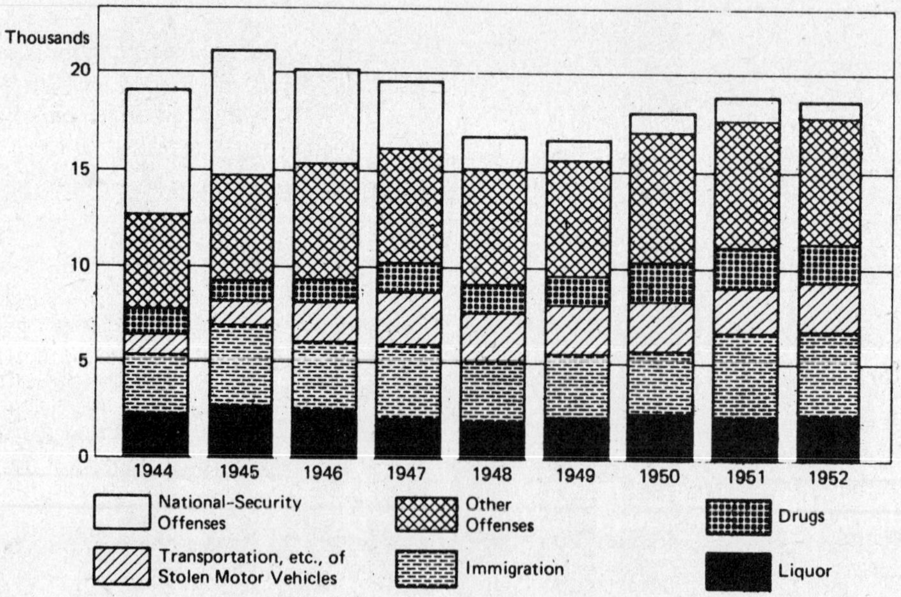

Source: Statistical Abstract of the U.S. 1953

1. In 1946, roughly what percent of the federal prisoners received from the courts were national-security offenders?

(A) 15
(B) 20
(C) 25
(D) 30
(E) 35

The total number of prisoners in 1946 was about 20,000, and national security offenders accounted for the part of the graph from just above 15,000 to just above 20,000. Therefore, there were about 20,000 − 15,000 = 5,000 prisoners convicted of national-security offenses. Since 5,000/20,000 = $\frac{1}{4}$ = 25%, the correct answer is (C).

2. Of the combined total for the four years 1947 through 1950, the largest number of offenders were in the category

(A) national-security offenses
(B) other offenses
(C) drugs
(D) immigration
(E) liquor

The correct answer is (B). Since other offenses have the most offenders in each year, that category must have the largest total number of offenders. [If this question specified the years 1944–1946, then (A) would be correct.]

3. Which of the following statements can be inferred from the graph?

I. The number of federal prisoners received from the courts decreased each year from 1946 to 1948.
II. More than 40% of the prisoners between 1944 and 1952 came from the other offenses category.
III. 2% of the federal prisoners received in 1952 were convicted on heroin charges.

(A) I only
(B) III only
(C) I and II only
(D) I and III only
(E) I, II, and III

Statement I is true, since the height of the bar for each year is lower than the height of the bar for the previous year in 1946, 1947, and 1948.

Statement II is not true. For most of the years, other offenses accounted for about 25–30%, and it never was more than 40% in any year. Therefore, it could not account for more than 40% of the total.

Statement III can not be inferred. There is a category of drug offenders, but there is no information about specific drugs.

So, the correct answer is (A).

SAMPLE PASSAGES

This section provides 23 sample reading passages. Each passage is followed by one or more questions. The questions include all of the types that are commonly used on the CBEST.

Read each passage carefully and then try to answer the question or questions that follow. Then check your answers by reading the Analysis that follows each reading passage.

PASSAGE 1

Your mind, like your body, is a thing whereof the powers are developed by effort. That is a principal use, as I see it, of hard work in studies. Unless you train your body you cannot be an athlete, and unless you train your mind you cannot be much of a scholar. The four miles an oarsman covers at top speed is in itself nothing to the good, but the physical capacity to hold out over the course is thought to be of some worth. So a good part of what you learn by hard study may not be permanently retained, and may not seem to be of much final value, but your mind is a better and more powerful instrument because you have learned it. "Knowledge is power," but still more the faculty of acquiring and using knowledge is power. If you have a trained and powerful mind, you are bound to have stored it with something, but its value is more in what it can do, what it can grasp and use, than in what it contains; and if it were possible, as it is not, to come out of college with a trained and disciplined mind and nothing useful in it, you would still be ahead, and still, in a manner, educated.

The title that best expresses the ideas of this passage is

1. "Knowledge Is Power"
2. **How to Retain and Use Facts**
3. **Why Acquire Knowledge**
4. **Physical and Mental Effort**
5. **The Trained Mind**

ANALYSIS OF PASSAGE 1

In this passage, the author stresses the need for "hard work in studies." He compares the training the athlete gets to the training the scholar needs. He concedes that much knowledge that one learns may be forgotten, but he emphasizes the value of knowing how to get and use knowledge. This comes from training. It is not the knowledge that one gets from college but the training of the mind that is valuable. Realizing this, we may eliminate choice 1 ("Knowledge is Power") because the author states that the faculty of acquiring knowledge is more important. Choice 2 (How to Retain and Use Facts) is not discussed in the paragraph. Choice 3 (Why Acquire Knowledge) may be supported by the statement that "Knowledge is Power," but we realize that the author is de-emphasizing this statement in the sentence in which he states it. Choice 4 (Physical and Mental Effort) may be taken by some students who notice that the author makes an analogy between the training of the athlete and the necessary training of the scholar. However, it is not as good as Choice 5 (The Trained Mind) because, throughout the paragraph, the author is stressing that the trained mind is something that must be developed by effort and in itself is a valuable and important faculty.

PASSAGE 2

The teacher suspected cheating as soon as she noticed the pupil's *furtive* glances at his classmate's paper.

In this context the word *furtive* means

1. overt
2. futile
3. few
4. sly
5. friendly

ANALYSIS OF PASSAGE 2

Overt glances are open and unconcealed. If the pupil had glanced overtly at his classmate's paper, the teacher would not have merely suspected him of cheating. She would have been sure of it. Futile means having no useful results; we are told nothing about results. Neither are we told anything about the number of glances, and we have no reason to think the glances are friendly. Rather, since cheating is suspected, we can assume that the glances were sly and underhanded. The best choice is Choice 4.

PASSAGE 3

The characteristic American believes, first, in justice as the foundation of civilized government and society, and, next, in freedom for the individual, so far as that freedom is possible without interference with the equal rights of others. He conceives that both justice and freedom are to be secured through popular respect for the laws enacted by the elected representatives of the people and through the faithful observance of those laws. It should be observed, however, that American justice in general keeps in view the present common good of the vast majority, and the restoration rather than the punishment of the exceptional malignant or defective individual. It is essentially democratic; and especially it finds sufferings inflicted on the innocent unintelligible and abhorrent.

The main idea of this selection may be best expressed as:

1. American justice
2. A plea for cooperation
3. The American government
4. Liberty as the foundation of government
5. The basis of American democracy

ANALYSIS OF PASSAGE 3

The author in his opening sentence couples justice and freedom of the individual as the foundations of civilized government. Any title which does not include both aspects is incomplete. Choices 1 and 4 are inadequate for this reason.

Choice 2 is inaccurate because this passage is a presentation of the American belief in cooperation. The author does not have to plead for cooperation on the part of Americans. It is already part of their basic philosophy.

Choice 3 (The American government) is not discussed in the passage. The author is discussing the factors, justice and liberty, which Americans regard as the basis of good government.

Choice 5 is best because the author is expounding on the factors which form the "basis of American democracy."

PASSAGE 4

There are exceptions to the rule of male insects being smaller than the females, and some of these exceptions are intelligible. Size and strength would be an advantage to the males which fight for the possession of the females, and in these cases, as with the stag-beetle (Lucanus), the males are larger than the females. There are, however, other beetles which are not known to fight together, of which the males exceed the females in size, and the meaning of this fact is not known, but in some of these cases, as with the huge Dynastes and Megasoma, we can at least see that there would be no necessity for the males to be smaller than the females, in order to be matured before them, for these beetles are not short-lived, and there would be ample time for the pairing of the sexes.

1. According to the author
   1. male insects are always smaller than females
   2. in a given species nature provides differences between sexes to insure successful reproduction
   3. size and strength protect females from other females
   4. longevity is characteristic of the Dynastes and Megasoma
   5. in the stag-beetle females are larger than the males

2. Where male beetles are smaller than female beetles, it is because
   1. they have to fight for their mates
   2. they are more intelligent
   3. they are ephemeral creatures
   4. there is ample time for mating
   5. they do not have to fight for their mates

3. The paragraph preceding this one probably
   1. discusses a generalization about the size of animals
   2. develops the idea that male insects do not live long after maturity
   3. discusses male and female beetles
   4. emphasizes that beetles are belligerent animals
   5. discusses insect behavior

4. The male Lucanus is particularly
   1. adaptable
   2. strong
   3. intelligent
   4. belligerent
   5. stagnant

ANALYSIS OF PASSAGE 4

1. The answer is 4. We can eliminate Choice 1 because in line 1 we are told that "there are exceptions" to the rule. Lines 9 and 12 contain additional references to male insects that are larger than females. (Incidentally, this illustrates one area where students should exercise caution. Whenever an answer is in the superlative—best, worst, etc.—or is all-inclusive—always, all—or all-exclusive—none—, be sure to reread the paragraph to make certain that the author actually makes the statement.) Choice 2 may be correct biologically and logically, but the author has not stated it in the paragraph; you are adding your own interpretation to the paragraph if you select this choice. Choice 3 is not stated in the paragraph. Choice 4 is found in lines 14 and 15; longevity means long life. Choice 5 is wrong; in line 6, the author states that males are larger.

2. The answer is 3. Choice 3 can be supported by analyzing lines 11-16. While the author is discussing large male beetles in these lines, we learn why other male beetles are smaller than female beetles. Male beetles are smaller (1) because they mature earlier and (2) because they are short lived. The word *ephemeral* means short lived. Choice 1 is incorrect; in lines 3 and 4 we find that male beetles are larger if they have to fight for their mates. Choice 2 is not stated in the paragraph. Choice 4 is incorrect; beetles grow *large* when there is ample time for mating. Choice 5 is likewise incorrect; size is important when males have to fight for their mates and therefore would explain the largeness of male beetles rather than the smallness.

3. This question calls for inferences. The clue lies in the first sentence. It is fair to assume that, if the author discusses exceptions to a rule, he has explained the rule in the preceding paragraph. There is no evidence in the paragraph that any of the other ideas were discussed previously. The correct choice is 1.

4. The answer is 4. The second sentence of this paragraph (lines 3 through 7) develops the idea that the male Lucanus is larger and stronger than the female beetle. However, we cannot accept either 2 or 3 as the answer because strong and large are relative terms. We are told in the same sentence that the males fight for the females. The word *belligerent* fits this situation. Choices 1 and 5 are not found in the paragraph.

PASSAGE 5

Despite his many hours of hard work at his bench, he realized that his progress was *tenuous*.

We can also describe his progress as
1. excellent
2. laudable
3. time-consuming
4. steady
5. insubstantial

ANALYSIS OF PASSAGE 5

This sentence indicates that the young man's hard work did not have its expected result. Instead of making excellent, laudable (praise-worthy), or steady progress, he made barely any progress at all; his progress was tenuous, or insubstantial (Choice 5). Be aware that words like *despite, although, instead of,* and *unlike* may signal a contrast.

PASSAGE 6

The six year old is about the best example that can be found of that type of inquisitiveness that causes irritated adults to exclaim, "Curiosity killed the cat." To him, the world is a fascinating place to be explored and investigated quite thoroughly, but such a world is bounded by the environment in which he or the people he knows live. It is constantly expanding through new experiences, which bring many eager questions from members of any group of first graders, as each one tries to figure out new relationships—to know and accept his place within the family, the school, and the community—to understand all around him. There are adults who find it quite annoying to be presented with such rank inquisitiveness. But this is no purposeless prying, no idle curiosity! It is that quality, characteristic of the successful adult, inherent in the good citizen—intellectual curiosity.

In this passage the author's attitude toward children is one of
1. despair
2. confidence
3. indifference
4. sharp criticism
5. exaggerated optimism

ANALYSIS OF PASSAGE 6

Although the author discusses the irritation adults sometimes feel at the incessant questions asked by six year old children, he feels that these questions are not purposeless. He feels that this intellectual curiosity is a characteristic of the adult citizen, and he is happy and confident when children display this trait (Choice 2).

PASSAGE 7

Good American English is simply good English, English that differs a little in pronunciation, vocabulary, and occasionally in idiom from good English as spoken in London or South Africa, but differs no more than our physical surroundings, our political and social institutions, and the other circumstances reflected in language differ from those of other English-speaking areas. It rests upon the same basis as that which the standard speech of England rests upon, —the usage of reputable speakers and writers throughout the country. No American student of language is so provincial as to hope, or wish, that the American standard may some day be adopted in England. Nor does he share the views of such in England as think that we would do well to take our standard readymade from them. He will be content with the opinion of Henry Bradley that "the wiser sort among us will not dispute that Americans have acquired the right to frame their own standards of correct English on the usage of their best writers and speakers."

1. The author considers good American English to be
   1. proper for use in America
   2. superior to the English spoken in South Africa
   3. inferior to the English spoken in England
   4. too idiomatic for general acceptance
   5. suitable as a standard for English-speaking countries

2. According to the author, correctness in language is determined by
   1. the majority of those who speak it
   2. the dominant social and political institutions
   3. geographical conditions
   4. good speakers and writers
   5. those who wish to standardize the language

ANALYSIS OF PASSAGE 7

The statement of Henry Bradley in the last sentence justifies the selection of Choice 1 as the answer to the first question.

The justification for Choice 4 as the best answer to the second question can be found in two sentences in the passage. Mr. Bradley's quotation mentions the usage of the "best writers and speakers." Likewise, the same thought is found in the second sentence ("the usage of reputable speakers and writers throughout the country").

PASSAGE 8

Today in America vast concourses of youth are flocking to our colleges, eager for something, just what they do not know. It makes much difference what they get. They will be prone to demand something they can immediately use: science, economics, business administration, law in its narrower sense. I submit that the shepherds should not first feed the flock with these. I argue for what used to go as a liberal education—not in the sense that young folks should waste precious years in efforts to master ancient tongues; but I speak for an introduction into the thoughts and deeds of men who have lived before them, in other countries than their own, with other strifes and other needs. This I maintain, not in the interest of that general cultural background which is so often a cloak for the prig, the snob and the pedant. But I submit to you that in some such way alone can we meet and master the high-power salesman of political patent medicines.

The title that best expresses the ideas of this passage is

1. **Why Pupils Go to College**
2. **Foreign Languages for Culture**
3. **The Need for Vocational Training**
4. **The Shepherd and His Student Flock**
5. **The Importance of a Liberal Education**

ANALYSIS OF PASSAGE 8

The author maintains that the young people flocking to our colleges do not know exactly what they are seeking. They often desire materials which they can put to immediate use; they seek subjects which have practical application. The author urges a study of the ideas and actions of men in other countries and other times. This liberal education is valuable not for its snobbishness or pedantry but for the insight it gives the student which will enable him to meet the problems of current society.

By paraphrasing the ideas of the passage in some such manner, the student can see that the writer is stressing "the importance of a liberal education." Thus, Choice 5 is best. Choice 1 is inadequate because it is not discussed in the passage. We are told that students are flocking to the colleges but we are not told why. Choice 2 is mentioned only by indirection. The author talks of mastering ancient tongues. He does not mention the study of contemporary foreign languages in this passage. Similarly, the author does not discuss the need for vocational training. Instead he implies that students, mistakenly, often seek vocational training because of its immediacy of application. Choice 4 is so broad that it becomes vague. The author is more interested in what the teacher gives his pupils than in the general idea of teacher and pupil.

PASSAGE 9

Many educators argued that a *homogeneous* grouping of students would improve instruction because the range of student abilities would be limited.

Such a grouping of students would be

1. varied
2. irregular
3. cognitive
4. heterodox
5. undiversified

ANALYSIS OF PASSAGE 9

The roots *homo*, same, and *gen*, kind, indicate that a homogeneous student grouping is made up of students of the same kind or level of ability. It is therefore an *undiversified* group (Choice 5).

PASSAGE 10

Most people do not think of fishes and other marine animals as having voices, and of those who are aware of the fact that many of them can "speak," few understand that these "conversations" have significance. Actually, their talk may be as meaningful as much of our own. For example, some sea animals use their "voices" to locate their food in the ocean expanses; others, to let their fellows know of their whereabouts; and still others, as a means of obtaining mates. Sometimes, "speaking" may even mean the difference between life and death to a marine animal. It appears in some cases that when a predator approaches, the prey depends on no more than the sounds it makes to escape.

Fish sounds are important to man, also. By listening to them he can learn a great deal about the habits of the creatures that make them, the size of the schools they form, the patterns of their migrations, and the nature of the environments in which they live. He can also apply this information to the more effective utilization of the listening posts he has set up to detect enemy submarines. A knowledge of fish sounds can avoid confusion and unneeded effort when a "new" sound is picked up and the sound sentry must decide whether or not to call an alert.

1. Which of the following statements is *best* supported by the information given? Noises produced by fish
   1. are apparently random
   2. are used by fishermen to increase their catch
   3. can be utilized to tell whether or not a submarine is nearby
   4. can confuse users of submarine-detection equipment

2. Which of the following statements can *best* be inferred from the information given?
   1. Fish noises cannot be transmitted through air.
   2. Hearing in fishes is more acute than in people.
   3. The chief use of "fish voices" is to enable one fish to communicate with another fish.
   4. The significance of some fish noises has been studied.

ANALYSIS OF PASSAGE 10

1. The passage informs us that the noises produced by fish are "meaningful" and therefore not apparently random. This eliminates Choice 1. Statement 2 may be inferred from the text but is not mentioned in the passage. Fish sounds apparently interfere with listening posts for submarines. These sounds cannot be used to detect

submarines. The listener must learn to differentiate between fish sounds and the sounds made by submarines. If he does not differentiate, he will be confused. Thus, 4 is the best answer.

2. Choice 4 is best because it is obvious that what we know about fish sounds is based on study. Choices 1 and 2 are not mentioned in the text and are therefore assumptions made by the reader. We can object to Choice 3 because we cannot find any justification for the statement that the ''chief'' use of these voices is for communication. It is, again, an unwarranted conclusion.

PASSAGE 11

We must discover and develop each student's *intrinsic* talents.

The student's talents are
1. inner
2. unwanted
3. objective
4. specious
5. extraneous

ANALYSIS OF PASSAGE 11

If the student's talents are in need of discovery, they are not obvious talents easily spotted by observers. If they must be developed, we can assume they are not unwanted or specious (deceptive). Choice 1 is best; the talents are inner and inborn.

PASSAGE 12

But there is more to the Library of Congress for the American dream than merely the wise appropriation of public money. The Library of Congress could not have become what it is today, with all the generous aid of Congress, without such a citizen as Dr. Herbert Putnam at the directing head of it. He and his staff have devoted their lives to making the four million and more books and pamphlets serve the public to a degree that cannot be approached by any similar great institution in the Old World. Then there is the public that uses these facilities. As one looks down on the general reading room, which alone contains ten thousand volumes that may be read without even the asking, one sees the seats filled with silent readers, old and young, rich and poor, black and white, the executive and the laborer, the general and the private, the noted scholar and the schoolboy, all reading at their own library provided by their own democracy.

The title that best expresses the ideas of the passage is
1. **Wise Use of Public Funds**
2. **An Institution of Democracy**
3. **Intelligent Use of Books**
4. **Generosity of Congress to the Public**
5. **The Old World and the New**

ANALYSIS OF PASSAGE 12

The quick or careless reader may find words or phrases which seem to justify the selection of several of the choices as the best title. A more careful reading will reveal shortcomings in most of these. In the first sentence, the author talks of the "wise appropriation of public money." This is not the same as "wise use." Likewise, Congress's generosity to the library should not be broadened to include the public. Thus, we can find fault with Choices 1 and 4. The reference to libraries in the Old World as a means of contrasting them with our own Library of Congress is too limited to justify the very broad implications of Choice 5. While the library makes books and pamphlets available to readers, we can not find any statement in the passage to justify the concept that these books are being used wisely. By elimination, we arrive at 2 (An Institution of Democracy) as the best of the choices. This concept is supported by the author's emphasis on the varied and contrasting groups using the facilities of the library provided through democratic processes for the use of all.

PASSAGE 13

The plot of this story is so *trite* that I can predict the outcome.

The plot can also be said to be
1. clever
2. involved
3. insipid
4. familiar
5. whimsical

ANALYSIS OF PASSAGE 13

Something predictable must be well-known or *familiar*. The best answer is Choice 4.

PASSAGE 14

Any young writer who may imagine that the power of clear and concise literary expression comes by nature, cannot do better than study in Goldsmith's writings the continual and minute alterations which the author considered necessary even after the first edition—sometimes when the second and third editions had been published. Many of these, especially in the poetical works, were merely improvements in sound, as suggested by a singularly sensitive ear. But the majority of the omissions and corrections were prompted by a careful taste, which abhorred everything redundant or slovenly. The English people are very fond of good English; and thus it is that couplets from "The Traveller" and "The Deserted Village" have come into the common stock of our language and that sometimes not so much on account of the ideas they convey as through their singular precision of epithet and musical sound.

1. Goldsmith avoided
    1. omissions
    2. alterations
    3. redundancy
    4. poetry
    5. criticism
2. By studying the work of Goldsmith
    1. we see the necessity for avoiding errors in first editions
    2. we see the importance of euphony in poetry
    3. we see why first editions are valuable
    4. we learn to avoid slovenly writing
    5. we learn to avoid common language

ANALYSIS OF PASSAGE 14

In this passage the reader is told that Goldsmith improved his poetry by making alterations and omissions. Thus, in question 1, Choices 1 and 2 are not correct. Goldsmith made alterations because he hated sloppy, redundant work. He therefore made them to avoid redundancy, and the correct answer is Choice 3.

The concluding sentence of the passage commends the verses of Goldsmith for their singular precision of epithet and musical sound; earlier in the passage the author remarks on Goldsmith's singularly sensitive ear. By studying Goldsmith, we learn about how important sound is in poetry. Euphony is the quality of being pleasing in sound. The answer to question 2, therefore, is Choice 2.

PASSAGE 15

Let us consider how voice training may contribute to personality development and an improved social adjustment. In the first place, it has been fairly well established that individuals tend to become what they believe other people think them to be. When people react more favorably toward us because our voices convey the impression that we are friendly, competent, and interesting, there is a strong tendency for us to develop those qualities in our personality. If we are treated with respect by others, we soon come to have more respect for ourselves. Then, too, one's own consciousness of having a pleasant, effective voice of which he does not need to be ashamed contributes materially to a feeling of poise, self-confidence, and a just pride in himself. A good voice, like good clothes, can do much for an ego that otherwise might be inclined to droop.

1. The title that best expresses the ideas of this passage is:
    1. Our Ego
    2. The Reflection of Our Personality
    3. How to Acquire a Pleasant Voice
    4. Voice Training in Personality Development
    5. Social Adjustment and Self-respect
2. A good voice
    1. contributes greatly to a feeling of poise
    2. conveys the impression that we are friendly
    3. is less important than good clothes
    4. is more important than good clothes
    5. makes others unconscious of our faults

ANALYSIS OF PASSAGE 15

In the opening sentence we are asked to consider how voice training may contribute to personality development. This, then, is the topic of the paragraph, and the best title for the paragraph is Choice 4. We may eliminate Choices 1, 2, and 5 as titles because they do not specifically mention voice training. Similarly, we may eliminate Choice 3 because, although it emphasizes voice training, it does not indicate that such training will influence the person's social development.

The main idea of the passage is that possessing a good voice will help us feel better about ourselves. Thus, while a good voice may well convey the impression that we are friendly, it does far more for us than that, and Choice 1, "A good voice contributes greatly to a feeling of poise," is preferable to Choice 2.

PASSAGE 16

One of the most urgent problems in teaching handwriting is presented by the left-handed child. The traditional policy has been to attempt to induce all children to write with their right hands. Parents and teachers alike have an antipathy to the child's using his left hand. On the other hand, psychologists have shown beyond a doubt that some persons are naturally left-handed and that it is much more difficult for them to do any skillful act with the right hand than with the left hand. Some believe, furthermore, that to compel a left-handed child to write with his right hand may make him nervous and may cause stammering. There seems to be some cases in which this is true, although in the vast majority of children who change over, no ill effects are noticed. In addition to these difficulties, left-handedness sometimes seems to cause mirror writing—writing from right to left—and reversals in reading, as reading "was" for "saw."

1. The title below that best expresses the ideas of this passage is:
    1. Nervous Aspects Connected with Handwriting
    2. Teaching Handwriting
    3. The Problems of the Left-handed Child
    4. A Special Problem in Teaching Handwriting
    5. Stammering, Mirror Writing and Reversals
2. The author implies that
    1. parents should break children of left-handedness
    2. left-handed children need special consideration

3. left-handed persons are inclined to stutter
4. left-handed persons are not more brilliant than right-handed ones
5. left-handed persons are less skillful than right-handed ones

3. The traditional policy in teaching handwriting has
1. dismayed the experts
2. resulted in failure to learn to write
3. aimed at mirror writing
4. made many children skillful with both hands
5. resulted in unsolved problems

ANALYSIS OF PASSAGE 16

The opening sentence of the passage indicates that its topic is an urgent problem in teaching handwriting. That problem is the difficulty of teaching handwriting to left-handed children. Note that the author is not discussing general problems of left-handed children. The author is discussing the problem parents and teachers have in teaching their left-handed children to write. Thus, Choice 3, The Problems of the Left-Handed Child, is inadequate because it is too general. So is Choice 2, Teaching Handwriting. Choices 1 and 5, on the other hand, are too specific. The best title is Choice 4.

The second question asks us to go beyond what the author states and see what the statements imply. The author does not imply that left-handed persons are less skillful than right-handed ones (Choice 5); instead, the author merely states that left-handed persons have a hard time performing skillful acts *with their right hand,* and that some psychologists believe left-handed persons *who are forced to write with their right hands* may stutter. However, we cannot logically conclude from this statement that left-handed persons are inclined to stutter (Choice 3), and indeed the author states that most children who learn to switch hands do so with no ill effects. The author never discusses the brilliance of left-handed persons (Choice 4). Only two answers are left. However, Choice 1 is faulty, because the author has shown that many problems may arise from attempts to induce left-handed children to write with their right hands. The author is trying to solve problems, not perpetuate them. Thus, the correct answer is Choice 2.

As we examine the choices in the third question, we should realize that Choices 1, 2, and 4 are not mentioned. Mirror-writing, in Choice 3, was not the *aim* of traditional policy (though it may have been an unfortunate unforeseen result of that policy). Choice 5 is the best answer.

PASSAGE 17

It was difficult for the teacher to enforce the new rules because they were too *stringent*.

The rules were
1. lucid
2. strict
3. wry
4. beneficial
5. pertinent

ANALYSIS OF PASSAGE 17

The best answer is Choice 2. Rules may be hard to enforce because they are too *stringent* or strict; they should not be hard to enforce because they are clear (Choice 1), helpful (Choice 4), or relevant (Choice 5).

PASSAGE 18

A more significant manifestation of the concern of the community with the general welfare is the collection and dissemination of statistics. This statement may cause the reader to smile, for statistics seem to be drab and prosaic things. The great growth of statistics, however, is one of the most remarkable characteristics of the age. Never before has a community kept track from month to month, and in some cases from week to week, of how many people are born, how many die and from what causes, how many are sick, how much is being produced, how much is being sold, how many people are at work, how many people are unemployed, how long they have been out of work, what prices people pay, how much income they receive and from what sources, how much they owe, what they intend to buy. These elaborate attempts of the country to keep informed about what is happening mean that the community is concerned with how its members are faring and with the conditions under which they live. For this reason the present age may take pride in its numerous and regular statistical reports and in the rapid increase in the number of these reports. No other age has evidenced such a keen interest in the conditions of the people.

1. The title below that best expresses the ideas of this passage is:
1. Remarkable Statistics
2. The Concerned Community
3. The Nature of Statistics
4. Statistics and Human Welfare
5. How to Keep Informed

2. The writer implies that statistics are
1. too scientific for general use
2. too elaborate and too drab
3. related to the improvement of living conditions
4. frequently misinterpreted
5. a product of the machine age

ANALYSIS OF PASSAGE 18

The author does not describe statistics themselves as remarkable but rather calls their great growth a remarkable characteristic of this age. Similarly, while mentioning several sorts of data gathered, the author does not define the nature of statistics itself. Thus, Choices 1 and 3 introduce ideas not presented by the author and are, therefore, unsuitable as appropriate titles. The passage concerns itself with the collection of statistics as a manifestation of a community's concern for the welfare of its members. Thus, any title should include the key word statistics. Choices 2 and 5 fail to do so. The best title, therefore, is Statistics and Human Welfare, Choice 4.

The opening and closing sentences of this passage tell us that statistics are collected out of consideration for the "general welfare" and are the result of a "keen interest in the conditions of the people." Thus, for the second question Choice 3 is justified. Nowhere in the passage does the author state that statistics are too scientific or misinterpreted. The author, likewise, does not state that statistics are too elaborate. The author does state that they may *seem* drab. The use of the word *seem* implies that the author does not believe that the statement is correct. Choice 5 is not justified by the text.

PASSAGE 19

I am amazed to see such fine work done by a mere *tyro*.

The work was done by a
1. specialist
2. libertine
3. novice
4. amateur
5. artisan

ANALYSIS OF PASSAGE 19

As observers of amateur sports know, amateurs often do very fine work. So do specialists and artisans. It is surprising, however, when a beginner does expert work. Therefore, the correct answer is Choice 3, *novice*.

PASSAGE 20

You should *delete* this paragraph in order to make your essay more succinct.

The word *delete* means
1. finish
2. expand
3. omit
4. censor
5. develop

ANALYSIS OF PASSAGE 20

A succinct essay is brief. To make an essay brief, you must cut out entire sections. You must do more than expurgate it by censoring an occasional objectionable word. The best choice is Choice 3, *omit*.

PASSAGE 21

As we know the short story today it is largely a product of the nineteenth and twentieth centuries and its development parallels the rapid development of industrialism in America. We have been a busy people, busy principally in evolving a production system supremely efficient. Railroads and factories have blossomed almost overnight; mines and oil fields have been discovered and exploited; mechanical inventions by the thousands have been made and perfected. Speed has been an essential element in our endeavors, and it has affected our lives, our very natures. Leisurely reading has been, for most Americans, impossible. As with our meals, we have grabbed bits of reading standing up, cafeteria style, and gulped down cups of sentiment on the run. We have had to read while hanging on to a strap in a swaying trolley car or in a rushing subway or while tending to a clamoring telephone switchboard. Our popular magazine has been our literary automat and its stories have often been no more substantial than sandwiches.

1. The title below that best expresses the ideas of this paragraph is:
   1. **"Quick-lunch" Literature**
   2. **Life in the Machine Age**
   3. **Cultûre in Modern Life**
   4. **Reading while Traveling**
   5. **The Development of Industrialism**

2. The short story today owes its popularity to its
   1. **settings**
   2. **plots**
   3. **style**
   4. **length**
   5. **characters**

3. The short story has developed because of Americans'
   1. **reactions against the classics**
   2. **need for reassurance**
   3. **lack of culture**
   4. **lack of education**
   5. **taste for speed**

4. From this selection one would assume that the author's attitude toward short stories is one of
   1. **approval**
   2. **indifference**
   3. **contempt**
   4. **impartiality**
   5. **regret**

ANALYSIS OF PASSAGE 21

The opening sentence of this passage defines the topic: the short story as a product of modern, fast-paced society. Any title which does not include both the idea of literature and the idea of speed is incomplete. Only Choice 1 will do.

If leisurely reading is impossible in modern times, then readers must content themselves with reading matter that is short. Thus, the short story owes its popularity to its length (Choice 4).

In answering question 3, we must remember that the author throughout stresses the effects of speed on our lives. Nowhere does the author refer to an American reaction against the classics or a need for reassurance. While the author mentions the sentimentality and lack of substance of our reading matter, he never asserts that these stem from a lack of culture or education on our parts. Instead, it is the author's thesis that the short story grew in response to our fast-paced way of life (Choice 5).

If the author believes that Americans *have had to* read on the run and that their literary tastes have been inevitably affected by the pace of their lives, then his attitude toward the short stories they read is more likely one of regret (Choice 5) rather than one of contempt (Choice 3). While he would prefer Americans to read more substantial literature than stories in popular magazines, he understands the reasons behind their choice and does not view the short story with scorn. The best answer is Choice 5.

PASSAGE 22

We need more men of culture and enlightenment in our society; we have too many *philistines* among us.

Philistines are
1. pedants
2. barbarians
3. moralists
4. paragons
5. humanists

ANALYSIS OF PASSAGE 22

The best answer is Choice 2. Men of culture and enlightenment are contrasted with philistines. Therefore, philistines are neither cultured nor enlightened. Pedants and moralists may have their faults, but they do not necessarily lack culture or a certain enlightenment. Those lacking culture are barbarians.

PASSAGE 23

Nationalism is not a harmonious natural growth, qualitatively identical with the love for family and home. It is frequently assumed that man loves in widening circles—his family, his village, his tribe or clan, the nation, and finally humanity and the supreme good. But love of home and family is a concrete feeling, accessible to everyone in daily experience, while nationalism, and in an even higher degree cosmopolitanism, is a highly complex and originally an abstract feeling. Nationalism—our identification with the life and aspirations of uncounted millions whom we shall never know, with a territory which we shall never visit in its entirety—is qualitatively different from love of family or of home surroundings. It is qualitatively akin to the love of humanity or of the whole earth.

1. The title below that best expresses the ideas of this paragraph is:
   1. A Distinction without a Difference
   2. Love of One's Fellow Beings
   3. The Nature of Nationalism
   4. An Abstract Affection
   5. Our Complex Emotions

2. Compared with love of family and home, nationalism is more
   1. natural
   2. clannish
   3. accessible
   4. concrete
   5. inclusive

3. A common assumption regarding nationalism is that it is
   1. an outgrowth of love of home and family
   2. more nearly related to humanity than to the home
   3. highly abstract and complex
   4. identified with the lives of millions whom we do not know
   5. stimulated by travel within one's own country

ANALYSIS OF PASSAGE 23

The subject of the opening sentence is nationalism. Only Choice 3, The Nature of Nationalism, contains this key word. The other choices are too vague to serve as titles for this text.

Love of home and family is described as accessible and concrete. It is contrasted with nationalism, which therefore is neither particularly accessible nor concrete. The opening sentence states that nationalism is not a natural growth. Thus, for question 2 Choices 1, 3, and 4 are incorrect. Nationalism is described as our identification with millions of people whom we shall never know; it therefore goes beyond mere clannishness, and can best be described as inclusive (Choice 5).

In the third question we are looking for a common assumption about nationalism. Sentence 2 begins "It is frequently assumed that man loves in widening circles—his family, his village, . . ." The assumption is that love of one's fellows grows out of the love of one's home and family. This is Choice 1.

CHAPTER **4**

MATHEMATICS REVIEW

The mathematics questions on the CBEST require you to know mathematical principles and to understand the basics of arithmetic, algebra, and geometry. You should also be able to translate problems into formulas and to interpret graphs.

Four basic types of questions are covered on the mathematics part of the test:

1) Recognizing Processes Used in Problem Solving (tell how you would solve a particular problem; choose which set of mathematical symbols translates a verbal problem, etc.)
2) Solving Word Problems (applied arithmetic, ratio and proportion, algebra, geometry, averaging, etc.)
3) Understanding Mathematical Concepts and Relationships (recognize numerical order; identify the meaning of key terms, such as area; understand relationships illustrated by graphs, etc.)
4) Functionally Transferring Knowledge (interpret a graph; analyze the logic of a relationship)

Approximately one half of the questions on the CBEST will test arithmetic concepts and skills. None of the questions will test computation as such, but you will have to perform some computations in answering many of the verbal problems.

You will have 70 minutes to solve 50 problems, a little over one minute each. Do the easy problems first. Learn to spot the time-consuming problems quickly so that you can skip them and return to them if you have time.

Review the basics. Then try the practice exercises. You should then be set for the model tests.

REVIEW

This section provides a concise review of the mathematics you need to know for the CBEST. It is divided into five major sections: Arithmetic, Algebra, Geometry, Formulas, and Hints. Several of the sections contain practice questions to help you sharpen your skills.

I. Arithmetic

I–A. Whole Numbers

A-1

The numbers 0, 1, 2, 3, . . . are called whole numbers or *integers*. So 75 is an integer but $4\frac{1}{3}$ is not an integer.

A-2

If the integer k divides m evenly, then we say *m is divisible by k* or *k is a factor of m*. For example, 12 is divisible by 4, but 12 is not divisible by 5. 1, 2, 3, 4, 6, 12 are all factors of 12.

If k is a factor of m, then there is another integer n such that $m = k \times n$; in this case, m is called a *multiple of k*.

Since $12 = 4 \times 3$, 12 is a multiple of 4 and also 12 is a multiple of 3. 5,10, 15, and 20 are all multiples of 5 but 15 and 5 are not multiples of 10.

Any integer is a multiple of each of its factors.

A-3

Any whole number is divisible by itself and by 1. If p is a whole number greater than 1, which has *only* p and 1 as factors, then p is called a *prime number*. 2, 3, 5, 7, 11, 13, 17, 19 and 23 are all primes. 14 is not a prime since it is divisible by 2 and by 7.

A whole number which is divisible by 2 is called an *even* number; if a whole number is not even, then it is an *odd* number. 2, 4, 6, 8, 10 are even numbers, and 1, 3, 5, 7 and 9 are odd numbers.

A collection of numbers is *consecutive* if each number is the successor of the number which precedes it. For example, 7, 8, 9 and 10 are consecutive, but 7, 8, 10, 13 are not. 4, 6, 8, 10 are consecutive even numbers. 7, 11, 13, 17 are consecutive primes. 7, 13, 19, 23 are not consecutive primes since 11 is a prime between 7 and 13.

A-4

Any whole number can be written as a product of factors which are prime numbers.

To write a number as a *product of prime factors:*

(A) Divide the number by 2 if possible; continue to divide by 2 until the factor you get is not divisible by 2.
(B) Divide the result from (A) by 3 if possible; continue to divide by 3 until the factor you get is not divisible by 3.
(C) Divide the result from (B) by 5 if possible; continue to divide by 5 until the factor you get is not divisible by 5.
(D) Continue the procedure with 7,11, and so on, until all the factors are primes.

EXAMPLE 1: Express 24 as a product of prime factors.

(A) $24 = 2 \times 12$, $12 = 2 \times 6$, $6 = 2 \times 3$ so $24 = 2 \times 2 \times 2 \times 3$. Since each factor (2 and 3) is prime, $24 = 2 \times 2 \times 2 \times 3$.

EXAMPLE 2: Express 252 as a product of primes.

(A) $252 = 2 \times 126$, $126 = 2 \times 63$ and 63 is not divisible by 2, so $252 = 2 \times 2 \times 63$.
(B) $63 = 3 \times 21$, $21 = 3 \times 7$ and 7 is not divisible by 3. Since 7 is a prime, then $252 = 2 \times 2 \times 3 \times 3 \times 7$ and all the factors are primes.

A-5

A number m is a *common multiple* of two other numbers k and j if it is a multiple of each of them. For example, 12 is a common multiple of 4 and 6, since $3 \times 4 = 12$ and $2 \times 6 = 12$. 15 is not a common multiple of 3 and 6, because 15 is not a multiple of 6.

A number k is a *common factor* of two other numbers m and n if k is a factor of m and k is a factor of n.

The *least common multiple* (L.C.M.) of two numbers is the smallest number which is a common multiple of both numbers. To find the least common multiple of two numbers k and j:

(A) Write k as a product of primes and j as a product of primes.
(B) If there are any common factors *delete* them in *one* of the products.
(C) Multiply the remaining factors; the result is the least common multiple.

EXAMPLE 1: Find the L.C.M. of 12 and 11.

(A) $12 = 2 \times 2 \times 3$, $11 = 11 \times 1$.
(B) There are no common factors.
(C) The L.C.M. is $12 \times 11 = 132$.

EXAMPLE 2: Find the L.C.M. of 27 and 63.

(A) $27 = 3 \times 3 \times 3$, $63 = 3 \times 3 \times 7$.
(B) $3 \times 3 = 9$ is a common factor so delete it once.
(C) The L.C.M. is $3 \times 3 \times 3 \times 7 = 189$.

You can find the L.C.M. of a collection of numbers in the same way except that if in step (B) the common factors are factors of more than two of the numbers, then delete the common factor in *all but one* of the products.

EXAMPLE 3: Find the L.C.M. of 27, 63 and 72.

(A) $27 = 3 \times 3 \times 3$, $63 = 3 \times 3 \times 7$, $72 = 2 \times 2 \times 2 \times 3 \times 3$.
(B) Delete 3×3 from two of the products.
(C) The L.C.M. is $3 \times 7 \times 2 \times 2 \times 2 \times 3 \times 3 = 21 \times 72 = 1{,}512$.

I–B. Fractions

B–1

A FRACTION is a number which represents a ratio or division of two whole numbers (integers). A fraction is written in the form $\frac{a}{b}$. The number on the top, a, is called the numerator; the number on the bottom, b, is called the denominator. The denominator tells how many equal parts there are (for example, parts of a pie); the numerator tells how many of these equal parts are taken. For example, $\frac{5}{8}$ is a fraction whose numerator is 5 and whose denominator is 8; it represents taking 5 of 8 equal parts, or dividing 8 into 5.

A fraction can not have 0 as a denominator since division by 0 is not defined.

A fraction with 1 as the denominator is the same as the whole number which is its numerator. For example, $\frac{12}{1}$ is 12, $\frac{0}{1}$ is 0.

If the numerator and denominator of a fraction are identical, the fraction represents 1. For example, $\frac{3}{3} = \frac{9}{9} = \frac{13}{13} = 1$. Any whole number, k, is represented by a fraction with a numerator equal to k times the denominator. For example, $\frac{18}{6} = 3$, and $\frac{30}{5} = 6$.

B–2

Mixed Numbers. A mixed number consists of a whole number and a fraction. For example, $7\frac{1}{4}$ is a mixed number; it means $7 + \frac{1}{4}$ and $\frac{1}{4}$ is called the fractional part of the mixed number $7\frac{1}{4}$. Any mixed number can be changed into a fraction:

(A) Multiply the whole number by the denominator of the fraction.
(B) Add the numerator of the fraction to the result of step A.
(C) Use the result of step B as the numerator and use the denominator of the fractional part of the mixed number as the denominator. This fraction is equal to the mixed number.

EXAMPLE 1: Write $7\frac{1}{4}$ as a fraction.

(A) $4 \cdot 7 = 28$
(B) $28 + 1 = 29$
(C) so $7\frac{1}{4} = \frac{29}{4}$

A fraction whose numerator is larger than its denominator can be changed into a mixed number.

(A) Divide the denominator into the numerator; the result is the whole number of the mixed number.
(B) Put the remainder from step A over the denominator; this is the fractional part of the mixed number.

EXAMPLE 2: Change $\frac{35}{8}$ into a mixed number.

(A) Divide 8 into 35; the result is 4 with a remainder of 3.
(B) $\frac{3}{8}$ is the fractional part of the mixed number.
(C) So $\frac{35}{8} = 4\frac{3}{8}$.

In calculations with mixed numbers, change the mixed numbers into fractions.

B–3

Multiplying Fractions. To multiply two fractions, multiply their numerators, multiply their denominators, and then divide the denominator of the resulting fraction into its numerator.

In word problems, *of* usually indicates multiplication.

EXAMPLE: John saves $\frac{1}{3}$ of \$240. How much does he save?

$$\frac{1}{3} \cdot \frac{240}{1} = \frac{240}{3} = \$80, \text{ the amount John saves.}$$

B–4

Dividing Fractions. One fraction is a *reciprocal* of another if their product is 1. So $\frac{1}{2}$ and 2 are reciprocals $\left(\frac{1}{2} \cdot 2 = \frac{1}{2} \cdot \frac{2}{1} = \frac{2}{2} = 1\right)$. To find the reciprocal of a fraction, simply interchange the numerator and denominator (turn the fraction upside down). This is called *inverting* the fraction. So when you invert $\frac{15}{17}$ you get $\frac{17}{15}$. When a fraction is inverted the inverted fraction and the original fraction are reciprocals. Thus $\frac{15}{17} \cdot \frac{17}{15} = \frac{255}{255} = \frac{1}{1} = 1$.

To divide one fraction (the dividend) by another fraction (the divisor), invert the divisor and multiply.

EXAMPLE 1: $\frac{5}{6} \div \frac{3}{4} = \frac{5}{6} \cdot \frac{4}{3} = \frac{20}{18}$

EXAMPLE 2: A worker makes a basket every $\frac{2}{3}$ hour. If the worker works for $7\frac{1}{2}$ hours, how many baskets will he make? We want to divide $\frac{2}{3}$ into $7\frac{1}{2}$. $7\frac{1}{2} = \frac{15}{2}$, so we want to divide $\frac{15}{2}$ by $\frac{2}{3}$. Thus

$$\frac{15}{2} \div \frac{2}{3} = \frac{15}{2} \cdot \frac{3}{2} = \frac{45}{4} = 11\frac{1}{4} \text{ baskets.}$$

B–5

Dividing and Multiplying by the Same Number. Since multiplication or division by 1 does not change the value of a number, you can multiply or divide any fraction by 1 and the fraction will remain the same. Remember that $\frac{a}{a} = 1$ for any non-zero number a. Therefore, if you multiply or divide any fraction by $\frac{a}{a}$, the result is the same as if you multiplied the numerator by a and denominator by a or divided the numerator by a and the denominator by a.

If you multiply the numerator and denominator of a fraction by the same non-zero number, the value of the fraction remains the same.

If you divide the numerator and denominator of any fraction by the same non-zero number, the value of the fraction remains the same.

Consider the fraction $\frac{3}{4}$. If we multiply 3 by 10 and 4 by 10, then $\frac{30}{40}$ must equal

$\frac{3}{4}$ (In $\frac{30}{40}$, 10 is a common factor of 30 and 40.)

When we multiply fractions, if any of the numerators and denominators have a common factor (see page 206 for factors) we can divide each of them by the common factor and the fraction remains the same. This process is called *cancelling* and can be a great time-saver.

EXAMPLE: Multiply $\frac{4}{9} \cdot \frac{75}{8}$. Since 4 is a common factor of 4 and 8, divide 4 and 8 by 4 getting $\frac{4}{9} \cdot \frac{75}{8} = \frac{1}{9} \cdot \frac{75}{2}$. Since 3 is a common factor of 9 and 75 divide 9 and 75 by 3 to get $\frac{1}{9} \cdot \frac{75}{2} = \frac{1}{3} \cdot \frac{25}{2}$. So $\frac{4}{9} \cdot \frac{75}{8} = \frac{1}{3} \cdot \frac{25}{2} = \frac{25}{6}$.

B–6

Equivalent Fractions. Two fractions are equivalent or equal if they represent the same ratio or number. In the last section, you saw that if you multiply or divide the numerator and denominator of a fraction by the same non-zero number, the result is equivalent to the original fraction. For example, $\frac{7}{8} = \frac{70}{80}$ since $70 = 10 \times 7$ and $80 = 10 \times 8$.

> In a multiple-choice test, your answer to a problem may not be the same as any of the given choices, yet one choice may be equivalent. Therefore, you may have to express your answer as an equivalent fraction.

To find a fraction with a known denominator equal to a given fraction:

(A) divide the denominator of the given fraction into the known denominator;

(B) multiply the result of (A) by the numerator of the given fraction; this is the numerator of the required equivalent fraction.

EXAMPLE: Your answer is $\frac{2}{5}$ One of the test answers has a denominator of 30.

Find a fraction with denominator 30 which is equal to $\frac{2}{5}$:

(A) 5 into 30 is 6;

(B) $6 \cdot 2 = 12$ so $\frac{12}{30} = \frac{2}{5}$.

Check your result. Divide numerator and denominator by the same number. $12 \div 6 = 2$ and $30 \div 6 = 5$

B–7

Reducing a Fraction to Lowest Terms. A fraction has been reduced to lowest terms when the numerator and denominator have no common factors.

For example, $\frac{3}{4}$ is reduced to lowest terms, but $\frac{3}{6}$ is not because 3 is a common factor of 3 and 6.

To reduce a fraction to lowest terms, cancel all the common factors of the numerator and denominator. (Cancelling common factors will not change the value of the fraction.)

For example, $\frac{100}{150} = \frac{10 \cdot 10}{10 \cdot 15} = \frac{10}{15} = \frac{5 \cdot 2}{5 \cdot 3} = \frac{2}{3}$. Since 2 and 3 have no common factors, $\frac{2}{3}$ is $\frac{100}{150}$ reduced to lowest terms. A fraction is equivalent to its reduction to lowest terms.

If you write the numerator and denominator as products of primes, it is easy to cancel all the common factors.

$$\frac{63}{81} = \frac{3 \cdot 3 \cdot 7}{3 \cdot 3 \cdot 3 \cdot 3} = \frac{7}{9}$$

B–8

Adding Fractions. If the fractions have the same denominator, then the denominator is called a *common denominator.* Add the numerators, and use this sum as the new numerator, retaining the common denominator as the denominator of the new fraction. Reduce the new fraction to lowest terms.

EXAMPLE 1: $\frac{5}{12} + \frac{3}{12} = \frac{5+3}{12} = \frac{8}{12} = \frac{2}{3}$

EXAMPLE 2: Jim uses 7 eggs to make breakfast and 8 eggs for supper. How many dozen eggs has he used? 7 eggs are $\frac{7}{12}$ of a dozen and 8 eggs are $\frac{8}{12}$ of a dozen. He used $\frac{7}{12} + \frac{8}{12} = \frac{7+8}{12} = \frac{15}{12} = \frac{5}{4} = 1\frac{1}{4}$ dozen eggs.

If the fractions don't have the same denominator, you must first find a common denominator. Multiply all the denominators together; the result is a common denominator.

EXAMPLE: To add $\frac{1}{2} + \frac{2}{3} + \frac{7}{4}$, $2 \cdot 3 \cdot 4 = 24$ is a common denominator.

There are many common denominators; the smallest one is called the *least common denominator.* For the previous example, 12 is the least common denominator.

Once you have found a common denominator, express each fraction as an equivalent fraction with the common denominator, and add as you did when the fractions had the same denominator.

EXAMPLE: $\frac{1}{2}+\frac{2}{3}+\frac{7}{4}=?$

(A) 24 is a common denominator.

(B) $\frac{1}{2}=\frac{12}{24}, \frac{2}{3}=\frac{16}{24}, \frac{7}{4}=\frac{42}{24}$.

(C) $\frac{1}{2}+\frac{2}{3}+\frac{7}{4}=\frac{12}{24}+\frac{16}{24}+\frac{42}{24}=\frac{12+16+42}{24}=\frac{70}{24}=\frac{35}{12}$.

B–9

Subtracting Fractions. When the fractions have the same denominator, subtract the numerators and place the result over the denominator.

EXAMPLE: $\frac{3}{5}-\frac{2}{5}=\frac{3-2}{5}=\frac{1}{5}$

When the fractions have different denominators

(A) Find a common denominator.
(B) Express the fractions as equivalent fractions with the same denominator.
(C) Subtract.

EXAMPLE: $\frac{3}{5}-\frac{2}{7}=?$

(A) A common denominator is $5 \cdot 7 = 35$.

(B) $\frac{3}{5}=\frac{21}{35}, \frac{2}{7}=\frac{10}{35}$.

(C) $\frac{3}{5}-\frac{2}{7}=\frac{21}{35}-\frac{10}{35}=\frac{21-10}{35}=\frac{11}{35}$.

B–10

Complex Fractions. A fraction whose numerator and denominator are themselves fractions is called a *complex fraction*. For example $\frac{2/3}{4/5}$ is a complex fraction. A complex fraction can always be simplified by dividing the fraction.

EXAMPLE 1: $\frac{2}{3} \div \frac{4}{5}=\frac{\cancel{2}^{1}}{3}\cdot\frac{5}{\cancel{4}_{2}}=\frac{1}{3}\cdot\frac{5}{2}=\frac{5}{6}$

EXAMPLE 2: It takes $2\frac{1}{2}$ hours to get from Buffalo to Cleveland traveling at a constant rate of speed. What part of the distance is traveled in $\frac{3}{4}$ of an hour?

$\frac{3/4}{2\ 1/2}=\frac{3/4}{5/2}=\frac{3}{4}\cdot\frac{2}{5}=\frac{3}{2}\cdot\frac{1}{5}=\frac{3}{10}$ of the distance.

I–C. Decimals

C–1

A collection of digits (the digits are 0,1,2, . . . ,9) after a period (called the decimal point) is called a *decimal fraction*. For example, these are all decimal fractions:

.503
.5602
.32
.4

Every decimal fraction represents a fraction. To find the fraction a decimal fraction represents:

(A) Take the fraction whose denominator is 10 and whose numerator is the first digit to the right of the decimal point.
(B) Take the fraction whose denominator is 100 and whose numerator is the second digit to the right of the decimal point.
(C) Take the fraction whose denominator is 1,000 and whose numerator is the third digit to the right of the decimal point.
(D) Continue the procedure until you have used each digit to the right of the decimal place. The denominator in each step is 10 times the denominator in the previous step.
(E) The *sum* of the fractions you have obtained in (A), (B), (C), and (D) is the fraction that the decimal fraction represents.

EXAMPLE 1: Find the fraction .503 represents.

(A) $\frac{5}{10}$

(B) $\frac{0}{100}$

(C) $\frac{3}{1000}$

(D) All the digits have already been used.

(E) So $.503 = \frac{5}{10} + \frac{0}{100} + \frac{3}{1000} = \frac{500}{1000} + \frac{0}{1000} + \frac{3}{1000} = \frac{503}{1000}$.

EXAMPLE 2: What fraction does .78934 represent?

(A) $\frac{7}{10}$

(B) $\frac{8}{100}$

(C) $\frac{9}{1000}$

(D) $\frac{3}{10{,}000}, \frac{4}{100{,}000}$

(E) So $.78934 = \frac{7}{10} + \frac{8}{100} + \frac{9}{1000} + \frac{3}{10{,}000} + \frac{4}{100{,}000} = \frac{78{,}934}{100{,}000}$.

Notice that the denominator of the last fraction you obtain in step (D) is a common denominator for all the previous denominators. Since each denominator is 10 times the previous one, the denominator of the final fraction of part (D) will be the product of *r* copies of 10 multiplied together (called 10^r) where *r* is the number of digits which appear in the decimal fraction. Therefore, a decimal fraction represents a fraction whose denominator is 10^r where *r* is the number of digits in the decimal fraction and whose numerator is the number represented by the digits of the decimal fraction.

EXAMPLE 3: What fraction does .5702 represent?

There are 4 digits in .5702. Therefore, the denominator is $10 \times 10 \times 10 \times 10 =$ 10,000, and the numerator is 5,702. Therefore, $.5702 = \frac{5{,}702}{10{,}000}$.

> ***You can add any number of zeros to the right of a decimal fraction without changing its value.***

EXAMPLE: $.3 = \frac{3}{10} = \frac{30}{100} = .30 = .30000 = \frac{30{,}000}{100{,}000} = .300000000\ldots$

C–2

We call the first position to the right of the decimal point the tenths place, since the digit in that position tells you how many tenths you should take. (It is the numerator of a fraction whose denominator is 10.) In the same way, we call the second position to the right the hundredths place, the third position to the right the thousandths, and so on. This is similar to the way whole numbers are expressed, since 568 means $5 \times 100 + 6 \times 10 + 8 \times 1$. The various digits represent different numbers depending on their position: the first place to the left of the decimal point represents units, the second place to the left represents tens, and so on.

The following diagram may be helpful:

```
T H T U   T H T
H U E N   E U H
O N N I . N N O
U D S T   T D U
S R   S   H R S
A E       S E A
N D         D N
D S         T D
S           H T
            S H
              S
```

Thus, 5,342.061 means 5 thousands + 3 hundreds + 4 tens + 2 + 0 tenths + 6 hundredths + 1 thousandth.

C–3

A DECIMAL is a whole number plus a decimal fraction; the decimal point separates the whole number from the decimal fraction. For example, 4,307.206 is a decimal which represents 4,307 added to the decimal fraction .206. A decimal fraction is a decimal with zero as the whole number.

C–4

A fraction whose denominator is a multiple of 10 is equivalent to a decimal. The denominator tells you the last place that is filled to the right of the decimal point. Place the decimal point in the numerator so that the last place to the right of the decimal point corresponds to the denominator. If the numerator does not have enough digits, add the appropriate number of zeros *before* the numerator.

EXAMPLE 1: Find the decimal equivalent of $\frac{5{,}732}{100}$.

Since the denominator is 100, you need two places to the right of the decimal point so $\frac{5{,}732}{100} = 57.32$.

EXAMPLE 2: What is the decimal equivalent of $\frac{57}{10{,}000}$?

The denominator is 10,000, so you need 4 decimal places. Since 57 only has two places, we add two zeros in front of 57; thus, $\frac{57}{10{,}000} = .0057$.

Do not make the error of adding the zeros to the right instead of to the left of 57; .5700 means $\frac{5{,}700}{10{,}000}$ not $\frac{57}{10{,}000}$.

C–5

Adding Decimals. Decimals are much easier to add than fractions. To add a collection of decimals:

(A) Write the decimals in a column with the decimal points vertically aligned.
(B) Add enough zeros to the right of the decimal point so that every number has an entry in each column to the right of the decimal point.
(C) Add the numbers in the same way as whole numbers.
(D) Place a decimal point in the sum so that it is directly beneath the decimal points in the decimals added.

EXAMPLE 1: How much is 5 + 3.43 + 16.021 + 3.1?

(A)
```
     5
     3.43
    16.021
  + 3.1
```

(B)
```
     5.000
     3.430
    16.021
  + 3.100
```

(C)
```
     5.000
     3.430
    16.021
  + 3.100
```

(D)
```
    27.551
```

The answer is **27.551**.

EXAMPLE 2: If John has \$.50, \$3.25, and \$6.05, how much does he have altogether?

$$\begin{array}{r} \$\ .50 \\ 3.25 \\ +\ 6.05 \\ \hline \$9.80 \end{array}$$ So John has \$9.80.

C–6

Subtracting Decimals. To subtract one decimal from another:

(A) Put the decimals in a column so that the decimal points are vertically aligned.
(B) Add zeros sc that every decimal has an entry in each column to the right of the decımal point.
(C) Subtract the numbers as you would whole numbers.
(D) Place the decimal point in the result so that it is directly beneath the decimal points of the numbers you subtracted.

EXAMPLE 1: Solve 5.053 − 2.09.

(A) $\begin{array}{r} 5.053 \\ -\ 2.09\ \ \\ \hline \end{array}$ (B) $\begin{array}{r} 5.053 \\ -\ 2.090 \\ \hline \end{array}$

(C) $\begin{array}{r} 5.053 \\ -\ 2.090 \\ \hline \end{array}$
(D) 2.963 The answer is **2.963.**

EXAMPLE 2: If Joe has \$12 and he loses \$8.40, how much money does he have left?

Since \$12.00 − \$8.40 = \$3.60, he has \$3.60 left.

C–7

Multiplying Decimals. Decimals are multiplied like whole numbers. *The decimal point of the product is placed so that the number of decimal places in the product is equal to the total of the number of decimal places in all of the numbers multiplied.*

EXAMPLE 1: What is (5.02)(.6)?

(502)(6) = 3012. There were 2 decimal places in 5.02 and 1 decimal place in .6, so the product must have 2 + 1 = 3 decimal places. Therefore, (5.02)(.6) = 3.012.

EXAMPLE 2: If eggs cost \$.06 each, how much should a dozen eggs cost?

Since (12)(.06) = .72, a dozen eggs should cost \$.72.

Computing Tip. To multiply a decimal by 10, just move the decimal point to the right one place; to multiply by 100, move the decimal point two places to the right and so on.

EXAMPLE: 9,983.456 × 100 = 998,345.6

C–8

Dividing Decimals. To divide one decimal (the dividend) by another decimal (the divisor):

(A) Move the decimal point in the divisor to the right until there is no decimal fraction in the divisor (this is the same as multiplying the divisor by a multiple of 10).
(B) Move the decimal point in the dividend the same number of places to the right as you moved the decimal point in step (A).
(C) Divide the result of (B) by the result of (A) as if they were whole numbers.
(D) The number of decimal places in the result (quotient) should be equal to the number of decimal places in the result of step (B).

EXAMPLE 1: Divide .05 into 25.155.

(A) Move the decimal point two places to the right in .05; the result is 5.
(B) Move the decimal point two places to the right in 25.155; the result is 2515.5.
(C) Divide 5 into 25155; the result is 5031.
(D) Since there was one decimal place in the result of (B); the answer is 503.1.

The work for this example might look like this:

$$\begin{array}{r} 503.1 \\ .05\,\overline{)25.15\,5} \end{array}$$

You can always check division by multiplying.

(503.1)(.05) = 25.155 so we were correct.

If you write division as a fraction, example 1 would be expressed as $\frac{25.155}{.05}$.

You can multiply both the numerator and denominator by 100 without changing the value of the fraction, so

$$\frac{25.155}{.05} = \frac{25.155 \times 100}{.05 \times 100} = \frac{2515.5}{5.}$$

So step (A) and (B) always change the division of a decimal by a decimal into the division by a whole number.

To divide a decimal by a whole number, divide them as if they were whole numbers. Then place the decimal point in the quotient so that the quotient has as many decimal places as the decimal (the dividend).

EXAMPLE 2: $\frac{55.033}{1.1} = \frac{550.33}{11.} = 50.03.$

EXAMPLE 3: If oranges cost 6¢ each, how many oranges can you buy for $2.52?

$$6¢ = \$.06,$$

so the number of oranges is

$$\frac{2.52}{.06} = \frac{252}{6} = 42.$$

Computing Tip. To divide a decimal by 10, move the decimal point *to the left* one place; to divide by 100, move the decimal point two places to the left, and so on.

EXAMPLE: Divide 5,637.6471 by 1,000.

The answer is 5.6376471, since to divide by 1,000 you move the decimal point 3 places to the left.

C–9

Converting a Fraction Into a Decimal. To convert a fraction into a decimal, divide the denominator into the numerator. For example, $\frac{3}{4} = 4\sqrt{3.00} =$ .75. Some fractions give an infinite decimal when you divide the denominator into the numerator, for example, $\frac{1}{3} = .333\ldots$ where the three dots mean you keep on getting 3 with each step of division. .333 . . . is an *infinite decimal.*

If a fraction has an infinite decimal, use the fraction in any computation.

EXAMPLE 1: What is $\frac{2}{9}$ of $3,690.90?

Since the decimal for $\frac{2}{9}$ is .2222 . . . use the fraction $\frac{2}{9}$.
$\frac{2}{9} \times \$3{,}690.90 = 2 \times \$410.10 = \$820.20.$

You should know the following decimal equivalents of fractions:

$\frac{1}{100} = .01$	$\frac{1}{6} = .1666\ldots$
$\frac{1}{50} = .02$	$\frac{1}{5} = .2$
$\frac{1}{40} = .025$	$\frac{1}{4} = .25$
$\frac{1}{25} = .04$	$\frac{1}{3} = .333\ldots$
$\frac{1}{20} = .05$	$\frac{3}{8} = .375$
$\frac{1}{16} = .0625$	$\frac{2}{5} = .4$
$\frac{1}{15} = .0666\ldots$	$\frac{1}{2} = .5$
$\frac{1}{12} = .0833\ldots$	$\frac{5}{8} = .625$
$\frac{1}{10} = .1$	$\frac{2}{3} = .666\ldots$
$\frac{1}{9} = .111\ldots$	$\frac{3}{4} = .75$
$\frac{1}{8} = .125$	$\frac{7}{8} = .875$
$\frac{3}{2} = 1.5$	

Any decimal with . . . is an infinite decimal.

I–D. Percentage

D–1

PERCENTAGE is another method of expressing fractions or parts of an object. Percentages are expressed in terms of hundredths, so 100% means 100 hundredths or 1. In the same way, 50% would be 50 hundredths or $\frac{50}{100}$ or $\frac{1}{2}$.

A decimal is converted to a percentage by multiplying the decimal by 100. Since multiplying a decimal by 100 is accomplished by moving the decimal point two places to the right, *you convert a decimal into a percentage by moving the decimal point two places to the right*. For example, .134 = 13.4%.

If you wish to convert a percentage into a decimal, you divide the percentage by 100. There is a shortcut for this also. To divide by 100 you move the decimal point two places to the left.

Therefore, *to convert a percentage into a decimal, move the decimal point two places to the left*. For example, 24% = .24.

A fraction is converted into a percentage by changing the fraction to a decimal and then changing the decimal to a percentage. A percentage is changed into a fraction by first converting the percentage into a decimal and then changing the decimal to a fraction. You should know the following fractional equivalents of percentages:

$1\% = \frac{1}{100}$	$25\% = \frac{1}{4}$	$80\% = \frac{4}{5}$
$2\% = \frac{1}{50}$	$33\frac{1}{3}\% = \frac{1}{3}$	$83\frac{1}{3}\% = \frac{5}{6}$
$4\% = \frac{1}{25}$	$37\frac{1}{2}\% = \frac{3}{8}$	$87\frac{1}{2}\% = \frac{7}{8}$
$5\% = \frac{1}{20}$	$40\% = \frac{2}{5}$	$100\% = 1$
$8\frac{1}{3}\% = \frac{1}{12}$	$50\% = \frac{1}{2}$	$120\% = \frac{6}{5}$
$10\% = \frac{1}{10}$	$60\% = \frac{3}{5}$	$125\% = \frac{5}{4}$
$12\frac{1}{2}\% = \frac{1}{8}$	$62\frac{1}{2}\% = \frac{5}{8}$	$133\frac{1}{3}\% = \frac{4}{3}$
$16\frac{2}{3}\% = \frac{1}{6}$	$66\frac{2}{3}\% = \frac{2}{3}$	$150\% = \frac{3}{2}$
$20\% = \frac{1}{5}$	$75\% = \frac{3}{4}$	

Note, for example, that $133\frac{1}{3}\% = 1.33\frac{1}{3} = 1\frac{1}{3} = \frac{4}{3}$.

When you compute with percentages, it is usually easier to change the percentages to decimals or fractions.

EXAMPLE 1: A company has 6,435 bars of soap. If the company sells 20% of its bars of soap, how many bars of soap did it sell?

Change 20% into .2. Thus, the company sold (.2)(6,435) = 1287.0 = 1,287 bars of soap. An alternative method would be to convert 20% to $\frac{1}{5}$. Then, $\frac{1}{5} \times 6{,}435 = 1{,}287$.

EXAMPLE 2: In a class of 60 students, 18 students received a grade of B. What percentage of the class received a grade of B?

$\frac{18}{60}$ of the class received a grade of B. $\frac{18}{60} = \frac{3}{10} = .3$ and $.3 = 30\%$, so 30% of the class received a grade of B.

EXAMPLE 3: If the population of Dryden was 10,000 in 1960 and the population of Dryden increased by 15% between 1960 and 1970, what was the population of Dryden in 1970?

The population increased by 15% between 1960 and 1970, so the increase was (.15)(10,000) which is 1,500. The population in 1970 was 10,000 + 1,500 = 11,500.

A quicker method: the population increased 15%, so the population in 1970 is 115% of the population in 1960. Therefore, the population in 1970 is 115% of 10,000 which is (1.15)(10,000) = 11,500.

D–2

Interest and Discount. Two of the most common uses of percentages are in interest and discount problems.

The rate of interest is usually given as a percentage. The basic formula for interest problems is:

INTEREST = AMOUNT × TIME × RATE

You can assume the rate of interest is the annual rate of interest unless the problem states otherwise; so you should express the time in years.

EXAMPLE 1: How much interest will $10,000 earn in 9 months at an annual rate of 6%?

9 months is $\frac{3}{4}$ of a year and $6\% = \frac{3}{50}$, so using the formula, the interest is $10,000 $\times \frac{3}{4} \times \frac{3}{50} = \$50 \times 9 = \$450$.

EXAMPLE 2: What annual rate of interest was paid if $5,000 earned $300 in interest in 2 years?

Since the interest was earned in 2 years, $150 is the interest earned in one year. $\frac{150}{5{,}000} = .03 = 3\%$, so the annual rate of interest was 3%.

This type of interest is called *simple interest.*

There is another method of computing interest called *compound interest.* In computing compound interest, the interest is periodically added to the amount (or principal) which is earning interest.

EXAMPLE 3: What will $1,000 be worth after three years if it earns interest at the rate of 5% compounded annually?

Compounded annually means that the interest earned during one year is added to the amount (or principal) at the end of each year. The interest on $1,000 at

5% for one year is \$(1,000)(.05) = \$50. So you must compute the interest on \$1,050 (not \$1,000) for the second year. The interest is \$(1,050)(.05) = \$52.50. Therefore, during the third year interest will be computed for \$1,102.50. During the third year the interest is \$(1,102.50)(.05) = \$55.125 = \$55.13. Therefore, after 3 years the original \$1000 will be worth \$1,157.63.

If you calculated simple interest on \$1,000 at 5% for three years, the answer would be \$(1,000)(.05)(3) = \$150. Therefore, using simple interest, \$1,000 is worth \$1,150 after 3 years. Notice that this is not the same as the money was worth using compound interest.

You can assume that interest means simple interest unless a problem states otherwise.

The basic formula for discount problems is:

$$\boxed{\text{DISCOUNT} = \text{COST} \times \text{RATE OF DISCOUNT}}$$

EXAMPLE 1: What is the discount if a car which cost \$3,000 is discounted 7%?

The discount is \$3,000 × .07 = \$210.00 since 7% = .07.

If we know the cost of an item and its discounted price, we can find the rate of discount by using the formula

$$\text{rate of discount} = \frac{\text{cost} - \text{price}}{\text{cost}}$$

EXAMPLE 2: What was the rate of discount if a boat which cost \$5,000 was sold for \$4,800?

Using this formula, we find that the rate of discount equals

$$\frac{5{,}000 - 4{,}800}{5{,}000} = \frac{200}{5{,}000} = \frac{1}{25} = .04 = 4\%.$$

After an item has been discounted once, it may be discounted again. This procedure is called *successive* discounting.

EXAMPLE 3: A bicycle originally cost \$100 and was discounted 10%. After three months it was sold after being discounted 15%. How much was the bicycle sold for?

After the 10% discount the bicycle was selling for \$100(.90) = \$90. An item which costs \$90 and is discounted 15% will sell for \$90(.85) = \$76.50, so the bicycle was sold for \$76.50.

Notice that if you added the two discounts of 10% and 15% and treated the successive discounts as a single discount of 25%, your answer would be that the bicycle sold for \$75, which is incorrect. Successive discounts are *not* identical to a single discount of the sum of the discounts. The previous example shows that successive discounts of 10% and 15% are not identical to a single discount of 25%.

I-E. Rounding off Numbers

E-1

Many times an approximate answer can be found more quickly and may be more useful than the exact answer. For example, if a company had sales of $998,875.63 during a year, it is easier to remember that the sales were about $1 million.

Rounding off a number to a decimal place means finding the multiple of the representative of that decimal place which is closest to the original number. Thus, rounding off a number to the nearest hundred means finding the multiple of 100 which is closest to the original number. Rounding off to the nearest tenth means finding the multiple of $\frac{1}{10}$ which is closest to the original number. After a number has been rounded off to a particular decimal place, all the digits to the right of that particular decimal place will be zero.

EXAMPLE 1: Round off 9,403,420.71 to the nearest hundred.

You must find the multiple of one hundred which is closest to 9,403,420.71.

The answer is 9,403,400.

Most problems dealing with money are rounded off if the answer contains a fractional part of a cent.

To round off a number to the rth decimal place:

(A) Look at the digit in the place to the right of the rth place;
(B) *If the digit is 0, 1, 2, 3, or 4, change all the digits in places to the right of the* rth *place to 0* to round off the number.
(C) *If the digit is 5, 6, 7, 8, or 9, add 1 to the digit in the* rth *place and change all the digits in places to the right of the* rth *place to 0* to round off the number.

EXAMPLE 2: If 16 donuts cost $1.00, how much should three donuts cost?

Three donuts should cost $\frac{3}{16}$ of $1.00. Since $\frac{3}{16} \times 1. = .1875$, the cost would be $.1875. In practice, you would round it up to $.19 or 19¢.

Rounding off numbers can help you get quick, approximate answers. Since many questions require only rough answers, you can sometimes save time on the test by rounding off numbers.

EXAMPLE 3: Round off 43.79 to the nearest tenth.

The place to the right of tenths is hundredths, so look in the hundredths place. Since 9 is bigger than 5, add 1 to the tenths place. Therefore, 43.79 is 43.8 rounded off to the nearest tenth.

If the digit in the *r*th place is 9 and you need to add 1 to the digit to round off the number to the *r*th decimal place, put a zero in the *r*th place and add 1 to the digit in the position to the left of the *r*th place. For example, 298 rounded off to the nearest 10 is 300; 99,752 to the nearest thousand is 100,000.

I–F. Signed Numbers

F–1

A number preceded by either a plus or a minus sign is called a SIGNED NUMBER. For example, +5, −6, −4.2, and +$^3/_4$ are all signed numbers. If no sign is given with a number, a plus sign is assumed; thus, 5 is interpreted as +5.

Signed numbers can often be used to distinguish different concepts. For example, a profit of $10 can be denoted by +$10 and a loss of $10 by −$10. A temperature of 20 degrees below zero can be denoted −20°.

F–2

Signed numbers are also called DIRECTED NUMBERS. You can think of numbers arranged on a line, called a number line, in the following manner:

Take a line which extends indefinitely in both directions, pick a point on the line and call it 0, pick another point on the line to the right of 0 and call it 1. The point to the right of 1 which is exactly as far from 1 as 1 is from 0 is called 2, the point to the right of 2 just as far from 2 as 1 is from 0 is called 3, and so on. The point halfway between 0 and 1 is called $^1/_2$, the point halfway between $^1/_2$ and 1 is called $^3/_4$. In this way, you can identify any whole number or any fraction with a point on the line.

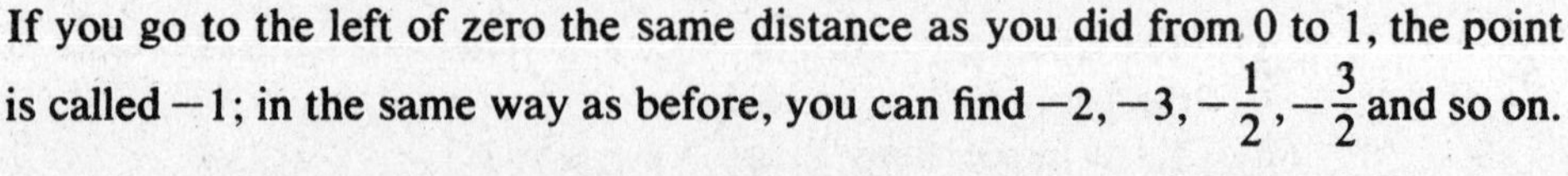

All the numbers which correspond to points to the right of 0 are called *positive numbers*. The sign of a positive number is +.

If you go to the left of zero the same distance as you did from 0 to 1, the point is called −1; in the same way as before, you can find −2, −3, $-\frac{1}{2}$, $-\frac{3}{2}$ and so on.

All the numbers which correspond to points to the left of zero are called *negative numbers*. Negative numbers are signed numbers whose sign is −. For example, −3, −5.15, −.003 are all negative numbers.

0 is neither positive nor negative; any nonzero number is positive or negative but not both. So $-0 = 0$.

F–3

Absolute Value. The absolute value of a signed number is the distance of the number from 0. The absolute value of any nonzero number is *positive*. For example, the absolute value of 2 is 2; the absolute value of -2 is 2. The absolute value of a number a is denoted by $|a|$, so $|-2| = 2$. The absolute value of any number can be found by dropping its sign, $|-12| = 12$, $|4| = 4$. *Thus* $|-a| = |a|$ *for any number a.* The only number whose absolute value is zero is zero.

F–4

Adding Signed Numbers:

Case I. Adding numbers with the *same sign:*

(A) The sign of the sum is the same as the sign of the numbers being added.
(B) Add the absolute values.
(C) Put the sign from step (A) in front of the number you obtained in step (B).

EXAMPLE 1: What is $-2 + (-3.1) + (-.02)$?

(A) The sign of the sum will be $-$.
(B) $|-2| = 2$, $|-3.1| = 3.1$, $|-.02| = .02$, and $2 + 3.1 + .02 = 5.12$.
(C) The answer is -5.12.

Case II. Adding *two* numbers with *different signs:*

(A) The sign of the sum is the sign of the number which is largest in absolute value.
(B) Subtract the absolute value of the number with the smaller absolute value from the absolute value of the number with the larger absolute value.
(C) The answer is the number you obtained in step (B) preceded by the sign from part (A).

EXAMPLE 2: How much is $-5.1 + 3$?

(A) The absolute value of -5.1 is 5.1 and the absolute value of 3 is 3, so the sign of the sum will be $-$.
(B) 5.1 is larger than 3, and $5.1 - 3 = 2.1$.
(C) The sum is -2.1.

Case III. Adding *more than two* numbers with *different signs:*

(A) Add all the positive numbers; the result is positive (this is Case I).
(B) Add all the negative numbers; the result is negative (this is Case I).
(C) Add the result of step (A) to the result of step (B), by using Case II.

EXAMPLE 3: Find the value of $5 + 52 + (-3) + 7 + (-5.1)$.

(A) $5+52+7=64$.
(B) $-3+(-5.1)=-8.1$.
(C) $64+(-8.1)=55.9$, so the answer is 55.9.

EXAMPLE 4: If a store made a profit of \$23.50 on Monday, lost \$2.05 on Tuesday, lost \$5.03 on Wednesday, made a profit of \$30.10 on Thursday, and made a profit of \$41.25 on Friday, what was its total profit (or loss) for the week? Use + for profit and − for loss.

The total is $23.50+(-2.05)+(-5.03)+30.10+41.25$ which is $94.85+(-7.08)=87.77$. So the store made a profit of \$87.77.

F–5

Subtracting Signed Numbers. When subtracting signed numbers:

(A) Change the sign of the number you are subtracting (the subtrahend).
(B) Add the result of step (A) to the number being subtracted from (the minuend) using the rules of the preceding section.

EXAMPLE 1: Subtract 4.1 from 6.5.

(A) 4.1 becomes -4.1.
(B) $6.5+(-4.1)=2.4$.

EXAMPLE 2: What is $7.8-(-10.1)$?

(A) -10.1 becomes 10.1.
(B) $7.8+10.1=17.9$.

So we subtract a negative number by adding a positive number with the same absolute value, and we subtract a positive number by adding a negative number of the same absolute value.

F–6

Multiplying Signed Numbers.

Case I. Multiplying two numbers:

(A) Multiply the absolute values of the numbers.
(B) If both numbers have the same sign, the result of step (A) is the answer, i.e. the product is positive. If the numbers have different signs, then the answer is the result of step (A) with a minus sign.

EXAMPLE 1: $(-5)(-12)=?$

(A) $5\times 12=60$
(B) Both signs are the same, so the answer is 60.

EXAMPLE 2: (4) (−3)= ?

(A) $4 \times 3 = 12$
(B) The signs are different, so the answer is −12. You can remember the sign of the product in the following way:

$$(-)(-) = +$$
$$(+)(+) = +$$
$$(-)(+) = -$$
$$(+)(-) = -$$

Case II. Multiplying more than two numbers:

(A) Multiply the first two factors using Case I.
(B) Multiply the result of (A) by the third factor.
(C) Multiply the result of (B) by the fourth factor.
(D) Continue until you have used each factor.

EXAMPLE 3: $(-5)(4)(2)(-\frac{1}{2})(\frac{3}{4}) = ?$

(A) $(-5)(4) = -20$
(B) $(-20)(2) = -40$
(C) $(-40)(-\frac{1}{2}) = 20$
(D) $(20)(\frac{3}{4}) = 15$, so the answer is 15.

> *The sign of the product is + if there are no negative factors or an even number of negative factors. The sign of the product is − if there are an odd number of negative factors.*

F–7

Dividing Signed Numbers: Divide the absolute values of the numbers; the sign of the quotient is determined by the same rules as you used to determine the sign of a product. Thus,

$$+ \div + = +$$
$$- \div - = +$$
$$+ \div - = -$$
$$- \div + = -$$

EXAMPLE 1: Divide 53.2 by −4.

53.2 divided by 4 is 13.3. Since one of the numbers is positive and the other negative, the answer is −13.3.

EXAMPLE 2: $\frac{-5}{-2} = \frac{5}{2}$

I–G. Averages, Medians, Ranges, and Modes

G–1

Mean. The *average* or *arithmetic mean* of a collection of N numbers is the result of dividing the sum of all the numbers in the collection by N.

EXAMPLE 1: The scores of 9 students on a test were 72, 78, 81, 64, 85, 92, 95, 60, and 55. What was the average score of the students?

Since there are 9 students, the average is the total of all the scores divided by 9. So the average is $\frac{1}{9}$ of $(72 + 78 + 81 + 64 + 85 + 92 + 95 + 60 + 55)$, which is $\frac{1}{9}$ of (682) or $75\frac{7}{9}$.

EXAMPLE 2: The temperature at noon in Coldtown, U.S.A. was 5° on Monday, 10° on Tuesday, 2° below zero on Wednesday, 5° below zero on Thursday, 0° on Friday, 4° on Saturday, and 1° below zero on Sunday. What was the average temperature at noon for the week?

Use negative numbers for the temperatures below zero. The average temperature is the average of 5, 10, −2, −5, 0, 4 and −1, which is $\frac{5 + 10 + (-2) + (-5) + 0 + 4 + (-1)}{7} = \frac{11}{7} = 1\frac{4}{7}$. Therefore, the average temperature at noon for the week is $1\frac{4}{7}°$.

EXAMPLE 3: If the average annual income of 10 workers is $15,665 and two of the workers each made $20,000 for the year, what is the average annual income of the remaining 8 workers?

The total income of all 10 workers is 10 times the average income which is $156,650. The two workers made a total of $40,000, so the total income of the remaining 8 workers was $156,650 − $40,000 = $116,650. Therefore, the average annual income of the 8 remaining workers is $\frac{\$116,650}{8} = \$14,581.25$.

G–2

The Median. The number which is in the middle if the numbers in a collection of numbers are arranged in order is called the *median*. In example 1 above, the median score was 78, and in example 2, the median temperature for the week was 0. Notice that the medians were different from the averages. In example 3, we don't have enough data to find the median although we know the average.

In general, the median and the average of a collection of numbers are different.

If the number of objects in the collection is even, the median is the average of the two numbers in the middle of the array. For example, the median of 64, 66, 72, 75, 76, and 77 is the average of 72 and 75 which is 73.5.

G–3

The Range. If you subtract the smallest from the largest of a collection of numbers, you will have that collection of number's *range*. In example 1 above, the lowest score was 55, and the highest score was 95. The range of scores was 95 − 55 = 40.

G–4

The Mode. In a collection of numbers, the most frequently appearing number is the *mode*. If the scores of the 9 students in example 1 were 72, 78, 81, 64, 78, 92, 95, 78, and 55, the mode of these scores would be 78.

I–H. Powers, Exponents, and Roots

H–1

If b is any number and n is a whole number greater than 0, b^n means the product of n factors each of which is equal to b. Thus,

$$b^n = b \times b \times b \times \cdots \times b \text{ where there are } n \text{ copies of } b.$$

If $n = 1$, there is only one copy of b so $b^1 = b$. Here are some examples.

$$2^5 = 2 \times 2 \times 2 \times 2 \times 2 = 32, (-4)^3 = (-4) \times (-4) \times (-4) = -64, \frac{3^2}{4} = \frac{3 \times 3}{4} = \frac{9}{4},$$

$$1^n = 1 \text{ for any } n, 0^n = 0 \text{ for any } n.$$

b^n is read as "b raised to the nth power." b^2 is read "b squared." b^2 is always greater than 0 (positive) if b is not zero, since the product of two negative numbers is positive. b^3 is read "b cubed," b^3 can be negative or positive.

You should know the following squares and cubes:

If you raise a fraction, $\frac{p}{q}$, to a power, then $\left(\frac{p}{q}\right)^n = \frac{p^n}{q^n}$. For example,

$$\left(\frac{5}{4}\right)^3 = \frac{5^3}{4^3} = \frac{125}{64}.$$

$1^2 = 1$	$8^2 = 64$	$1^3 = 1$
$2^2 = 4$	$9^2 = 81$	$2^3 = 8$
$3^2 = 9$	$10^2 = 100$	$3^3 = 27$
$4^2 = 16$	$11^2 = 121$	$4^3 = 64$
$5^2 = 25$	$12^2 = 144$	$5^3 = 125$
$6^2 = 36$	$13^2 = 169$	
$7^2 = 49$	$14^2 = 196$	
	$15^2 = 225$	

EXAMPLE 1: If the value of an investment triples each year, what percent of its value today will the investment be worth in 4 years?

The value increases by a factor of 3 each year. Since the time is 4 years, there will be four factors of 3. So the investment will be worth $3 \times 3 \times 3 \times 3 = 3^4$ as much as it is today. $3^4 = 81$, so the investment will be worth 8,100% of its value today in four years.

H–2

Exponents. In the expression b^n, b is called the base and n is called the *exponent*. In the expression 2^5, 2 is the base and 5 is the exponent. The exponent tells how many factors there are.

> The *two basic formulas for problems involving exponents* are:
>
> (A) $b^n \times b^m = b^{n+m}$
> (B) $a^n \times b^n = (a \cdot b)^n$
>
> (A) and (B) are called *laws of exponents.*

EXAMPLE 1: What is 6^3?

$$\text{Since } 6 = 3 \times 2,\ 6^3 = 3^3 \times 2^3 = 27 \times 8 = 216.$$

or

$$6^3 = 6 \times 6 \times 6 = 216.$$

EXAMPLE 2: Find the value of $2^3 \times 2^2$.

Using (A), $2^3 \times 2^2 = 2^{2+3} = 2^5$ which is 32. You can check this, since $2^3 = 8$ and $2^2 = 4$; $2^3 \times 2^2 = 8 \times 4 = 32$.

H-3

Negative Exponents. $b^0 = 1$ *for any nonzero number b.* By one of the laws of exponents (A) above, $b^n \times b^0$ should be $b^{n+0} = b^n$. If we still want (A) to be true, then b^0 must be 1. (NOTE: 0^0 is not defined.)

Using the law of exponents once more, you can define b^{-n} where n is a positive number. If (A) holds, $b^{-n} \times b^n = b^{-n+n} = b^0 = 1$, so $b^{-n} = \frac{1}{b^n}$. *Multiplying by b^{-n} is the same as dividing by b^n.*

EXAMPLE 1: $$2^0 = 1$$

EXAMPLE 2: $$2^{-3} = \frac{1}{2^3} = \frac{1}{8}$$

EXAMPLE 3: $$\left(\frac{1}{2}\right)^{-1} = \frac{1}{1/2} = 2$$

EXAMPLE 4: Find the value of $\frac{6^4}{3^3}$.

$$\frac{6^4}{3^3} = \frac{(3 \cdot 2)^4}{3^3} = \frac{3^4 \cdot 2^4}{3^3} = 3^4 \times 2^4 \times 3^{-3} = 3^4 \times 3^{-3} \times 2^4 = 3^1 \times 2^4 = 48.$$

H-4

Roots. If you raise a number d to the nth power and the result is b, then d is called the nth root of b, which is usually written $\sqrt[n]{b} = d$. Since $2^5 = 32$, then $\sqrt[5]{32} = 2$. The second root is called the square root and is written $\sqrt{\ }$; the third root is called the cube root. If you read the columns of the table on page 229 from right to left, you have a table of square roots and cube roots. For example, $\sqrt{225} = 15$; $\sqrt{81} = 9$; $\sqrt[3]{64} = 4$.

There are two possibilities for the square root of a positive number; the positive one is called the square root. Thus we say $\sqrt{9} = 3$ although $(-3) \times (-3) = 9$.

Since the square of any nonzero number is positive *the square root of a nega-*

tive number is not defined as a real number. Thus $\sqrt{-2}$ is not a real number. There are cube roots of negative numbers. $\sqrt[3]{-8} = -2$, because $(-2) \times (-2) \times (-2) = -8$.

You can also write roots as exponents; for example,

$$\sqrt[n]{b} = b^{1/n}; \text{ so } \sqrt{b} = b^{1/2}, \sqrt[3]{b} = b^{1/3}.$$

Since you can write roots as exponents, formula (B) above is especially useful.

$a^{1/n} \times b^{1/n} = (a \cdot b)^{1/n}$ or $\sqrt[n]{a \times b} = \sqrt[n]{a} \times \sqrt[n]{b}$. This formula is the basic formula for simplifying square roots, cube roots and so on. *On the test you must state your answer in a form which matches one of the choices given.*

EXAMPLE 1: $\sqrt{54} = ?$

Since $54 = 9 \times 6$, $\sqrt{54} = \sqrt{9 \times 6} = \sqrt{9} \times \sqrt{6}$. Since $\sqrt{9} = 3$, $\sqrt{54} = 3\sqrt{6}$.

You can not simplify by adding square roots unless you are taking square roots of the same number. For example,

$$\sqrt{3} + 2\sqrt{3} - 4\sqrt{3} = -\sqrt{3}, \text{ but } \sqrt{3} + \sqrt{2} \text{ is not equal to } \sqrt{5}.$$

EXAMPLE 2: Simplify $6\sqrt{12} + 2\sqrt{75} - 3\sqrt{98}$.

Since $12 = 4 \times 3$, $\sqrt{12} = \sqrt{4 \times 3} = \sqrt{4} \times \sqrt{3} = 2\sqrt{3}$;
$75 = 25 \times 3$, so $\sqrt{75} = \sqrt{25} \times \sqrt{3} = 5\sqrt{3}$;
and $98 = 49 \times 2$, so $\sqrt{98} = \sqrt{49} \times \sqrt{2} = 7\sqrt{2}$.
Therefore, $6\sqrt{12} + 2\sqrt{75} - 3\sqrt{98} = 6 \times 2\sqrt{3} + 2 \times 5\sqrt{3} - 3 \times 7\sqrt{2} = 12\sqrt{3} + 10\sqrt{3} - 21\sqrt{2} = 22\sqrt{3} - 21\sqrt{2}$.

EXAMPLE 3: Simplify $27^{1/3} \times 8^{1/3}$.

$27^{1/3} = \sqrt[3]{27} = 3$ and $8^{1/3} = \sqrt[3]{8} = 2$, so $27^{1/3} \times 8^{1/3} = 3 \times 2 = 6$. Notice that 6 is $\sqrt[3]{216}$ and $27^{1/3} \times 8^{1/3} = (27 \times 8)^{1/3} = 216^{1/3}$.

II. Algebra

II–A. Algebraic Expressions

A–1

Often it is necessary to deal with quantities which have a numerical value which is unknown. For example, we may know that Tom's salary is twice as much as

Joe's salary. If we let the value of Tom's salary be called T and the value of Joe's salary be J, then T and J are numbers which are unknown. However, we do know that the value of T must be twice the value of J, or $T = 2J$.

T and $2J$ are examples of algebraic expressions. An algebraic expression may involve letters in addition to numbers and symbols; however, *in an algebraic expression a letter always stands for a number.* Therefore, you can multiply, divide, add, subtract and perform other mathematical operations on a letter. Thus, x^2 would mean x times x. Some examples of algebraic expressions are: $2x + y$, $y^3 + 9y$, $z^3 - 5ab$, $c + d + 4$, $5x + 2y(6x - 4y + z)$. When letters or numbers are written together without any sign or symbol between them, multiplication is assumed. Thus $6xy$ means 6 times x times y. $6xy$ is called a term; terms are separated by + or − signs. The expression $5z + 2 + 4x^2$ has three terms, $5z$, 2, and $4x^2$. Terms are often called monomials (mono = one). If an expression has more than one term, it is called a *polynomial,* (poly = many). The letters in an algebraic expression are called *variables* or *unknowns.* When a variable is multiplied by a number, the number is called the *coefficient* of the variable. So in the expression $5x^2 + 2yz$, the coefficient of x^2 is 5, and the coefficient of yz is 2.

A–2

Simplifying Algebraic Expressions. *You must be able to recognize algebraic expressions which are equal.* It will also save time when you are working problems if you can change a complicated expression into a simpler one.

Case I. Simplifying expressions which don't contain parentheses:

(A) Perform any multiplications or divisions before performing additions or subtractions. Thus, the expression $6x + y \div x$ means add $6x$ to the quotient of y divided by x. Another way of writing the expression would be $6x + \frac{y}{x}$. This is not the same as $\frac{6x + y}{x}$.

(B) The order in which you multiply numbers and letters in a term does not matter. So $6xy$ is the same as $6yx$.

(C) The order in which you add terms does not matter; for instance, $6x + 2y - x = 6x - x + 2y$.

(D) If there are roots or powers in any terms, you may be able to simplify the term by using the laws of exponents. For example, $5xy \cdot 3x^2y = 15x^3y^2$.

(E) Combine like terms. *Like terms* (or similar terms) are terms which have exactly the same letters raised to the same powers. So x, $-2x$, $\frac{1}{3}x$ are like terms. For example, $6x - 2x + x + y$ is equal to $5x + y$. In combining like terms, you simply add or subtract the coefficients of the like terms, and the result is the coefficient of that term in the simplified expression. In our example above, the coefficients of x were +6, −2, and +1; since $6 - 2 + 1 = 5$ the coefficient of x in the simplified expression is 5.

(F) Algebraic expressions which involve divisions or factors can be simplified by using the techniques for handling fractions and the laws of exponents. Remember dividing by b^n is the same as multiplying by b^{-n}.

EXAMPLE 1: $3x^2 - 4\sqrt{x} + \sqrt{4x} + xy + 7x^2 = ?$

(D) $\sqrt{4x} = \sqrt{4}\sqrt{x} = 2\sqrt{x}$.
(E) $3x^2 + 7x^2 = 10x^2$, $-4\sqrt{x} + 2\sqrt{x} = -2\sqrt{x}$.

The original expression equals $3x^2 + 7x^2 - 4\sqrt{x} + 2\sqrt{x} + xy$. Therefore, the simplified expression is $10x^2 - 2\sqrt{x} + xy$.

EXAMPLE 2: Simplify $\frac{21x^4y^2}{3x^6y}$.

(F) $\frac{21}{3}x^4y^2x^{-6}y^{-1}$.
(B) $7x^4x^{-6}y^2y^{-1}$.
(D) $7x^{-2}y$, so the simplified term is $\frac{7y}{x^2}$.

EXAMPLE 3: Write $\frac{2x}{y} - \frac{4}{x}$ as a single fraction.

(F) A common denominator is xy so $\frac{2x}{y} = \frac{2x \cdot x}{y \cdot x} = \frac{2x^2}{xy}$, and $\frac{4}{x} = \frac{4y}{xy}$.

Therefore, $\frac{2x}{y} - \frac{4}{x} = \frac{2x^2}{xy} - \frac{4y}{xy} = \frac{2x^2 - 4y}{xy}$

Case II. Simplifying expressions which have parentheses:

The first rule is to perform the operations inside parentheses first. So $(6x + y) \div x$ means divide the sum of $6x$ and y by x. Notice that $(6x + y) \div x$ is different from $6x + y \div x$.

The main rule for getting rid of parentheses is the distributive law, which is expressed as $a(b + c) = ab + ac$. In other words, if any monomial is followed by an expression contained in a parenthesis, then *each* term of the expression is multiplied by the monomial. Once we have gotten rid of the parentheses, we proceed as we did in Case I.

EXAMPLE 4: $2x(6x - 4y + 2) = (2x)(6x) + (2x)(-4y) + (2x)(2) = 12x^2 - 8xy + 4x$.

If an expression has more than one set of parentheses, get rid of the *inner parentheses first* and then *work out* through the rest of the parentheses.

EXAMPLE 5: $2x - (x + 6(x - 3y) + 4y) = ?$

To remove the inner parentheses we multiply $6(x - 3y)$ getting $6x - 18y$. Now we have $2x - (x + 6x - 18y + 4y)$ which equals $2x - (7x - 14y)$. Distribute the minus sign (multiply by -1), getting $2x - 7x - (-14y) = -5x + 14y$.

Sometimes brackets are used instead of parentheses.

EXAMPLE 6: Simplify $-3x\left[\frac{1}{2}(3x - 2y) - 2(x(3 + y) + 4y)\right]$

$$= -3x\left[\frac{1}{2}(3x - 2y) - 2(3x + xy + 4y)\right]$$

$$= -3x\left[\frac{3}{2}x - y - 6x - 2xy - 8y\right]$$

$$= -3x\left[-\frac{9}{2}x - 2xy - 9y\right]$$

$$= \frac{27}{2}x^2 + 6x^2y + 27xy.$$

A–3

Adding and Subtracting Algebraic Expressions. Since algebraic expressions are numbers, they can be added and subtracted.

The only algebraic terms which can be combined are like terms.

EXAMPLE 1: $(3x + 4y - xy^2) + (3x + 2x(x - y)) = ?$

The expression $= (3x + 4y - xy^2) + (3x + 2x^2 - 2xy)$, removing the inner parentheses;
$= 6x + 4y + 2x^2 - xy^2 - 2xy$, combining like terms.

EXAMPLE 2: $(2a + 3a^2 - 4) - 2(4a^2 - 2(a + 4)) = ?$

It equals $(2a + 3a^2 - 4) - 2(4a^2 - 2a - 8)$, removing inner parentheses;
$= 2a + 3a^2 - 4 - 8a^2 + 4a + 16$, removing outer parentheses;
$= -5a^2 + 6a + 12$, combining like terms.

A–4

Multiplying Algebraic Expressions. When you multiply two expressions, you multiply *each term of the first by each term of the second.*

EXAMPLE 1: $(b - 4)(b + a) = b(b + a) - 4(b + a) = ?$

$$= b^2 + ab - 4b - 4a.$$

EXAMPLE 2: $(2h - 4)(h + 2h^2 + h^3) = ?$

$$= 2h(h + 2h^2 + h^3) - 4(h + 2h^2 + h^3)$$
$$= 2h^2 + 4h^3 + 2h^4 - 4h - 8h^2 - 4h^3$$
$= -4h - 6h^2 + 2h^4$, which is the product.

If you need to multiply more than two expressions, multiply the first two expressions, then multiply the result by the third expression, and so on until you have used each factor. Since algebraic expressions can be multiplied, they can be squared, cubed, or raised to other powers.

EXAMPLE 3: $(x-2y)^3 = (x-2y)(x-2y)(x-2y)$.

Since $(x-2y)(x-2y) = x^2 - 2yx - 2yx + 4y^2$
$= x^2 - 4xy + 4y^2$,

$$\begin{aligned}(x-y)^3 &= (x^2 - 4xy + 4y^2)(x-2y)\\ &= x(x^2 - 4xy + 4y^2) - 2y(x^2 - 4xy + 4y^2)\\ &= x^3 - 4x^2y + 4xy^2 - 2x^2y + 8xy^2 - 8y^3\\ &= x^3 - 6x^2y + 12xy^2 - 8y^3.\end{aligned}$$

The order in which you multiply algebraic expressions does not matter. Thus $(2a+b)(x^2+2x) = (x^2+2x)(2a+b)$.

A–5

Factoring Algebraic Expressions. If an algebraic expression is the product of other algebraic expressions, then the expressions are called factors of the original expression. For instance, we claim that $(2h-4)$ and $(h+2h^2+h^3)$ are factors of $-4h - 6h^2 + 2h^4$. We can always check to see if we have the correct factors by multiplying; so by example 2 above we see that our claim is correct. We need to be able to factor algebraic expressions in order to solve quadratic equations. It also can be helpful in dividing algebraic expressions.

First remove any monomial factor which appears in every term of the expression.

Some examples:

$3x + 3y = 3(x+y)$: 3 is a monomial factor.

$15a^2b + 10ab = 5ab(3a+2)$: $5ab$ is a monomial factor.

$$\frac{1}{2}hy - 3h^3 + 4hy = h\left(\frac{1}{2}y - 3h^2 + 4y\right),$$

$$= h\left(\frac{9}{2}y - 3h^2\right)\text{: } h \text{ is a monomial factor.}$$

You may also need to factor expressions which contain squares or higher powers into factors which only contain linear terms. (Linear terms are terms in which variables are raised only to the first power.) The first rule to remember is that since $(a+b)(a-b) = a^2 + ba - ba - b^2 = a^2 - b^2$, the difference of two squares can always be factored.

EXAMPLE 1: Factor $(9m^2 - 16)$.

$9m^2 = (3m)^2$ and $16 = 4^2$, so the factors are $(3m-4)(3m+4)$.

Since $(3m-4)(3m+4) = 9m^2 - 16$, these factors are correct.

EXAMPLE 2: Factor $x^4y^4 - 4x^2$.

$x^4y^4 = (x^2y^2)^2$ and $4x^2 = (2x)^2$, so the factors are $x^2y^2 + 2x$ and $x^2y^2 - 2x$.

You also may need to factor expressions which contain squared terms and linear terms, such as $x^2 + 4x + 3$. The factors will be of the form $(x+a)$ and $(x+b)$. Since $(x+a)(x+b) = x^2 + (a+b)x + ab$, you must look for a pair of numbers a and b such that $a \cdot b$ is the numerical term in the expression and $a+b$ is the coefficient of the linear term (the term with exponent 1).

EXAMPLE 3: Factor $x^2 + 4x + 3$.

You want numbers whose product is 3 and whose sum is 4. Look at the possible factors of three and check whether they add up to 4. Since $3 = 3 \times 1$ and $3 + 1$ is 4, the factors are $(x+3)$ and $(x+1)$. Remember to check by multiplying.

EXAMPLE 4: Factor $y^2 + y - 6$.

Since -6 is negative, the two numbers a and b must be of opposite sign. Possible pairs of factors for -6 are -6 and $+1$, 6 and -1, 3 and -2, and -3 and 2. Since $-2 + 3 = 1$, the factors are $(y + 3)$ and $(y - 2)$. So $(y + 3)(y - 2) = y^2 + y - 6$.

EXAMPLE 5: Factor $a^3 + 4a^2 + 4a$.

Factor out a, so $a^3 + 4a^2 + 4a = a(a^2 + 4a + 4)$. Consider $a^2 + 4a + 4$; since $2 + 2 = 4$ and $2 \times 2 = 4$, the factors are $(a + 2)$ and $(a + 2)$. Therefore, $a^3 + 4a^2 + 4a = a(a + 2)^2$.

If the term with the highest exponent has a coefficient unequal to 1, divide the entire expression by that coefficient. For example, to factor $3a^3 + 12a^2 + 12a$, factor out a 3 from each term, and the result is $a^3 + 4a^2 + 4a$ which is $a(a+2)^2$. Thus, $3a^3 + 12a^2 + 12a = 3a(a + 2)^2$.

There are some expressions which can not be factored, for example, $x^2 + 4x + 6$. In general, if you can't factor something by using the methods given above, don't waste a lot of time on the question. Sometimes you may be able to check the answers given to find out what the correct factors are.

A–6

Division of Algebraic Expressions. The main things to remember in division are:

(1) When you divide a sum, you can get the same result by dividing each term and adding quotients. For example, $\frac{9x + 4xy + y^2}{x} = \frac{9x}{x} + \frac{4xy}{x} + \frac{y^2}{x} = 9 + 4y + \frac{y^2}{x}$.

(2) You can cancel common factors, so the results on factoring will be helpful. For example, $\frac{x^2 - 2x}{x - 2} = \frac{x(x - 2)}{x - 2} = x$.

You can also divide one algebraic expression by another using long division.

EXAMPLE 1: $(15x^2 + 2x - 4) \div 3x - 1$.

$$
\begin{array}{r}
5x + 2 \\
3x - 1\,\overline{)\,15x^2 + 2x - 4} \\
\underline{15x^2 - 5x} \\
7x - 4 \\
\underline{6x - 2} \\
x - 2
\end{array}
$$

So the answer is $5x + 2$ with a remainder of $x - 2$.

You can check by multiplying,

$(5x + 2)(3x - 1) = 15x^2 + 6x - 5x - 2$

$= 15x^2 + x - 2$; now add the remainder $x - 2$

and the result is $15x^2 + x - 2 + x - 2 = 15x^2 + 2x - 4$.

Division problems where you need to use (1) and (2) are more likely than problems involving long division.

II–B. Equations

B–1

AN EQUATION is a statement that says two algebraic expressions are equal. $x+2=3$, $4+2=6$, $3x^2+2x-6=0$, $x^2+y^2=z^2$, $\frac{y}{x}=2+z$, and $A=LW$ are all examples of equations. We will refer to the algebraic expressions on each side of the equals sign as the left side and the right side of the equation. Thus, in the equation $2x + 4 = 6y + x$, $2x + 4$ is the left side and $6y + x$ is the right side.

B–2

If we assign specific numbers to each variable or unknown in an algebraic expression, then the algebraic expression will be equal to a number. This is called *evaluating* the expression. For example, if you evaluate $2x + 4y^2 + 3$ for $x = -1$ and $y = 2$, the expression is equal to $2(-1) + 4 \cdot 2^2 + 3 = -2 + 4 \cdot 4 + 3 = 17$.

If we evaluate each side of an equation and the number obtained is the same for each side of the equation, then the specific values assigned to the unknowns are called a *solution of the equation.* Another way of saying this is that the choices for the unknowns satisfy the equation.

EXAMPLE 1: Consider the equation $2x + 3 = 9$.

If $x = 3$, then the left side of the equation becomes $2 \cdot 3 + 3 = 6 + 3 = 9$, so both sides equal 9, and $x = 3$ is a solution of $2x + 3 = 9$. If $x = 4$, then the left side is $2 \cdot 4 + 3 = 11$. Since 11 is not equal to 9, $x = 4$ is *not* a solution of $2x + 3 = 9$.

EXAMPLE 2: Consider the equation $x^2 + y^2 = 5x$.

If $x = 1$ and $y = 2$, then the left side is $1^2 + 2^2$ which equals $1 + 4 = 5$. The right side is $5 \cdot 1 = 5$, since both sides are equal to 5, $x = 1$ and $y = 2$ is a solution.

If $x = 5$ and $y = 0$, then the left side is $5^2 + 0^2 = 25$ and the right side is $5 \cdot 5 = 25$, so $x = 5$ and $y = 0$ is also a solution.

If $x = 1$ and $y = 1$, then the left side is $1^2 + 1^2 = 2$ and the right side is $5 \cdot 1 = 5$. Therefore, since $2 \neq 5$, $x = 1$ and $y = 1$ is not a solution.

There are some equations which *do not have any solutions which are real numbers*. Since the square of any real number is positive or zero, the equation $x^2 = -4$ does not have any solutions which are real numbers.

B–3

Equivalence. One equation is *equivalent* to another equation, if they have exactly the same solutions. The basic idea in solving equations is to transform a given equation into an equivalent equation whose solutions are obvious.

> The two main tools for solving equations are:
>
> (A) If you add or subtract the same algebraic expression to or from *each side* of an equation, the resulting equation is equivalent to the original equation.
>
> (B) If you multiply or divide both sides of an equation by the same *nonzero* algebraic expression, the resulting equation is equivalent to the original equation.

The most common type of equation is the linear equation with only one unknown. $6z = 4z - 3$, $3 + a = 2a - 4$, $3b + 2b = b - 4b$, are all examples of linear equations with only one unknown.

Using (A) and (B), you can solve a linear equation in one unknown in the following way:

(1) Group all the terms which involve the unknown on one side of the equation and all the terms which are purely numerical on the other side of the equation. This is called *isolating the unknown.*

(2) Combine the terms on each side.

(3) Divide each side by the coefficient of the unknown.

EXAMPLE 1: Solve $6x + 2 = 3$ for x.

(1) Using (A) subtract 2 from each side of the equation. Then $6x + 2 - 2 = 3 - 2$ or $6x = 3 - 2$.

(2) $6x = 1$.

(3) Divide each side by 6. Therefore, $x = \frac{1}{6}$.

You should always check your answer in the original equation.

$$\text{Since } 6\left(\frac{1}{6}\right) + 2 = 1 + 2 = 3,\ x = \frac{1}{6} \text{ is a solution.}$$

EXAMPLE 2: Solve $3x + 15 = 3 - 4x$ for x.

(1) Add $4x$ to each side and subtract 15 from each side; $3x + 15 - 15 + 4x = 3 - 15 - 4x + 4x$.

(2) $7x = -12$.

(3) Divide each side by 7, so $x = \frac{-12}{7}$ is the solution.

CHECK:

$$3\left(\frac{-12}{7}\right) + 15 = \frac{-36}{7} + 15 = \frac{69}{7} \text{ and } 3 - 4\left(\frac{-12}{7}\right) = 3 + \frac{48}{7} = \frac{69}{7}.$$

If you do the same thing to each side of an equation, the result is still an equation but it may not be equivalent to the original equation. Be especially careful if you square each side of an equation. For example, $x = -4$ is an equation; square both sides and you get $x^2 = 16$ which has both $x = 4$ and $x = -4$ as solutions. *Always check your answer in the original equation.*

If the equation you want to solve involves square roots, get rid of the square roots by squaring each side of the equation. Remember to check your answer since squaring each side does not always give an equivalent equation.

EXAMPLE 3: Solve $\sqrt{4x+3} = 5$.

Square both sides: $(\sqrt{4x+3})^2 = 4x + 3$ and $5^2 = 25$, so the new equation is $4x + 3 = 25$. Subtract 3 from each side to get $4x = 22$ and now divide each side by 4. The solution is $x = \frac{22}{4} = 5.5$. Since $4(5.5) + 3 = 25$ and $\sqrt{25} = 5$, $x = 5.5$ is a solution to the equation $\sqrt{4x+3} = 5$.

If an equation involves fractions, multiply through by a common denominator and then solve. Check your answer to make sure you did not multiply or divide by zero.

EXAMPLE 4: Solve $\frac{3}{a} = 9$ for a.

Multiply each side by a: the result is $3 = 9a$. Divide each side by 9, and you obtain $\frac{3}{9} = a$ or $a = \frac{1}{3}$. Since $\frac{3}{1/3} = 3 \cdot 3 = 9$, $a = \frac{1}{3}$ is a solution.

B–4

You may be asked to solve two equations in two unknowns. Use one equation to solve for one unknown in terms of the other; now change the second equation into an equation in only one unknown which can be solved by the methods of the preceding section.

EXAMPLE 1: Solve for x and y: $\begin{cases} \frac{x}{y} = 3 \\ 2x + 4y = 20. \end{cases}$

The first equation gives $x = 3y$. Using $x = 3y$, the second equation is $2(3y) + 4y = 6y + 4y$ or $10y = 20$, so $y = \frac{20}{10} = 2$. Since $x = 3y$, $x = 6$.

CHECK:

$\frac{6}{2} = 3$, and $2 \cdot 6 + 4 \cdot 2 = 20$, so $x = 6$ and $y = 2$ is a solution.

EXAMPLE 2: If $2x + y = 5$ and $x + y = 4$, find x and y.

Since $x + y = 4$, $y = 4 - x$, so $2x + y = 2x + 4 - x = x + 4 = 5$ and $x = 1$. If $x = 1$, then $y = 4 - 1 = 3$. So $x = 1$ and $y = 3$ is the solution.

CHECK:

$$2 \cdot 1 + 3 = 5 \text{ and } 1 + 3 = 4.$$

Sometimes we can solve two equations by adding them or by subtracting one from the other. If we subtract $x + y = 4$ from $2x + y = 5$ in example 2, we have $x = 1$. However, the previous method will work in cases when the addition method does not work.

B–5

Solving Quadratic Equations. If the terms of an equation contain squares of the unknown as well as linear terms, the equation is called *quadratic*. Some examples of quadratic equations are $x^2 + 4x = 3$, $2z^2 - 1 = 3z^2 - 2z$, and $a + 6 = a^2 + 6$.

To solve a quadratic equation:

(A) Group all the terms on one side of the equation so that the other side is *zero*.
(B) Combine the terms on the nonzero side.
(C) Factor the expression into linear expressions.
(D) Set the linear factors equal to zero and solve.

The method depends on the fact that if a product of expressions is zero then at least one of the expressions must be zero.

EXAMPLE 1: Solve $x^2 + 4x = -3$.

(A) $x^2 + 4x + 3 = 0$
(C) $x^2 + 4x + 3 = (x + 3)(x + 1) = 0$
(D) So $x + 3 = 0$ or $x + 1 = 0$. Therefore, the solutions are $x = -3$ and $x = -1$.

CHECK:

$(-3)^2 + 4(-3) = 9 - 12 = -3$
$(-1)^2 + 4(-1) = 1 - 4 = -3$, so $x = -3$ and $x = -1$ are solutions.

A quadratic equation will usually have 2 different solutions, but it is possible for a quadratic to have only one solution or even no solution.

EXAMPLE 2: If $2z^2 - 1 = 3z^2 - 2z$, what is z?

(A) $0 = 3z^2 - 2z^2 - 2z + 1$
(B) $z^2 - 2z + 1 = 0$
(C) $z^2 - 2z + 1 = (z - 1)^2 = 0$
(D) $z - 1 = 0$ or $z = 1$

CHECK:

$2 \cdot 1^2 - 1 = 2 - 1 = 1$ and $3 \cdot 1^2 - 2 \cdot 1 = 3 - 2 = 1$,
so $z = 1$ is a solution.

Equations which may not look like quadratics may be changed into quadratics.

EXAMPLE 3: Find a if $a - 3 = \frac{10}{a}$.

Multiply each side of the equation by a to obtain $a^2 - 3a = 10$, which is quadratic.

(A) $a^2 - 3a - 10 = 0$
(C) $a^2 - 3a - 10 = (a - 5)(a + 2)$
(D) So $a - 5 = 0$ or $a + 2 = 0$.

Therefore, $a = 5$ and $a = -2$ are the solutions.

CHECK:

$5 - 3 = 2 = \frac{10}{5}$ so $a = 5$ is a solution.

$-2 - 3 = -5 = \frac{10}{-2}$ so $a = -2$ is a solution.

You can also solve quadratic equations by using the *quadratic formula.* The quadratic formula states that the solutions of the quadratic equation $ax^2 + bx + c = 0$ are $x = \frac{1}{2a}[-b + \sqrt{b^2 - 4ac}]$ and $x = \frac{1}{2a}[-b - \sqrt{b^2 - 4ac}]$. This is usually written $x = \frac{1}{2a}[-b \pm \sqrt{b^2 - 4ac}]$. Use of the quadratic formula would replace steps (C) and (D).

EXAMPLE 4: Find x if $x^2 + 5x = 12 - x^2$.

(A) $x^2 + 5x + x^2 - 12 = 0$
(B) $2x^2 + 5x - 12 = 0$

So $a = 2$, $b = 5$ and $c = -12$. Therefore, using the quadratic formula, the solutions are $x = \frac{1}{4}[-5 \pm \sqrt{25 - 4 \cdot 2 \cdot (-12)}] = \frac{1}{4}[-5 \pm \sqrt{25 + 96}] = \frac{1}{4}[-5 \pm \sqrt{121}]$. So we have $x = \frac{1}{4}[-5 \pm 11]$. The solutions are $x = \frac{3}{2}$ and $x = -4$.

CHECK:

$$\left(\frac{3}{2}\right)^2 + 5 \cdot \frac{3}{2} = \frac{9}{4} + \frac{15}{2} = \frac{39}{4} = 12 - \frac{9}{4} = 12 - \left(\frac{3}{2}\right)^2$$
$$(-4)^2 + 5(-4) = 16 - 20 = -4 = 12 - 16 = 12 - (-4)^2$$

NOTE: If $b^2 - 4ac$ is negative, then the quadratic equation $ax^2 + bx + c = 0$ has no real solutions because negative numbers do not have real square roots.

The quadratic formula will always give you the solutions to a quadratic equation. If you can factor the equation, factoring will usually give you the solution in less time. Remember, you want to answer as many questions as you can in the time given. So factor if you can. If you don't see the factor immediately, then use the formula.

PRACTICE

1. If $r = \frac{s}{3}$ and $4r = 5t$, what is s in terms of t?
   (A) $\frac{4t}{15}$ (B) $\frac{15t}{4}$ (C) $4t$ (D) $5t$ (E) $60t$

2. If $\frac{1}{r} = 3$ and $s = 3$, what is r in terms of s?
   (A) s (B) $3 - s$ (C) $\frac{1}{s}$ (D) $-s$ (E) $9s$

3. $\frac{a}{b} = c$; $b = c$; $b = ?$
   (A) $\frac{a}{2}$ (B) $\sqrt{a}$ (C) $\frac{a}{6}$ (D) $2a$ (E) a^2

4. $z + \frac{1}{z} = 2$; $z = ?$
   (A) $\frac{1}{2}$ (B) 1 (C) $1\frac{1}{2}$ (D) 2 (E) $2\frac{1}{2}$

5. If $\frac{n}{7} + \frac{n}{5} = \frac{12}{35}$, what is the numerical value of n?
   (A) 1 (B) $\sqrt{12}$ (C) 6 (D) 17.5 (E) 35

6. $\frac{ca^2 - cb^2}{-a - b}$ is equivalent to $cb + ?$
   (A) ac (B) $-ca$ (C) 1 (D) -1 (E) c

7. $x\sqrt{.09} = 3$; $x = ?$
   (A) $\frac{1}{10}$ (B) $\frac{3}{10}$ (C) $\frac{1}{3}$ (D) 1 (E) 10

8. $7x - 5y = 13$
   $2x - 7y = 26$
   $9x - 12y = ?$
   (A) 13 (B) 26 (C) 39 (D) 40 (E) 52

9. $ab - 2cd = p$
   $ab - 2cd = q$
   $6cd - 3ab = r$
   $p = (?)r$
   (A) -3 (B) $-\frac{1}{3}$ (C) $\frac{1}{3}$ (D) 1 (E) 3

10. $\sqrt{\frac{16}{36} + \frac{1}{4}} = ?$
    (A) $\frac{2}{5}$ (B) $\frac{1}{3}$ (C) $\frac{5}{6}$ (D) $\frac{11}{12}$ (E) $\frac{7}{6}$

11. $z + \frac{2}{z} = 2z$; $z^2 = (?)$
    (A) 0 (B) $\frac{1}{2}$ (C) 1 (D) $1\frac{1}{2}$ (E) 2

12. $\frac{1}{\frac{1}{N}} \div \frac{1}{N} = ?$
    (A) 1 (B) $\frac{1}{N^2}$ (C) $\frac{1}{N}$ (D) N (E) N^2

13. If $\frac{1}{x} = \frac{a}{b}$ then x equals the
    (A) sum of a and b
    (B) product of a and b
    (C) difference of a and b
    (D) quotient of b and a
    (E) quotient a and b

14. $x^2 + y = 9$
    $x^2 - y = -1$
    $y = ?$
    (A) 1 (B) ± 3 (C) 5 (D) 8 (E) 10

15. $2x - 4y = -10$
    $5x - 3y = 3$
    $3x - 6y = (?)$
    (A) $\frac{3}{5}$ (B) $\frac{2}{3}$ (C) -7 (D) 15 (E) -15

16. $5x - 3y = 3$
    $2x - 4y = -10$
    $3x + y = (?)$
    (A) -30 (B) -13 (C) -7 (D) 7 (E) 1

17. $4y - x = 10$
    $3x = 2y$
    $xy = ?$
    (A) 2 (B) 3 (C) 6 (D) 12 (E) 24

18. $3x + 10 = 9x - 20$
    $(x + 5)^2 = (?)$
    (A) 5 (B) 10 (C) 15 (D) 25 (E) 100

19. $\frac{a}{b} = c$; $b = c$. Find b in terms of a.
    (A) a (B) b (C) $\pm\sqrt{b}$ (D) $\pm\sqrt{a}$ (E) $\pm\sqrt{}$

20. $17xy = 22xy - 5$
    $x^2y^2 = (?)$
    (A) 0 (B) 1 (C) -5 (D) 5 (E) $7\frac{4}{5}$

ANSWER KEY

1. B	8. C	15. E
2. C	9. B	16. E
3. B	10. C	17. C
4. B	11. E	18. E
5. A	12. E	19. D
6. B	13. D	20. B
7. E	14. C	

II–C. Verbal Problems

C–1

The general method for solving word problems is to translate them into algebraic problems. The quantities you are seeking are the unknowns, which are usually represented by letters. The information you are given in the problem is then turned into equations. Words such as "is," "was," "are," and "were" mean equals, and words like "of" and "as much as" mean multiplication.

EXAMPLE 1: A coat was sold for \$75. The coat was sold for 150% of the cost of the coat. How much did the coat cost?

You want to find the cost of the coat. Let $\$C$ be the cost of the coat. You know that the coat was sold for \$75 and that \$75 was 150% of the cost. So $\$75 = 150\%$ of $\$C$ or $75 = 1.5C$. Solving for C you get $C = \frac{75}{1.5} = 50$, so the coat cost \$50.

CHECK:

$$(1.5)\ \$50 = \$75.$$

EXAMPLE 2: Tom's salary is 125% of Joe's salary. Mary's salary is 80% of Joe's salary. The total of all three salaries is \$61,000. What is Mary's salary?

Let $M =$ Mary's salary, $J =$ Joe's salary and $T =$ Tom's salary. The first sentence says $T = 125\%$ of J or $T = \frac{5}{4}J$, and $M = 80\%$ of J or $M = \frac{4}{5}J$. The second sentence says that $T + M + J = \$61{,}000$. Using the information from the first sentence, $T + M + J = \frac{5}{4}J + \frac{4}{5}J + J = \frac{25}{20}J + \frac{16}{20}J + J = \frac{61}{20}J$. So $\frac{61}{20}J = 61{,}000$; solving for J you have $J = \frac{20}{61} \times 61{,}000 = 20{,}000$. Therefore, $T = \frac{5}{4} \times \$20{,}000 = \$25{,}000$ and $M = \frac{4}{5} \times \$20{,}000 = \$16{,}000$.

CHECK:

$$\$25{,}000 + \$16{,}000 + \$20{,}000 = \$61{,}000.$$

So Mary's salary is \$16,000.

EXAMPLE 3: Steve weighs 25 pounds more than Jim. Their combined weight is 325 pounds. How much does Jim weigh?

Let $S =$ Steve's weight in pounds and $J =$ Jim's weight in pounds. The first sentence says $S = J + 25$, and the second sentence becomes $S + J = 325$. Since $S = J + 25$, $S + J = 325$ becomes $(J + 25) + J = 2J + 25 = 325$. So $2J = 300$ and $J = 150$. Therefore, Jim weighs 150 pounds.

CHECK:

If Jim weighs 150 pounds, then Steve weighs
175 pounds and $150 + 175 = 325$.

EXAMPLE 4: **A carpenter is designing a closet. The floor will be in the shape of a rectangle whose length is 2 feet more than its width. How long should the closet be if the carpenter wants the area of the floor to be 15 square feet?**

The area of a rectangle is length times width, usually written $A = LW$, where A is the area, L is the length, and W is the width. We know $A = 15$ and $L = 2 + W$. Therefore, $LW = (2 + W)\ W = W^2 + 2W$; this must equal 15. So we need to solve $W^2 + 2W = 15$ or $W^2 + 2W - 15 = 0$. Since $W^2 + 2W - 15$ factors into $(W + 5)(W - 3)$, the only possible solutions are $W = -5$ and $W = 3$. Since W represents a width, -5 cannot be the answer; therefore the width is 3 feet. The length is the width plus two feet, so the length is 5 feet. Since $5 \times 3 = 15$, the answer checks.

PRACTICE

1. How many cents are there in $2x - 1$ dimes?

   (A) $10x$ (B) $20x - 10$ (C) $19x$ (D) $\frac{2x - 1}{10}$

   (E) $\frac{x}{5} - 1$

2. How many nickels are there in c cents and q quarters?

   (A) $\frac{c}{5} + 5q$ (B) $5(c + q)$ (C) $5c + \frac{q}{5}$

   (D) $\frac{c + q}{5}$ (E) $c + 25q$

3. How many days are there in w weeks and w days?

   (A) $7w^2$ (B) 7 (C) $8w$ (D) $14w$ (E) $7w$

4. How many pupils can be seated in a room with s single seats and d double seats?

   (A) sd (B) $2sd$ (C) $2(s + d)$ (D) $2d + s$
   (E) $2s + d$

5. A classroom has r rows of desks with d desks in each row. On a particular day when all pupils are present 3 seats are left vacant. The number of pupils in this class is

   (A) $dr - 3$ (B) $d + r + 3$ (C) $dr + 3$

   (D) $\frac{r}{d} + 3$ (E) $\frac{d}{r} + 3$

6. A storekeeper had n loaves of bread. By noon he had s loaves left. How many loaves did he sell?

   (A) $s - n$ (B) $n - s$ (C) $n + s$ (D) $sn - s$

   (E) $\frac{n}{s}$

7. A man has d dollars and spends s cents. How many dollars has he left?

   (A) $d - s$ (B) $s - d$ (C) $100d - s$

   (D) $\frac{100d - s}{100}$ (E) $\frac{d - s}{100}$

8. How much change (in cents) would a woman receiv if she purchases p pounds of sugar at c cents per poun after she gives the clerk a one-dollar bill?

   (A) $100 - p - c$ (B) $pc - 100$ (C) $100 - pc$
   (D) $100 - p + c$ (E) $pc + 100$

9. Sylvia is two years younger than Mary. If Mary is m years old, how old was Sylvia two years ago?

   (A) $m + 2$ (B) $m - 2$ (C) $m - 4$
   (D) $m + 4$ (E) $2m - 2$

10. A storekeeper sold n articles at $\$D$ each and thereb made a profit of r dollars. The cost to the storekeepe for each article was

    (A) $Dn - r$ (B) $D(n - r)$ (C) $\frac{Dn - r}{n}$

    (D) $\frac{D(n - r)}{n}$ (E) $\frac{Dn + r}{n}$

ANSWER KEY

1. B	5. A	9. C
2. A	6. B	10. C
3. C	7. D	
4. D	8. C	

C–2

Distance Problems. A common type of word problem is a distance or velocity problem. The basic formula is

DISTANCE TRAVELED = RATE × TIME.

The formula is abbreviated $d = rt$.

The distance an object travels is the product of its *average* speed (rate) and the time it is traveling. This formula can be readily converted to express time in terms of distance and rate by dividing each side by r.

$$t = \frac{d}{r}$$

It can also be changed to a formula for rate by dividing it by t,

$$r = \frac{d}{t}.$$

You should memorize the original formula, $d = rt$, and know how to convert it quickly to the others.

EXAMPLE 1: A train travels at an average speed of 50 miles per hour for $2\frac{1}{2}$ hours and then travels at a speed of 70 miles per hour for $1\frac{1}{2}$ hours. How far did the train travel in the entire 4 hours?

The train traveled for $2\frac{1}{2}$ hours at an average speed of 50 miles per hour, so it traveled $50 \times \frac{5}{2} = 125$ miles in the first $2\frac{1}{2}$ hours. Traveling at a speed of 70 miles per hour for $1\frac{1}{2}$ hours, the distance traveled will be equal to $r \times t$ where $r = 70$ m.p.h. and $t = 1\frac{1}{2}$, so the distance is $70 \times \frac{3}{2} = 105$ miles. Therefore, the total distance traveled is $125 + 105 = 230$ miles.

EXAMPLE 2: The distance from Cleveland to Buffalo is 200 miles. A train takes $3\frac{1}{2}$ hours to go from Buffalo to Cleveland and $4\frac{1}{2}$ hours to go back from Cleveland to Buffalo. What was the average speed of the train for the round trip from Buffalo to Cleveland and back?

The train took $3\frac{1}{2} + 4\frac{1}{2} = 8$ hours for the trip. The distance of a round trip is $2(200) = 400$ miles. Since $d = rt$ then 400 miles $= r \times 8$ hours. Solve for r and you have $r = \frac{400 \text{ miles}}{8 \text{ hours}} = 50$ miles per hour. Therefore the average speed is 50 miles per hour.

The speed in the formula is the average speed. If you know that there are different speeds for different lengths of time, then you must use the formula more than once, as we did in example 1.

PRACTICE

1. An automobile travels at the rate of 55 miles per hour on the Pennsylvania Turnpike. How many minutes will it take to travel $\frac{2}{3}$ of a mile at this rate?
(A) 0.2 (B) 0.72 (C) 2.2 (D) 13.5 (E) 22
2. Miguel leaves at 9:00 A.M. and stops for repairs at 9:20 A.M. If the distance covered was 18 miles, what was the average velocity for this part of the trip?
(A) 5.4 (B) 6 (C) 54 (D) 36 (E) 60
3. A man runs y yards in m minutes. What is his rate in yards per hour?
(A) $\frac{y}{60m}$ (B) $\frac{m}{60y}$ (C) $60my$ (D) $\frac{60y}{m}$ (E) $\frac{60m}{y}$
4. Ten minutes after a plane leaves the airport, it is reported that the plane is 40 miles away. What is the average speed of the plane, in miles per hour?
(A) 66 (B) 240 (C) 400 (D) 600 (E) 660
5. An automobile passes City X at 9:55 A.M. and City Y at 10:15 A.M. City X is 30 miles from City Y. What is the average rate of the automobile in miles per hour?
(A) 10 (B) 30 (C) 90 (D) 120 (E) 360
6. The distance between two cities is 1800 miles. How many gallons of gasoline will a motorist use with an automobile that uses (on the average) 1 gallon of gasoline for each 12 miles?
(A) 150 (B) 160 (C) 216 (D) 1500 (E) 2160
7. How many miles does a car travel if it averages a rate of 35 miles per hour for 3 hours and 24 minutes?
(A) 109 (B) 112 (C) 113 (D) 119 (E) 129
8. Two cars start towards each other from points 200 miles apart. One car travels at 40 miles an hour and the other travels at 35 miles an hour. How far apart will the two cars be after four hours of continuous traveling?
(A) 20 (B) 40 (C) 75 (D) 100 (E) 160
9. A motorist travels for 3 hours at 40 miles per hour and then covers a distance of 80 miles in two hours and 40 minutes. His average rate for the entire trip was
(A) 35 m.p.h. (B) 35.3 m.p.h. (C) 35.5 m.p.h.
(D) 36 m.p.h. (E) 37 m.p.h.
10. A man driving a distance of 90 miles, averages 30 miles per hour. On the return trip he averages 45 miles per hour. His average for the round trip, in miles per hour, is
(A) 34 (B) 36 (C) $37\frac{1}{2}$ (D) 40 (E) 75
11. The El Capitan of the Santa Fe travels a distance of 152.5 miles from La Junta to Garden City in two hours. What is the average speed in m.p.h.?
(A) 15.25 (B) 31.5 (C) 30.5 (D) 71 (E) 76.3
12. The distance between Portland, Oregon, and Santa Fe New Mexico is 1800 miles. How long would it take a train with an average speed of 60 miles per hour to make the trip? (Give answer in hours)
(A) 30 (B) 39 (C) 48 (D) 300 (E) 480
13. A man travels for 5 hours at an average rate of 40 m.p.h. He develops some motor trouble and returns to his original starting point in 10 hours. What was his average rate on the return trip?
(A) 10 (B) 15 (C) 20 (D) 26.6 (E) 40
14. If a man walks W miles in H hours, and then rides R miles in the same length of time, what is his average rate for the entire trip?
(A) $\frac{R+W}{H}$ (B) $\frac{2(R+W)}{H}$ (C) $\frac{R+W}{2H}$
(D) $\frac{H}{R-W}$ (E) $\frac{RW-H}{2}$
15. How long would it take a car traveling at 30 miles per hour to cover a distance of 44 feet? (1 mile = 5280 feet)
(A) 1 second (B) 2.64 seconds (C) 5.2 seconds
(D) 1 minute (E) 7.7 minutes

ANSWER KEY

1. B	6. A	11. E
2. C	7. D	12. A
3. D	8. D	13. C
4. B	9. B	14. C
5. C	10. B	15. A

C–3

Work Problems. In this type of problem you can assume all workers in the same category work at the same rate. The main idea is: If it takes k workers 1 hour to do a job then *each worker does* $\frac{1}{k}$ *of the job in an hour* or he works at the rate of $\frac{1}{k}$ of the job per hour. If it takes m workers h hours to finish a job then each worker does $\frac{1}{m}$ of the job in h hours so he does $\frac{1}{h}$ of $\frac{1}{m}$ in an hour. Therefore, each worker *works at the rate of* $\frac{1}{mh}$ *of the job per hour.*

EXAMPLE 1: If 5 men take an hour to dig a ditch, how long should it take 12 men to dig a ditch of the same type?

Since 5 workers took an hour, each worker does $\frac{1}{5}$ of the job in an hour. So 12 workers will work at the rate of $\frac{12}{5}$ of the job per hour. Thus if T is the time it takes for 12 workers to do the job, $\frac{12}{5} \times T = 1$ job and $T = \frac{5}{12} \times 1$, so

$$T = \frac{5}{12} \text{ hours or 25 minutes.}$$

EXAMPLE 2: Worker A takes 8 hours to do a job. Worker B takes 10 hours to do the same job. How long should it take worker A and worker B working together, but independently, to do the same job?

Worker A works at a rate of $\frac{1}{8}$ of the job per hour, since he takes 8 hours to finish the job. Worker B finished the job in 10 hours, so he works at a rate of $\frac{1}{10}$ of the job per hour. Therefore, if they work together they should complete $\frac{1}{8} + \frac{1}{10} = \frac{18}{80} = \frac{9}{40}$, so they work at a rate of $\frac{9}{40}$ of the job per hour together. So if T is the time it takes them to finish the job, $\frac{9}{40}$ of the job per hour $\times$ T hours must equal 1 job. Therefore,

$$\frac{9}{40} \times T = 1 \text{ and } T = \frac{40}{9} = 4\frac{4}{9} \text{ hours.}$$

EXAMPLE 3: There are two taps, tap 1 and tap 2, in a keg. If both taps are opened, the keg is drained in 20 minutes. If tap 1 is closed and tap 2 is open, the keg will be drained in 30 minutes. If tap 2 is closed and tap 1 is open, how long will it take to drain the keg?

Tap 1 and tap 2 together take 20 minutes to drain the keg, so together they drain the keg at a rate of $\frac{1}{20}$ of the keg per minute. Tap 2 takes 30 minutes to drain the keg by itself, so it drains the keg at the rate of $\frac{1}{30}$ of the keg per minute. Let r be the rate at which tap 1 will drain the keg by itself. Then $\left(r + \frac{1}{30}\right)$ of the keg per minute is the rate at which both taps together will drain the keg, so $r + \frac{1}{30} = \frac{1}{20}$. Therefore, $r = \frac{1}{20} - \frac{1}{30} = \frac{1}{60}$, and tap 1 drains the keg at the rate of $\frac{1}{60}$ of the keg per minute, so it will take 60 minutes or 1 hour for tap 1 to drain the keg if tap 2 is closed.

PRACTICE

1. One boy can deliver newspapers on his route in $1\frac{1}{4}$ hours. A boy who takes his place one day finds it takes him 15 minutes longer to deliver these papers. How long would it take to deliver the papers if they worked together?
(A) $22\frac{1}{2}$ min. (B) $37\frac{1}{2}$ min. (C) 40 min. (D) 50 min. (E) 65 min.

2. A contractor estimates that he can paint a house in 5 days by using 6 men. If he actually uses only 5 men for the job how many days will it take to do this job?
(A) 5 (B) $5\frac{1}{4}$ (C) $5\frac{1}{2}$ (D) 6 (E) $6\frac{1}{2}$

3. A club decided to build a cabin. The job can be done by 3 skilled workmen in 20 days or by 5 of the boys in 30 days. How many days will it take if all work together?
(A) 10 days (B) 12 days (C) $12\frac{2}{3}$ days (D) 14 days (E) 5 days

4. Andrew can do a piece of work in r days and Bill, who works faster, can do the same work in s days. Which of the following expressions, if any, represents the number of days it would take the two of them to do the work if they worked together?
(A) $\frac{r+s}{2}$ (B) $\frac{1}{r}+\frac{1}{s}$ (C) $r-s$ (D) $\frac{rs}{r+s}$
(E) none of these

5. Four tractors working together can plow a field in 12 hours. How long will it take 6 tractors to plow a field of the same size, if all tractors work at the same rate?
(A) 6 hrs. (B) 9 hrs. (C) 10 hrs. (D) 18 hrs. (E) 8 hrs.

6. A small factory with 3 machines has a job of stamping out a number of pan covers. The newest machine can do the job in 3 days, another machine can do it in 4 days, and the third machine can do it in 6 days. How many days will it take the factory to do the job, using all three machines.
(A) $1\frac{1}{3}$ days (B) $4\frac{1}{3}$ days (C) 6 days (D) 13 days (E) $1\frac{4}{9}$ days

7. Steven can mow a lawn in 20 minutes and Bernard can mow the same lawn in 30 minutes. How long will it take them working together to mow the lawn?
(A) 10 min. (B) $12\frac{1}{2}$ min. (C) 15 min. (D) 25 min. (E) 12 min.

8. It takes Bert an hour to do a job that Harry can do in 40 minutes. One morning they worked together for 12 minutes, then Bert went away and Harry finished the job. How long did it take him to finish?
(A) 8 min. (B) 16 min. (C) 20 min. (D) 28 min. (E) 33 min.

9. One man can paint a house in r days and another man s days. If together they can do the work in d days, the equation that expresses the amount of work done by both men in one day is
(A) $d=\frac{1}{r+s}$ (B) $\frac{1}{r}=\frac{d}{r+s}$ (C) $\frac{1}{d}=\frac{r+s}{rs}$
(D) $\frac{r+s}{d}=1$ (E) $\frac{d}{rs}=1$

10. Linda has m minutes of homework in each of her s subjects. What part of her homework does she complete in an hour?
(A) $\frac{1}{ms}$ (B) $\frac{ms}{60}$ (C) $\frac{60}{ms}$ (D) $\frac{s}{60m}$ (E) $\frac{60m}{s}$

11. Sam can mow a lawn in 20 minutes, while Mark takes 10 minutes longer to mow this lawn. How long will it take them to mow the lawn if they both work together?
(A) 10 minutes
(B) 12 minutes
(C) $12\frac{1}{2}$ minutes
(D) 15 minutes
(E) more than 15 minutes

12. It takes h hours to mow a lawn. What part of the lawn is mowed in one hour?
(A) h (B) $\frac{h}{x}$ (C) hx (D) $\frac{1}{h}$ (E) $\frac{x}{h}$

13. If M men can complete a job in H hours, how long will it take 5 men to do this job?
(A) $\frac{5M}{H}$ (B) $\frac{M}{5H}$ (C) $\frac{MH}{5}$ (D) $\frac{5}{MH}$
(E) $\frac{5H}{M}$

14. Ann can type a manuscript in 10 hours. Florence can type this manuscript in 5 hours. If they both type the manuscript together it can be completed in
(A) 2 hours 30 minutes
(B) 3 hours
(C) 3 hours 20 minutes
(D) 5 hours
(E) 7 hours 30 minutes

15. It was calculated that 75 men could complete a strip on a new highway in 20 days. When work was scheduled to commence, it was found necessary to send 25 men on another road project. How much longer will it take to complete the strip?
(A) 10 days (B) 20 days (C) 30 days
(D) 40 days (E) 60 days

ANSWER KEY

1. C	6. A	11. B
2. D	7. E	12. D
3. B	8. C	13. C
4. D	9. C	14. C
5. E	10. C	15. A

II-D. Counting Problems

D–1

An example of the first type of counting problem is: 50 students signed up for both English and Math. 90 students signed up for either English or Math. If 25 students are taking English but not taking Math, how many students are taking Math but not taking English?

In these problems, "either . . . or . . ." means you can take both, so the people taking both are counted among the people taking either Math or English.

You must avoid counting the same people twice in these problems. The formula is:

the number taking English or Math = the number taking English + the number taking Math − the number taking both.

You have to subtract the number taking both subjects since they are counted once with those taking English and counted again with those taking Math.

A person taking English is either taking Math or not taking Math, so there are 50 + 25 = 75 people taking English, 50 taking English and Math and 25 taking English but not taking Math. Since 75 are taking English, 90 = 75 + number taking Math − 50; so there are 90 − 25 = 65 people taking Math. 50 of the people taking Math are taking English so 65 − 50 or 15 are taking Math but not English.

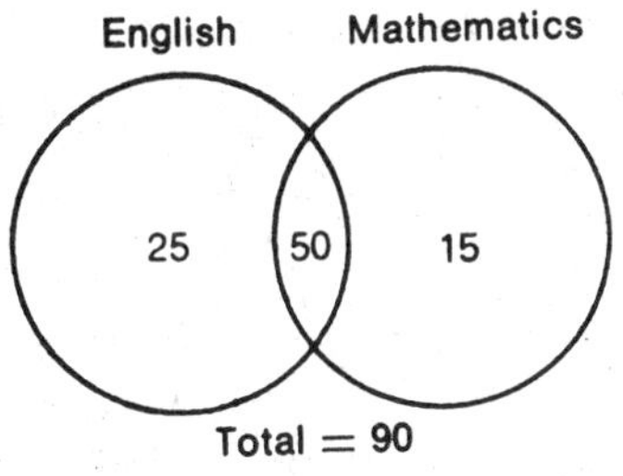

The figure shows what is given. Since 90 students signed up for English or Mathematics, 15 must be taking Mathematics but not English.

EXAMPLE 1: In a survey, 60% of those surveyed owned a car and 80% of those surveyed owned a T.V. If 55% owned both a car and a T.V., what percent of those surveyed owned a car or a T.V. but not both?

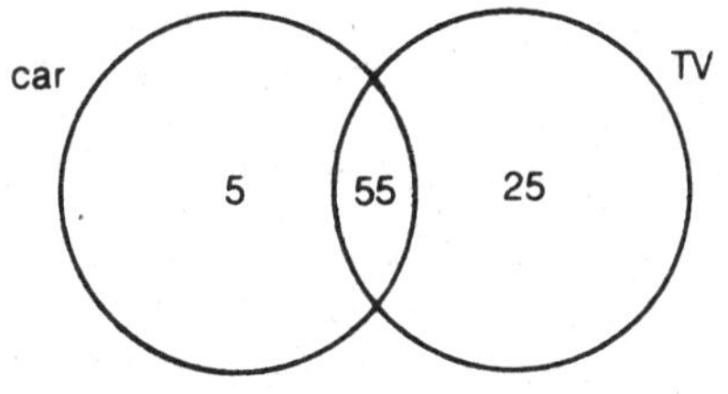

The basic formula is:

people who own a car or a T.V. = people who own a car + people who own a T.V. − people who own both a car and a T.V.

So the people who own a car or a T.V. = 60% + 80% − 55% = 85%. Therefore, 85% of the people surveyed own either a car or a T.V.

If we just add 60% and 80% the result is 140% which is impossible. This is because the 55% who own both are counted twice.

D–2

> If an event can happen in m different ways, and each of the m ways is followed by a second event which can occur in k different ways, then the first event can be followed by the second event in $m \cdot k$ different ways. This is called the *fundamental principle of counting.*

EXAMPLE 1: If there are 3 different roads from Syracuse to Binghamton and 4 different roads from Binghamton to Scranton, how many different routes are there from Syracuse to Scranton which go through Binghamton?

There are 3 different ways to go from Syracuse to Binghamton. Once you are in Binghamton, there are 4 different ways to get to Scranton. So using the fundamental principle of counting, there are $3 \times 4 = 12$ different ways to get from Syracuse to Scranton going through Binghamton.

EXAMPLE 2: A club has 20 members. They are electing a president and a vice president. How many different outcomes of the election are possible? (Assume the president and vice president must be different members of the club.)

There are 20 members, so there are 20 choices for president. Once a president is chosen, there are 19 members left who can be vice president. So there are $20 \cdot 19 = 380$ different possible outcomes of the election.

II–E. Ratio and Proportion

E–1

Ratio. A ratio is a comparison of two numbers by division. The ratio of a to b is written as $a{:}b = \frac{a}{b} = a \div b$. We can handle ratios as fractions, since a ratio is a fraction. In the ratio $a{:}b$, a and b are called the *terms* of the ratio. *Since* a:b *is a fraction,* b *can never be zero.* The fraction $\frac{a}{b}$ is usually different from the fraction $\frac{b}{a}$ $\left(\text{for example } \frac{3}{2} \text{ is not the same as } \frac{2}{3}\right)$ so *the order of the terms in a ratio is important.*

EXAMPLE 1: If an orange costs 20¢ and an apple costs 12¢, what is the ratio of the cost of an orange to the cost of an apple?

The ratio is $\frac{20¢}{12¢} = \frac{5}{3}$ or 5:3. Notice that the ratio of the cost of an apple to the cost of an orange is $\frac{12¢}{20¢} = \frac{3}{5}$ or 3:5. So the order of the terms is important.

A ratio is a number, so if you want to find the ratio of two quantities they must be expressed in the same units.

EXAMPLE 2: What is the ratio of 8 inches to 6 feet?

Change 6 feet into inches. Since there are 12 inches in a foot, 6 feet $= 6 \times 12$ inches $= 72$ inches. So the ratio is $\frac{8 \text{ inches}}{72 \text{ inches}} = \frac{1}{9}$ or 1:9. If you regard ratios as fractions, the units must cancel out. In example 2, if you did not change units the ratio would be $\frac{8 \text{ inches}}{6 \text{ feet}} = \frac{4}{3}$ inches/feet, which is not a number.

If two numbers measure different quantities, their quotient is usually called a rate. For example, $\frac{50 \text{ miles}}{2 \text{ hours}}$ which equals 25 miles per hour is a rate of speed.

E–2

Proportion. A proportion is a statement that two ratios are equal. For example, $\frac{3}{12} = \frac{1}{4}$ is a proportion; it could also be expressed as 3:12 = 1:4 or 3:12 :: 1:4.

In the proportion $a{:}b = c{:}d$, the terms on the outside, (a and d), are called the *extremes*, and the terms on the inside, (b and c), are called the *means*. Since $a{:}b$ and $c{:}d$ are ratios, b and d are both different from zero, so $bd \neq 0$. Multiply each side of $\frac{a}{b} = \frac{c}{d}$ by bd; you get $(bd)\left(\frac{a}{b}\right) = ad$ and $(bd)\left(\frac{c}{d}\right) = bc$. Since $bd \neq 0$, the proportion $\frac{a}{b} = \frac{c}{d}$ is equivalent to the equation $ad = bc$. This is usually expressed in the following way.

In a proportion the product of the extremes is equal to the product of the means.

EXAMPLE 1: Find x if $\frac{4}{5} = \frac{10}{x}$.

In the proportion $\frac{4}{5} = \frac{10}{x}$, 4 and x are the extremes and 5 and 10 are the means, so $4x = 5 \cdot 10 = 50$.

Solve for x and we get $x = \frac{50}{4} = 12.5$.

Finding the products ad and bc is also called <u>*cross-multiplying the proportion:*</u> $\frac{a}{b} \times \frac{c}{d}$. So cross-multiplying a proportion gives two equal numbers. The proportion $\frac{a}{b} = \frac{c}{d}$ is read "a is to b as c is to d."

EXAMPLE 2: Two numbers are in the ratio 5:4 and their difference is 10. What is the larger number?

Let m and n be the two numbers. Then $\frac{m}{n} = \frac{5}{4}$ and $m - n = 10$. Cross-multiply the proportion and you get $5n = 4m$ or $n = \frac{4}{5}m$. So $m - n = m - \frac{4}{5}m = \frac{1}{5}m = 10$ and $m = 50$, which means $n = \frac{4}{5} \cdot 50 = 40$. Therefore, the larger number is 50.

CHECK:

$$\frac{50}{40} = \frac{5}{4} \text{ and } 50 - 40 = 10.$$

Two variables, a and b, are *directly proportional* if they satisfy a relationship of the form $a = kb$, where k is a number. The distance a car travels in two hours and its average speed for the two hours are directly proportional, since $d = 2s$ where d is the distance and s is the average speed expressed in miles per hour. Here $k = 2$. Sometimes the word *directly* is omitted, so *a and b are proportional* means $a = kb$.

EXAMPLE 3: If m is proportional to n and $m = 5$ when $n = 4$, what is the value of m when $n = 18$?

There are two different ways to work the problem.

I. Since m and n are directly proportional, $m = kn$; and $m = 5$ when $n = 4$, so $5 = k \cdot 4$ which means $k = \frac{5}{4}$. Therefore, $m = \frac{5}{4}n$. So when $n = 18$, $m = \frac{5}{4} \cdot 18 = \frac{90}{4} = 22.5$.

II. Since m and n are directly proportional, $m = kn$. If n' is some value of n, then the value of m corresponding to n' we will call m', and $m' = kn'$. So $\frac{m}{n} = k$ and $\frac{m'}{n'} = k$; therefore, $\frac{m}{n} = \frac{m'}{n'}$ is a proportion. Since $m = 5$ when $n = 4$, $\frac{m}{n} = \frac{5}{4} = \frac{m'}{18}$. Cross-multiply and we have $4m' = 90$ or $m' = \frac{90}{4} = 22.5$.

If two quantities are proportional, you can always set up a proportion in this manner.

EXAMPLE 4: If a machine makes 3 yards of cloth in 2 minutes, how many yards of cloth will the machine make in 50 minutes?

The amount of cloth is proportional to the time the machine operates. Let y be the number of yards of cloth the machine makes in 50 minutes; then $\frac{2 \text{ minutes}}{50 \text{ minutes}} = \frac{3 \text{ yards}}{y \text{ yards}}$, so $\frac{2}{50} = \frac{3}{y}$. Cross multiply, and you have $2y = 150$, so $y = 75$. Therefore, the machine makes 75 yards of cloth in 50 minutes.

Since a ratio is a number, the units must cancel; so put the numbers which measure the same quantity in the same ratio.

Any two units of measurement of the same quantity are directly proportional.

EXAMPLE 5: How many ounces are there in $4\frac{3}{4}$ pounds?

Let x be the number of ounces in $4\frac{3}{4}$ pounds. Since there are 16 ounces in a pound, $\frac{x \text{ ounces}}{16 \text{ ounces}} = \frac{4\,^3\!/_4 \text{ pounds}}{1 \text{ pound}}$. Cross-multiply to get $x = 16 \cdot 4\frac{3}{4} = 16 \cdot \frac{19}{4} = 76$; so $4\frac{3}{4}$ pounds = 76 ounces.

You can always change units by using a proportion. You should know the following measurements:

LENGTH:	1 foot = 12 inches
	1 yard = 3 feet
AREA:	1 square foot = 144 square inches
	1 square yard = 9 square feet
TIME:	1 minute = 60 seconds
	1 hour = 60 minutes
	1 day = 24 hours
	1 week = 7 days
	1 year = 52 weeks
VOLUME:	1 quart = 2 pints
	1 gallon = 4 quarts
WEIGHT:	1 ounce = 16 drams
	1 pound = 16 ounces
	1 ton = 2000 pounds

EXAMPLE 6: On a map, it is $2\frac{1}{2}$ inches from Harrisburg to Gary. The actual distance from Harrisburg to Gary is 750 miles. What is the actual distance from town A to town B if they are 4 inches apart on the map?

Let d miles be the distance from A to B; then $\frac{2\,^1\!/_2 \text{ inches}}{4 \text{ inches}} = \frac{750 \text{ miles}}{d \text{ miles}}$. Cross-multiply and we have $\left(2\frac{1}{2}\right)d = 4 \times 750 = 3{,}000$, so $d = \frac{2}{5} \times 3{,}000 = 1{,}200$. Therefore, the distance from A to B is 1,200 miles. Problems like this one are often called scale problems.

Two variables, a and b, are *indirectly proportional* if they satisfy a relationship of the form $k = ab$, where k is a number. So the average speed of a car and the time it takes the car to travel 300 miles are indirectly proportional, since $st = 300$ where s is the speed and t is the time.

EXAMPLE 7: m is indirectly proportional to n and $m = 5$ when $n = 4$. What is the value of m when $n = 18$?

Since m and n are indirectly proportional, $m \cdot n = k$, and $k = 5 \cdot 4 = 20$ because $m = 5$ when $n = 4$. Therefore, $18m = k = 20$, so $m = \frac{20}{18} = \frac{10}{9}$ when $n = 18$.

Other examples of indirect proportion are work problems (see page 246).

> If two quantities are directly proportional, then when one increases, the other increases. If two quantities are indirectly proportional when one quantity increases, the other decreases.

E–3

It is also possible to compare three or more numbers by a ratio. The numbers A, B, and C are in the ratio 2:4:3 means $A{:}B = 2{:}4$, $A{:}C = 2{:}3$, and $B{:}C = 4{:}3$. The order of the terms is important. $A{:}B{:}C$ is read "*A is to B is to C*."

EXAMPLE 1: What is the ratio of Tom's salary to Martha's salary to Anne's salary if Tom makes $15,000, Martha makes $12,000 and Anne makes $10,000?

The ratio is 15,000:12,000:10,000 which is the same as 15:12:10. You can cancel a factor which appears in *every* term.

EXAMPLE 2: The angles of a triangle are in the ratio 5:4:3; how many degrees are there is the largest angle?

The sum of the angles in a triangle is 180°. If the angles are $a°$, $b°$, and $c°$, then $a + b + c = 180$, and $a{:}b{:}c{:} = 5{:}4{:}3$. You could find b in terms of a since $\frac{a}{b} = \frac{5}{4}$ and c in terms of a since $\frac{a}{c} = \frac{5}{3}$ and then solve the equation for a.

A quicker method for this type of problem is:

(1) Add all the numbers, so $5 + 4 + 3 = 12$.
(2) Use each number as the numerator of a fraction whose denominator is the result of step (1), getting $\frac{5}{12}, \frac{4}{12}, \frac{3}{12}$.
(3) Each quantity is the corresponding fraction (from step (2)), of the total.

Thus

$a = \frac{5}{12}$ of 180 or 75, $b = \frac{4}{12}$ of 180 or 60, and $c = \frac{3}{12}$ of 180 or 45.
So the largest angle is 75°.

CHECK:

$$75{:}60{:}45 = 5{:}4{:}3 \text{ and } 75 + 60 + 45 = 180.$$

PRACTICE

1. An Erlenmeyer flask can hold 0.6 liters. How many flasks are necessary to hold 3.6 liters?
(A) 3 (B) 4.2 (C) 6 (D) 12 (E) 21.6

2. At 13° Centigrade a cubic centimeter of uranium weighs 18.7 grams. What is the weight (in grams) of 0.1 cubic centimeters of uranium at 13° Centigrade?
(A) 1 (B) 1.87 (C) .187 (D) 100 (E) 1870

3. If the cost of 500 articles is d dollars, how many of these articles can be bought for x dollars?
(A) $\frac{500d}{x}$ (B) $\frac{500}{dx}$ (C) $\frac{dx}{500}$ (D) $\frac{500x}{d}$ (E) $\frac{d}{500x}$

4. A man left $5,000.00 to his three sons. For every dollar Abraham received, Benjamin received $1.50 and Charles received $2.50. How much money was lef to Benjamin?
(A) $750 (B) $1000 (C) $1100 (D) $1500 (E) $3000

5. The Wey of Scotland is equivalent to 40 bushels. How many Weys are there in 4 bushels?
(A) $\frac{1}{10}$ (B) 1 (C) 10 (D) 44 (E) 160

6. The Japanese ken is equivalent to 5.97 feet. How man feet are there in 59.7 ken?
(A) 0.1 (B) 10 (C) 248 (D) 356 (E) 360

7. 640 acres = 1 square mile
1 acre = 4,840 square yards
1 square mile = ? square yards

(A) $\frac{16}{121}$ (B) $\frac{121}{16}$ (C) 1760 (D) 309,760
(E) 3,097,600

8. A bag of chicken feed will feed 18 chickens for 54 days. How long will it feed 12 chickens?
(A) 36 (B) 37 (C) 53 (D) 72 (E) 81

9. If it requires 9 men 15 days to complete a task, how long would it take to complete this task if three additional men were employed?
(A) $4\frac{3}{4}$ (B) 10 (C) $11\frac{1}{4}$ (D) 12 (E) 16

0. A man works 5 days a week and binds 35 sets of books each week. If there are 7 books in a set, what is the number of books he binds each day?
(A) 1 (B) 7 (C) 25 (D) 35 (E) 49

1. Three men invested $2,000, $3,000, and $5,000 respectively upon the formation of a partnership. The net profits at the end of the year amounted to $960.00. How much should the man who invested the least money receive as his share if the profits are divided in accordance with the amount each partner invested?
(A) $192 (B) $220 (C) $240 (D) $384 (E) $480

2. Three boys have marbles in the ratio of 19:5:3. If the boy with the least number has 9 marbles, how many marbles does the boy with the greatest number have?
(A) 27 (B) 33 (C) 57 (D) 81 (E) 171

3. Snow is accumulating f feet per minute. How much snow will fall in h hours if it continues falling at that rate?
(A) $60fh$ (B) fh (C) $\frac{60f}{h}$ (D) $\frac{60h}{f}$ (E) $\frac{f}{h}$

4. A diagram of a plane drawn to the scale of 0.5 inch equals 80 feet. If the length of the diagram is 4.5 inches the actual length of the plane is
(A) 320 ft. (B) 360 ft. (C) 640 ft. (D) 680 ft.
(E) 720 ft.

15. Joan can wire x radios in $\frac{3}{4}$ minute. At this rate, how many radios can she wire in $\frac{3}{4}$ of an hour?
(A) $\frac{x}{60}$ (B) $\frac{60}{x}$ (C) $60x$ (D) 60 (E) $x + 60$

16. If a light flashes every 6 seconds, how many times will it flash in $\frac{3}{4}$ of an hour?
(A) 225 (B) 250 (C) 360 (D) 450 (E) 480

17. Samuel, Martin, and Miguel invest $5000, $7000, and $12,000 respectively in a business. If the profits are distributed proportionately, what share of a $1111 profit should Miguel receive?
(A) $231.40 (B) $264.00 (C) $333.33 (D) $370.33
(E) $555.50

18. If there are 5 to 8 eggs in a pound, what is the maximum number of eggs in 40 pounds?
(A) 5 (B) 8 (C) 160 (D) 200 (E) 320

19. 24-carat gold is pure gold
18-carat gold is $\frac{3}{4}$ gold
20-carat gold is $\frac{5}{6}$ gold
The ratio of pure gold in 18-carat gold to 20-carat gold is
(A) 5:8 (B) 9:10 (C) 15:24 (D) 8:5 (E) 10:9

20. A cup of oatmeal weighs 3 ounces. A cup of pancake mix weighs 5 ounces. How many cups of oatmeal will have the same weight as 3 cups of pancake mix?
(A) $\frac{3}{5}$ (B) $1\frac{2}{3}$ (C) 3 (D) 5 (E) 15

ANSWER KEY

1.	C	8.	E	15.	C
2.	B	9.	C	16.	D
3.	D	10.	E	17.	E
4.	D	11.	A	18.	E
5.	A	12.	C	19.	B
6.	D	13.	A	20.	D
7.	E	14.	E		

II–F. Sequence and Progressions

F–1

A SEQUENCE is an ordered collection of numbers. For example, 2,4,6,8,10, . . . is a sequence. 2,4,6,8,10 are called the *terms* of the sequence. We identify the terms by their position in the sequence; so 2 is the first term, 8 is the 4th term and so on. The dots mean the sequence continues; you should be able to figure out the succeeding terms. In the example, the sequence is the sequence of even integers, and the next term after 10 would be 12.

EXAMPLE 1: What is the eighth term of the sequence 1,4,9,16,25, . . . ?

Since $1^2 = 1$, $2^2 = 4$, $3^2 = 9$, the sequence is the sequence of squares of integers, so the eighth term is $8^2 = 64$.

F–2

An *arithmetical progression* is a sequence of numbers with the property that the *difference* of any two consecutive numbers is always the same. The numbers 2,6,10,14,18,22, . . . constitute an arithmetical progression, since each term is 4 more than the term before it. 4 is called the common difference of the progression.

If d is the common difference and a is the first term of the progression, then the nth term will be $a + (n - 1)d$. So a progression with common difference 4 and initial term 5 will have $5 + 6(4) = 29$ as its 7th term. You can check your answer. The sequence would be 5,9,13,17,21,25,29, . . . so 29 is the seventh term.

A sequence of numbers is called a *geometric progression* if the *ratio* of consecutive terms is always the same. So 3,6,12,24,48, . . . is a geometric progression since $\frac{6}{3} = 2 = \frac{12}{6} = \frac{24}{12} = \frac{48}{24}, \ldots$. *The nth term of a geometric series is* ar^{n-1} where a is the first term and r is the common ratio. If a geometric progression started with 2 and the common ratio was 3, then the fifth term should be $2 \cdot 3^4 = 2 \cdot 81 = 162$. The sequence would be 2,6,18,54,162, . . . so 162 is indeed the fifth term of the progression.

We can quickly add up the first n terms of a geometric progression which starts with a and has common ratio r. *The formula for the sum of the first n terms is* $\frac{ar^n - a}{r - 1}$ when $r \neq 1$. (If $r = 1$ all the terms are the same so the sum is na.)

EXAMPLE 1: Find the sum of the first 7 terms of the sequence 5,10,20,40, ...

Since $\frac{10}{5} = \frac{20}{10} = \frac{40}{20} = 2$, the sequence is a geometric sequence with common ratio 2. The first term is 5, so $a = 5$ and the common ratio is 2. The sum of the first seven terms means $n = 7$. Thus, the sum is

$$\frac{5 \cdot 2^7 - 5}{2 - 1} = 5(2^7 - 1) = 5(128 - 1) = 5 \cdot 127 = 635.$$

CHECK:

The first seven terms are 5,10,20,40,80,160,320, and $5 + 10 + 20 + 40 + 80 + 160 + 320 = 635$.

II–G. Inequalities

G–1

A number is positive if it is greater than 0, so 1, $\frac{1}{1000}$, and 53.4 are all positive numbers. Positive numbers are signed numbers whose sign is +. If you think of numbers as points on a number line (see section I-F-2, page 244), positive numbers correspond to points to the right of 0.

A number is negative if it is less than 0. $-\frac{4}{5}$, −50, and −.0001 are all negative numbers. Negative numbers are signed numbers whose sign is $-$ Negative numbers correspond to points to the left of 0 on a number line.

0 is the only number which is neither positive nor negative.

$a > b$ means the number a is greater than the number b, that is $a = b + x$ where x is a positive number. If we look at a number line, $a > b$ means a is to the right of b. $a > b$ can also be read as b is less than a, which is also written $b < a$. For example, $-5 > -7.5$ because $-5 = -7.5 + 2.5$ and 2.5 is positive.

The notation $a \leqslant b$ means a is less than or equal to b, or b is greater than or equal to a. For example, $5 \geqslant 4$; also $4 \geqslant 4$. $a \neq b$ means a is not equal to b.

If you need to know whether one fraction is greater than another fraction, put the fractions over a common denominator and compare the numerators.

EXAMPLE 1: Which is larger, $\frac{13}{16}$ or $\frac{31}{40}$?

A common denominator is 80.

$\frac{13}{16} = \frac{65}{80}$, and $\frac{31}{40} = \frac{62}{80}$;

since $65 > 62$,

$\frac{65}{80} > \frac{62}{80}$,

so $\frac{13}{16} > \frac{31}{40}$.

G–2

Inequalities have certain properties which are similar to equations. We can talk about the left side and the right side of an inequality, and we can use algebraic expressions for the sides of an inequality. For example, $6x < 5x + 4$. A value for an unknown *satisfies an inequality*, if when you evaluate each side of the inequality the numbers satisfy the inequality. So if $x = 2$, then $6x = 12$ and $5x + 4 = 14$ and since $12 < 14$, $x = 2$ satisfies $6x < 5x + 4$. Two inequalities are equivalent if the same collection of numbers satisfies both inequalities.

The following basic principles are used in work with inequalities:

(A) Adding the same expression to *each* side of an inequality gives an equivalent inequality (written $a < b \Leftrightarrow a + c < b + c$ where $\Leftrightarrow$ means equivalent).
(B) Subtracting the same expression from *each* side of an inequality gives an equivalent inequality ($a < b \Leftrightarrow a - c < b - c$).
(C) Multiplying or dividing *each* side of an inequality by the same *positive* expression gives an equivalent inequality ($a < b \Leftrightarrow ca < cb$ for $c > 0$).
(D) Multiplying or dividing each side of an inequality by the same *negative* expression *reverses* the inequality ($a < b \Leftrightarrow ca > cb$ for $c < 0$).
(E) If both sides of an inequality have the same sign, inverting both sides of the inequality *reverses* the inequality.

$$0 < a < b \Leftrightarrow 0 < \frac{1}{b} < \frac{1}{a}$$

$$a < b < 0 \Leftrightarrow \frac{1}{b} < \frac{1}{a} < 0$$

(F) If two inequalities are of the same type (both greater or both less), adding the respective sides gives the same type of inequality.

$$(a < b \text{ and } c < d, \text{ then } a + c < b + d)$$

Note that the inequalities are *not* equivalent.

(G) If $a < b$ and $b < c$ then $a < c$.

EXAMPLE 1: Find the values of x for which $5x - 4 < 7x + 2$.

Using principle (B) subtract $5x + 2$ from each side, so $(5x - 4 < 7x + 2) \Leftrightarrow -6 < 2x$. Now use principle (C) and divide each side by 2, so $-6 < 2x \Leftrightarrow -3 < x$.

So any x greater than -3 satisfies the inequality. It is a good idea to make a spot check. -1 is > -3; let $x = -1$ then $5x - 4 = -9$ and $7x + 2 = -5$. Since $-9 < -5$, the answer is correct for at least the particular value $x = -1$.

EXAMPLE 2: Find the values of a which satisfy $a^2 + 1 > 2a + 4$.

Subtract $2a$ from each side, so
$(a^2 + 1 > 2a + 4) \Leftrightarrow a^2 - 2a + 1 > 4$.
$a^2 - 2a + 1 = (a - 1)^2$ so
$a^2 - 2a + 1 > 4 \Leftrightarrow (a - 1)^2 > 2^2$.

We need to be careful when we take the square roots of inequalities. If $q^2 > 4$ and if $q > 0$, then $q > 2$; but if $q < 0$, then $q < -2$. We must look at two cases in example 2. First, if $(a - 1) \geq 0$ then

$(a - 1)^2 > 2^2 \Leftrightarrow a - 1 > 2$ or $a > 3$.
If $(a - 1) < 0$ then $(a - 1)^2 > 2^2 \Leftrightarrow a - 1 < -2 \Leftrightarrow a < -1$.
So the inequality is satisfied if $a > 3$ or if $a < -1$.

CHECK:

$$(-2)^2 + 1 = 5 > 2(-2) + 4 = 0, \text{ and } 5^2 + 1 = 26 > 14 = 2 \cdot 5 + 4.$$

Some inequalities are not satisfied by *any* real number. For example, since $x^2 \geq 0$ for all x, there is no real number x such that $x^2 < -9$.

You may be given an inequality and asked whether other inequalities follow from the original inequality. You should be able to answer such questions by using principles (A) through (G).

If there is any property of inequalities you can't remember, try out some specific numbers. If $x < y$, then what is the relation between $-x$ and $-y$? Since $4 < 5$ but $-5 < -4$, the relation is probably $-x > -y$, which is true by (D).

Probably the most common mistake is forgetting to reverse the inequalities if you multiply or divide by a negative number.

PRACTICE

1. Point P is on line segment AB. Which of the following is always true?
   (A) $AP = PB$ (B) $AP > PB$ (C) $PB > AP$
   (D) $AB > AP$ (E) $AB > AP + PB$

2. If $x < y$ and $a = b$ then
   (A) $x + a = y + b$ (B) $x + a < y + b$
   (C) $x + a > y + b$ (D) $x + a = y$
   (E) $x + a = b$

3. If $x < y$ and $z = \frac{1}{2}x$ and $a = \frac{1}{2}y$ then
   (A) $z > a$ (B) $a > z$ (C) $\frac{1}{2}a = \frac{1}{2}z$
   (D) $2x > 2z$ (E) $2a > y$

4. If $b < d$ and $a = 2b$ and $c = 2d$ then
   (A) $b = d$ (B) $a = c$ (C) $a < c$
   (D) $b > d$ (E) $a > c$

5. If $p < q$ and $r < s$ then
   (A) $p = r > q + s$ (B) $p + r < q + s$
   (C) $pr < qs$ (D) $pr > qs$ (E) $p + r = q + s$

6. If $-1 < x \leqq 1$ then the value of x is
   (A) zero only (B) one only (C) one and zero
   (D) one value more than one
   (E) one value less than one

7. In the inequality $5x + 2 < 2x + 5$ all of the following may be a value of x except
   (A) 0 (B) 1 (C) -1 (D) -2 (E) -3

8. If $a > b$ and $b > c$ then
   (A) $a < c$ (B) $a > c$ (C) $a = c$
   (D) $c > a$ (E) $b < a$

9. If $a > b > 1$ then which of the following is true?
   (A) $b + a > 2a$ (B) $a^2 < ab$ (C) $a - b < 0$
   (D) $a < b + 1$ (E) $a^2 > b^2$

10. If $2y > 5$ then
   (A) $y > 2.5$ (B) $y < 2.5$ (C) $y = 2.5$
   (D) $y = 10$ (E) $y = 5.2$

11. If $3x - 4 > 8$ then
   (A) $x = 4$ (B) $x = 0$ (C) $x = 4, 0$
   (D) $x > 4$ (E) $x < 4$

12. In triangle ABC $AB = AC$. All of the following statements are true except
   (A) $AB < AC + BC$ (B) $AC < AB + BC$
   (C) $BC < AB + AC$ (D) $AC + BC = AB + BC$
   (E) $BC + AC > AB + BC$

13. In triangle KLM the measure of angle M > the measure of angle L. Which of the following is true?
   (A) $KM > KL$ (B) $KL > KM$ (C) $KL < KM$
   (D) $KM + LM < KL$ (E) $KL + LM < KM$

14. In triangles ABC and DEF, AC = DF, BC = EF and AB > DE, then
   (A) $m\angle C = m\angle F$ (B) $m\angle F > m\angle C$
   (C) $m\angle F < m\angle C$ (D) $m\angle A = m\angle D$
   (E) $m\angle B = m\angle E$

15. If $x < y$ and $a < b$, then
   (A) $a + x < b + y$ (B) $a + x > b + y$
   (C) $a = y$ (D) $x = b$ (E) $ax = by$

ANSWER KEY

1.	D	6.	C	11.	D
2.	B	7.	B	12.	E
3.	B	8.	B	13.	B
4.	C	9.	E	14.	C
5.	B	10.	A	15.	A

III. Geometry

III–A. Angles

A–1

If two straight lines meet at a point they form an *angle*. The point is called the *vertex* of the angle and the lines are called the *sides* or *rays* of the angle. The sign for angle is $\angle$ and an angle can be denoted in the following ways:

(A) $\angle ABC$ where B is the vertex, A is a point on one side, and C a point on the other side.

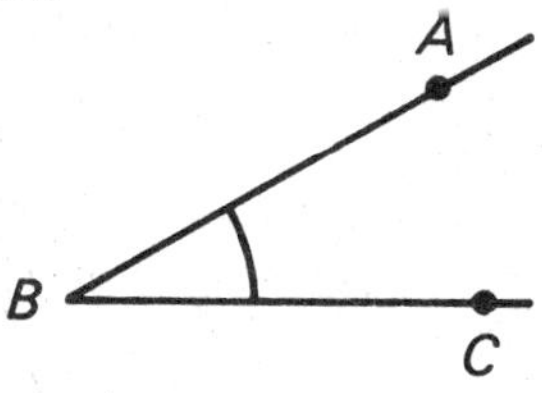

(B) $\angle B$ where B is the vertex.

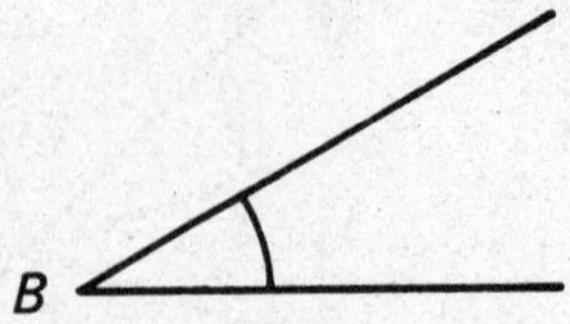

(C) $\angle 1$ or $\angle x$ where x or 1 is written inside the angle.

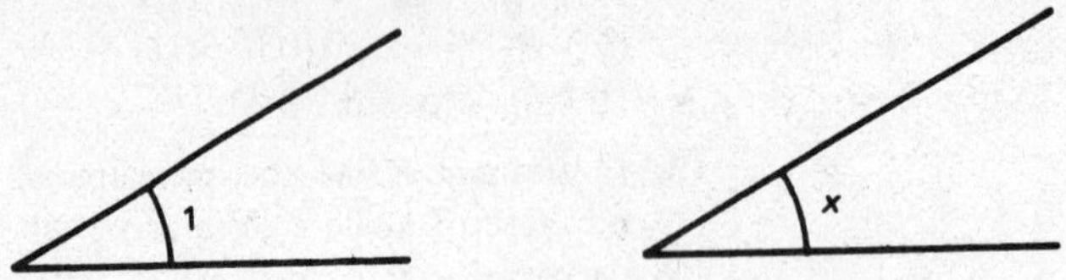

Angles are usually measured in degrees. We say that an angle equals x degrees, when its measure is x degrees. Degrees are denoted by °. An angle of 50 degrees is 50°. $60' = 1°$, $60'' = 1'$ where ′ is read minutes and ″ is read seconds.

A–2

Two angles are *adjacent* if they have the same vertex and a common side and one angle is not inside the other.

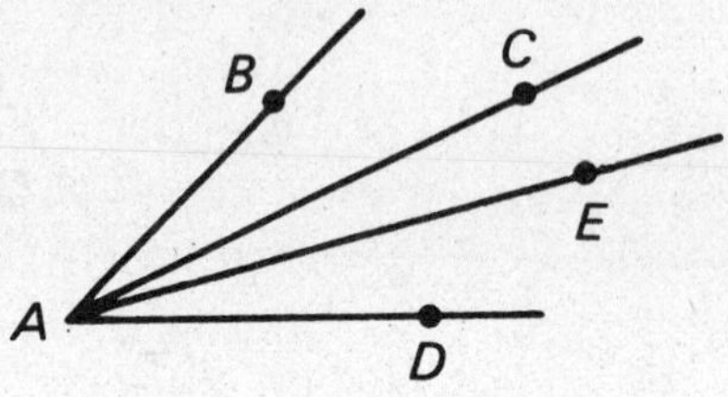

$\angle BAC$ and $\angle CAD$ are adjacent, but $\angle CAD$ and $\angle EAD$ are not adjacent.

If two lines intersect at a point, they form 4 angles. The angles opposite each other are called *vertical* angles. $\angle 1$ and $\angle 3$ are vertical angles. $\angle 2$ and $\angle 4$ are vertical angles.

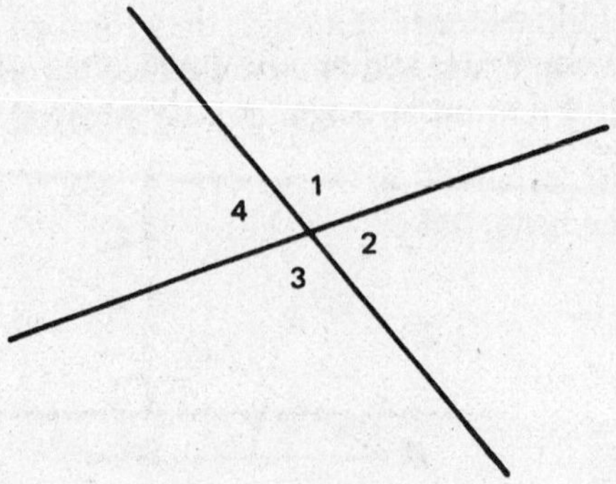

Vertical angles are equal,

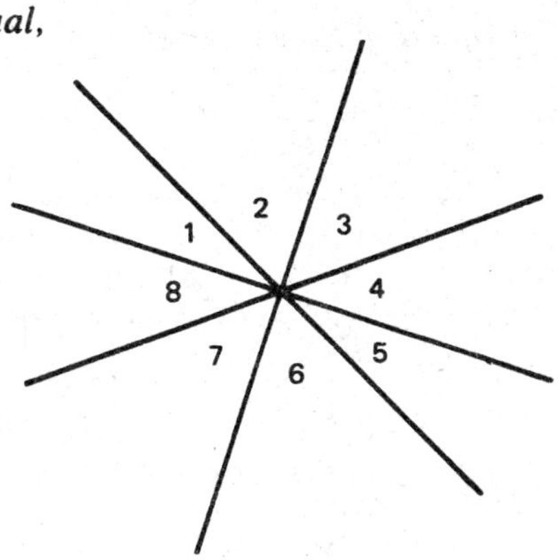

so $\angle 1 = \angle 5$, $\angle 2 = \angle 6$, $\angle 3 = \angle 7$, $\angle 4 = \angle 8$.

A–3

A straight angle is an angle whose sides lie on a straight line. *A straight angle equals 180°.*

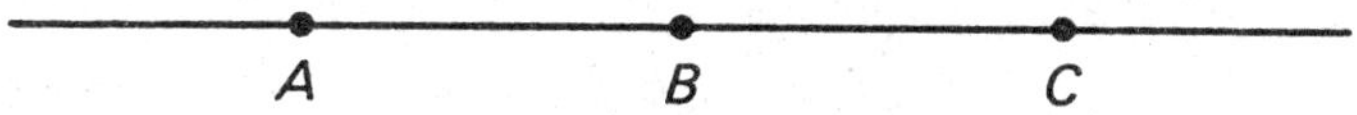

$\angle ABC$ is a straight angle.

If the sum of two adjacent angles is a straight angle, then the angles are *supplementary* and each angle is the supplement of the other.

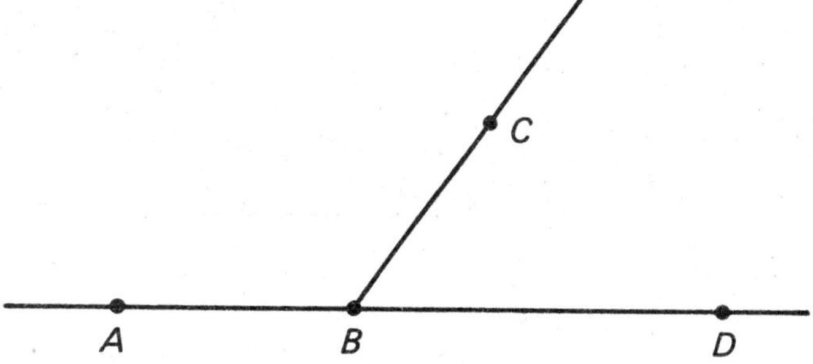

$\angle ABC$ and $\angle CBD$ are supplementary.

If an angle of $x°$ and an angle of $y°$ are supplements, then $x + y = 180$.

If two supplementary angles are equal, they are both *right angles.* A right angle is half of a straight angle. A right angle $= 90°$.

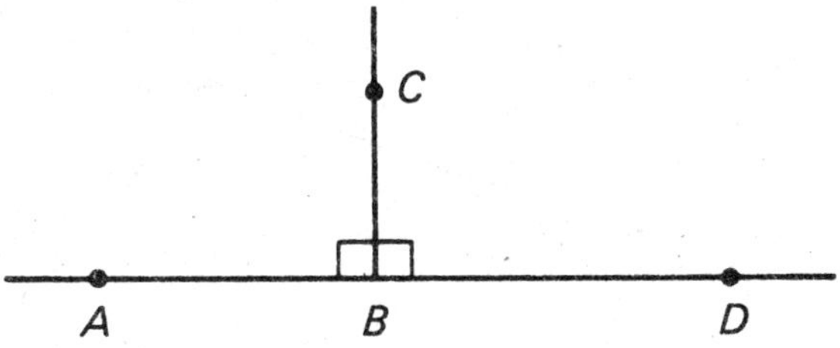

$\angle ABC = \angle CBD$ and they are both right angles. A right angle is denoted by ∟. When 2 lines intersect and all four of the angles are equal, then each of the angles is a right angle.

If the sum of two adjacent angles is a right angle, then the angles are *complementary* and each angle is the complement of the other.

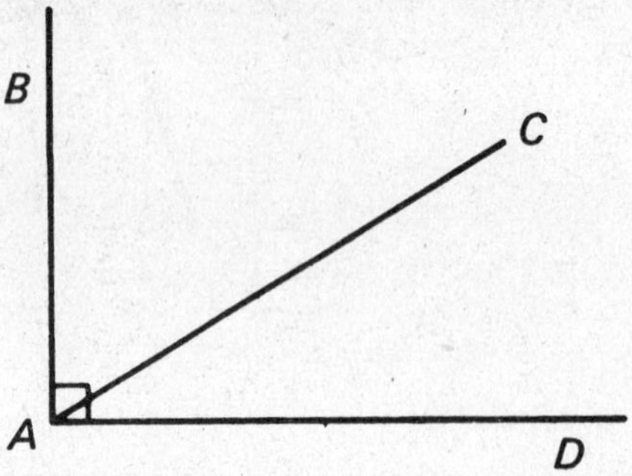

$\angle BAC$ and $\angle CAD$ are complementary.

If an angle of $x°$ and an angle of $y°$ are complementary, then $x + y = 90$.

EXAMPLE 1: If the supplement of angle x is three times as much as the complement of angle x, how many degrees is angle x?

Let d be the number of degrees in angle x; then the supplement of x is $(180-d)°$, and the complement of x is $(90-d)°$. Since the supplement is 3 times the complement, $180 - d = 3(90 - d) = 270 - 3d$ which gives $2d = 90$, so $d = 45$.

Therefore, angle x is 45°.

If an angle is divided into two equal parts by a straight line, then the angle has been *bisected* and the line is called the *bisector* of the angle.

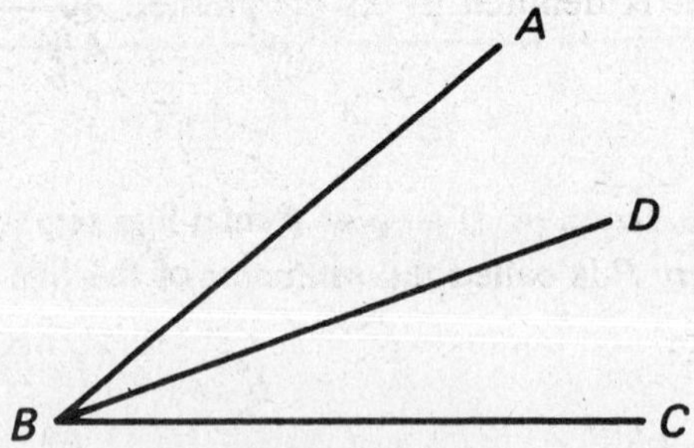

BD bisects $\angle ABC$; so $\angle ABD = \angle DBC$.

An *acute angle* is an angle less than a right angle. An *obtuse* angle is an angle greater than a right angle, but less than a straight angle.

∠1 is an acute angle, and ∠2 is an obtuse angle.

III–B. Lines

B–1

A line is understood to be a straight line. A line is assumed to extend indefinitely in both directions. *There is one and only one line between two distinct points.* There are two ways to denote a line:

(1) (A) by a single letter: *l* is a line;

(2) (B) by two points on the line:

AB is a line.

A *line segment* is the part of a line between two points called *endpoints.* A line segment is denoted by its endpoints.

AB is a line segment. If a point *P* on a line segment is equidistant from the endpoints, then *P* is called the *midpoint* of the line segment.

P is the midpoint of *AB* if the length of $AP =$ the length of *PB*. Two line segments are equal if their lengths are equal; so $AP = PB$ means the line segment *AP* has the same length as the line segment *PB*.

When a line segment is extended indefinitely in one direction, it is called a *ray*. A ray has one endpoint.

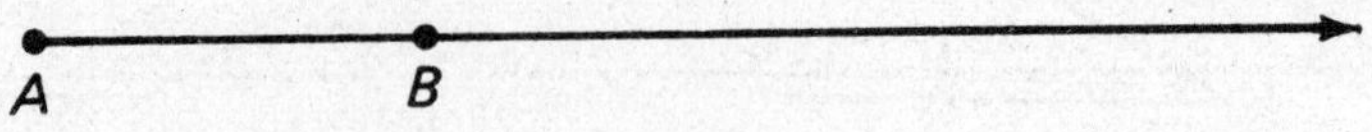

AB is a ray which has *A* as its endpoint.

B–2

P is a *point of intersection* of two lines if *P* is a point which is on both of the lines. *Two different lines can not have more than one point of intersection*, because there is only one line between two points.

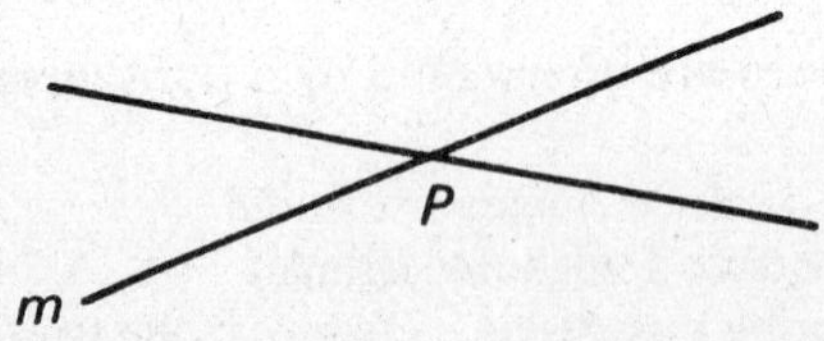

P is the point of intersection of *m* and *n*. We also say *m and n intersect at P*.

Two lines in the same plane are parallel if they do not intersect no matter how far they are extended.

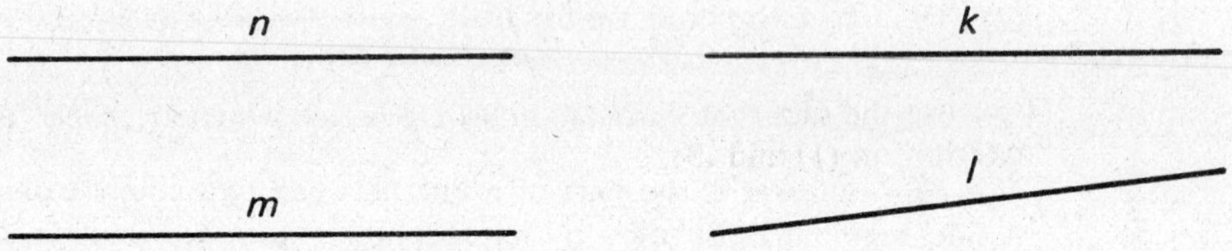

m and *n* are parallel, but *k* and *l* are not parallel since if *k* and *l* are extended they will intersect. Parallel lines are denoted by the symbol ||; so $m \parallel n$ means *m* is parallel to *n*.

If two lines are parallel to a third line, then they are parallel to each other.

If a third line intersects two given lines, it is called a *transversal*. A transversal and the two given lines form eight angles. The four inside angles are called *interior* angles. The four outside angles are called *exterior* angles. If two angles are on opposite sides of the transversal they are called *alternate* angles.

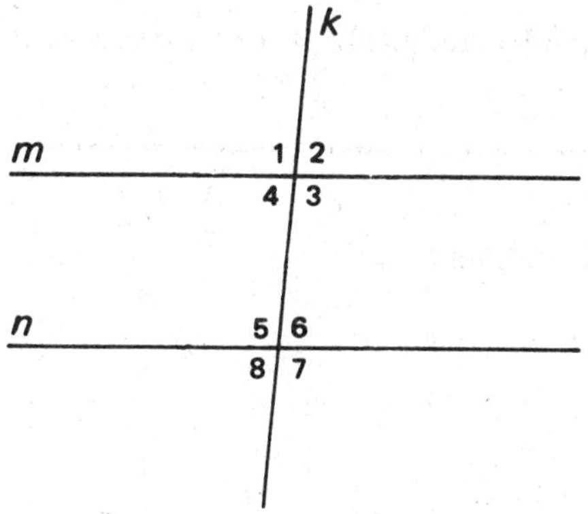

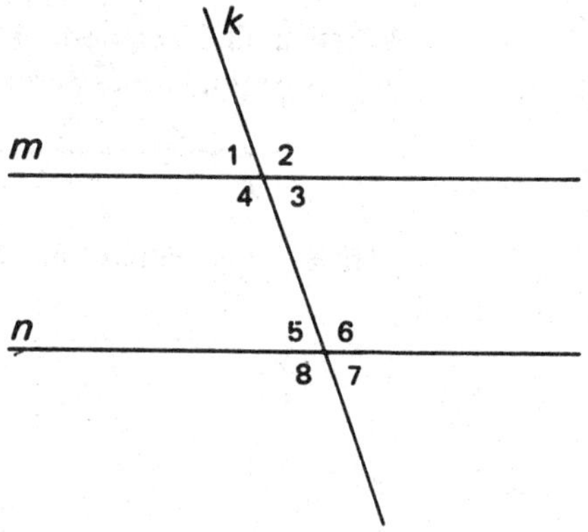

k is a transversal of the lines *m* and *n*. Angles 1, 2, 7, and 8 are the exterior angles, and angles 3, 4, 5, and 6 are the interior angles. $\angle 4$ and $\angle 6$ are an example of a pair of alternate angles. $\angle 1$ and $\angle 5$, $\angle 2$ and $\angle 6$, $\angle 3$ and $\angle 7$, and $\angle 4$ and $\angle 8$ are pairs of *corresponding* angles.

If two parallel lines are intersected by a transversal then:

(1) Alternate interior angles are equal.
(2) Corresponding angles are equal.
(3) Interior angles on the same side of the transversal are supplementary.

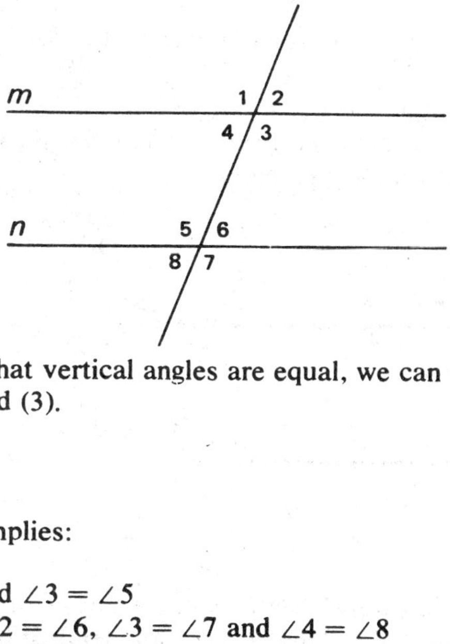

If we use the fact that vertical angles are equal, we can replace "interior" by "exterior" in (1) and (3).

m is parallel to *n* implies:

(1) $\angle 4 = \angle 6$ and $\angle 3 = \angle 5$
(2) $\angle 1 = \angle 5$, $\angle 2 = \angle 6$, $\angle 3 = \angle 7$ and $\angle 4 = \angle 8$
(3) $\angle 3 + \angle 6 = 180°$ and $\angle 4 + \angle 5 = 180°$

The reverse is also true. Let *m* and *n* be two lines which have *k* as a transversal.

(1) If a pair of alternate interior angles are equal, then *m* and *n* are parallel.
(2) If a pair of corresponding angles are equal, then *m* and *n* are parallel.
(3) If a pair of interior angles on the same side of the transversal are supplementary, then *m* is parallel to *n*.

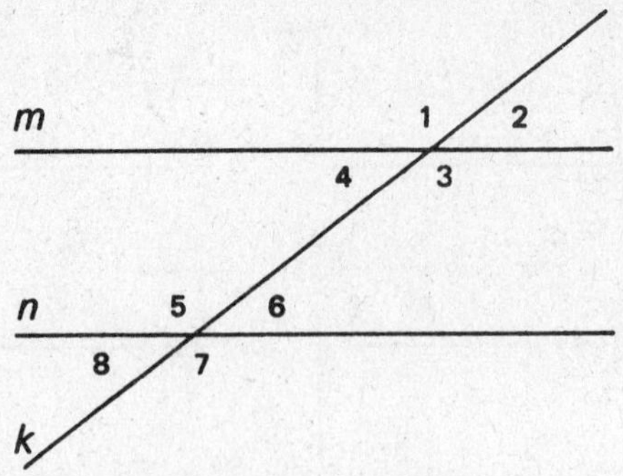

If $\angle 3 = \angle 5$, then $m \parallel n$. If $\angle 4 = \angle 6$ then $m \parallel n$. If $\angle 2 = \angle 6$ then $m \parallel n$. If $\angle 3 + \angle 6 = 180°$, then $m \parallel n$.

EXAMPLE 1: If m and n are two parallel lines and angle 1 is 60°, how many degrees is angle 2?

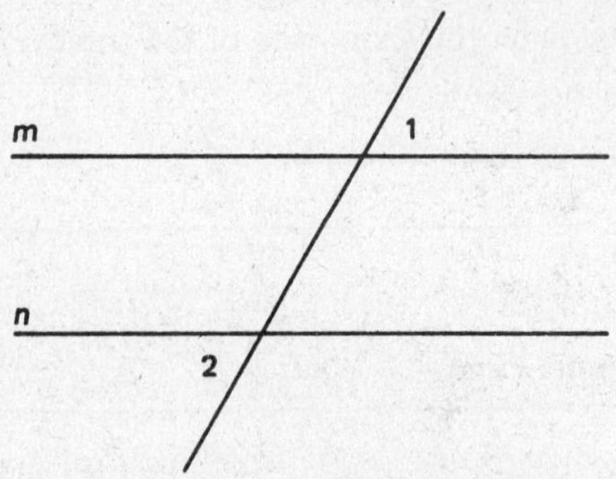

Let $\angle 3$ be the vertical angle equal to angle 2.

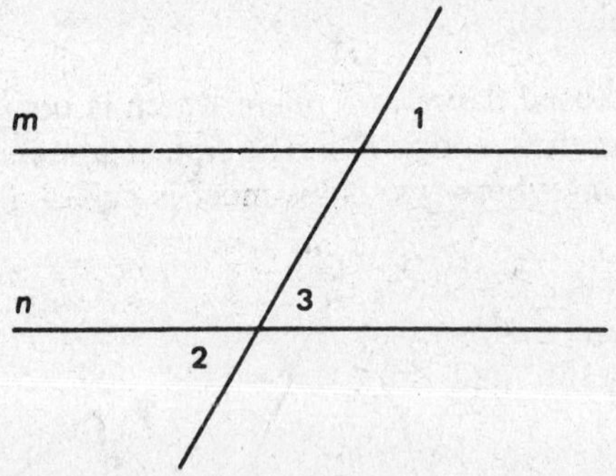

$\angle 3 = \angle 2$. Since m and n are parallel, corresponding angles are equal. Since $\angle 1$ and $\angle 3$ are corresponding angles, $\angle 1 = \angle 3$. Therefore, $\angle 1 = \angle 2$, and $\angle 2$ equals 60° since $\angle 1 = 60°$.

B–3

When two lines intersect and all four of the angles formed are equal, the lines are said to be *perpendicular*. If two lines are perpendicular, they are the sides of right angles whose vertex is the point of intersection.

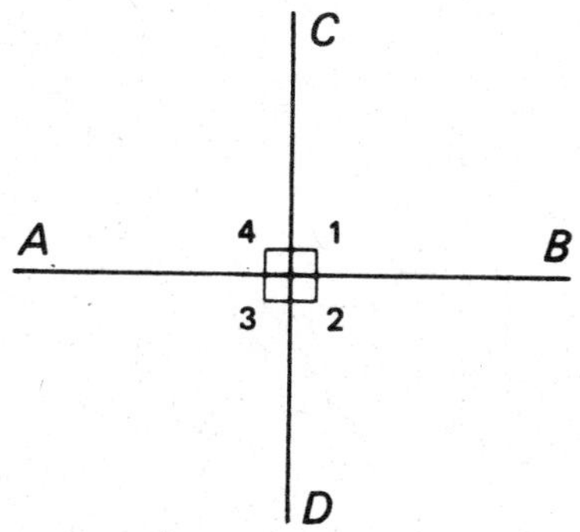

AB is perpendicular to *CD*, and angles 1, 2, 3, and 4 are all right angles. $\perp$ is the symbol for perpendicular; so $AB \perp CD$.

If two lines in a plane are perpendicular to the same line, then the two lines are parallel.

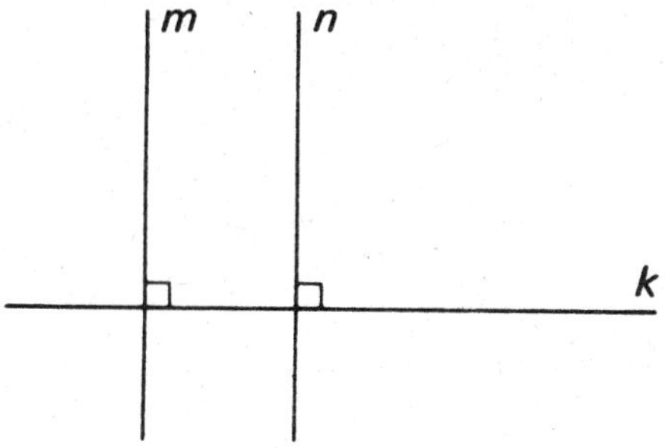

$m \perp k$ and $n \perp k$ implies that $m \parallel n$.

If *any one* of the angles formed when two lines intersect is a right angle, then the lines are perpendicular.

III–C. Polygons

A POLYGON is a closed figure in a plane which is composed of line segments which meet only at their endpoints. The line segments are called *sides* of the polygon, and a point where two sides meet is called a *vertex* (plural *vertices*) of the polygon.

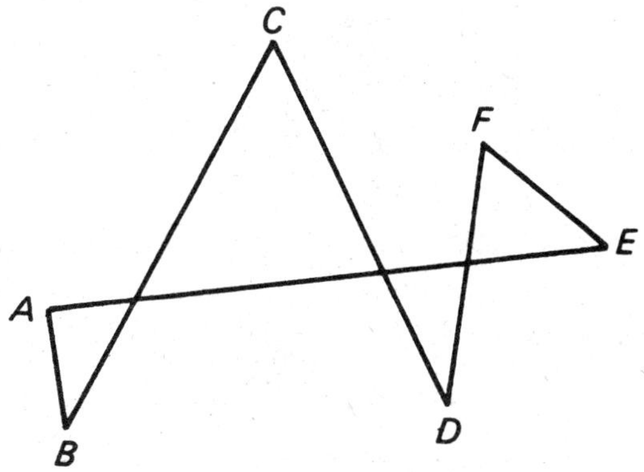

ABCDEF is not a polygon since the line segments intersect at points which are not endpoints.

Some examples of polygons are:

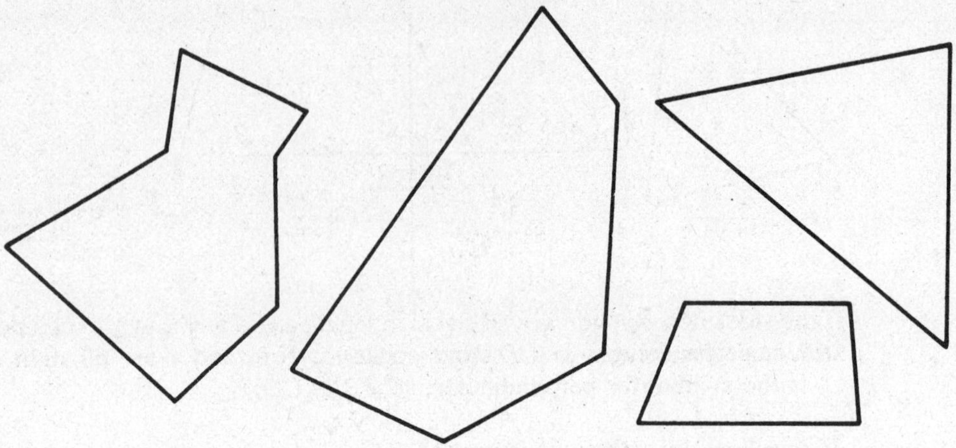

A polygon is usually denoted by the vertices given in order.

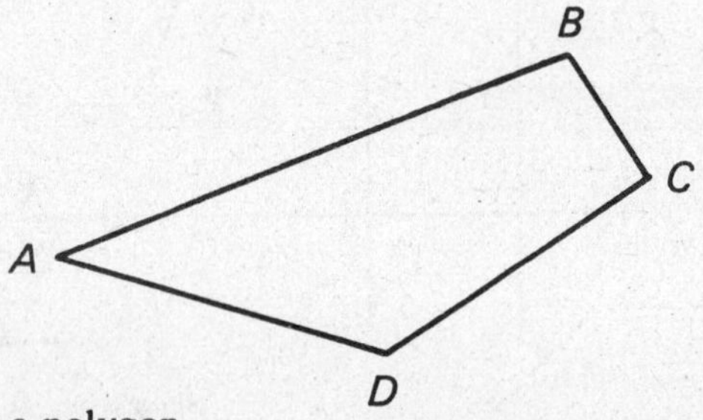

ABCD is a polygon.

A *diagonal* of a polygon is a line segment whose endpoints are nonadjacent vertices. The *altitude* from a vertex *P* to a side is the line segment with endpoint *P* which is perpendicular to the side.

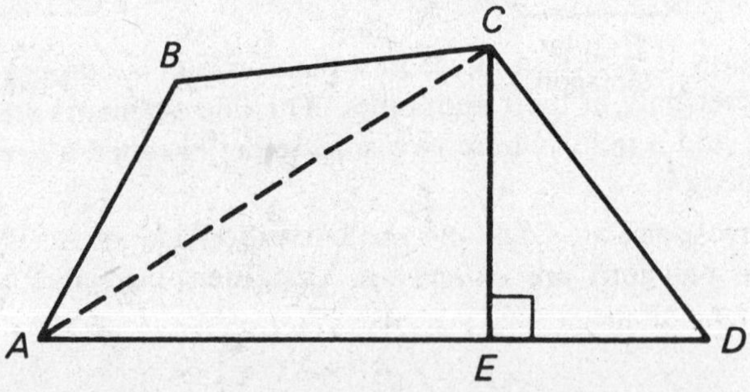

AC is a diagonal, and *CE* is the altitude from *C* to *AD*.

Polygons are classified by the number of angles or sides they have. A polygon with three angles is called a *triangle;* a four-sided polygon is a *quadrilateral;* a polygon with five angles is a *pentagon;* a polygon with six angles is a *hexagon;* an eight-sided polygon is an *octagon*. The number of angles is always equal to the number of sides in a polygon, so a six-sided polygon is a hexagon. The term *n*-gon refers to a polygon with *n* sides.

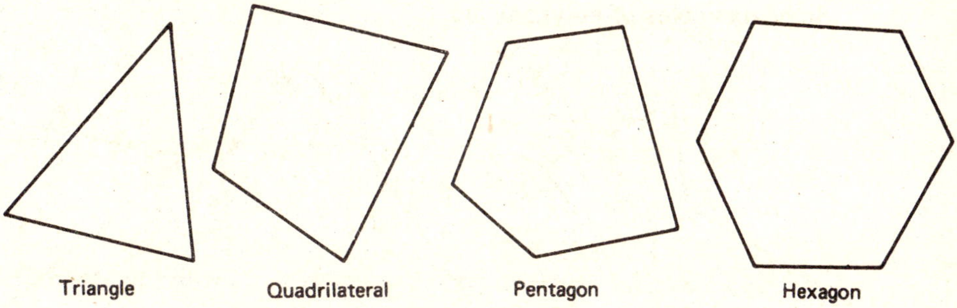

If the sides of a polygon are all equal in length and if all the angles of a polygon are equal, the polygon is called a *regular* polygon.

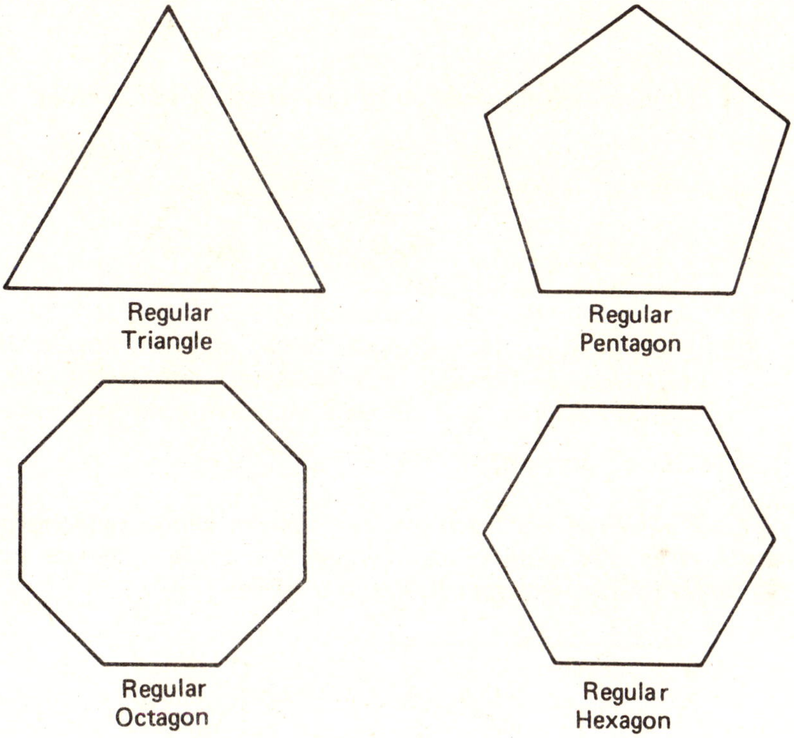

If the corresponding sides and the corresponding angles of two polygons are equal, the polygons are *congruent*. Congruent polygons have the same size and the same shape.

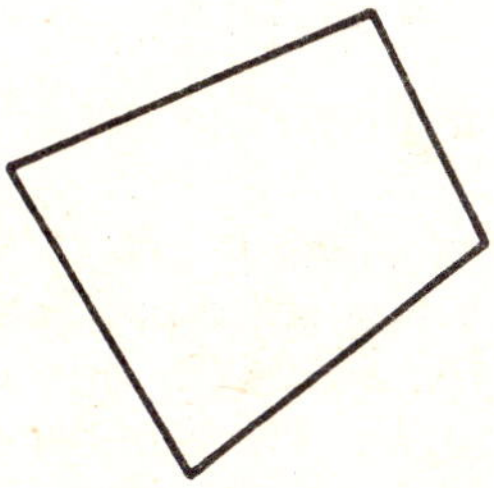

and

are congruent but

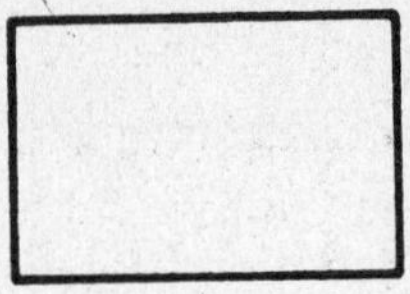 and 

are not congruent.

In figures for problems on congruence, sides with the same number of strokes through them are equal.

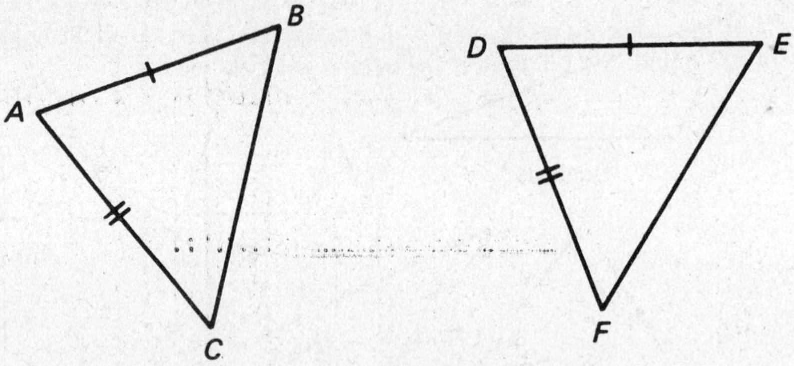

This figure indicates that $AB = DE$ and $AC = DF$.

If all the corresponding angles of two polygons are equal and the lengths of the corresponding sides are proportional, the polygons are said to be *similar*. Similar polygons have the same shape but need not be the same size.

(1) 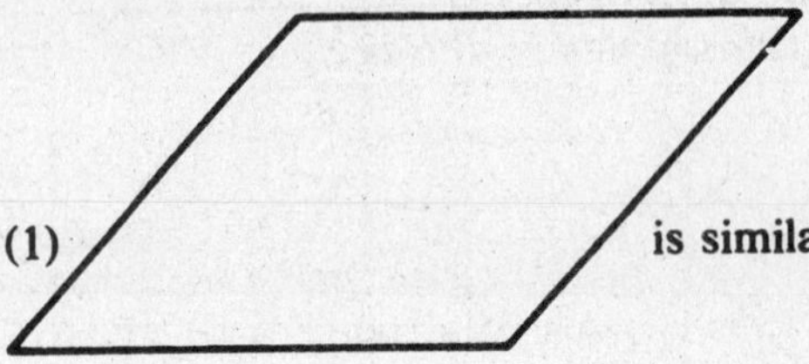 is similar to 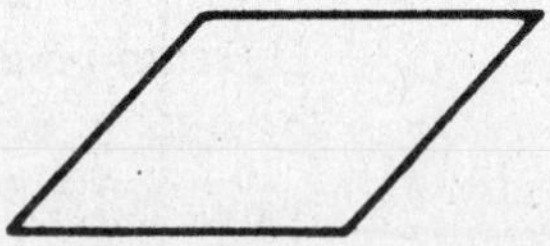

(2) 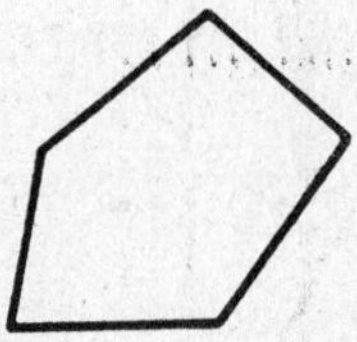 is not similar to 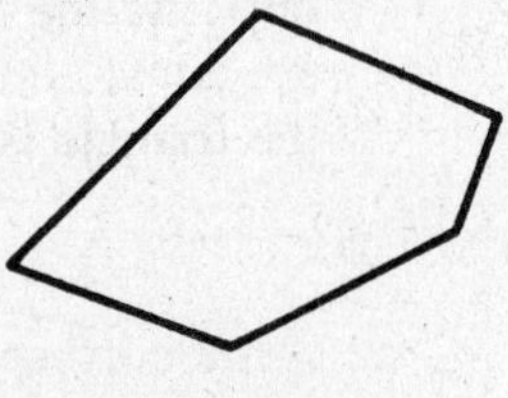

(3)  is not similar to 

In (3) the corresponding angles are equal, but the corresponding sides are not proportional.

The sum of all the angles of an n-gon is $(n-2)180°$. So the sum of the angles in a hexagon is $(6-2)180° = 720°$.

III–D. Triangles

D–1

A TRIANGLE is a 3-sided polygon. If two sides of a triangle are equal, it is called *isosceles*. If all three sides are equal, it is an *equilateral* triangle. If all of the sides have different lengths, the triangle is *scalene*. When one of the angles in a triangle is a right angle, the triangle is a *right triangle*. If one of the angles is obtuse we have an *obtuse triangle*. If all the angles are acute, the triangle is an *acute triangle*.

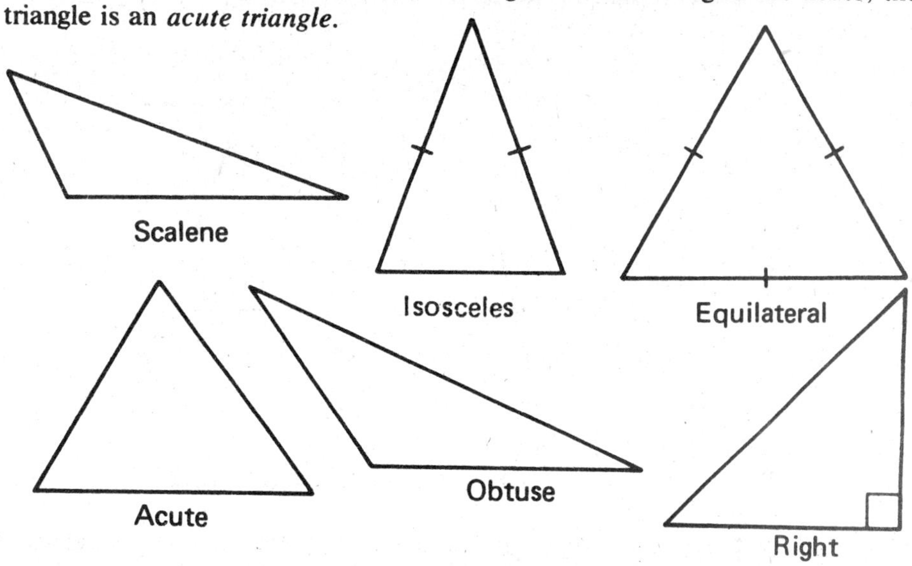

The symbol for a triangle is $\triangle$; so $\triangle ABC$ means a triangle whose vertices are *A*, *B*, and *C*.

The sum of the angles in a triangle is 180°.

The sum of the lengths of any two sides of a triangle must be longer than the remaining side.

If two angles in a triangle are equal, then the lengths of the sides opposite the equal angles are equal. If two sides of a triangle are equal, then the angles opposite the two equal sides are equal. In an equilateral triangle all the angles are equal and each angle = 60°. If each of the angles in a triangle is 60°, then the triangle is equilateral.

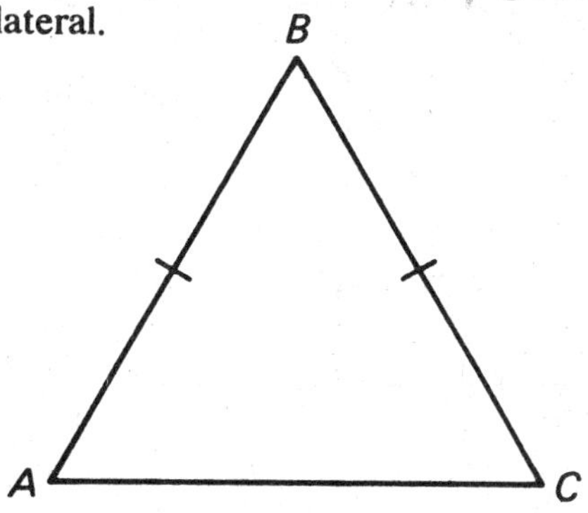

If $AB = BC$, then $\angle BAC = \angle BCA$.

If one angle in a triangle is larger than another angle, the side opposite the larger angle is longer than the side opposite the smaller angle. If one side is longer than another side, then the angle opposite the longer side is larger than the angle opposite the shorter side.

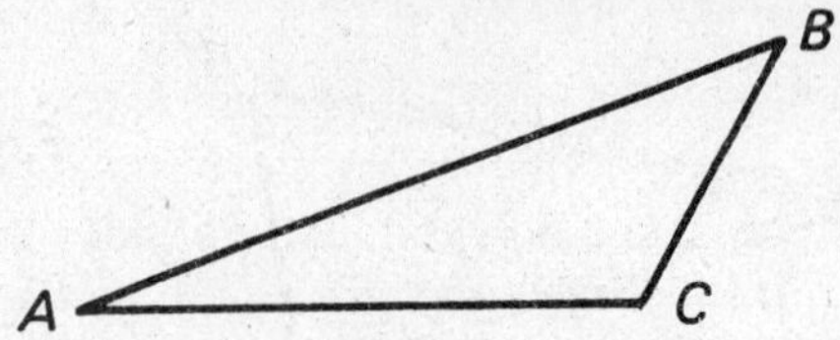

$AB > AC$ implies $\angle BCA > \angle ABC$.

In a right triangle, the side opposite the right angle is called the *hypotenuse*, and the remaining two sides are called *legs*.

The Pythagorean Theorem states that the square of the length of the hypotenuse is equal to the sum of the squares of the lengths of the legs.

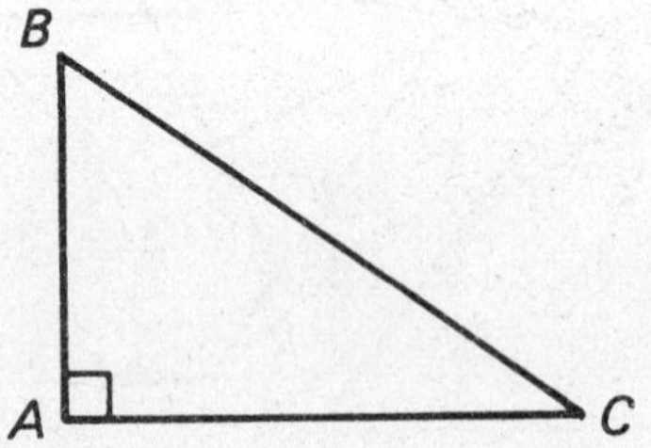

$(BC)^2 = (AB)^2 + (AC)^2$

If $AB = 4$ and $AC = 3$ then $(BC)^2 = 4^2 + 3^2 = 25$ so $BC = 5$. If $BC = 13$ and $AC = 5$, then $13^2 = 169 = (AB)^2 + 5^2$. So $(AB)^2 = 169 - 25 = 144$ and $AB = 12$.

If the lengths of the three sides of a triangle are a, b, and c and $a^2 = b^2 + c^2$, then the triangle is a right triangle where a is the length of the hypotenuse.

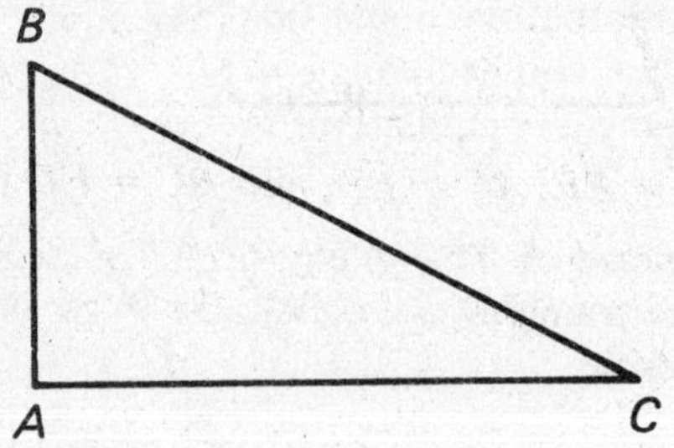

If $AB = 8$, $AC = 15$, and $BC = 17$, then since $17^2 = 8^2 + 15^2$, $\angle BAC$ is a right angle.

D–2

CONGRUENCE. Two triangles are congruent, if two pairs of corresponding sides and the corresponding *included* angles are equal. This is called *Side-Angle-Side* and is denoted by S.A.S.

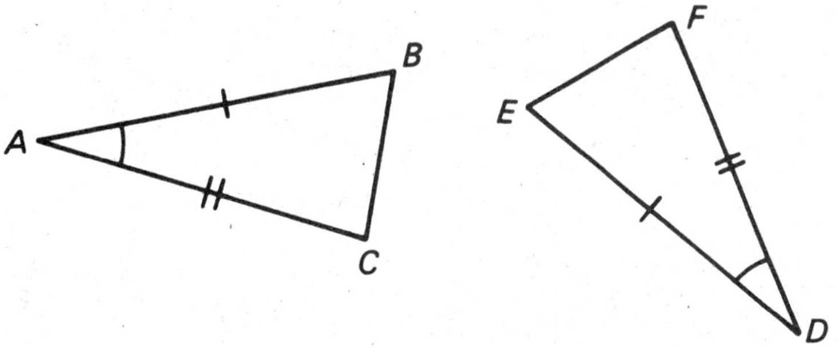

$AB = DE$, $AC = DF$ and $\angle BAC = \angle EDF$ imply that $\triangle ABC \cong \triangle DEF$. $\cong$ means congruent.

Two triangles are congruent if two pairs of corresponding angles and the corresponding *included* side are equal. This is called *Angle-Side-Angle* or A.S.A.

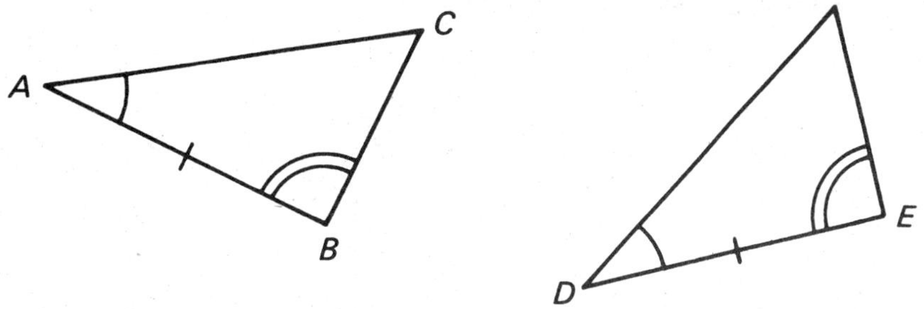

If $AB = DE$, $\angle BAC = \angle EDF$, and $\angle CBA = \angle FED$ then $\triangle ABC \cong \triangle DEF$.

If all three pairs of corresponding sides of two triangles are equal, then the triangles are congruent. This is called *Side-Side-Side* or S.S.S.

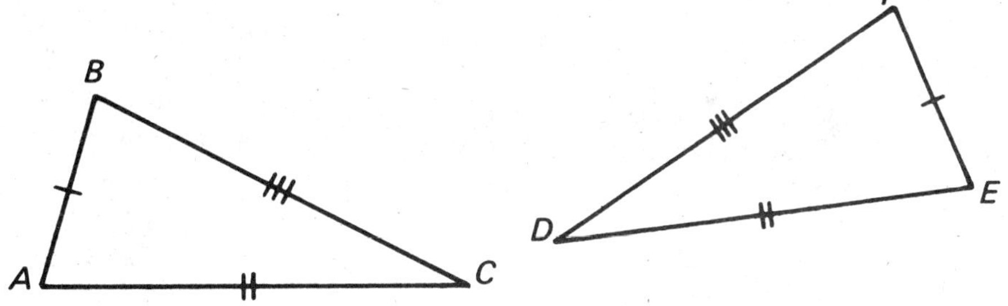

$AB = EF$, $AC = ED$, and $BC = FD$ imply that $\triangle ABC \cong \triangle EFD$.

Because of the Pythagorean Theorem, if any two corresponding sides of two right triangles are equal, the third sides are equal and the triangles are congruent.

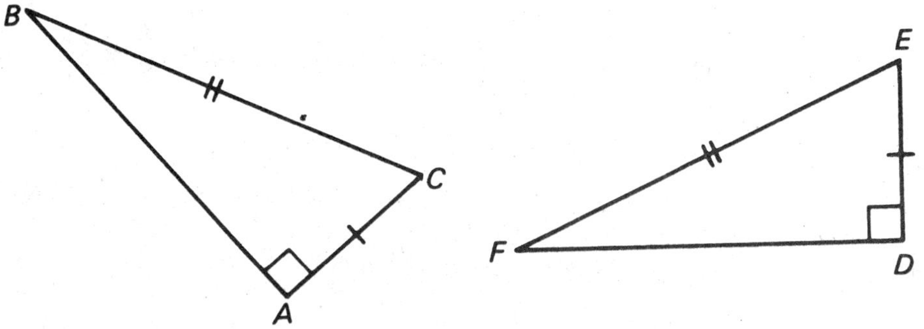

$AC = DE$ and $BC = EF$ imply $\triangle ABC \cong \triangle DFE$.

In general, if two corresponding sides of two triangles are equal, we cannot infer that the triangles are congruent.

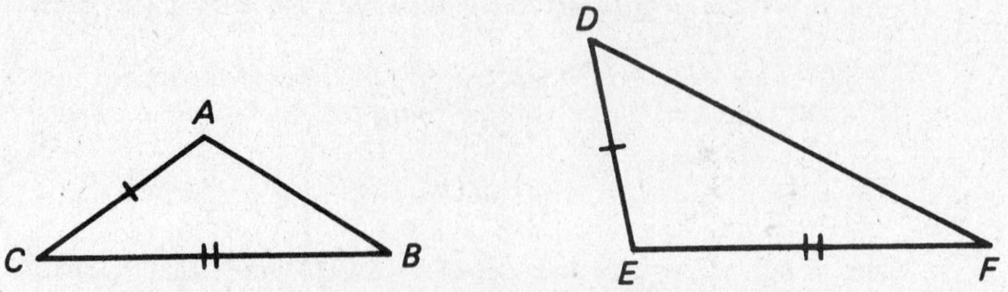

$AC = DE$ and $CB = EF$, but the triangles are not congruent.

If two sides of a triangle are equal, then the altitude to the third side divides the triangle into two congruent triangles.

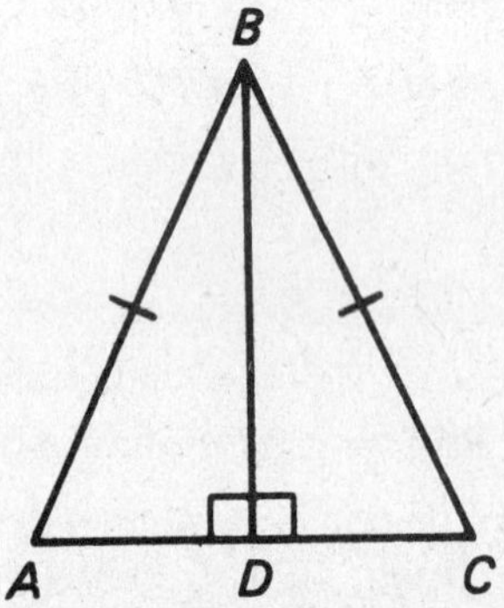

$AB = BC$ and $BD \perp AC$ implies $\triangle ADB \cong \triangle CDB$.

Therefore, $\angle ABD = \angle CBD$, so BD bisects $\angle ABC$. Since $AD = DC$, D is the midpoint of AC so BD is the median from B to AC. A *median* is the segment from a vertex to the midpoint of the side opposite the vertex.

EXAMPLE 1: $EF = ?$

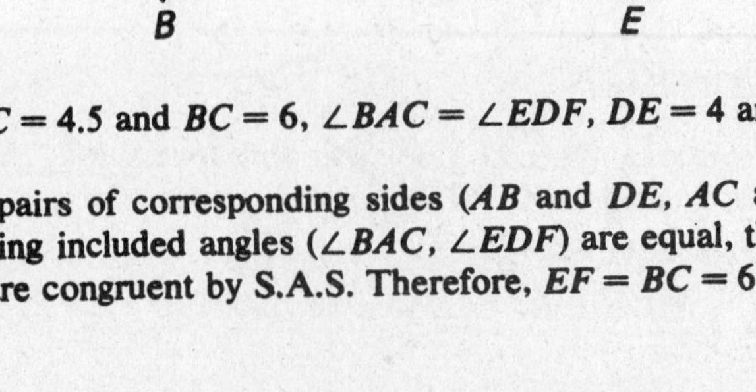

$AB = 4$, $AC = 4.5$ and $BC = 6$, $\angle BAC = \angle EDF$, $DE = 4$ and $DF = 4.5$

Since two pairs of corresponding sides (AB and DE, AC and DF) and the corresponding included angles ($\angle BAC$, $\angle EDF$) are equal, the triangles ABC and DEF are congruent by S.A.S. Therefore, $EF = BC = 6$.

D–3

Similarity. *Two triangles are similar if all three pairs of corresponding angles are equal.* Since the sum of the angles in a triangle is 180°, it follows that if two corresponding angles are equal, the third angles must be equal.

If you draw a line which passes through a triangle and is parallel to one of the sides of the triangle, the triangle formed is similar to the original triangle.

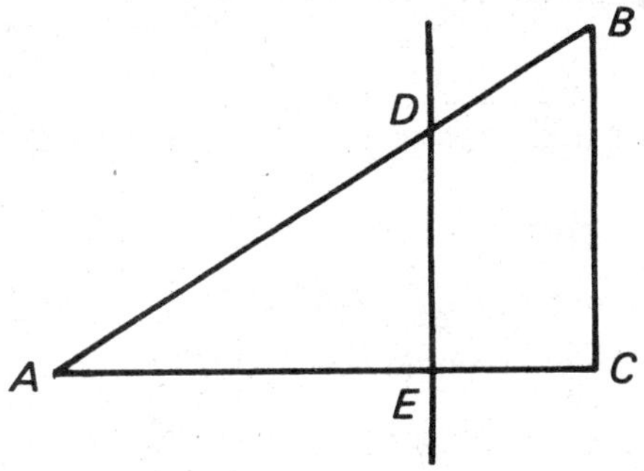

If $DE \parallel BC$ then $\triangle ADE \sim \triangle ABC$. The symbol $\sim$ means similar.

EXAMPLE 1: A man 6 feet tall casts a shadow 4 feet long; at the same time a flagpole casts a shadow which is 50 feet long. How tall is the flagpole?

The man with his shadow and the flagpole with its shadow can be regarded as the pairs of corresponding sides of two similar triangles.

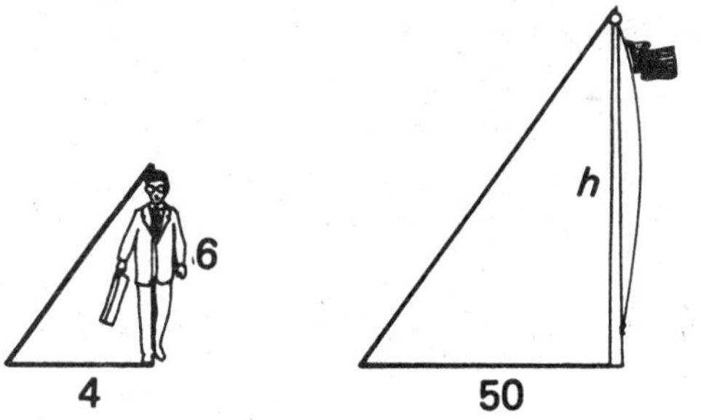

Let h be the height of the flagpole. Since corresponding sides of similar triangles are proportional, $\frac{4}{50} = \frac{6}{h}$. Cross-multiply getting $4h = 6 \cdot 50 = 300$; so $h = 75$. Therefore, the flagpole is 75 feet high.

III–E. Quadrilaterals

A QUADRILATERAL is a polygon with four sides. The sum of the angles in a quadrilateral is 360°. If the opposite sides of a quadrilateral are parallel, the figure is a *parallelogram*.

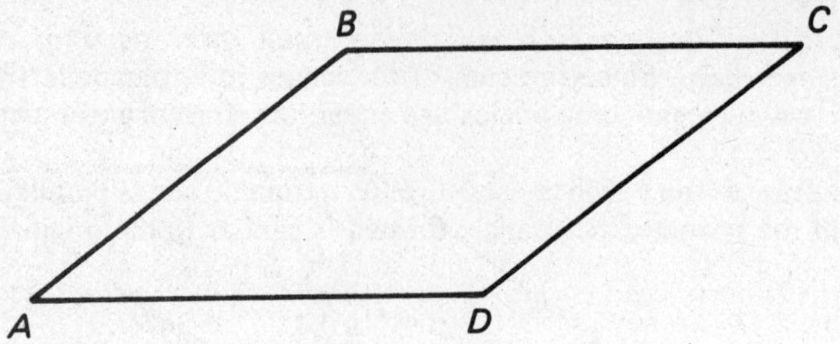

ABCD is a parallelogram.

In a parallelogram:

(1) The opposite sides are equal.
(2) The opposite angles are equal.
(3) A diagonal divides the parallelogram into two congruent triangles.
(4) The diagonals bisect each other. (A line *bisects* a line segment if it intersects the segment at the midpoint of the segment.)

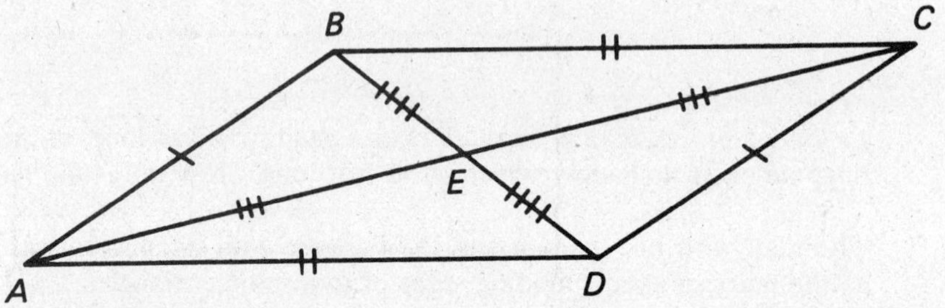

ABCD is a parallelogram.

(1) $AB = DC$, $BC = AD$.
(2) $\angle BCD = \angle BAD$, $\angle ABC = \angle ADC$.
(3) $\triangle ABC \cong \triangle ADC$, $\triangle ABD \cong \triangle CDB$.
(4) $AE = EC$ and $BE = ED$.

If *any* of the statements (1), (2), (3) and (4) are true for a quadrilateral, then the quadrilateral is a parallelogram.

If all of the sides of a parallelogram are equal, the figure is called a *rhombus*.

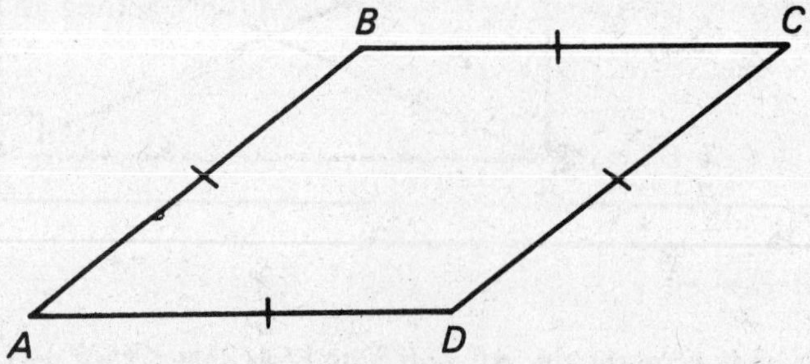

ABCD is a rhombus.

The diagonals of a rhombus are perpendicular.

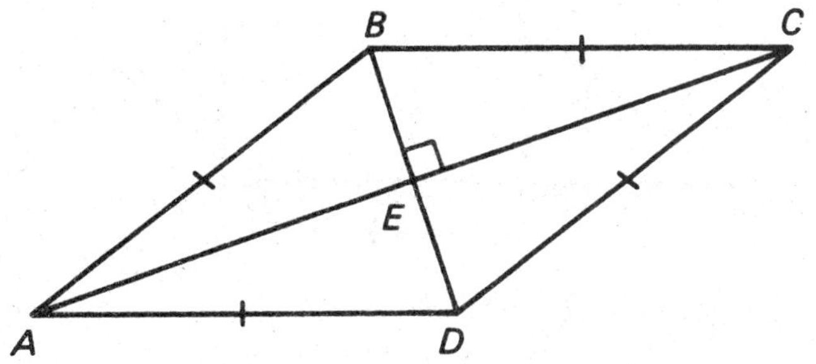

$BD \perp AC$; $\angle BEC = \angle CED = \angle AED = \angle AEB = 90°$.

If all the angles of a parallelogram are right angles, the figure is a *rectangle*.

ABCD is a rectangle.

Since the sum of the angles in a quadrilateral is 360°, if *all* the angles of a quadrilateral are equal then the figure is a rectangle. The diagonals of a rectangle are equal. The length of a diagonal can be found by using the Pythagorean Theorem.

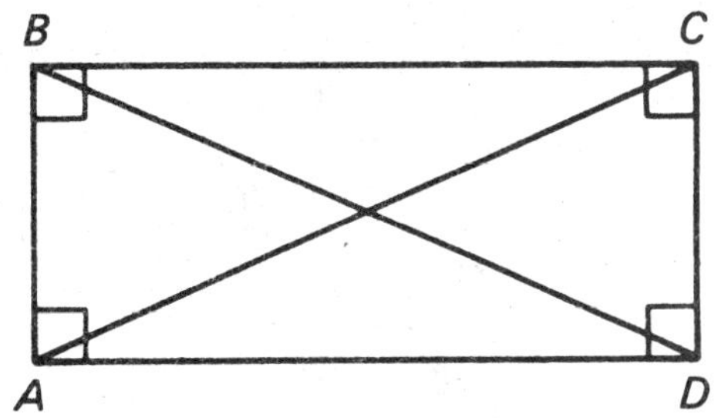

If *ABCD* is a rectangle, $AC = BD$ and $(AC)^2 = (AD)^2 + (DC)^2$.

If all the sides of a rectangle are equal, the figure is a *square*.

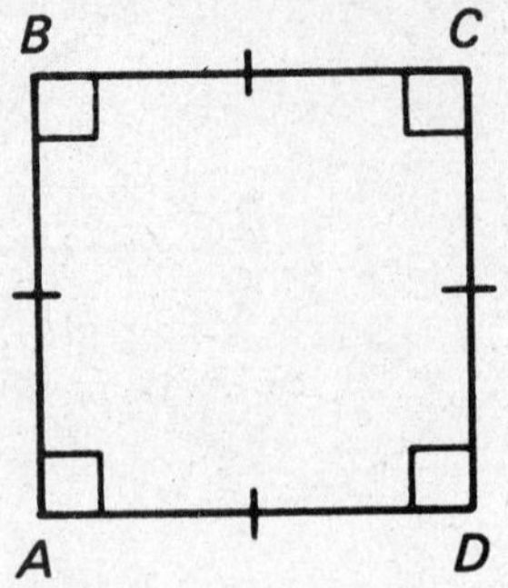

ABCD is a square.

If all the angles of a rhombus are equal, the figure is a square. The length of the diagonal of a square is $\sqrt{2}\,s$ where s is the length of a side.

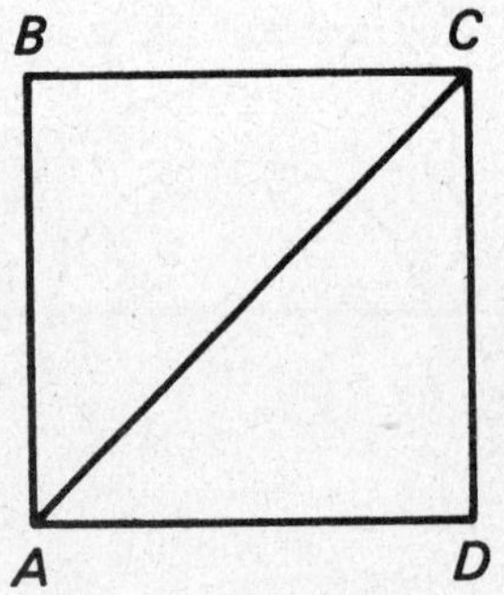

In square $ABCD$, $AC = (\sqrt{2})AD$.

A quadrilateral with two parallel sides and two sides which are not parallel is called a *trapezoid.* The parallel sides are called *bases*, and the non-parallel sides are called *legs*.

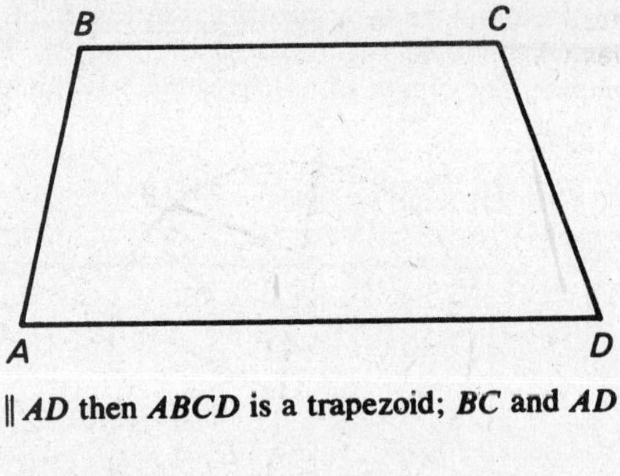

If $BC \parallel AD$ then $ABCD$ is a trapezoid; BC and AD are the bases.

III–F. Circles

A CIRCLE is a figure in a plane consisting of all the points which are the same distance from a fixed point called the *center* of the circle. A line segment from any point on the circle to the center of the circle is called a *radius* (plural: radii) of the circle. All radii of the same circle have the same length.

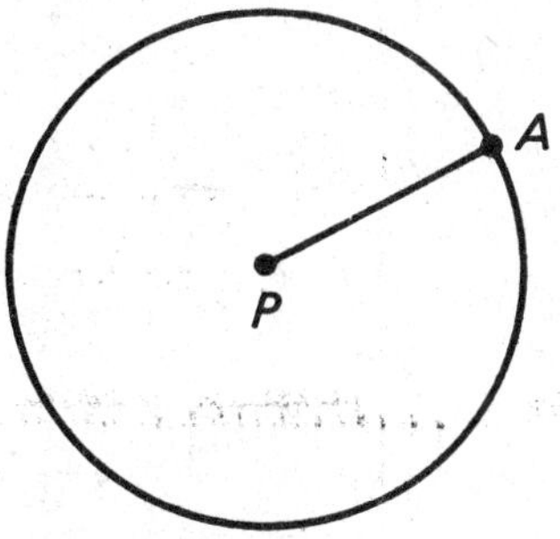

This circle has center *P* and radius *AP*.

A circle is denoted by a single letter, usually its center. Two circles with the same center are *concentric*.

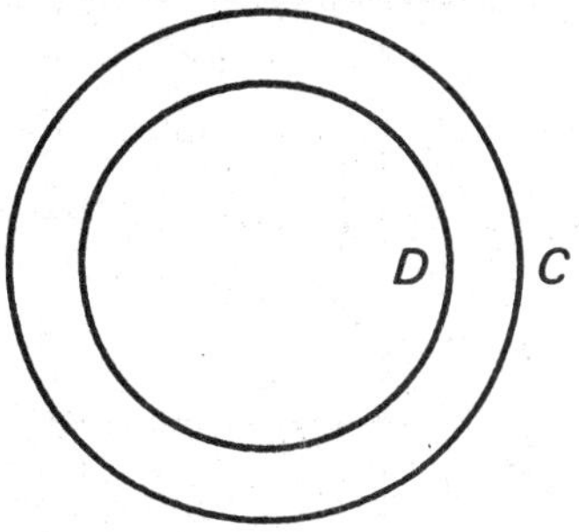

C and *D* are concentric circles.

A line segment whose endpoints are on a circle is called a *chord*. A chord which passes through the center of the circle is a *diameter*. *The length of a diameter is twice the length of a radius*. A diameter divides a circle into two congruent halves which are called *semicircles*.

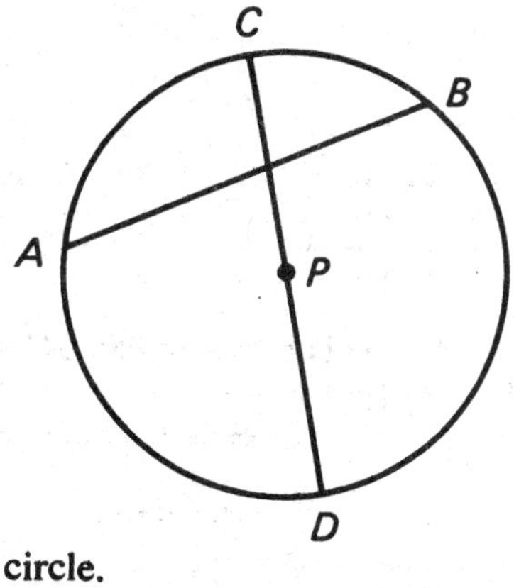

P is the center of the circle.
AB is a chord and *CD* is a diameter.

A diameter which is perpendicular to a chord bisects the chord.

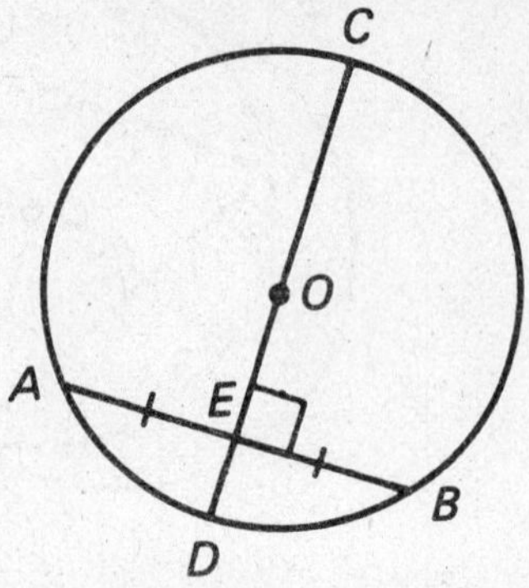

O is the center of this circle and $AB \perp CD$; then $AE = EB$.

If a line intersects a circle at one and only one point, the line is said to be a *tangent* to the circle. The point common to a circle and a tangent to the circle is called the *point of tangency*. The radius from the center to the point of tangency is perpendicular to the tangent.

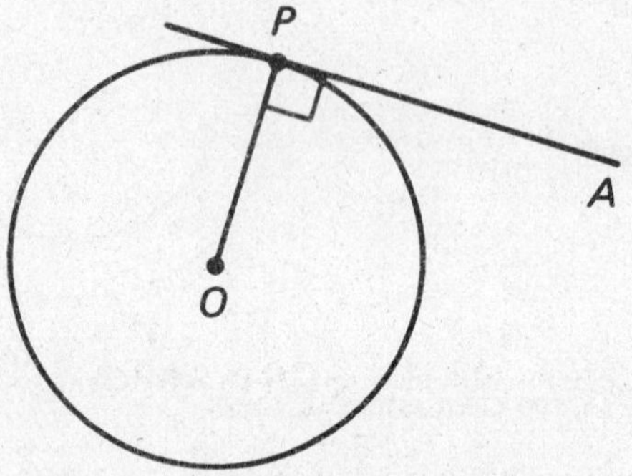

AP is tangent to the circle with center *O*. *P* is the point of tangency and $OP \perp PA$.

A polygon is *inscribed* in a circle if all of its vertices are points on the circle.

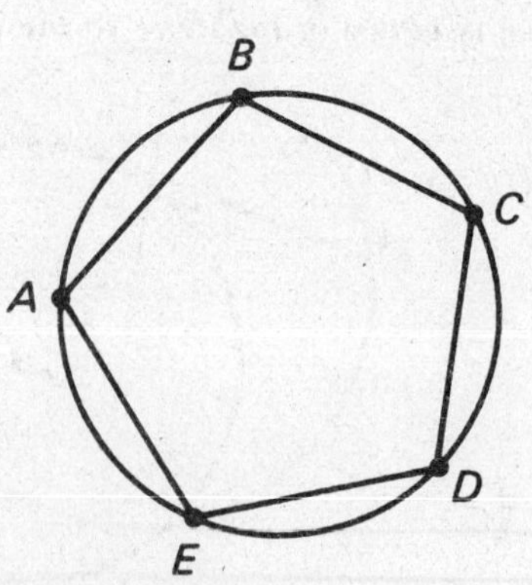

ABCDE is an inscribed pentagon.

An angle whose vertex is a point on a circle and whose sides are chords of the circle is called an *inscribed angle*. An angle whose vertex is the center of a circle and whose sides are radii of the circle is called a *central angle*.

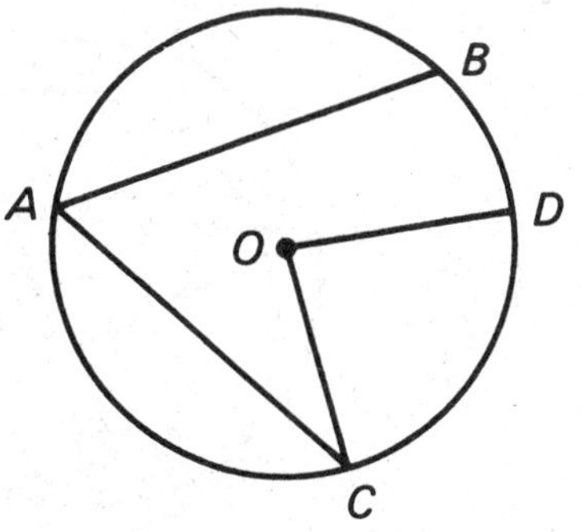

$\angle BAC$ is an inscribed angle.
$\angle DOC$ is a central angle.

An *arc* is a part of a circle.

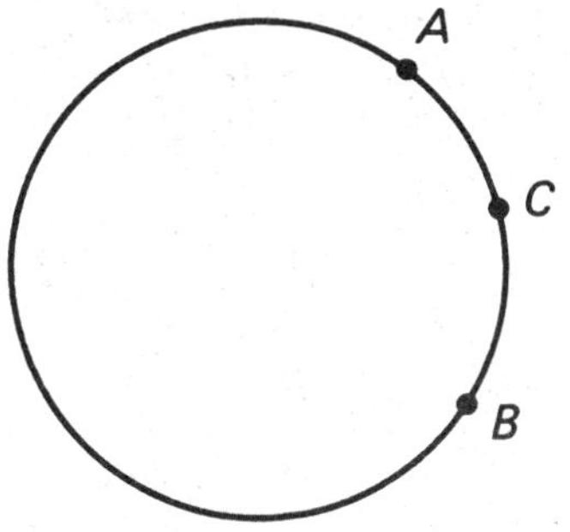

ACB is an arc. Arc ACB is written $\widehat{ACB}$.

If two letters are used to denote an arc, they represent the smaller of the two possible arcs. So $\widehat{AB} = \widehat{ACB}$.

An arc can be measured in degrees. The entire circle is 360°; thus an arc of 120° would be $\frac{1}{3}$ of a circle.

A central angle is equal in measure to the arc it intercepts.

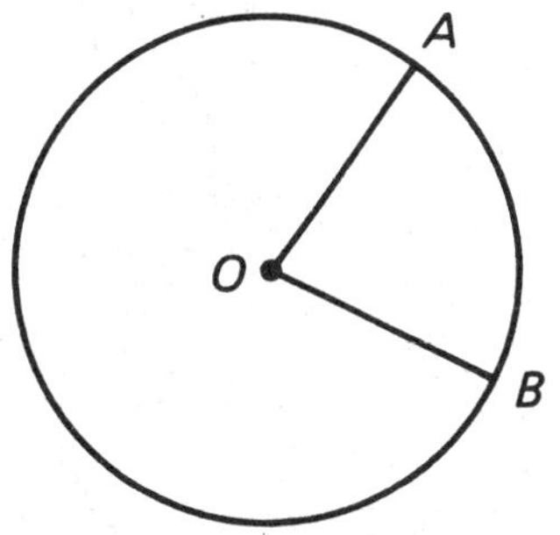

$\angle AOB = \widehat{AB}$

An inscribed angle is equal in measure to $\frac{1}{2}$ the arc it intercepts.

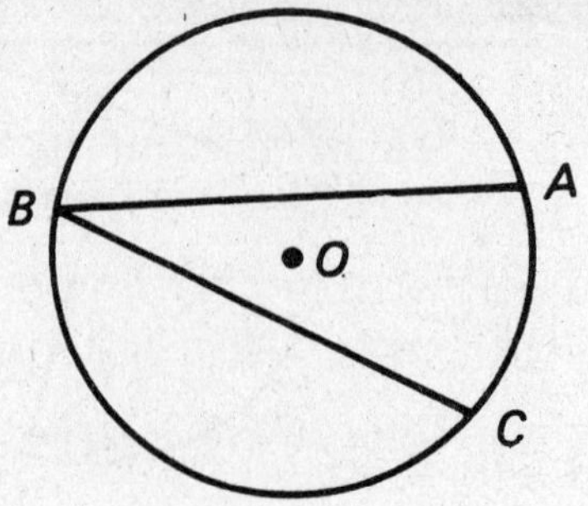

$\angle ABC = \frac{1}{2}\widehat{AC}$.

An angle inscribed in a semicircle is a *right angle.*

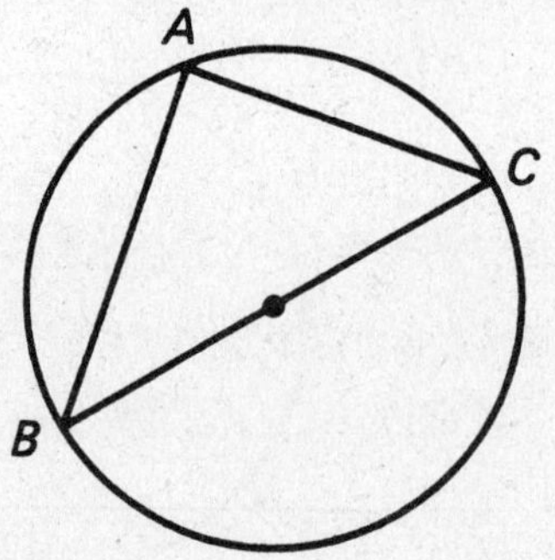

If BC is a diameter, then $\angle BAC$ is inscribed in a semicircle; so $\angle BAC = 90°$.

III–G. Area, Perimeter, and Volume

G–1

The area A of a square equals s^2, where s is the length of a side of the square. Thus, $A = s^2$.

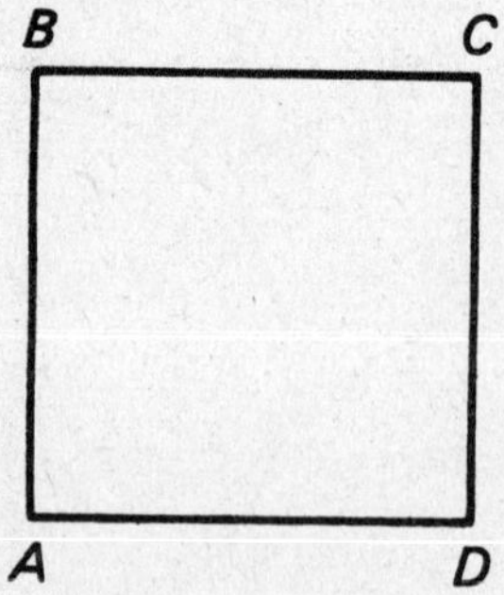

If $AD = 5$ inches, the area of square $ABCD$ is 25 square inches.

The area of a rectangle equals length times width; if L is the length of one side and W is the length of a perpendicular side, then the area $A = LW$.

If $AB = 5$ feet and $AD = 8$ feet, then the area of rectangle $ABCD$ is 40 square feet.

The area of a parallelogram is base × height; $A = bh$, where b is the length of a side and h is the length of an altitude to the base.

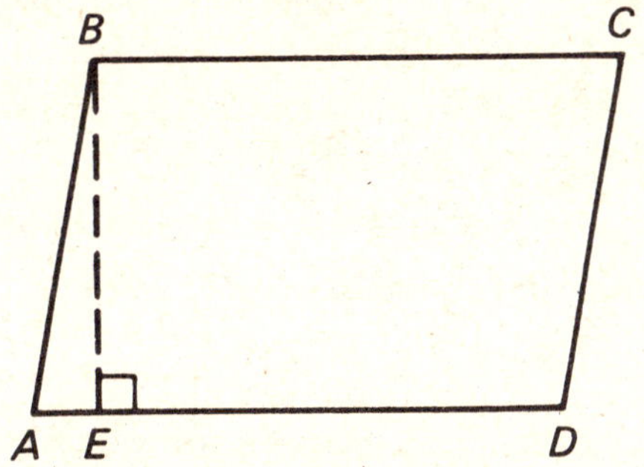

If $AD = 6$ yards and $BE = 4$ yards, then the area of the parallelogram $ABCD$ is $6 \cdot 4$ or 24 square yards.

The area of a trapezoid is the (average of the bases) × height. $A = [(b_1 + b_2)/2]\, h$ where b_1 and b_2 are the lengths of the parallel sides and h is the length of an altitude to one of the bases.

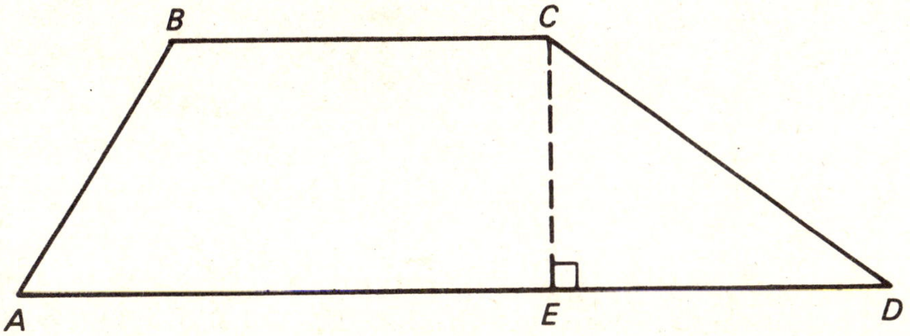

If $BC = 3$ miles, $AD = 7$ miles, and $CE = 2$ miles, then the area of trapezoid $ABCD$ is $[(3 + 7)/2] \cdot 2 = 10$ square miles.

The area of a triangle is $\frac{1}{2}$ (base × height); $A = \frac{1}{2}bh$, where b is the length of a side and h is the length of the altitude to that side.

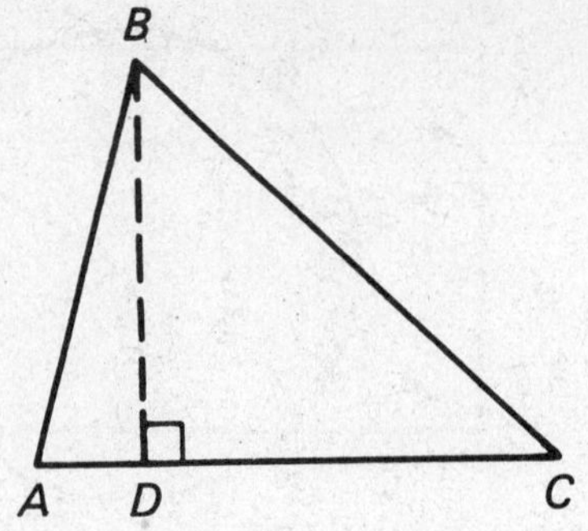

If $AC = 5$ miles and $BD = 4$ miles, then the area of the triangle is $\frac{1}{2} \times 5 \times 4 = 10$ square miles.

Since the legs of a right triangle are perpendicular to each other, the area of a right triangle is one-half the product of the lengths of the legs.

EXAMPLE 1: If the lengths of the sides of a triangle are 5 feet, 12 feet, and 13 feet, what is the area of the triangle?

Since $5^2 + 12^2 = 25 + 144 = 169 = 13^2$, the triangle is a right triangle and the legs are the sides with lengths 5 feet and 12 feet. Therefore, the area is $\frac{1}{2} \times 5 \times 12 = 30$ square feet.

If we want to find the area of a polygon which is not of a type already mentioned, we break the polygon up into smaller figures such as triangles or rectangles, find the area of each piece, and add these to get the area of the given polygon.

The area of a circle is πr^2 where r is the length of a radius. Since $d = 2r$ where d is the length of a diameter, $A = \pi\left(\frac{d}{2}\right)^2 = \pi\frac{d^2}{4}$. π is a number which is approximately $\frac{22}{7}$ or 3.14; however, there is *no fraction which is exactly equal to* π. π is called an *irrational number*.

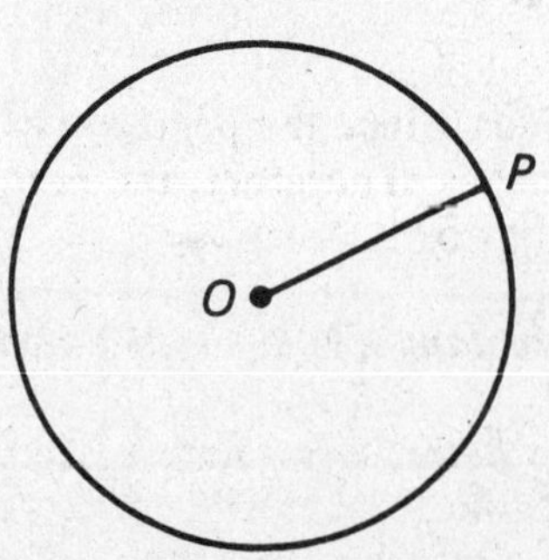

If $OP = 2$ inches, then the area of the circle with center O is $\pi 2^2$ or 4π square inches. The portion of the plane bounded by a circle and a central angle is called a *sector* of the circle.

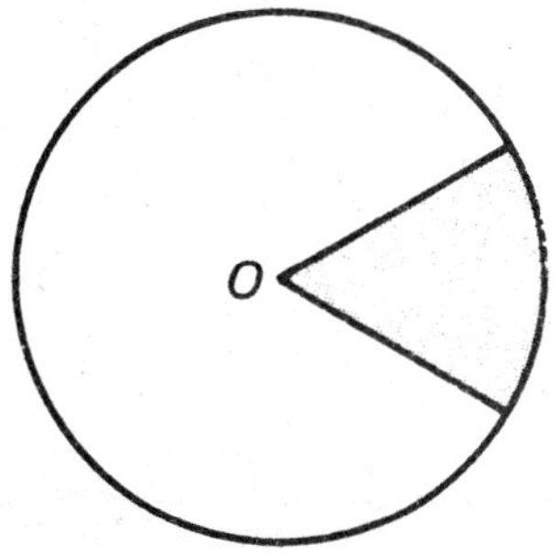

The shaded region is a sector of the circle with center O. The area of a sector with central angle $n°$ in a circle of radius r is $\frac{n}{360}\pi r^2$.

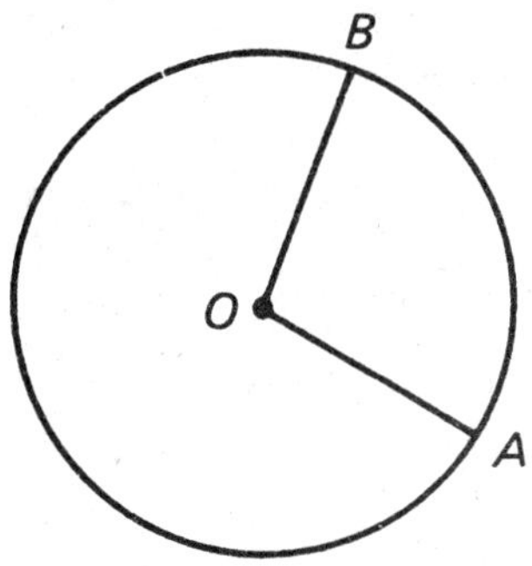

If $OB = 4$ inches and $\angle BOA = 100°$, then the area of the sector is $\frac{100}{360}\pi \cdot 4^2 = \frac{5}{18} \cdot 16\pi = \frac{40}{9}\pi$ square inches.

G–2

The *perimeter* of a polygon is the sum of the lengths of the sides.

EXAMPLE 1: What is the perimeter of a regular pentagon whose sides are 6 inches long?

A pentagon has 5 sides. Since the pentagon is regular, all sides have the same length which is 6 inches. Therefore, the perimeter of the pentagon is 5×6 which equals 30 inches or 2.5 feet.

The *perimeter of a rectangle is* $2(L + W)$ where L is the length and W is the width.
The *perimeter of a square is* $4s$ where s is the length of a side of the square.

The *perimeter of a circle* is called the *circumference* of the circle. The *circumference of a circle is* πd *or* $2\pi r$, where d is the length of a diameter and r is the length of a radius.

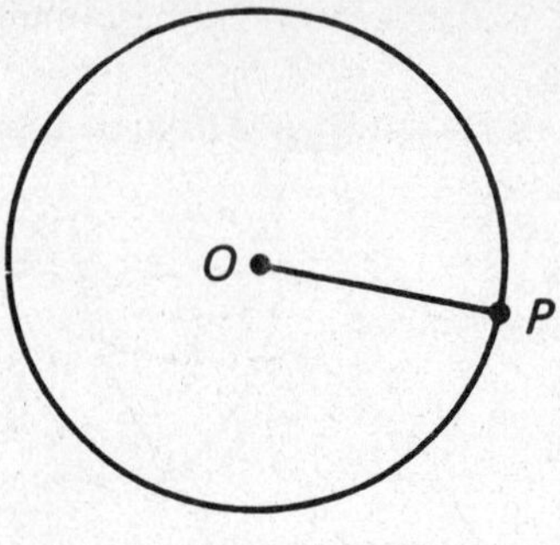

If O is the center of a circle and $OP = 5$ feet, then the circumference of the circle is $2 \times 5\pi$ or 10π feet.

The length of an arc of a circle is $(n/360)\ \pi d$ where the central angle of the arc is $n°$.

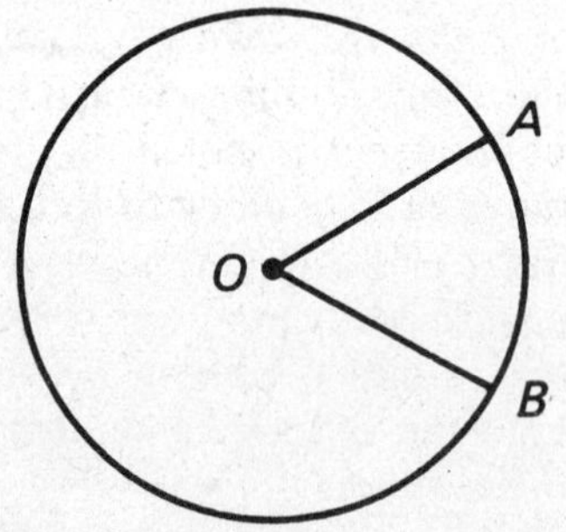

If O is the center of a circle where $OA = 5$ yards and $\angle AOB = 60°$, then the length of arc AB is $\frac{60}{360}\pi \times 10 = \frac{10}{6}\pi = \frac{5}{3}\pi$ yards.

EXAMPLE 2: How far will a wheel of radius 2 feet travel in 500 revolutions? (Assume the wheel does not slip.)

The diameter of the wheel is 4 feet; so the circumference is 4π feet. Therefore, the wheel will travel $500 \times 4\pi$ or $2{,}000\pi$ feet in 500 revolutions.

G–3

A *rectangular parallelepiped* is a solid figure all of whose faces are rectangles. It has six such faces. Its volume is the product of the length times the width times the height.

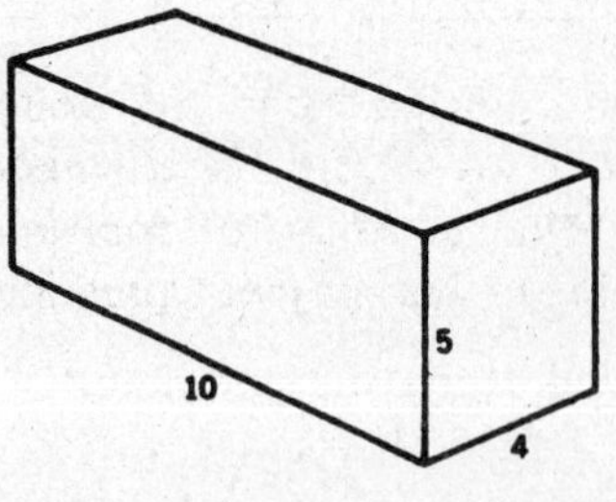

$V = 10 \times 5 \times 4$

A *cube* is a special kind of rectangular parallelepiped with length, width, and height all equal. If x is the length, width, or height, then $V = x^3$.

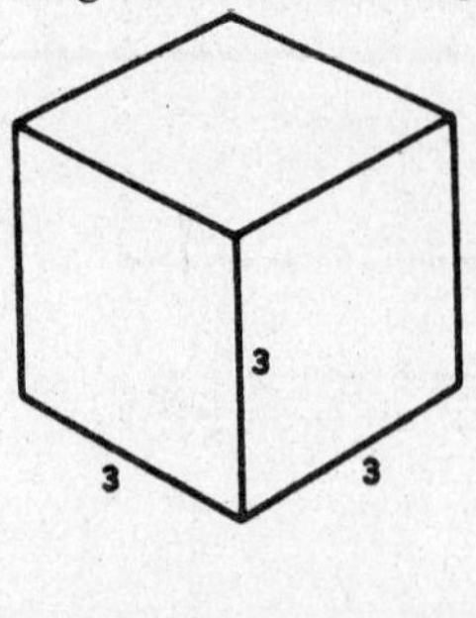

$V = 3^3 = 3 \times 3 \times 3 = 27$

The volume of a *cylinder* is the area of the base multiplied by the height. If the cylinder has a circular base, then $V = h(\pi r^2)$. If two cylinders have the same height and the same base, they will have the same volume regardless of the angle between the base and the line of centers.

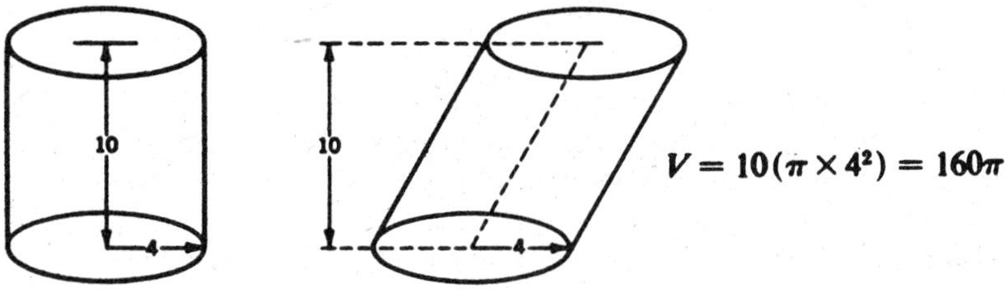

III–H. Coordinate Geometry

In coordinate geometry, every point in the plane is associated with an ordered pair of numbers called *coordinates*. Two perpendicular lines are drawn; the horizontal line is called the *x*-axis and the vertical line is called the *y*-axis. The point where the two axes intersect is called the *origin*. Both of the axes are number lines with the origin corresponding to zero (see I–6.) Positive numbers on the *x*-axis are to the right of the origin, negative numbers to the left. Positive numbers on the *y*-axis are above the origin, negative numbers below the origin. The coordinates of a point *P* are (x,y) if *P* is located by moving *x* units along the *x*-axis from the origin and then moving *y* units up or down. *The distance along the x-axis is always given first.*

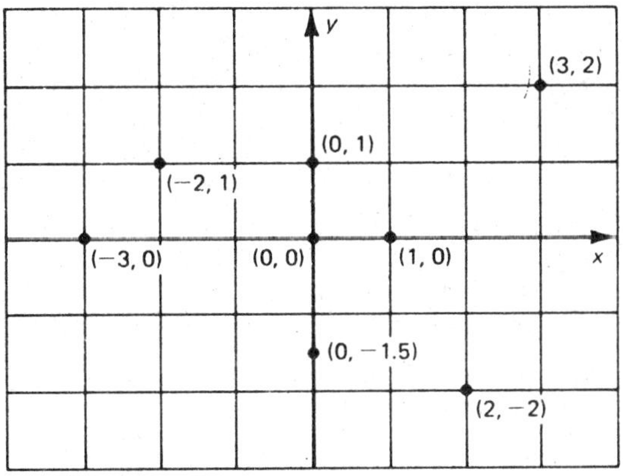

The numbers in parentheses are the coordinates of the point. Thus "$P = (3,2)$" means that the coordinates of *P* are (3,2). *The distance between the point with coordinates (x,y) and the point with coordinates (a,b) is* $\sqrt{(x-a)^2 + (y-b)^2}$. You should be able to answer most questions by using the distance formula.

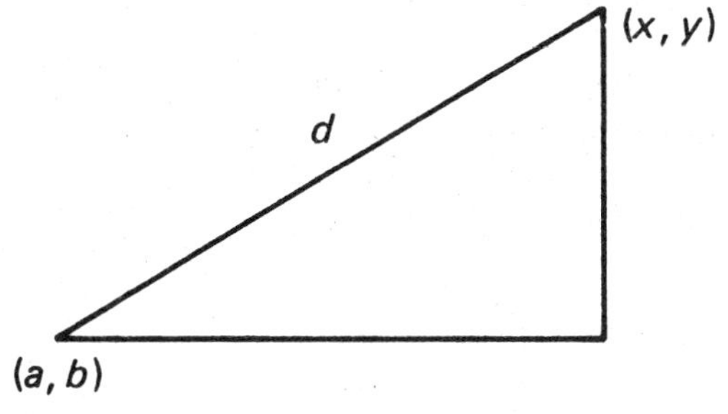

$$d = \sqrt{(x-a)^2 + (y-b)^2}$$

EXAMPLE 1: Is $ABCD$ a parallelogram? $A = (3,2)$, $B = (1,-2)$, $C = (-2,1)$, $D = (1,5)$.

The length of AB is $\sqrt{(3-1)^2 + (2-(-2))^2} = \sqrt{2^2 + 4^2} = \sqrt{20}$. The length of CD is $\sqrt{(-2-1)^2 + (1-5)^2} = \sqrt{(-3)^2 + (-4)^2} = \sqrt{25}$. Therefore, $AB \neq CD$, so $ABCD$ cannot be a parallelogram, since in a parallelogram the lengths of opposite sides are equal.

Geometry problems occur frequently. *If you are not provided with a diagram, draw one for yourself.* Think of any conditions which will help you answer the question; perhaps you can see how to answer a different question which will lead to an answer to the original question. It may help to draw in some diagonals, altitudes, or other auxiliary lines in your diagram.

PRACTICE

1. Using formulas
   Circumference $= 2\pi r$
   Area $= \pi r^2$
   where r = radius, find the area of a circle whose circumference is x.
   (A) $\frac{x^2}{4\pi^2}$ (B) $\frac{x^2}{4\pi}$ (C) $\frac{x^2}{4}$ (D) πx^2 (E) πx

2. One side of a rectangle is x inches. If the perimeter is p inches, what is the length (in inches) of the other side?
   (A) $p - x$ (B) $p - 2x$ (C) $\frac{p-x}{2}$
   (D) $\frac{p-2x}{2}$ (E) $2p - 2x$

3. C is the midpoint of line AE. B and D are on line AE so that $AB = BC$ and $CD = DE$. What percent of AC is AD?
   (A) 33 (B) 50 (C) 66 (D) 133 (E) 150

4. A picture in an art museum is six feet wide and eight feet long. If its frame has a width of six inches, what is the ratio of the area of the frame to the area of the picture?
   (A) $\frac{5}{16}$ (B) $\frac{5}{4}$ (C) $\frac{4}{5}$ (D) $\frac{5}{12}$ (E) $\frac{3\frac{1}{5}}{1}$

5. To represent a family budget on a circle graph, how many degrees of the circle should be used to represent an item that is 20% of the total budget?
   (A) 20 (B) 36 (C) 60 (D) 72 (E) 90

6. What is the maximum number of glass tumblers (each with a circumference of 4π inches) that can be placed on a table 48″ × 32″?
   (A) 36 (B) 48 (C) 92 (D) 96 (E) 192

7. To avoid paying a toll on a direct road, I go west 10 miles, south 5 miles, west 30 miles, and north 35 miles. The length of the toll road is (?) miles.
   (A) 30 (B) 45 (C) 50 (D) 70 (E) 85

8. The length of a rectangle is increased by 50%. By what per cent would the width have to be decreased to maintain the same area?
   (A) $33\frac{1}{3}$ (B) 50 (C) $66\frac{2}{3}$ (D) 150 (E) 200

9. Area of circle O $= 9\pi$. What is the area of $ABCD$?
   (A) 24 (B) 30 (C) 35
   (D) 36 (E) 48

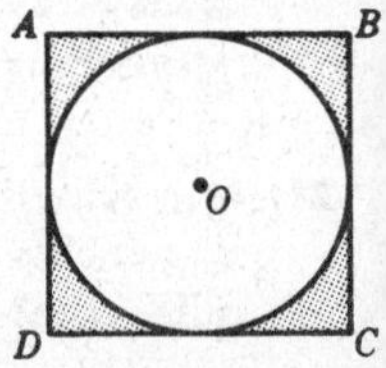

10. A man travels four miles north, twelve miles east, and then twelve miles north. How far (to the nearest mile) is he from the starting point?
    (A) 17 (B) 20 (C) 21 (D) 24 (E) 28

11. If angle DBA equals 39° and angle FBE equals 79°, then angle GBC has a measure of
    (A) 39° (B) 51° (C) 62°
    (D) 118° (E) 152°

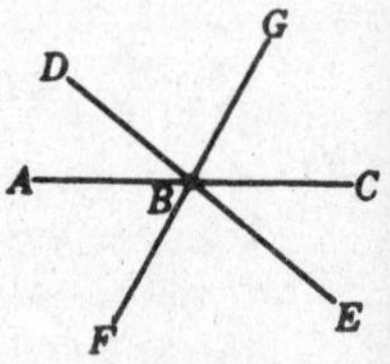

12. The length of a rectangle is l and the width is w. If the width is increased by 2 units, by how many units will the perimeter be increased?
    (A) 2 (B) 4 (C) $2w$ (D) $2w + 2$ (E) $2w + 4$

13. If the radius of a wheel is f feet, how many revolutions does the wheel make per mile? (1 mile equals 5,280 feet)
    (A) $5280f$ (B) $\frac{2640}{\pi f}$ (C) $5280\pi f^2$ (D) $\frac{\pi f}{2640}$ (E) $\frac{\pi f^2}{5280}$

14. The length of a wire fence around a circular flower bed is 100π feet. What is the area (in square feet) of a two-foot concrete walk surrounding this fence?
    (A) 98π (B) 100π (C) 102π (D) 202π (E) 204π

15. How many tiles (each one foot square) are necessary to form a one-foot border around the inside of a room 24 feet by 14 feet?
    (A) 36 (B) 37 (C) 72 (D) 74 (E) 76

16. When the radius of a circle is doubled the area is multiplied by
    (A) 2 (B) 2π (C) $2\pi r$ (D) 3.14 (E) 4

17. $AD = 14$
$EF = 6$
$BC = ?$
(A) 8 (B) 12 (C) 20
(D) 26 (E) 36

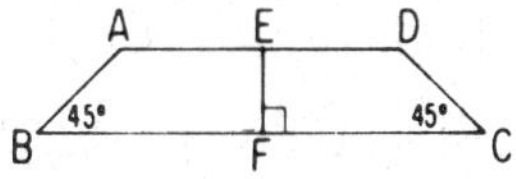

18. If the diagonal of a table with a square top is 6 feet, what is the area of the table top (in square feet)?
(A) $\sqrt{18}$ (B) 9π (C) 18 (D) $18\sqrt{2}$ (E) 36

19. How many spokes are there in the wheel of a sports car if any two spokes form an angle of 15°?
(A) 12 (B) 15 (C) 22 (D) 24 (E) 36

20. How many degrees are there in an angle formed by the hands of a clock at 2:30?
(A) 100° (B) 105° (C) 110° (D) 115° (E) 120°

21. One side of a rectangle is x inches. If the perimeter is p inches, what is the length (in inches) of the other side? Answer in terms of p and x.
(A) $p - x$ (B) $p - 2x$ (C) $\frac{p - x}{2}$
(D) $\frac{p - 2x}{2}$ (E) $2p - 2x$

22. Base RT of triangle RST is $\frac{4}{5}$ of altitude SV. If SV equals c, which of the following is an expression for the area of the triangle RST?
(A) $\frac{2c}{5}$ (B) $\frac{2c^2}{5}$ (C) $\frac{c^2}{2}$ (D) $\frac{4c^2}{5}$ (E) $\frac{8c^2}{5}$

23. A triangle has a base b and an altitude a. A second triangle has a base twice the altitude of the first triangle, and an altitude twice the base of the first triangle. What is the area of the second triangle?
(A) $\frac{1}{2}ab$ (B) ab (C) $2ab$ (D) $4ab$ (E) $\frac{1}{2}a^2b^2$

24. A pond 100 feet in diameter is surrounded by a circular grass walk which is 2 feet wide. How many square feet of grass are there on the walk? (Answer in terms of π.)
(A) 98π (B) 100π (C) 102π
(D) 202π (E) 204π

25. What is the area of $ABCD$?
(A) 5 (B) 8 (C) 10
(D) 16 (E) 20

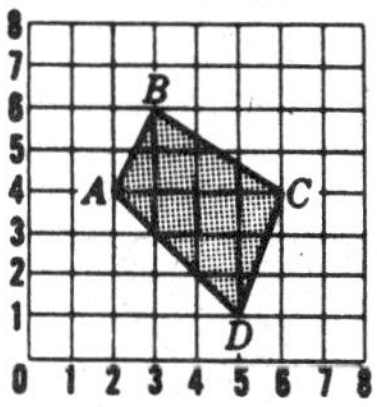

26. The distance from A to C in the square field $ABCD$ is 50 feet. What is the area of field $ABCD$ in square feet?
(A) $25\sqrt{2}$ (B) 625
(C) 1250 (D) 2500
(E) 5000

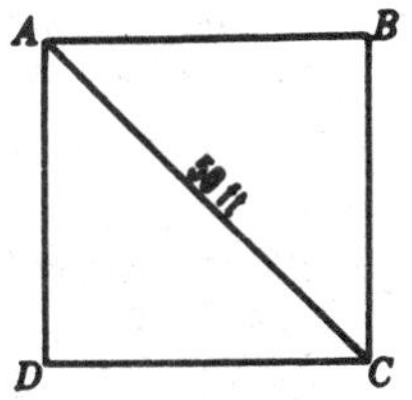

27. In the figure at the right, $ABCD$ is a square and semicircles and constructed on each side of the square. If AB is 2, what is the area of the entire figure?
(A) $2 + 4\pi$ (B) $2 - 4\pi$
(C) $4 + 8\pi$ (D) $4 - 2\pi$
(E) $4 + 2\pi$

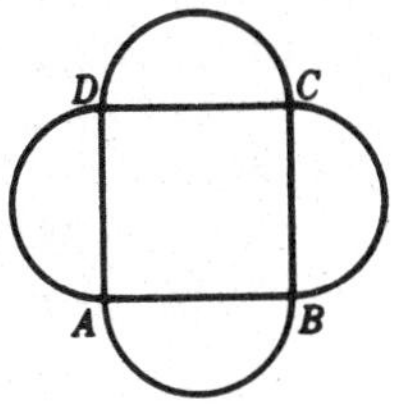

28. O is the center of the circle at the right. XO is perpendicular to YO and the area of triangle XOY is 32. What is the area of circle O?
(A) 16π (B) 32π (C) 64π
(D) 128π (E) 256π

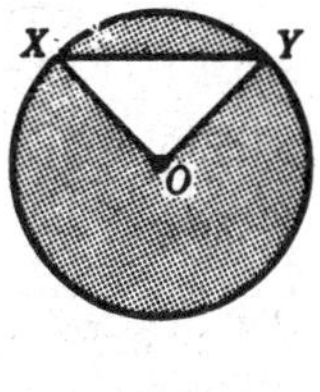

29. Square $QRST$ is inscribed in circle O.
$OV \perp TS$
$OV = 1$
The area of the shaded portion is
(A) $\pi - 4$ (B) $4\pi - 4$ (C) $2\pi - 4$
(D) $4\pi - 2$ (E) $2\pi - 2$

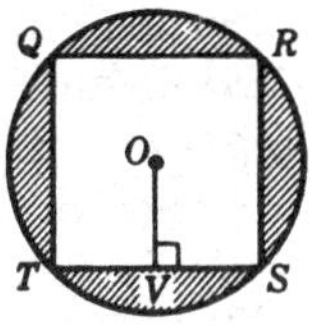

30. $QVR \perp SVT$
$\angle VSR = x°$
$\angle VRW = (?)°$
(A) $90 - x$
(B) $90 + x$
(C) $x - 90$
(D) $180 - x$
(E) 135

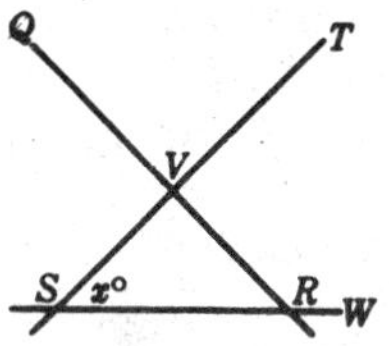

31. $ABJH$, $JDEF$, $ACEG$ are squares
$\frac{BC}{AB} = 3$
$\frac{\text{Area } BCDJ}{\text{Area } HJFG} = ?$
(A) $\frac{1}{9}$ (B) $\frac{1}{3}$ (C) 1 (D) 3 (E) 9

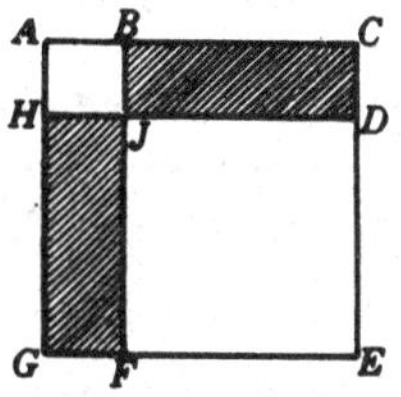

32. Rectangle $ABCD$ is made up of five equal squares. $AD = 30$. Find EF.
(A) 6 (B) 8
(C) 10 (D) 12
(E) 20

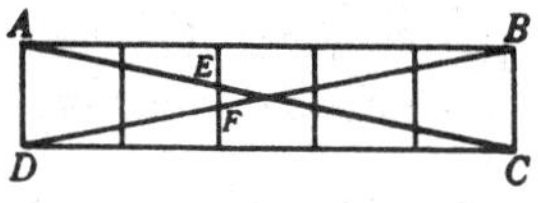

33. Radius $OA = 6.5$
Chord $AC = 5$
Area of triangle ABC equals
(A) 16 (B) 18
(C) 24 (D) 30
(E) 36

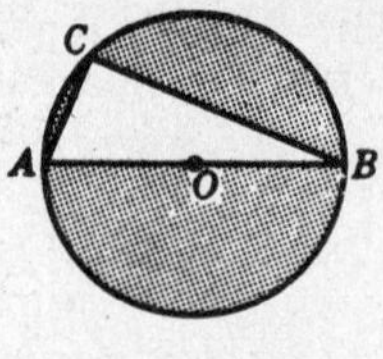

34. Angles a, b and c are in ratio of 1:3:2. How many degrees in angle b?
(A) 30 (B) 50
(C) 60 (D) 90
(E) 100

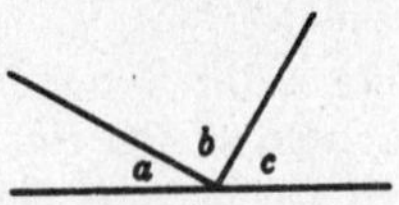

35. BC equals one half of AB. The area of right triangle ABC equals 64 square feet. Find hypotenuse AC to the nearest foot.
(A) 12 (B) 14
(C) 18 (D) 24
(E) 32

36. $ABCD$ is a square
$AE = 2$
$GC = 8$
Shaded area = 44
Area of $FBEJ$ = ?
(A) 36 (B) 56
(C) 64 (D) 68
(E) 80

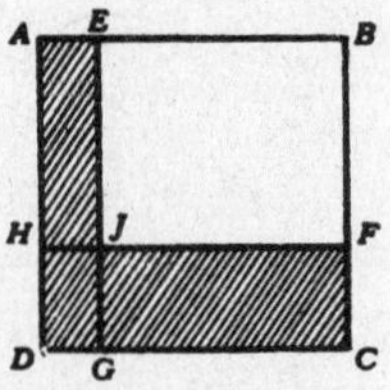

37. The area of a rectangle $KLMN$ equals 100. Base NM equals 20. What is the area of triangle ANM if A is any point on KL?
(A) 25 (B) 50 (C) 75
(D) 100 (E) cannot be determined

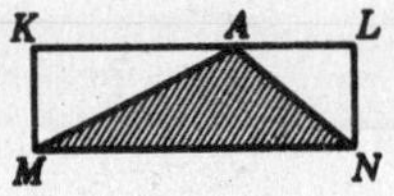

38. $ABCD$ is a rectangle.
$AD = 12$, $AB = 16$. DE = ?
(A) 8 (B) 10 (C) 14
(D) 15 (E) 20

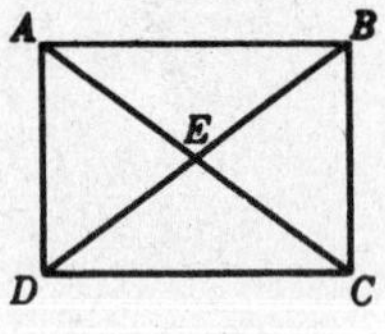

39. O is the center of the circle.
BC is parallel to AD.
$OA = 5$
$CB = 8$
$\frac{AB}{AD} = ?$
(A) $\frac{3}{4}$ (B) $\frac{4}{5}$ (C) 1
(D) $\frac{5}{4}$ (E) $\frac{4}{3}$

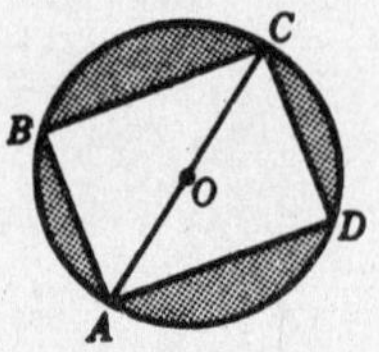

40. $BA = 2BC$
$EA = 2DE$
$BE = 14$
DC = ?
(A) 7 (B) 18 (C) 21
(D) 24 (E) 28

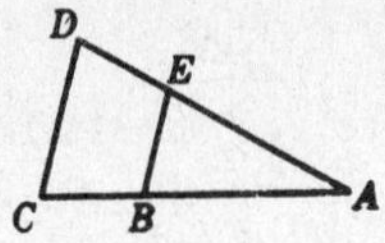

41. If angle DBG equals 79° and angle CBE equals 39° then angle GBE equals
(A) 51° (B) 62°
(C) 101° (D) 108°
(E) 202°

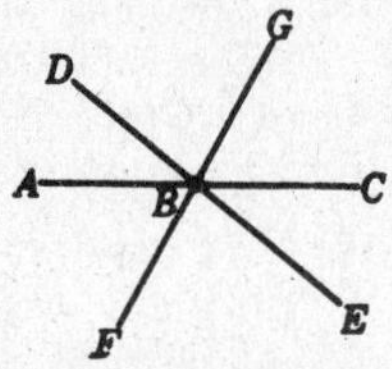

42. $\angle A = (?)^\circ$
(A) 15 (B) 45 (C) 60
(D) 80 (E) 120

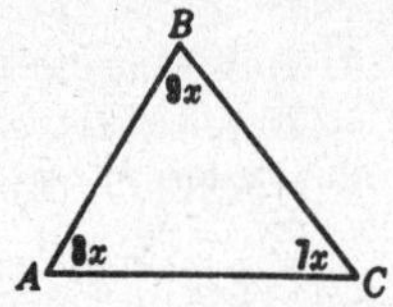

43. Four equal circles of diameter one foot touch at four points as shown in the figure. What is the area of the shaded portion (in feet)?
(A) $1 - \frac{\pi}{4}$ (B) $1 - \pi$
(C) $1 - 4\pi$ (D) π (E) $\frac{\pi}{4}$

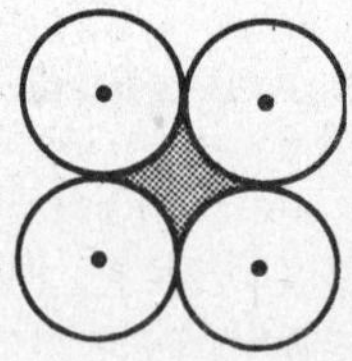

44. Perimeter of $ABCD$ = 24
The area of the shaded portion is
(A) 27π (B) $9\pi - 36$
(C) $9\pi - 24$ (D) $36 - 9\pi$
(E) $24 - 9\pi$

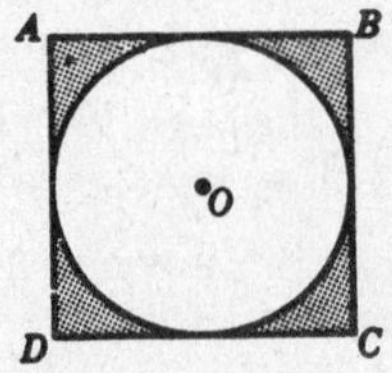

45. $ABIJ$, $BCHI$, $CDGH$, and $DEFG$ are congruent rectangles.
$AJ = 21$
KI = ?
(A) 3 (B) 5.25 (C) 7
(D) 10.5 (E) 14

46. The area of the shaded portion is
(A) $2r^2(4 - \pi)$
(B) $2r^2(2 - 2\pi)$
(C) $2r^2(\pi - 4)$
(D) $2r^2(\pi - 2)$
(E) $r^2(2 - \pi)$

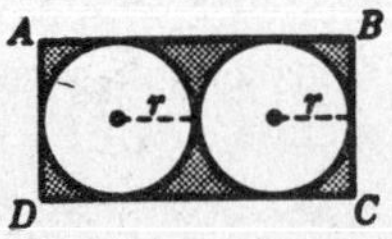

47. How many square units are there in the shaded triangle?
(A) 4 (B) 6 (C) 8
(D) 9 (E) 12

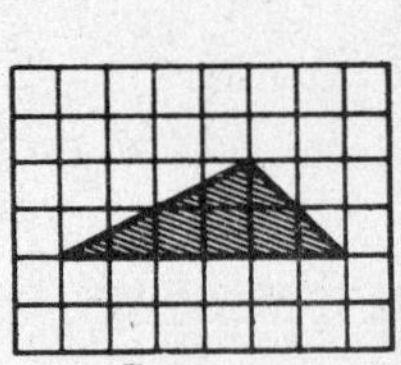

48. $AE \perp ED$ $ED = 13$
$CD \perp ED$ $CD = 3$
$DC \perp CB$ $CB = 2$
$AB = ?$ $AE = 11$
(A) 8 (B) 13 (C) 14
(D) 15 (E) 17

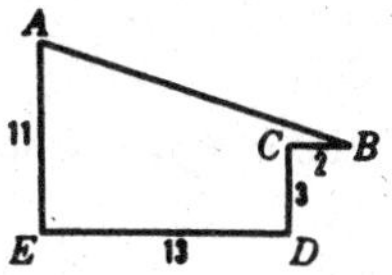

49. If an airplane starts at point R and travels 14 miles directly north to S, then 48 miles directly east to T, what is the straight line distance from T to R in miles?
(A) 25 (B) 34 (C) 50 (D) 62 (E) 2500

50. The area of a circle with radius r is equal to the area of a rectangle with base b. Find the altitude of the rectangle in terms of π, r, and b.
(A) $\sqrt{\pi r}$ (B) $\frac{2\pi r}{b}$ (C) $\pi r^2 b$ (D) $\frac{\pi r^2}{b}$ (E) $\frac{\pi r^2}{b^2}$

51. A line segment is drawn from point (8, −2) to point (4, 6). The coordinates of the midpoint of this line segment are
(A) 12, 4 (B) 12, 8 (C) 6, 4 (D) 6, 2
(E) 6, −2

52. Lines joining point (−4, 0) with point (0, 5) with point (4, 0) will form a (an)
(A) circle (B) right triangle (C) rectangle
(D) square (E) isosceles triangle

53. Point A (−3, −4) is drawn to point B (3, 4). Which of the following is true?
(A) the length of AB = 5 units (B) AB is parallel to the X axis (C) AB passes through point (6, 8) (D) AB passes through origin (E) AB is the radius of a circle with center at 0,0

54. Triangle ABC has the following vertices: A(1, 0), B(5,0), and C(3, 4). Which of the following is true?
(A) $AB = BC$ (B) $AB = AC$ (C) $CA = CB$
(D) $AC > BC$ (E) $AC < BC$

55. The area of a circle whose center is at (0, 0) is 25π. The circle passes through all of the following points EXCEPT
(A) −5, 0 (B) 5, 5 (C) 5, 0 (D) 0, 5
(E) 0, −5

56. The following points are vertices of quadrilateral $ABCD$ (0, 4), (4, 0), (0, −4) and (−4, 0). The area of $ABCD$ is
(A) 8 (B) 16 (C) 32 (D) 48 (E) 64

57. The vertices of triangle ABC are (4, 3), (4, 7) and (8, 3). The area of triangle ABC equals
(A) 4 (B) $4\sqrt{3}$ (C) 8 (D) 12.5
(E) 16

58. A line segment AB is drawn from point (2, 3) and point (4, 7). What are the coordinates of the midpoint?
(A) (5, 3) (B) (3, 5) (C) (6, 10)
(D) (2. 4) (E) (4, 2)

59. What is the distance from point A(3, 4) to Point B(−3, −4)?
(A) 0 (B) 5 (C) 10 (D) 13 (E) 14

60. Point P(4, 2) is the midpoint of line OPC, where O is at origin (O, O). The coordinates of C are
(A) (2, 1) (B) (4, 8) (C) (4, 4)
(D) (8, 2) (E) (8, 4)

ANSWER KEY

1.	B	21.	D	41.	C
2.	D	22.	B	42.	C
3.	E	23.	C	43.	A
4.	A	24.	E	44.	D
5.	D	25.	C	45.	C
6.	D	26.	C	46.	A
7.	C	27.	E	47.	B
8.	A	28.	C	48.	E
9.	D	29.	C	49.	C
10.	B	30.	B	50.	D
11.	C	31.	C	51.	D
12.	B	32.	A	52.	E
13.	B	33.	D	53.	D
14.	E	34.	D	54.	C
15.	C	35.	C	55.	B
16.	E	36.	B	56.	C
17.	D	37.	B	57.	C
18.	C	38.	B	58.	B
19.	D	39.	A	59.	C
20.	B	40.	C	60.	E

Formulas

(The number next to each formula refers to the section of the chapter where the formula is discussed.)

Interest = Amount × Time × Rate	I– D–2
Discount = Cost × Rate of Discount	I– D–2
$x = \frac{1}{2a}[-b \pm \sqrt{b^2 - 4ac}]$ (quadratic formula)	II– B–5
Distance = Rate × Time	II– C–2
$a^2 + b^2 = c^2$ when a and b are the legs and c is the hypotenuse of a right triangle (Pythagorean Theorem)	III– D–1
Diameter of a circle = 2 × Radius	III– F
Area of a square = s^2	III– G–1
Area of a rectangle = LW	III– G–1
Area of a triangle = $\frac{1}{2}bh$	III– G–1
Area of a circle = πr^2	III– G–1
Area of a parallelogram = bh	III– G–1
Area of a trapezoid = $\frac{1}{2}(b_1 + b_2)h$	III– G–1
Circumference of a circle = πd	III– G–2
Perimeter of a square = $4s$	III– G–2
Perimeter of a rectangle = $2(L + W)$	III– G–2
Distance between points (x,y) and (a,b) is $\sqrt{(x-a)^2 + (y-b)^2}$	III– H
Volume of a cube = S^3	III– G–3
Volume of a rectangular parallelepiped = LWH	III– G–3
Volume of a cylinder = $\pi r^2 h$	III– G–3
Distance between points (x,y) and (a,b) is $\sqrt{(x-a)^2 + (y-b)^2}$	III– H

Hints for Answering Mathematical Questions

1. Reread the question to make sure you have answered the question asked, and not what you anticipated.

2. You may save time by looking at the answers before you begin your computation. Some of the answers may be contrary to fact. Sometimes it is quicker to work back from the answers.

3. Don't waste time on superfluous computations.

4. Estimate the answer whenever you can, to save time.

5. Budget your time so you can try all the questions. (Bring a watch.)

6. You may not be able to answer all the questions; don't waste time worrying about it.

7. Do all the problems you know how to work *before* you start to think about those that will take a minute or two to answer.

8. If you skip a question, make sure to skip that number on the answer sheet.

9. Make sure you express your answer in the units asked for.

SAMPLE EXERCISES

This section provides two mathematical exercises, each with 25 questions. Take these practice exercises, check your answers, and study the answer explanations provided.

The exercises that follow will give you an indication of your ability to handle these mathematical questions. The time for Exercises A and B is 30 minutes each. Scoring for each of the exercises may be interpreted as follows:

20–25	SUPERIOR
16–19	ABOVE AVERAGE
11–15	AVERAGE
7–10	BELOW AVERAGE
0– 6	UNSATISFACTORY

MATHEMATICS EXERCISE A

1. In 1955, it cost \$12 to purchase one hundred pounds of potatoes. In 1975, it cost \$34 to purchase one hundred pounds of potatoes. The price of one hundred pounds of potatoes increased X dollars between 1955 and 1975 with X equal to:
(A) 1.20 (B) 2.20 (C) 3.40 (D) 22 (E) 34

2. A house cost Ms. Jones C dollars in 1965. Three years later she sold the house for 25% more than she paid for it. She has to pay a tax of 50% of the gain. (The gain is the selling price minus the cost.) How much tax must Ms. Jones pay?
(A) $\frac{1}{24}C$ (B) $\frac{C}{8}$ (C) $\frac{1}{4}C$ (D) $\frac{C}{2}$ (E) $.6C$

3. If the length of a rectangle is increased by 20%, and the width of the same rectangle is decreased by 20%, then the area of the rectangle
(A) decreases by 20% (B) decreases by 4% (C) is unchanged (D) increases by 20% (E) increases by 40%

Use the following graph for questions 4-7.

Worldwide Military Expenditures

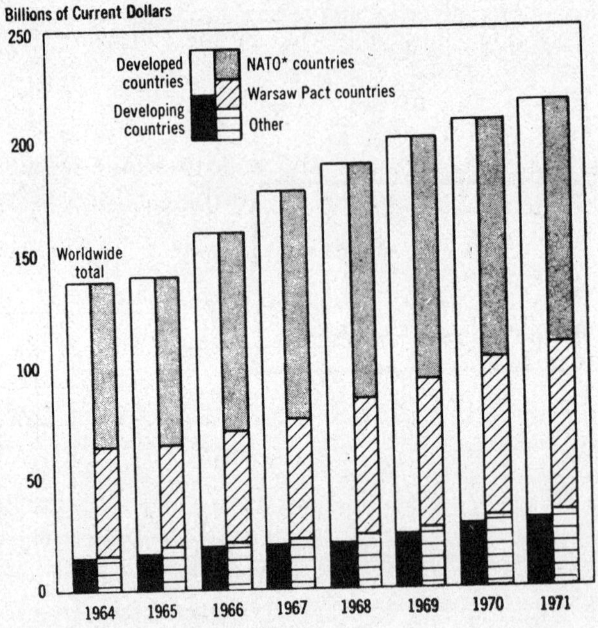

* North Atlantic Treaty Organization

Source: Pocket Data Book U.S.A. 1973. Bureau of the Census.

4. Between 1964 and 1969, worldwide military expenditures (A) increased by about 50% (B) roughly doubled (C) increased by about 150% (D) almost tripled (E) increased by 10%

5. The average yearly military expenditure by the developing countries between 1964 and 1971 was approximately how many billions of current dollars? (A) 20 (B) 50 (C) 100 (D) 140 (E) 175

6. Which of the following statements can be inferred from the graph?
I. The NATO countries have higher incomes than the Warsaw Pact countries.
II. Worldwide military expenditures have increased each year between 1964 and 1971.
III. In 1972 worldwide military expenditures were more than 230 billion current dollars.
(A) I only (B) II only (C) I and II only (D) II and III only (E) I, II, and III

7. A speaker claims that the NATO countries customarily spend ⅓ of their combined incomes on military expenditures. According to the speaker, the combined incomes of the NATO countries (in billions of current dollars) in 1971 was about
(A) 100 (B) 200 (C) 250 (D) 350 (E) 500

8. 8% of the people eligible to vote are between 18 and 21. In an election 85% of those eligible to vote who were between 18 and 21 actually voted. In that election, people between 18 and 21 who actually voted were what percent of those people eligible to vote?
(A) 4.2 (B) 6.4 (C) 6.8 (D) 8 (E) 8.5

9. If n and p are both odd numbers, which of the following numbers *must* be an even number?
(A) $n + p$ (B) np (C) $np + 2$ (D) $n + p + 1$ (E) $2n + p$

10. It costs g cents a mile for gasoline and m cents a mile for all other costs to run a car. How many *dollars* will it cost to run the car for 100 miles?
(A) $\frac{g + m}{100}$ (B) $100g + 100m$ (C) $g + m$ (D) $g + .1m$ (E) g

11. What is the length of the line segment which connects A to B?
(A) $\sqrt{3}$ (B) 2 (C) $2\sqrt{2}$ (D) 4 (E) 8

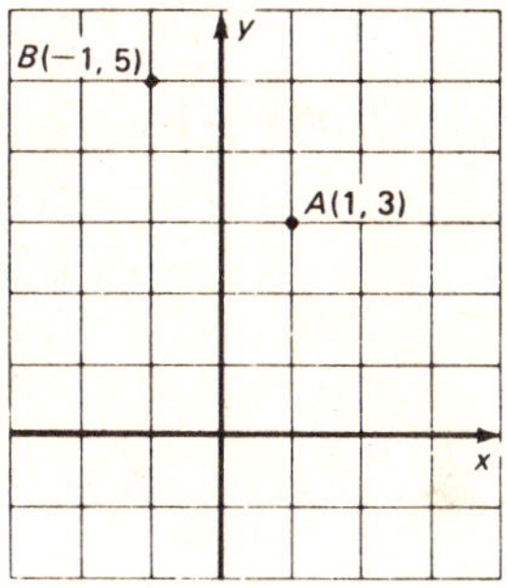

12. A cab driver's income consists of his salary and tips. His salary is $50 a week. During one week his tips were $\frac{5}{4}$ of his salary. What fraction of his income for the week came from tips?
(A) $\frac{4}{9}$ (B) $\frac{1}{2}$ (C) $\frac{5}{9}$ (D) $\frac{5}{8}$ (E) $\frac{5}{4}$

Use the table below for questions 13–17.

INCOME (IN DOLLARS)	TAX (IN DOLLARS)
0– 4,000	1% of income
4,000– 6,000	40 + 2 % of income over 4,000
6,000– 8,000	80 + 3% of income over 6,000
8,000–10,000	140 + 4% of income over 8,000
10,000–15,000	220 + 5% of income over 10,000
15,000–25,000	470 + 6% of income over 15,000
25,000–50,000	1,070 + 7% of income over 25,000

13. How much tax is due on an income of $7,500?
(A) $75 (B) $80 (C) $125 (D) $150 (E) $225

14. Your income for a year is $26,000. You receive a raise so that next year your income will be $29,000. How much *more* will you pay in taxes next year if the tax rate remains the same?
(A) $70 (B) $180 (C) $200 (D) $210 (E) $700

15. Joan paid \$100 tax. If X was her income, which of the following statements is true?
(A) $0 < X < 4{,}000$ (B) $4{,}000 < X < 6{,}000$ (C) $6{,}000 < X < 8{,}000$
(D) $8{,}000 < X < 10{,}000$ (E) $10{,}000 < X < 15{,}000$

16. The town of Zenith has a population of 50,000. The average inçome of a person who lives in Zenith is \$3,700 per year. What is the total amount paid in taxes by the people of Zenith? Assume each person pays tax on \$3,700.
(A) \$37 (B) \$3700 (C) \$50,000 (D) \$185,000 (E) \$1,850,000

17. A person who has an income of \$10,000 pays what percent (to the nearest percent) of his or her income in taxes?
(A) 1 (B) 2 (C) 3 (D) 4 (E) 5

18. Given that x and y are real numbers, let $S(x,y) = x^2 - y^2$. Then $S(3, S(3,4)) =$
(A) -40 (B) -7 (C) 40 (D) 49 (E) 56

19. Eggs cost 90¢ a dozen. Peppers cost 20¢ each. An omelet consists of 3 eggs and ¼ of a pepper. How much will the ingredients for 8 omelets cost?
(A) \$.90 (B) \$1.30 (C) \$1.80 (D) \$2.20 (E) \$2.70

20. It is 185 miles from Binghamton to New York City. If a bus takes 2 hours to travel the first 85 miles, how long must the bus take to travel the final 100 miles in order to average 50 miles an hour for the entire trip?
(A) 60 min. (B) 75 min. (C) 94 min. (D) 102 min. (E) 112 min.

21. What is the area of the figure below? $ABDC$ is a rectangle and BDE is an isosceles right triangle.
(A) ab (B) ab^2 (C) $b\left(a + \frac{b}{2}\right)$
(D) cab (E) $\frac{1}{2}bc$

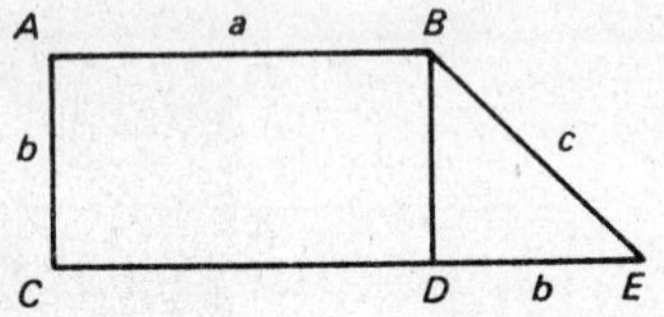

22. If $2x + y = 5$ then $4x + 2y$ is equal to
(A) 5 (B) 8 (C) 9 (D) 10 (E) none of these

23. In 1967, a new sedan cost \$2,500; in 1975, the same type of sedan cost \$4,800. The cost of that type of sedan has increased by what percent between 1967 and 1975?
(A) 48 (B) 52 (C) 92 (D) 152 (E) 192

24. What is the area of the square *ABCD*?
(A) 10 (B) 18 (C) 24 (D) 36
(E) 48

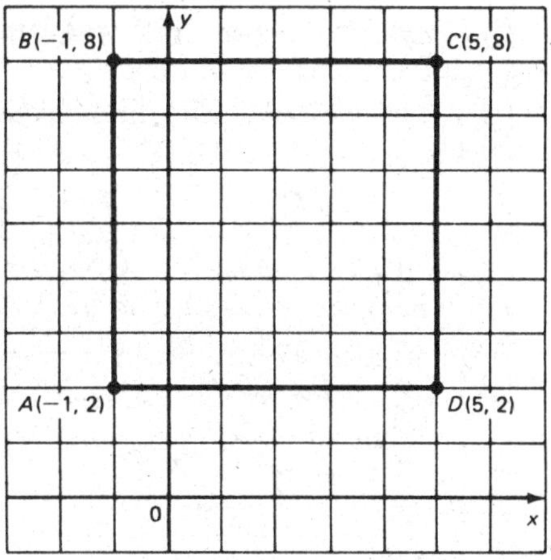

25. If $x + y = 6$ and $3x - y = 4$, then $x - y$ is equal to
(A) −1 (B) 0 (C) 2 (D) 4 (E) 6

MATHEMATICS
EXERCISE **B**

Use the graphs below for questions 1–5.

Women in the Labor Force

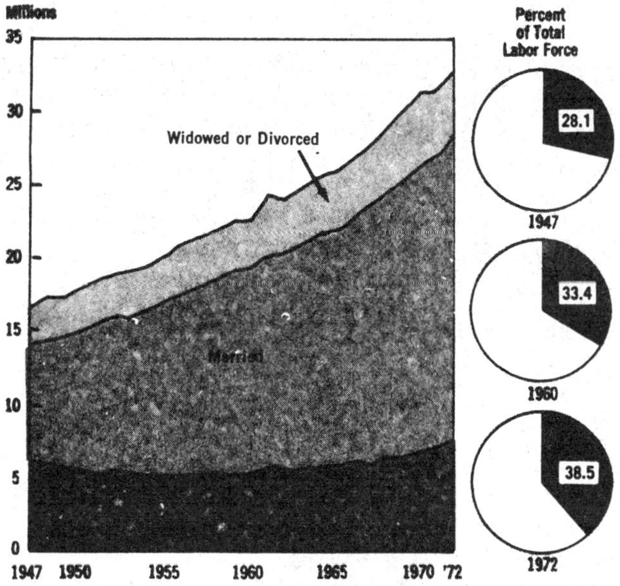

Source: Pocket Data Book U.S.A. 1973. Bureau of the Census.

1. The total labor force in 1960 was about *y* million with *y* equal to about
(A) 22 (B) 65 (C) 75 (D) 80 (E) 85

2. In 1947, the percentage of women in the labor force who were married was about
(A) 28 (B) 33 (C) 38 (D) 50 (E) 65

3. What was the first year when more than 20 million women were in the labor force?
(A) 1950 (B) 1953 (C) 1956 (D) 1958 (E) 1964

4. Between 1947 and 1972, the number of women in the labor force (A) increased by about 50% (B) increased by about 100% (C) increased by about 150% (D) increased by about 200% (E) increased by about 250%

5. Which of the following statements about the labor force can be inferred from the graphs?

I. Between 1947 and 1957, there were no years when more than 5 million widowed or divorced women were in the labor force.

II. In every year between 1947 and 1972, the number of single women in the labor force has increased.

III. In 1965, women made up more than ⅓ of the total labor force.

(A) I only (B) II only (C) I and II only (D) I and III only (E) I, II, and III

6. If $\frac{x}{y} = \frac{2}{3}$ then $\frac{y^2}{x^2}$ is equal to

(A) $\frac{4}{9}$ (B) $\frac{2}{3}$ (C) $\frac{3}{2}$ (D) $\frac{9}{4}$ (E) $\frac{5}{2}$

7. In the figure, BD is perpendicular to AC. BA and BC have length a. What is the area of the triangle ABC?

(A) $2x\sqrt{a^2 - x^2}$ (B) $x\sqrt{a^2 - x^2}$
(C) $a\sqrt{a^2 - x^2}$ (D) $2a\sqrt{x^2 - a^2}$
(E) $x\sqrt{x^2 - a^2}$

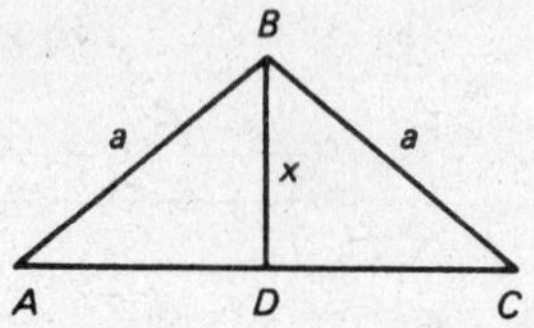

8. If two places are one inch apart on a map, then they are actually 160 miles apart. (The scale on the map is one inch equals 160 miles.) If Seton is 2⅞ inches from Monroe on the map, how many miles is it from Seton to Monroe?

(A) 3 (B) 27 (C) 300 (D) 360 (E) 460

9. In the accompanying diagram $ABCD$ is a rectangle. The area of isosceles right triangle $ABE = 7$, and $EC = 3(BE)$. The area of ABCD is

(A) 21 (B) 28
(C) 42 (D) 56
(E) 84

10. An automobile tire has two punctures. The first puncture by itself would make the tire flat in 9 minutes. The second puncture by itself would make the tire flat in 6 minutes. How long will it take for both punctures together to make the tire flat? (Assume the air leaks out at a constant rate.)

(A) $3\frac{3}{5}$ minutes (B) 4 minutes (C) $5\frac{1}{4}$ minutes (D) $7\frac{1}{2}$ minutes

(E) 15 minutes

11. If n^3 is odd, which of the following statements are true?
I. n is odd.
II. n^2 is odd.
III. n^2 is even.

(A) I only (B) II only (C) III only (D) I and II only
(E) I and III only

Use the table below for questions 12–15.

Participation in National Elections

Persons in millions. Civilian noninstitutional population as of Nov. 1. Based on post-election surveys of persons reporting whether or not they voted; differs from table 103 data which are based on actual vote counts.

Characteristic	1964 Persons of voting age	1964 Percent voted	1968 Persons of voting age	1968 Percent voted	1972 Persons of voting age	1972 Percent voted
Total	111	69	117	68	136	63
Male	52	72	54	70	64	64
Female	58	67	62	66	72	62
White	99	71	105	69	121	64
Negro and other	11	57	12	56	15	51
Negro	10	58	11	58	13	52
Region:						
North and West	78	75	82	71	94	66
South	32	57	35	60	43	55
Age:						
18–24 years	10	51	12	50	25	50
25–44 years	45	69	46	67	49	63
45–64 years	38	76	40	75	42	71
65 years and over	17	66	18	66	20	63

Source: U.S. Bureau of the Census.

12. Which of the following groups had the highest percentage of voters in 1968?
(A) 18–24 years (B) Female (C) South (D) 25–44 years (E) Male

13. In 1972, what percent (to the nearest percent) of persons of voting age were female?
(A) 52 (B) 53 (C) 62 (D) 64 (E) 72

14. In 1968, how many males of voting age voted?
(A) 37,440,000 (B) 37,800,000 (C) 42,160,000 (D) 62,000,000
(E) 374,400,000

15. Let X be the number (in millions) of persons of voting age in the range 25–44 years who lived in the North and West in 1964. Which of the following includes all possible values and only possible values of X?
(A) $0 \leqq X \leqq 45$ (B) $13 \leqq X \leqq 45$ (C) $13 \leqq X \leqq 78$ (D) $45 \leqq X \leqq 78$ (E) $75 \leqq X \leqq 78$

16. There are 50 students enrolled in Business 100. Of the enrolled students, 90% took the final exam. Two-thirds of the students who took the final exam passed the final exam. How many students passed the final exam?
(A) 30 (B) 33 (C) 34 (D) 35 (E) 45

17. If a is less than b, which of the following numbers is greater than a and less than b?
(A) $(a+b)/2$ (B) $(ab)/2$ (C) $b^2 - a^2$ (D) ab (E) $b - a$

18. In the figure, OR and PR are radii of circles. The length of OP is 4. If $OR = 2$, what is PR? PR is tangent to the circle with center O.

(A) 2 (B) $\frac{5}{2}$ (C) 3 (D) $2\sqrt{3}$

(E) $3\sqrt{2}$

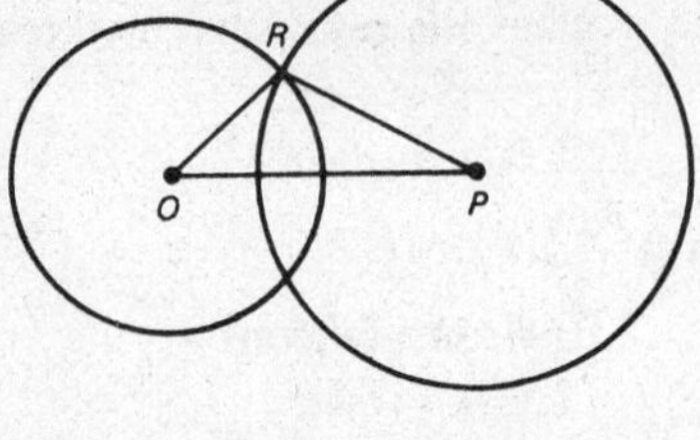

19. A bus uses one gallon of gasoline to travel 15 miles. After a tune-up, the bus travels 15% farther on one gallon. How many gallons of gasoline (to the nearest tenth) will it take for the bus to travel 150 miles after a tune-up?
(A) 8.5 (B) 8.7 (C) 8.9 (D) 9.0 (E) 10.0

20. If $x + 2y = 4$ and $x/y = 2$, then x is equal to

(A) 0 (B) $\frac{1}{2}$ (C) 1 (D) $\frac{3}{2}$ (E) 2

Use the following table for questions 21–23.

SPEED OF A TRAIN OVER A 3 HOUR PERIOD

TIMED PERIOD *(in minutes)*	0	30	45	60	90	120	150	180
SPEED AT TIME *(in m.p.h.)*	40	45	47.5	50	55	60	65	70

21. How fast was the train traveling 2½ hours after the beginning of the timed period?
(A) 50 m.p.h. (B) 55 m.p.h. (C) 60 m.p.h. (D) 65 m.p.h. (E) 70 m.p.h.

22. During the three hours shown on the table the speed of the train
(A) increased by 25% (B) increased by 50% (C) increased by 75%
(D) increased by 100% (E) increased by 125%

23. At time t measured in minutes after the beginning of the time period, which of the following gives the speed of the train in accordance with the table?
(A) $\frac{1}{6}t$ (B) $10t$ (C) $40 + t$ (D) $40 + \frac{1}{6}t$ (E) $40 + 10t$

24. It costs $1,000 to make the first thousand copies of a book and x dollars to make each subsequent copy. If it costs a total of $7,230 to make the first 8,000 copies of a book, what is x?
(A) .89 (B) .90375 (C) 1.00 (D) 89 (E) 90.375

25. If 16 workers can finish a job in three hours, how long should it take 5 workers to finish the same job?
(A) $3\frac{1}{2}$ hours (B) 4 hours (C) 5 hours (D) $7\frac{1}{16}$ hours (E) $9\frac{3}{5}$ hours

ANSWER KEYS

e letter following each question number is the correct answer. The numbers in parenthesis refer to the sec-
ıs of this chapter which explain the necessary mathematics principles. A more detailed explanation of all answers
ows:

ıthematics Exercise A

D (I-A)
B (I-D)
B (III-G, I-D)
A (IV-D, IV-E, I-D)
A (IV-D, I-G)
B (IV-D)
D (IV-D, I-B)
C (I-D)
A (I-A)
C (II-A)
C (III-H, I-H)
C (I-B)
C (I-D)

14. D (I-D)
15. C (I-D)
16. E (I-G, I-D)
17. B (I-D, I-E)
18. A (II-A)
19. D (I-B)
20. D (II-C)
21. C (III-G, II-A, I-H)
22. D (II-B)
23. C (I-D)
24. D (III-H, III-G)
25. A (II-B)

Mathematics Exercise B

1. B (IV-B, IV-C)
2. D (IV-C)
3. C (IV-C)
4. B (IV-C)
5. A (IV-C)
6. D (I-H)
7. B (III-D, III-G)
8. E (II-E)
9. D (III-G)
10. A (II-C)
11. D (I-A)
12. E (IV-A)
13. B (IV-A)
14. B (IV-A)
15. B (IV-A, II-G)
16. A (I-D, I-B)
17. A (II-G)
18. D (III-F, III-D)
19. B (I-D)
20. E (II-B)
21. D (IV-A)
22. C (IV-A)
23. D (II-A)
24. A (II-B)
25. E (II-C)

Explanation of Answers

Mathematics Exercise A

1. **D** The price increased by $34 - 12 = 22$ dollars.
2. **B** She sold the house for 125% of C or $\frac{5}{4}C$. Thus, the gain is $\frac{5}{4}C - C = \frac{C}{4}$. She must pay a tax of 50% of $\frac{C}{4}$ or $\frac{1}{2}$ of $\frac{C}{4}$. Therefore, the tax is $\frac{C}{8}$. Notice that the three years has nothing to do with the problem. Sometimes a question contains unnecessary information.
3. **B** The area of a rectangle is length times width. Let L and W denote the original length and width. Then the new length is $1.2L$ and the new width is $.8W$. Therefore, the new area is $(1.2L)(.8W) = .96LW$ or 96% of the original area. So the area has decreased by 4%.
4. **A** In 1964 military expenditures were about 140 billion and by 1969 they had increased to about 200 billion. $\frac{60}{140} = \frac{3}{7}$ which is almost 50%. By using a straight edge, you may see that the bar for 1969 is about half again as long as the bar for 1964.
5. **A** Since the developing countries' military expenditures for every year were less than 30 billion, choice A is the only possible answer. Notice that by reading the possible answers first, you save time. You don't need the exact answer.
6. **B** I can not be inferred since the graph indicates *only* the dollars spent on military expenditures, not the percent of income and not total income. II is true since each bar is higher than the previous bar to the left. III can not be inferred since the graph gives no information about 1972. So only statement II can be be inferred from the graph.
7. **D** In 1971 the NATO countries spent over 100 billion and less than 150 billion on military expenditures. Since this was $\frac{1}{3}$ of their combined incomes the combined income is between 300 billion and 450 billion. Thus choice D must be the correct answer.
8. **C** Voters between 18 and 21 who voted are 85% of the 8% of eligible voters. Thus, $(.08)(.85) = .068$, so 6.8% of the eligible voters were voters between 18 and 21 who voted.

9. **A** Odd numbers are of the form $2x + 1$ where x is an integer. Thus if $n = 2x + 1$ and $p = 2k + 1$, then $n + p = 2x + 1 + 2k + 1 = 2x + 2k + 2$ which is even. Using $n = 3$ and $p = 5$, all the other choices give an odd number. In general, if a problem involves odd or even numbers, try using the fact that odd numbers are of the form $2x + 1$ and even numbers of the form $2y$ where x and y are integers.

10. **C** To run a car 100 miles will cost $100\ (g + m)$ cents. Divide by 100 to convert to dollars. The result is $g + m$.

11. **C** Using the distance formula, the distance from A to B is $\sqrt{(1 - (-1))^2 + (3 - 5)^2} = \sqrt{4 + 4} = \sqrt{8} = \sqrt{4 \times 2} = \sqrt{4}\sqrt{2} = 2\sqrt{2}$. You have to be able to simplify $\sqrt{8}$ in order to obtain the correct answer.

12. **C** Tips for the week were $\frac{5}{4} \cdot 50$, so his total income was $50 + \frac{5}{4}(50) = \frac{9}{4}(50)$. Therefore, tips made up $\frac{5/4(50)}{9/4(50)} = \frac{5/4}{9/4} = \frac{5}{9}$ of his income. *Don't waste time figuring out the total income and the tip income. You can use the time to answer other questions.*

13. **C** 7,500 is in the 6,000–8,000 bracket so the tax will be 80 + 3% of the income over 6,000. Since 7,500 − 6,000 = 1,500, the income over 6,000 is 1,500. 3% of 1500 = (.03)(1500) = 45, so the tax is 80 + 45 = 125.

14. **D** The tax on 26,000 is 1,070 + 7% of (26,000 − 25,000). Thus, the tax is 1,070 + 70 = 1,140. The tax on 29,000 is 1.070 + 7% of (29,000 − 25,000). Thus, the tax on 29,000 is 1,070 + 280 = 1,350. Therefore, you will pay 1,350 − 1,140 = \$210 more in taxes next year.
A faster method is to use the fact that the \$3,000 raise is income over 25,000, so it will be taxed at 7%. Therefore, the tax on the extra \$3,000 will be (.07)(3,000) = 210.

15. **C** If income is less than 6,000, then the tax is less than 80. If income is greater than 8,000, then the tax is greater than 140. Therefore, if the tax is 100, the income must be between 6,000 and 8,000. You *do not* have to calculate her exact income.

16. **E** Each person pays the tax on \$3,700 which is 1% of 3700 or \$37. Since there are 50,000 people in Zenith, the total taxes are (37)(50,000) = \$1,850,000.

17. **B** The tax on 10,000 is 220, so taxes are $\frac{220}{10{,}000} = .022 = 2.2\%$ of income. 2.2% is 2% after rounding to the nearest percent.

18. **A** $S(3,4) = 3^2 - 4^2 = 9 - 16 = -7$. Therefore, $S(3,S(3,4)) = S(3,-7) = 3^2 - (-7)^2 = 9 - 49 = -40$.

19. **D** 8 omelets will use $8 \cdot 3 = 24$ eggs and $8 \cdot \frac{1}{4} = 2$ peppers. Since 24 is two dozen, the cost will be (2)(90¢) + (2)(20¢) = 220¢ or \$2.20.

20. **D** In order to average 50 m.p.h. for the trip, the bus must make the trip in $\frac{185}{50} = 3\frac{7}{10}$ hours which is 222 minutes. Since 2 hours or 120 minutes were needed for the first 85 miles, the final 100 miles must be completed in 222 − 120 which is 102 minutes.

21. **C** The area of a rectangle is length times width so the area of $ABDC$ is ab. The area of a triangle is one half of the height times the base. Since BDE is an isosceles right triangle, the base and height both are equal to b. Thus, the area of BDE is $\frac{1}{2}b^2$ Therefore, the area of the figure is $ab + \frac{1}{2}b^2$ which is equal to $b\ (a + \frac{b}{2})$. You have to express your answer as one of the possible answers, so you need to be able to simplify.

22. **D** Since $4x + 2y$ is equal to $2(2x + y)$ and $2x + y = 5$, $4x + 2y$ is equal to $2(5)$ or 10.

23. **C** The cost has increased by \$4800 minus \$2500 or \$2300 between 1967 and 1975. So the cost has increased by $\frac{2300}{2500}$ which is .92 or 92%. Answer (E) is incorrect. The price in 1975 is 192% of the price in 1967, but the *increase* is 92%.

24. **D** The distance from $(-1, 2)$ to $(5, 2)$ is 6. (You can use the distance formula or just count the blocks in this case.) The area of a square is the length of a side squared, so the area is 6^2 or 36.

25. **A** Since $x + y = 6$ and $3x - y = 4$, we may add the two equations to obtain $4x = 10$, or $x = 2.5$. Then, because $x + y = 6$, y must be 3.5. Therefore, $x - y = -1$.

Mathematics Exercise B

1. **B** In 1960 women made up 33.4% or about ⅓ of the labor force. Using the line graph, there were about 22 million women in the labor force in 1960. So the labor force was about 3(22) or 66 million. The closest answer among the choices is 65 million.

2. **D** In 1947, there were about 16 million women in the labor force, and about 14 − 6 or 8 million of them were married. Therefore, the percentage of women in the labor force who were married is $\frac{8}{16}$ or 50%

3. **C** Look at the possible answers first. You can use your pencil and admission card as straight edges.

4. **B** In 1947, there were about 16 million women in the labor force. By 1972 there were about 32 million. Therefore, the number of women doubled which is an increase of 100%. (Not of 200%.)

5. **A** I is true since the width of the band for widowed or divorced women was never more than 5 million between 1947 and 1957. II is false since the number of single women in the labor force decreased from 1947 to 1948. III can not be inferred since there is no information about the total labor force or women as a percent of it in 1965. Thus, only I can be inferred.

6. **D** If $\frac{x}{y}$ is $\frac{2}{3}$, then $\frac{y}{x}$ is $\frac{3}{2}$. Since $\left(\frac{y}{x}\right)^2$ is equal to $\frac{y^2}{x^2}$, $\frac{y^2}{x^2}$ is $\left(\frac{3}{2}\right)^2$ or $\frac{9}{4}$.

7. **B** The area of a triangle is $\frac{1}{2}$ altitude times base. Since BD is perpendicular to AC, x is the altitude. Using the Pythagorean theorem, $x^2 + (AD)^2 = a^2$ and $x^2 + (DC)^2 = a^2$. Thus, $AD = DC$, and $AD = \sqrt{a^2 - x^2}$. So the base is $2\sqrt{a^2 - x^2}$. Therefore, the area is $\frac{1}{2}(x)(2\sqrt{a^2 - x^2})$ which is choice B.

8. **E** $1 : 160 :: 2\frac{7}{8} : x$. $x = 2\frac{7}{8}(160)$. $2\frac{7}{8}$ is $\frac{23}{8}$ so the distance from Seton to Monroe is $\frac{23}{8}(160) = 460$ miles

9. **D** Let $EF = FG = GC$. Therefore, $BE = EF = FG = GC$. Draw perpendiculars EH, FI, GJ. Draw diagonals HF, IG, JC. The 8 triangles are equal in area since they each have the same altitude (AB or DC) and equal bases (BE, EF, FG, GC, AH, HI, IJ, JD). Since the area of $ABE = 7$, the area of $ABCD = (8)(7)$ or 56.

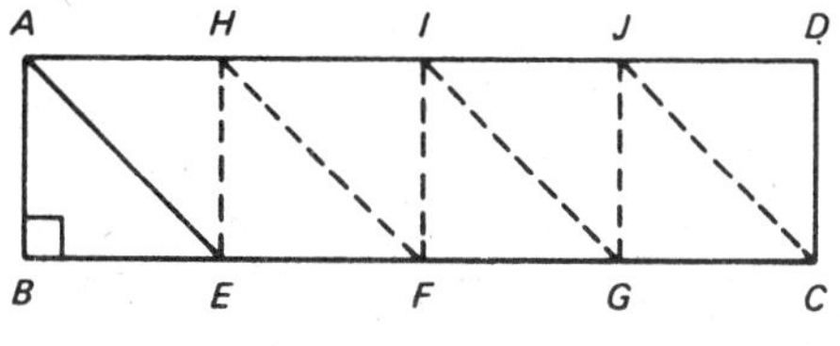

10. **A** In each minute the first puncture will leak $\frac{1}{9}$ of the air and the second puncture will leak $\frac{1}{6}$ of the air. Together $\frac{1}{9} + \frac{1}{6} = \frac{5}{18}$. So $\frac{5}{18}$ of the air will leak out in each minute. In $\frac{18}{5}$ or $3\frac{3}{5}$ minutes the tire will be flat.

11. **D** Since an even number times any number is even, and n times n^2 is od neither n or n^2 can be even. Therefore, n and n^2 must both be odd for to be odd. I and II are true, and III is false.
12. **E** Look in the fourth column.
13. **B** In 1972 there were 72 million females out of 136 million persons of voti age. $\frac{72}{136} = .529$ which is 53% to the nearest percent.
14. **B** In 1968, 70% of the 54 million males of voting age voted, a $(.7)(54{,}000{,}000) = 37{,}800{,}000$.
15. **B** Since 78 million persons of voting age lived in the North and West 1964, and there were 65 million persons of voting age not in the 25– year range, there must be at least $78 - 65 = 13$ million people in t North and West in the 25–44 year range. X must be greater than or eq to 13. Since there were 45 million people of voting age in the 25–44 y range, X must be less than or equal to 45.
16. **A** 90% of 50 is 45, so 45 students took the final. $\frac{2}{3}$ of 45 is 30. Therefo 30 students passed the final.
17. **A** The average of two different numbers is always between the two. If $a =$ and $b = 3$, then $b^2 - a^2 = 5$, $ab = 6$, and $b - a = 1$ so C, D, and must be false. If $a = ½$ and $b = 1$, then $(ab)/2 = ¼$, so B is also fal
18. **D** Since the radius to the point of tangency is perpendicular to the tang OR must be perpendicular to PR. Therefore, ORP is a right triangle, a $(PO)^2 = (OR)^2 + (PR)^2$. Then, $(PR)^2 = (PO)^2 - (OR)^2$. Th $(PR)^2 = 4^2 - 2^2$, and $PR = \sqrt{16-4} = \sqrt{12} = \sqrt{4}\sqrt{3} = 2\sqrt{3}$.
19. **B** After the tune-up, the bus will travel $(1.15)(15) = 17.25$ miles on a g lon of gas. Therefore, it will take $(150) \div (17.25) = 8.7$ (to the nea tenth) gallons of gasoline to travel 150 miles.
20. **E** If $x/y = 2$, then $x = 2y$, so $x + 2y = 2y + 2y = 4y$. But $x + 2y =$ so $4y = 4$, or $y = 1$. Since $x = 2y$, x must be 2.
21. **D** 2½ hours is 150 minutes.
22. **C** The train's speed increased by $70 - 40$ which is 30 miles per hour. 30 is 75%.
23. **D** When $t = 0$, the speed is 40, so A and B are incorrect. When $t = 1$ the speed is 70, so C and E are incorrect. Choice D gives all the val which appear in the table.
24. **A** The cost of producing the first 8,000 copies is $1{,}000 + 7{,}000x$. 1,000 $7{,}000x = \$7{,}230$. Therefore, $7{,}000x = 6230$ and $x = .89$.
25. **E** Assume all workers work at the same rate unless given different infor tion. Since 16 workers take 3 hours, each worker does $\frac{1}{48}$ of the job hour. Thus, the 5 workers will finish $\frac{5}{48}$ of the iob each hour. $\frac{5}{48}x =$ It will take $\frac{48}{5} = 9\frac{3}{5}$ hours for them to finish the job.

SELF-ASSESSMENT

As you went through these practice exercises, were you able to finish them in the time allotted? Did you have trouble handling the computations involved? Evaluate your performance. Did you spend so much time on one question that you never got to answer two or three others? Did you forget to leave yourself a minute or two to fill in your guesses? If you fell into these common errors during this practice, be sure to avoid them as you take the model tests.

Before you take the model tests:

If you had trouble with fractions, decimals, percentages, or exponents, review Section I.

If you had trouble with algebraic problems, review Section II.

If you had trouble with geometric problems, review Section III.

If you had trouble interpreting graphs, review the section on charts and graphs in the chapter on reading skills.

CHAPTER **5**

WRITING SKILLS REVIEW

Purpose of the Writing Test

(1) You demonstrate your ability to *think* by showing that you understand the topic of the essay, that you have a point to make about the topic, and that you have several substantial ideas to support or illustrate your point.

(2) Your ability to *organize* is shown by arranging ideas according to a purposeful plan. Good writers almost always use a plan instead of relying on the order in which ideas just happened to pop into their heads.

(3) You show your mastery of *English* by expressing yourself clearly, using language that is essentially correct—language that will enable your readers to understand exactly what you intended to tell them.

The CBEST writing test offers you an opportunity to demonstrate that you have what it takes to be a classroom teacher. The best essays are clear, interesting, and correct. Similarly, the best teachers present their material clearly, make it interesting, and use correct English to communicate with their students.

Design of the Test

You must write an essay on each of two topics. One topic asks you to express your thoughts about a given situation or a statement. The other topic asks you to write about a personal experience. Since you are allowed one hour to complete the test, you should plan to spend about 30 minutes on each essay. What you say in each essay is completely up to you. The only requirement is that you write only on the given topics. Readers will take a dim view of an essay that strays from the topic, regardless of how beautifully it is written.

Your essays need not follow a prescribed format. Three to six paragraphs are customary, but not essential. In general, your essays should have an appealing opening, a few paragraphs of development, and an appropriate conclusion. Variations are possible, of course. The form you use should follow the point and substance of your essays.

Evaluating Your Essays

Each essay will be evaluated by two different readers who have been instructed to read the essays *holistically*. That is, they are to spend no more than two or three minutes reading each essay and assign a grade based on their general impression of the writing. They won't mark you down a certain number of points for spelling errors or reduce your grade for each grammatical flaw in your paper. Rather, the strengths and weaknesses of each essay will create a cumulative effect on the readers.

Although the Information Bulletin on the CBEST specifically states that *Pass* papers "will be clearly reasoned, well-organized, and well developed," it's hard to put a finger on the precise meaning of each of those qualities. Holistic essay reading remains far from an exact science. Readers' personal reactions will count heavily in the assessment of your writing. Even though the judgments of experienced readers rarely differ by more than one grade, the rationale for assigning a specific number (from 1–4) to a paper often varies.

The most successful essays will earn 4, or *Pass,* a grade that indicates writing competence. A grade of 3, or *Marginal Pass,* means that the essay suggests competence. A 2, or *Marginal Fail,* suggests incompetence, and a grade of 1, or *Fail,* indicates that the writing is, quite frankly, unacceptable.

It is important to remember that your essays will be read not by machines but by people—real people with feelings, moods, likes, and dislikes, and the capacity to laugh, grow angry, and be moved. In most ways they are probably not much different from you, except that they have had more experience as teachers. Consequently, they will enjoy reading an essay that is informative, entertaining, interesting, and clear. On the other hand, they will be put off by writing that is garbled, phony, or downright dull. As you write, therefore, keep your readers in mind. Write as one human being to another. Let your essays be an exercise in person-to-person communication.

REVIEW

Preparing for the Test

Writing two essays in 60 minutes is a real challenge. Many professional writers couldn't do it because they work too slowly, agonizing over every word and sentence, rewriting often, and then rewriting what they've rewritten. Even some journalists, accustomed to working under the pressure of deadlines, would be hard-pressed to produce two good essays in an hour's time.

Unfortunately, however, you have no choice. You have to condense into a few minutes all the steps that another writer, enjoying the luxury of time, might ordinarily stretch into hours or even days. Certainly, you've had the experience before. Finals in college, for example, tested not only what you knew but how quickly you could fill up an exam booklet.

Unlike most final exams in, say, a psychology or a history course, though, the CBEST doesn't ask questions for which there are predetermined answers. For the CBEST, you cannot study. Whatever you need to know is already lodged inside you. The task you face is to locate it, organize it, and get it onto the page for someone to read. The only way to prepare for this test is to practice, practice, practice—practice writing similar types of essays in 30 minutes.

Choose any of the sample essay topics in this chapter. Write an essay a day for the next several days, until you get the feel of 30 minutes' writing time. How many words do you actually put down on paper? How long do you spend on figuring out a topic and making notes? How much time do you reserve for editing and proofreading? Practice all the steps until you can rely on your internal clock to tell you when you should be going on to the next step. In short, get the timing right. Grow accustomed to apportioning your time for each step in the writing process. Incidentally, during the test, no one will tell you the time. You have to pace yourself. A watch will help, of course, but without a sure grasp of time, you'll be handicapped.

Getting the Most out of Thirty Minutes

No one can tell you the proper amount of time to spend on each step in the writing process, nor even the best order for taking each step. What works for someone else may not work for you. Some people spill their thoughts willy nilly onto the page. Other writers work over each sentence carefully before going on to the next one. You have to find and practice your own best method. Adapt the following schedule to suit your own writing methods:

Prewriting . . . . 5–10 minutes
(Reading and analyzing the topic, thinking of ideas, making lists of ideas, freewriting, looping, clustering and branching, questioning, narrowing the subject, outlining, defining your main idea.)

Composing . . . . 15–20 minutes
(Setting your words on paper, using paragraphs to develop your ideas, writing an appealing opening and appropriate closing, using your natural "voice," and unifying your piece with transitions.)

Revising, editing, and proofreading . . . . 5–10 minutes
(Reordering ideas, trimming needless words, reviewing verb choice, checking for proper mechanics, and use of English.)

Notice that no time has been left for neatly recopying your essay. Indeed, you shouldn't waste time recopying. While neat handwriting helps, you won't be penalized for crossings-out or handwriting that is less that perfect. If the handwriting is legible, leave it. Do not waste time copying it over. Besides, you may not have enough paper. At present, you are given only two sheets of lined paper for each essay. If you make your letters too large, skip lines, or leave wide margins you may run out of space. Remember always to

THINK AHEAD

Notice also that no more than twenty minutes out of thirty should be spent actually composing. The rest—as much as half, perhaps—might be better spent doing preliminary work and adding the final touches to your essays. Again, though, be guided by techniques that work best for you.

The Length of Your Essays

Considering the time allotted for the test, don't expect to write long essays. An essay of 500 words is almost unheard of. Essays between 250 and 400 words are closer to the mark. Sometimes an even shorter piece may do, but not much shorter, since your ideas will seem too general or too superficial if you don't say enough about them. Ample development of ideas is always a sign of good writing. In the end, though, the length of your essays is less important than both their lucidity and their capacity to engage the readers' interest. Quality counts a lot more than quantity. Because your essays must be short, they must be well-focused. That is, you can't expect to say everything about a broad subject in 250–400 words. The sharper the focus, the better, for it's preferable to write a detailed essay about a small, well-defined subject than to generalize about big, global matters—which is about all one can do in half an hour.

Writing an Essay

If you had saved all the essays you ever wrote, you'd probably need a wheelbarrow to cart them away. In other words, you've already had plenty of practice. When you wrote all those essays, did you pour the words onto the page, or did you squeeze them out one by one? Did you preplan exactly what you wanted to say, or did you discover your point as you went along? Did you prepare an outline? Were you preoccupied with spelling and grammar as you wrote, or did you write freely? Did you reread as you went along or only at the end? Whatever you did, you used a process of some kind, changing it perhaps according to the purpose and importance of each piece and the amount of time you had to write it. Some processes probably worked better than others.

When you write the CBEST essays, you'd be well-advised to have a process in mind, since you don't have the time to devise one on the spot. No one can tell you exactly which process will work best for you. Try out several beforehand.

To get started, work with the simple and logical sequence of steps that is taught widely in schools and colleges and serves as the foundation of virtually all processes that writers use. It consists of three basic stages: Prewriting, Composing, and Revising and Proofreading. Take a close look at how each stage contributes to the writing of essays.

Prewriting

The prewriting stage, as the name suggests, consists of all you do before you actually begin writing the text of your essay.

1. *Reading the Topic.* Obviously, prewriting on the CBEST should begin with a careful reading of the assigned topic. Read it two or three times, underlining key ideas and words, until you are confident that you know *exactly* what you are being asked to do. For each topic, identify the following.

a. *The situation or circumstances.* Because writing does not take place in a vacuum, most CBEST topics will give you a hypothetical situation that calls for a written response.

dience. The topic will frequently tell you who will be interested in reading your
ommittee, a group of students, a school administrator, etc. The point is that
o adjust your writing for different readers.

re likely to be asked to express your opinion about an issue or to describe or
or set of circumstances. The overall purpose will be to inform your readers
nce or to sway them to believe as you do about a given issue.

ic often tells you to compose a letter, a newspaper article, or an entry in a
kind. If no format is specified, write a straightforward essay. Do not be
your creativity with an offbeat form such as a poem, play, or monologue. The
e for experiments in writing.

tion or material to include. Search the topic for suggestions about what the
n. Sometimes suggestions are explicit ("give two reasons for...," "explain
More often, however, the choice of material is left up to you.

nd analyze the following topic.

> ting seniors at your university have been asked to name, describe, and
> e worst professors they had during their time at the university. Each
> read by the university personnel committee. Keeping in mind that the
> eriously any statement in which the evaluation criteria are not explicitly
> description/evaluation.

a. *The situation or circumstances.* ______________________________

b. *The prospective audience.* ______________________________

c. *The purpose.* ______________________________

d. *The format.* ______________________________

e. *The kinds of information or material to include.* ______________________________

Your own analysis will probably not coincide word for word with the sample responses. Yet, the sense of your answers should be similar:

a. *The situation or circumstances.* As a graduating senior, you are being asked to write about the best and the worst professors you had in college.

b. *The prospective audience.* The personnel committee of your college or university.

c. *The purpose.* The committee is interested in gathering information from students about the quality of teaching at the university.

d. *The format.* A description and evaluation of both the best and the worst professors you had.

e. *The kinds of information or material to include.* 1. Descriptive material. 2. Evaluations. 3. Explicit criteria for evaluating your professors.

While taking the CBEST, you won't have time to write out an analysis of each topic, but take a few moments to identify precisely what you are expected to write. As you proceed, check the topic again and again to be sure you haven't strayed from it.

2. *Warming up.* The quality of your essay may well depend on the quality of your warmups—what you do to gather and arrange ideas for your essays. Some writers make lists of ideas, others write formal outlines. Still others prefer to write key words, draw boxes around them, and connect them with arrows. Some draw circles within circles, as though to create a visual image of their essay before putting ideas into words. No method excels another, as long as it helps you collect and organize ideas for your essays.

Before you walk into the CBEST exam room, have a warmup plan in mind. Any of the usual methods—listing, freewriting, looping, clustering and branching, questioning—will serve. Experiment with each method and adopt those that serve you best.

Topic #2:

Each of us has moments when we experience insights that offer a new awareness of the direction of our lives. These moments are exciting, joyful, possibly a little frightening. Later, such instances may appear trivial, but at the time they occur, they are important.

Write an essay that describes one of your moments of insight—perhaps when you realized that you wanted to be a teacher. Your essay should communicate both the *content* and the *feel* of your experience. Provide enough detail for your readers to share your new awareness, and be certain you clarify its significance in your life.

a. *Listing.* As rapidly as you can, write a list of anything—literally *anything*—that might qualify as a response to the topic you've been given. Like pulling out a stopper, making a list often starts the flow of ideas. Your mind makes connections as one idea calls up memories of another, and then another. Do not be particular. After a few minutes, review the list and choose the one subject which holds the most promise for your essay.

To show you how this and other techniques have been put to use, the work done by Franny Smith of San Francisco, an education major from a California state college, will be used as an illustration:

Franny's "list," written for Sample Essay #2

When I realized that most people have prejudices
When I understood that ultimately my life belongs to me alone.
When I discovered that I'm really smarter than I thought.
When I figured out the meaning of "ulterior motives"
When it hit me that I should be a teacher
When I understood the significance of faith
When I saw the difference between listening and hearing

b. *Free-writing.* Write nonstop for five minutes, paying no attention to grammar, spelling, or punctuation. Concentrate on telling the truth about matters related to the CBEST topic. The mind works far faster than your hand, but in a speedily written free-write, you may be able to capture flashes of thought before they get away or you may come across an idea you wouldn't have found in any other way.

Franny's Free-write

When did I first want to be a teacher? I remember my office job, in a bank. Wow, was that boring. Every day on my way to work, I used to think of how bored I would be that day, and I used to play a fantasy game, thinking of what I would tell a group of kids in my class about the news of the day. I read somewhere that if you want to know something well, teach it to someone else.Then you can't fake it. You have to know your stuff or they won't learn. That's what my job in the bank was—fake! I hated it. In teaching, though, I knew I'd have to be honest. It seemed like a clean, pure profession. Also I could have a good time. There would be no time to be bored, not with 25 or 30 kids all wanting your attention at the same time. So maybe it was on those mornings walking to work that I realized that I'd much rather be heading toward a schoolhouse than to a bank.

c. *Looping.* Once you have finished free-writing, reread what you have written. Circle any idea or phrase which you like or which holds promise for an essay. Take one of the circled items and free-write on that in order to generate more ideas and capture fleeting details.

Franny's "Loop"

Having a good time. Isn't that what it's all about? Yes, to get a teaching job maybe you have to say how much you like to help people or how much young kids need responsive and caring adults to work with, but those kinds of ideas, while true in principle, only *sound* good. They don't mean anything in reality. I remember having such a good time telling that little boy at the beach all about the waves and tides and what causes them. He asked so many questions, and he seemed to be so interested in my answers. Maybe I spoke with authority or he sensed that I took him seriously. Whatever happened, it was a moment I'll never forget. Maybe it was then that I experienced for the first time the joy of being a teacher.

d. *Clustering and Branching.* After you've chosen your subject, write it down and draw a circle around it. Surround the circle with smaller circles containing important qualities or features of your main subject. Branch out from those to still smaller details. Then number all the parts in the order you might use them in your essay. Let the numbered ideas guide you as you compose your essay.

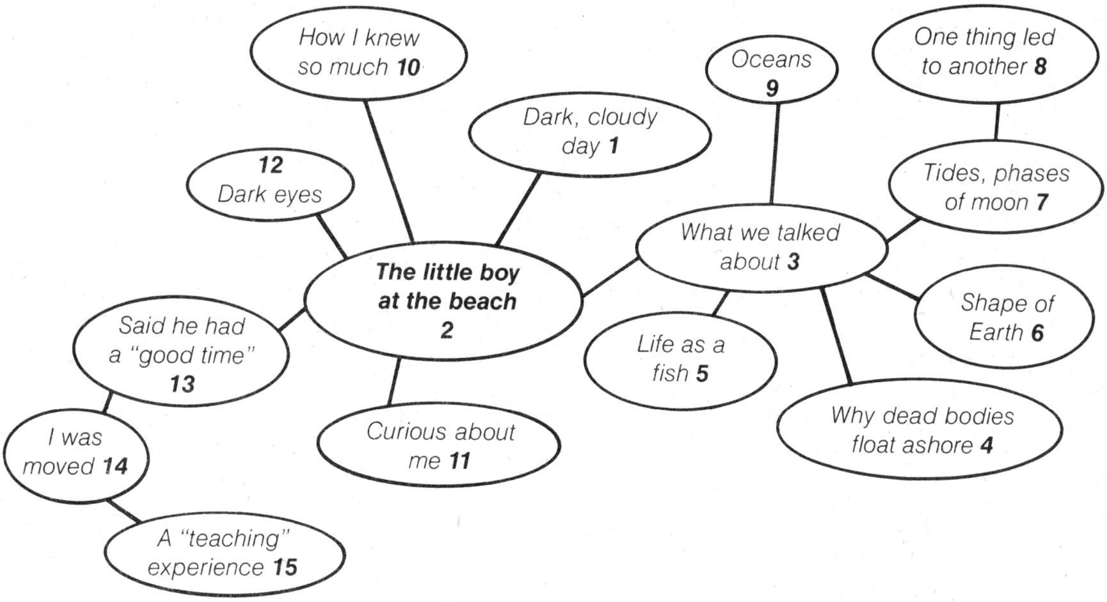

Franny's "Clusters" and "Branches"

e. *Questioning.* Assume the role of a self-interrogator by asking yourself questions about the topic. For instance, about a "moment of insight" you might ask such questions as these:

What triggered my moment of insight?
What was I doing at the time?
What insight did I have?
Did this insight change me in any way?
If I hadn't had that insight, how would my life be different?

To better understand the feelings provoked by the moment, you might ask:

If I were to paint the moment, what colors would I use?
If a movie were to be made of the moment, what background music would I choose?
Why do I like or dislike thinking about that moment?

Thoughtful answers to such questions may start the flow of any number of ideas to be included in your essay.

f. *Narrowing the focus.* Spend part of your warm-up time searching for the point, or focus of your essay. Identifying the subject isn't enough. Now you must focus on what you'll say about the subject. Many well-meaning essay writers have adhered closely to CBEST topics, but their pieces had no point. For instance, they told of a personal experience with a handicapped child or of their fondness for good old professor Jones, but after reading their essays, the best a reader could say was that the writers had told "about" the child or "about" Professor Jones. They neglected to focus on how their work with little Sarah taught them not to become too emotionally attached to their students, or to explain how the cynicism of Professor Jones persuaded them to teach in high school rather than college.

Prefer a sharp focus to a broad one, for you can't include everything in a short essay. Concentrate on one moment, one idea, one main point. Quickly set your limits and define them. If you don't, you could run out of time, not to mention space, before you're half finished.

Topic #2 sets the limits for you. It specially tells you to write about "moments" of insight rather than about protracted periods of growth. There's a lesson here: small is better!

Franny's Focused Essay

Revelation at the Beach

Some people claim a heightened sense of awareness while taking a shower, staring at a blazing hearth, or jogging.

Not I. My moments of revelation come mostly at the water's edge. The breezy salt air, the cool sand under my feet and the brush of surf upon the shore must release some special hormone in me that opens my brain to new ideas and insights.

I was sitting on the beach on a cloudy summer day a few years ago, for example, when I was struck with the thought that I should probably be a teacher. The thought didn't just come to me out of the blue but was inspired by a conversation I had with a little boy, about ten years old, who was walking along and asked me if I'd heard about the dead man they found washed up about a mile down the beach. I hadn't, so I was curious to know more.

The boy and I began to talk. Why do drowned men pop back up to the surface and float ashore, the boy asked me. An interesting question, I thought. It had never occurred to me to wonder why dead bodies didn't just stay put down among the fishes.

"I don't know," I said, "but I can tell you why floating things come ashore."

So I began to tell him about the wind and the waves, the tides and phases of the moon, the shape of the earth and the oceans of the world. One thought just seemed to lead directly into another. All the while, the boy seemed fascinated by my explanations, his dark eyes wide with the wonder of it all.

"How come you know all that?" he asked.

I then told him about how I had grown up with boats, how my father and I used to sail together almost every chance we had, and that knowledge of the water was just something I acquired, just as a child on a farm knows about animals and a city child learns the subway system.

When it came time to go, the boy told me how much fun it had been to talk to me. I said that I had fun too. Walking home, it struck me that I had just had a "teaching experience." I was good at it, and it was most enjoyable. If that is what teaching is like, I thought, why not spend more time at it. One could do worse things with one's life.

g. *Outlining.* Blessed are those writers with a distinct plan for getting from the beginning to the end—before they write their first word. Most writers, though, start more tentatively, knowing their general direction, but uncovering their specific route as they write. Because of the time limit on the CBEST, it's probably a good idea to plan your route as accurately as you can, taking special care to avoid time-consuming trips down side roads.

Some sort of outline is likely to help you plan. An outline is no more than a list of matters you plan to write about, arranged more or less in order. It can be elaborately constructed, with Roman numerals and A's, B's, C's, and so forth—although you may squander precious time building a formal outline during the CBEST—or better, it can be a variation of the formula for the widely used five-paragraph essay. *The Formula* is a simple, clearcut plan for turning a muddle of ideas into a model of clarity. Each part has its place and purpose:

The Formula

Title	
Introduction	
Body	Point 1 Point 2 Point 3
Conclusion	

In the *introduction,* writers lead up to what they plan to say. In the *body,* they say it. In the *conclusion*, they recall for their readers what they have said.

Notice, too, that the body consists of three points, each of which may be developed in a separate paragraph. Three is a good number to aim for, although it's not essential. Why three? Mainly because it's a number that works. If you can make three statements about a subject, you probably know what you're talking about. One is too simple, two is still pretty shallow, but three is thoughtful. Psychologically, three creates a sense of wholeness, like a complete story with a beginning, middle, and end. Each point, though, doesn't necessarily receive equal treatment. You might manage one point with a single paragraph, while others get more. But each point has to be distinctive. Your third point must not be a reworded version of your first or second.

There is no such thing as the "best" way to arrange your ideas. Order depends on the purpose of the piece. In stories, events are often arranged chronologically. But in persuasive essays, arguments, explanations, definitions, and descriptions, a different order is needed. Random order, unless you're very lucky, usually doesn't work. Therefore, rank your ideas in order of importance. Although your first idea may be your best, save it for last. Giving it away too soon will make all that follows anticlimactic. In other words, work toward your best point, not away from it. If you have three main points to make, start with your second best, and plug in your least favorite between the other two.

Franny's CBEST essay, "Revelation at the Beach," follows the formula. Whether Franny deliberately divided the body of the essay into three distinct points is impossible to say. The point, however, is that Franny's essay, which is generally clear, interesting, and correctly written, falls naturally into three parts and leaves readers with a sense that the essay is complete and that in telling about the experience on the beach, Franny has said neither too much nor too little.

Franny uses The Formula

Title		– Revelation at the Beach
Introduction		– moments of insight
Body	Point 1	– meeting the boy on the beach
	Point 2	– what we talked about
	Point 3	– taking leave
Conclusion		– what I learned from the experience

h. *Defining Your Main Idea.* At some point in the process of writing your essay, be sure to pause for a moment and say to yourself. "The point of my essay is. . . ." Complete the statement with one clear, straightforward, declarative sentence. If it takes more than a single statement, perhaps your main idea is too fuzzy. You may be trying to say more than you have time for, or the main point isn't yet clear to you. If you're not sure of your own main idea, you can bet that your readers won't understand it either.

Also, make sure that your main idea is an *idea,* not just a subject. The subject of Franny's essay is what happened at the beach. The main idea of the essay, however, is a complete statement: A chance encounter at the beach helped me decide to become a teacher.

After you've declared you main idea, try to say what each part of the essay adds to the whole. If any part won't contribute, discard it. All the pieces of the essay, when added together, should equal the whole.

Composing the Essay

There's usually no clearcut boundary between prewriting and composing. One stage of the writing process flows seamlessly into the next. As you compose you're apt to shuffle ideas, fine tune the focus, and change the route you had in mind at the start. Making too many changes, thought, might lead you into a labyrinth of confusion and leave you with no time to set things straight again. So if you can, try to be as faithful as possible to the essay you've planned. In half an hour you don't have the luxury of changing your mind too often.

As you set words on paper, be ever mindful of basic essay-writing principles. You probably adhere to these principles in most of your writing, anyway, but perhaps a quick refresher will give a boost to your preparation for the test.

Let's say you're going to write on the following topic:

Topic # 3:

Growing numbers of college students are choosing "practical" majors that seem directly related to career skills, majors such as business administration and computer science. At the same time, the numbers of students majoring in fields such as philosophy, English, and history are dwindling. Imagine that you are a department chairperson attending a meeting of other chairpeople, all of whom will present a statement about which academic major is most valuable for students. Prepare a statement of your position on this subject.

Base the statement that you write on these elementary principles:

a. Use paragraphs to develop your ideas.

b. Use a hook to catch the reader's interest.

c. Wrap up your essay with an appealing conclusion.

d. Use a natural voice.

e. Unify your piece with transitions.

a. *Use paragraphs to develop your ideas.* How many? Three to six paragraphs ought to be enough, but the number depends on what you have to say about the subject. Usually one or two won't be enough. It often takes more to crack open an idea.

Paragraphs serve as an aid to readers. The indentation is a signal to readers to get ready for a change in thought, somewhat like a directional blinker telling other drivers that you're about to turn. Yet, not every new paragraph signals a drastic change. You may simply want to move the essay ahead one step at a time, and paragraphs illuminate each step.

Whether readers skim the paragraphs or slog doggedly through every word, they need to find sentences now and then that, like landmarks, help them know where they are. Such guiding sentences differ from others because they define each paragraph's main topic. Hence the name *topic sentence.*

Not every paragraph contains a topic sentence. The topic of some paragraphs is so obvious that to state it would be redundant. Then, too, groups of paragraphs can be so closely knit that one topic sentence states the most important idea for all of them.

An acceptable response to Topic #3 might contain five paragraphs: An introductory paragraph, three paragraphs of development—each citing a different reason to defend your choice of the most valuable academic major—and a concluding paragraph.

To be sure, other perfectly good responses to the topic could be written in two or even ten paragraphs. No rule governs every possibility. Your sense of what readers need in order to follow your ideas must guide you.

b. *Use a hook to catch the readers' interest.* The opening of an essay should grab your readers' attention. Once you've got them, you can lead readers anywhere, but first you need a "hook" to pull them past the opening lines—a phrase, sentence, or idea that will entice them to read the next sentences almost in spite of themselves. CBEST readers force themselves to read essays because their job description says they have to. Make them read your essays because they want to—because they know from your opening lines that your essays are worth postponement of a coffee break.

Hooks that surprise, inform, or tickle readers come in a variety of shapes:

1. Start with an incident, real or imaginary, that leads directly into the point of your essay.

In a recent survey, college graduates were asked to identify their heroes, men and women of thought and action from both the past and present. The most frequently mentioned person turned out to be Lee Iacocco. He showed up far more often that Martin Luther King, Mother Theresa, Thomas Jefferson, and Jesus Christ.

2. State some facts about the topic to show its importance or timeliness.

During the last few years, several studies of higher education have been published. Although each study had a different focus and intent, each came to the same overwhelming conclusion: The quality of American undergraduate education leaves a lot to be desired!

3. Identify your subject—but not with an announcement like, "I am going to write about the most valuable academic major." An example such as this is more graceful and just as informative:

This afternoon, ladies and gentlemen, I am going to settle the perennial argument once and for all. I am going to tell you which academic major is the most valuable for our students.

4. Knock down a commonly held belief or assumption.

The ownership of a college degree, despite rumors to the contrary, does not certify that its owner can think creatively, write a decent paragraph, figure out alternative solutions to problems, or even know how to find answers to simple factual questions.

5. Ask a few pithy questions which you'll answer in your essay.

In the year 2010, what will our country need more: physicians or marketing experts? Social workers or bankers? Teachers or computer technicians? Writers or farmers?

6. Address your readers directly, as though you're having a conversation with them.

Have you noticed that more and more of our brightest students are shying away from our college's hardest courses?

In any selection of essays you'd probably find several other worthy techniques for writing an attractive opening. If you find yourself groping for a suitable hook as you begin to write your CBEST essays, don't put off writing the rest. Chances are that an idea will hit you as you compose the body of your essays. In fact, many essayists save their openings for last, writing them only after they've reread their work and figured out exactly what their essays say.

c. *Wrap up your essay with an appealing conclusion.* When you reach the end, you can lift your pen off the page and be done with it, or you can present your readers with a little gift—something to remember you by. A gift can be an idea to think about, a line to chuckle over, a memorable phrase or quotation. The best gifts often tie the ending of an essay to its opening, recalling for readers where it all began. Whatever you give, however, the gift must fit the content, style, and mood of your essay.

You have probably read enough stories and essays to know what endings sound like, what lends a sense of completeness to a piece of writing. For example when you tell readers how an unresolved issue was settled, or when you begin to speculate on what might occur in the future, readers know that an ending is at hand.

Even commonly used endings can bring any essay to a stylish resolution, as these examples show.

1. Show that you have a sense of humor. Even though your topic may be serious, readers always appreciate a lift at the end—provided, of course, that your humor is appropriate.

   Let's restore the original meaning to the word "gut." Let it be associated with the entrails of a cat or a chicken, not with the courses at our college.

2. End with an apt quotation drawn either from the essay itself or from elsewhere.

   Or, as Ogden Nash once said:
   "Farewell, farewell to my beloved language,
   Once English, now a vile orangutanguage."

3. Finish with a clear restatement of your essay's main point, using new words. Add a short tag line, perhaps.

   The student is discovering his own self and learning how to relate it to other selves. That is why we have to keep educational formalities to a minimum. The quality of the college experience rests ultimately on a series of individual responses of one person to another—whether in books or face to face. And that is the heart of the matter.

4. Bring the readers up to date or project them into the future.

   If we follow the course I've outlined in these remarks, the tree of knowledge will continue to bloom at this college.

Some essays don't need an extended conclusion. When they're over, they're over. But even a short conclusion is better than none at all. At the end, readers should feel as though they've arrived somewhere. Above all, though, avoid the summary ending. Trust your readers to remember the substance of your 250–400 words. To say it all again borders on being an insult to the readers' intelligence.

d. *Use a natural voice.* Do you know what you sound like on paper? Even though written words are silent, readers "hear" the voice behind the words. True, they won't hear your pitch or pronunciation, but they'll "hear" your personality.

Very often, test-takers hide their voices in words that portray someone else. They think, for instance, that in order to impress readers, they ought to sound clever or cute, sophisticated or scholarly, when they write. So they imitate people who are clever, cute, sophisticated, or scholarly. By using someone else's voice, though, they end up sounding unlike themselves—in short, sounding false or pretentious.

For virtually any CBEST essay, a natural, conversational style will be appropriate. You can be formal or informal—and still sound natural. You can be imaginative, humorous, ironical, cynical, worldly, earnest—any way at all, in fact, as long as you sound like you. So don't imitate. Let your genuine voice ring out.

That doesn't mean, of course, that you need to pepper your paper with pop expressions or use the sloppy half-formed sentences of conversation. Instead, think of your writing as the natural speech of someone who speaks well or the kind of speech you would use during a friendly talk with a professor you don't know well but whose literature course you want to take.

Here's a terrific idea phrased in extremely formal language: "The acquisition of knowledge needs no formal justification: Its true sanction is a much simpler affair, and inherent in itself."

Most modern Americans don't write like that. Those who do have practiced for years to sound cultivated without sounding pretentious. Unless you have successfully mastered that style of writing, stick to more casual, colloquial phrasing: Pursue knowledge for its own sake. No other justification is necessary. That sounds natural, more akin to everyday speech.

e. *Unify your piece with transitions.* You'll help your readers navigate through your piece and give your writing a sense of unity by choosing words that set up relationships between ideas. This can be done with words like *this*, which ties the sentence you are now reading, for example, to the previous one. Fortunately, English is supplied with an abundance of words and phrases for linking ideas to each other:

When you ADD ideas: moreover, in addition, further, besides, also, and then, then too, again, next, secondly, equally important...
When you make a CONTRAST: however, conversely, in contrast, on the other hand, on the contrary, but, nevertheless, and yet, still, even so...
When you make a COMPARISON or draw a PARALLEL: similarly, likewise, in comparison, in like manner...
When you give an EXAMPLE: for example, for instance...
When you show RESULTS: as a result, as a consequence, consequently, therefore, thus, hence, accordingly...
When you REINFORCE an idea: indeed, in fact, as a matter of fact, to be sure, of course, in any event, by all means...
When you express SEQUENCE or the passing of TIME: soon after, then, previously, meanwhile, in the meantime, later, at length, immediately, next...
When you show PLACES: here, nearby, at this spot, near at hand, in this vicinity, on the opposite side, across from, adjacent to...
When you CONCLUDE: finally, in short, in other words, in a word, to sum up, in conclusion, in the end...

Each time you link one sentence to another with a transitional word or phrase, you're doing a good turn for your readers. You're assuring them of a smooth trip through your writing. Without such help, or when every sentence stands like a disconnected link in a chain, readers bump along and often lose the point you're making.

Links between sentences lend a hand to writers, too. They help writers stick to the topic. Ideas that don't connect with others around them probably should be moved or thrown out.

Here's an essay written in response to Topic #3. Notice how the writer adheres to the principles of effective essay writing.

A brief hook asks the crucial question. It shows that the writer understands the topic.

Which is the most important major? The question would stump King Solomon.

The tone is conversational. The writer seems to be aware of the audience.

Many transitional words and phrases—at the start of each paragraph as well as between sentences: e.g., *after all, yet, for example, in like manner, but*

Since I represent the English faculty of this college, you probably expect me to proclaim that the study of language and literature is the most important major. The arguments in support of such a pronouncement are no doubt well-known to all of you. After all, our ability to use words, to voice and record our thoughts and emotions, to establish relationships, to report our history, to conduct commerce, to create works of literature—all these and more spring from our use of language. Our language separates us from the beasts and makes us unique in the universe, as far as we know.

Essay has three main paragraphs:
1. Importance of language
2. The need for other majors.
3. Need to improve *all* the majors. (Main point! —saved for last.)

Yet, language without something worthwhile to say, is language misused. Without the sciences, the humanities, the histories and the mathematics, we would be left with a language without substance. We could grunt at each other, as our ancestors did, but all the good things of the modern world would not exist. For example, in a world without at least a rudimentary understanding of physics, buildings would topple, engines would not exist, electricity would be unknown, our lives would be dominated by superstition. We would be primitives all, hunting and gathering our food, making crude tools, no better off than creatures of the stone age.

All paragraphs have a main idea supported by details and examples.

The writer attempts to identify the "most important major," acknowledges futility, and offers a thoughtful alternative.

In like manner, our world would be a far different place without chemistry, mathematics, the social sciences, biology, the fine and performing arts, engineering and all the other disciplines that students choose at this college. In truth, then, to identify the most important major is an impossibility. We need them all. A more important question is how we can make every major a greater challenge, a more exciting quest for important knowledge, a subject of study to help all of our students fulfill their potential as human beings. But that's the subject of another essay.

Language may be a bit grandiose in places, but it's consistent with alleged speaker—an English department head.

Conclusion ("gift") leaves the reader thinking about the future.

295 words—a reasonable length.

Revising and Proofreading

Use the few minutes remaining before time runs out to reread your essay. Although you won't have enough space or time to perform major surgery—shifting paragraphs or refocusing your paper, for example—you should be able to improve the style quickly and painlessly, first by cutting out needless words and second, by injecting active, lively verbs into your prose.

Brevity Works Best. Never use two words when one will do. Readers want to be told quickly and directly what you have to say. Otherwise they'll lose interest. Exercise your crossing-out muscles.

You should work through all of the sentences you've written by examining each one for words you don't really need. The sentence you just read contains 20 words. It could be stated more economically this way: *Examine every sentence and cross out all the extra words* (10 words). In fact, it could be trimmed still further: *Cut unneeded words out of every sentence* (7 words).

In lean writing every word counts. One missing word distorts or changes meaning. To trim fat, be tough on your sentences. Wring them through this three-step workout.

a. *Combine sentences*

FAT: We've heard that students are no longer interested in the humanistic studies. Instead, they are worried about their vocational plans for the future and career training (26 words).

LEAN: We've heard that students are more concerned about vocations and careers than about humanities (14 words).

b. *Look for telltale words like which, who, that, thing, and all.*
FAT: Edison was a man *who* was obsessed by the wonders of electricity (12).
LEAN: Edison was obsessed by the wonders of electricity (8).
FAT: The *thing* that most graduates lack is a sense of history (11).
LEAN: Most graduates lack a sense of history (7).

c. *Search for phrases that add words but no meaning.* Trim such phrases as *the fact that* and *due to the fact that*
FAT: The college was under pressure due to the fact more than half of its varsity football players failed to graduate (20).
LEAN: The college was under pressure because more than half of its varsity football players failed to graduate (17).

Other Fat Phrases	Lean
at this point in time	now
what I mean is...	I mean
on account of	because
as a result of	because
in the final analysis	finally
few and far between	few
each and every one	each
this is a subject that...	this subject
ten in number	ten
at the age of six years old	at age six
most unique	unique
true fact	fact
in regard to, with regard to, in relation to with reference to	about

After you have pared your sentences to the bone, reread them and try to trim still further. Be tough, even though it hurts to take out what you worked hard to put in. For the effort, your writing will be stronger, more readable, and more interesting.

Inject Life With Active Verbs. Writers need active verbs to excite reader interest. Active verbs perform, get up, and move around. They surpass all other words in their power to enliven a piece of writing. They add energy and vitality to sentences and also enable writers to cut unneeded words.

In contrast, being verbs (*is, are, was, were,* etc.) are still and stagnant. They don't do anything except join one part of a sentence to another. Because being verbs show no action, use active verbs whenever you can.

a. *Extract verbs from other words in the sentence.*
DEAD: My uncle was a teacher of history for 26 years.
Extract the verb "taught" from the noun "teacher."
ALIVE: My uncle taught history for 26 years.
DEAD: Physical education has been an appealing major to athletes.
Extract the verb "appeals" from the adjective "appealing."
ALIVE: Majoring in physical education appeals to athletes.

b. *Substitute altogether fresh verbs.*
DEAD: In the public's eyes, it is silly for a student to major in recreation.
ALIVE: The public scorns students who major in recreation.

Because being verbs occur so often in everyday language, writers sometimes can't avoid using them. Nor should you try to discard them altogether because frequently no other words will do. Be stingy with being verbs, though. If you find that more than one of every three sentences you write contains a being verb, you may be using too many. If you substitute active verbs, your writing will acquire life and vitality.

Proofreading. Do not hand in your essays without proofreading them first. If time permits, read your essays slowly, once for their sense and once for mechanics. Ideally, you should give them three or four more readings, each time trying to catch errors of a different sort: grammar, punctuation, and spelling. Read them a line at a time, keeping a hawklike watch on every letter, word, and mark of punctuation. To help you concentrate, you might use a spare piece of paper to cover everything but the line you are working on. Read the line forward and then back. On the backward reading you'll lose the sense of the meaning, allowing you to keep your mind on the spelling.

Pay particular attention to words that sound alike but take different spellings: *there, their,* and *they're; its* and *it's; to, two,* and *too.* Also such words as *principal* and *principle, stationery* and *stationary; weather* and *whether;* and the dozens of other homonyms that trap unwary writers. Watch out also for commonly misspelled demons like *a lot, all right, already, separate, doesn't, should've,* and of course, *eleemosynary!*

Grammar and Usage

This section contains a concise review of the basic rules of grammar and usage for standard written English. It is divided into three sections: Essentials, Common Problems, and Punctuation.

Grammar and Usage: The Essentials

The Parts of Speech

1. **Nouns** are words that name or designate persons, places, things, states, or qualities. *John Jones, Africa, book,* and *justice* are examples of nouns.
2. **Pronouns** are words used in place of nouns. *He, we, them, who, which, this, what, each, everyone,* and *myself* are examples of pronouns.
3. **Verbs** are words or phrases that express action or state of being. *Eat, memorize, believe, feel,* and *seem* are examples of verbs.
4. **Adjectives** are words that serve as modifiers of nouns. *Famous, attractive, tall,* and *devoted* are examples of adjectives.
5. **Adverbs** are words that modify verbs, adjectives, or other adverbs. *Too, very, happily,* and *quietly* are examples of adverbs.
6. **Prepositions** are words used with nouns or pronouns to form phrases. *From, with, between, of,* and *to* are examples of prepositions.
7. **Conjunctions** are words that serve to connect words, phrases, and clauses. *And, but, when,* and *because* are examples of conjunctions.
8. **Articles** are the words *the, a,* and *an.* These words serve to identify as a noun the word that they modify.
9. **Interjections** are grammatically independent words or expressions. *Alas, wow,* and *oh my* are examples of interjections.

NOUNS

Nouns are inflected; that is, they change in form to indicate number and case. *Number* refers to the distinction between singular and plural; *case* refers to the way in which a noun is related to other elements in the sentence.

Number

Nouns are either singular or plural. To form the plural of a noun:

1. Add *s* to the singular.
girl / girls — house / houses

2. Add *es* when the noun ends in *s, x, z, ch,* or *sh.*
dish / dishes — church / churches

3. Add *s* when the noun ends in *o* preceded by a vowel.
folio / folios — trio / trios

4. Add *es* when the noun ends in *o* preceded by a consonant.
tomato / tomatoes — potato / potatoes
(Exceptions to this rule: *contraltos, pianos, provisos, dynamos, Eskimos, sopranos.*)

5. Add *s* to nouns ending in *f* or *fe* after changing these letters to *ve.*
knife / knives — shelf / shelves
(Exceptions to this rule: *chiefs, dwarfs, griefs, reefs, roofs, safes.*)

6. Add *s* to nouns ending in *y* preceded by a vowel.
boy / boys — valley / valleys

7. Add *es* to nouns ending in *y* preceded by a consonant and change the *y* to *i.*
baby / babies — story / stories

8. Add *s* to the important part of a hyphenated word.
brother-in-law / brothers-in-law — passer-by / passers-by

9. Add *s* or *es* to proper nouns.
Frank / Franks — Smith / Smiths
Jones / Joneses — Charles / Charleses
(Note that the apostrophe (') is not used.)

10. Add *s* or *es* to either the title or the proper noun when both are mentioned.
Doctor Brown / Doctors Brown or Doctor Browns
Miss Smith / Misses Smith or Miss Smiths

11. Add *'s* to form the plural of letters, numerals and symbols.
e / e's — 9 / 9's
etc. / etc.'s — & / &'s

12. Change to a different form in the following cases:

foot / feet	tooth / teeth
goose / geese	woman / women
louse / lice	child / children
man / men	ox / oxen

13. Retain the foreign form with some words of foreign origin.

alumna / alumnae	focus / foci
alumnus / alumni	genus / genera
analysis / analyses	hypothesis / hypotheses
antithesis / antitheses	larva / larvae
bacillus / bacilli	matrix / matrices
bacterium / bacteria	monsieur / messieurs
basis / bases	oasis / oases
crisis / crises	parenthesis / parentheses
criterion / criteria	thesis / theses
erratum / errata	trousseau / trousseaux

Case

Nouns are also inflected to show possession. The possessive case of nouns is formed in the following manner:

1. If the noun ends in *s*, add an apostrophe (').

2. If the noun does not end in *s*, add an apostrophe (') and an *s*.
   The doctor's office (The office of the doctor)
   The doctors' office (The office of two or more doctors)
   The girl's books (The books of one girl)
   The girls' books (The books of two or more girls)

Note that in nouns of one syllable ending in *s*, either the apostrophe or the apostrophe and an *s* may be used.

James' hat and James's hat are both correct.

A noun preceding a gerund should be in the possessive case. (A gerund is a verb form—a verbal—that is used as a noun: Slicing raw onions made him cry.)

Incorrect: The teacher complained about John talking.
Correct: The teacher complained about John's talking.

PRONOUNS

Pronouns are classified as *personal, relative, interrogative, demonstrative, indefinite, intensive,* or *reflexive.*

Personal Pronouns

Personal pronouns indicate the person speaking, the person spoken to, or the person spoken about. They are inflected to indicate case and number. In the third person, they also indicate gender. *He* is the masculine pronoun, *she* is the feminine pronoun, and *it* is the neuter or common gender pronoun.

The *First Person*
(the person speaking or writing)

Case	*Singular*	*Plural*
Nominative	I	we
Possessive	my, mine	our, ours
Objective	me	us

The *Second Person*
(the person spoken or written to)

Case	*Singular*	*Plural*
Nominative	you	you
Possessive	your, yours	your, yours
Objective	you	you

The *Third Person*
(the person, place, or thing spoken or written about)

Third Person Masculine

Case	*Singular*	*Plural*
Nominative	he	they
Possessive	his	their, theirs
Objective	him	them

Third Person Feminine

Case	*Singular*	*Plural*
Nominative	she	they
Possessive	her, hers	their, theirs
Objective	her	them

Third Person Neuter

Case	*Singular*	*Plural*
Nominative	it	they
Possessive	its	their, theirs
Objective	it	them

Relative Pronouns

The relative pronouns are *who, which,* and *that.* They are used to relate a word in the independent clause (see the section on clauses later in this chapter) to a dependent clause. *Who* is used to refer to persons, *which* to things, and *that* to both persons and things. Like the personal pronouns, *who* has different forms according to case:

Case	*Singular*	*Plural*
Nominative	who	who
Possessive	whose	whose
Objective	whom	whom

Interrogative Pronouns

The interrogative pronouns are *who, which,* and *what.* They are used to ask questions. *Which* and *what* do not change according to case. *Who* follows the forms listed under "Relative Pronouns."

Demonstrative Pronouns

The demonstrative pronouns are *this, that, these,* and *those.* They serve to point out people, places, and things. The plural of *this* is *these*; the plural of *that* is *those.*

Indefinite Pronouns

The indefinite pronouns include *all, anyone, each, either, everyone, somebody, someone, whatever, whoever.* The objective case of *whoever* is *whomever*; all the other indefinite pronouns have the same form in the nominative and objective cases. The possessive case of any indefinite pronoun is formed by adding *'s: everyone's, somebody's.*

Intensive and Reflexive Pronouns

Intensive pronouns are used to intensify or emphasize a noun or pronoun.

I myself did it.

Reflexive pronouns refer back to the subject of the sentence.

I taught myself.

The intensive and reflexive pronouns have the same singular and plural forms:

Person	*Singular*	*Plural*
First	myself	ourselves
Second	yourself	yourselves
Third	himself	themselves
	herself	themselves

Some Problems Involving Pronouns

The major grammatical problems concerning pronouns involve agreement and case. These are discussed in the following section.

An intensive pronoun should not be used without the noun or pronoun to which it refers.

Incorrect: Herself baked the cake.
Correct: Mary herself baked the cake.

Like nouns, a pronoun preceding a gerund should be in the possessive case.

Incorrect: She objected to me going out too late.
Correct: She objected to my going out too late.

VERBS

Conjugation of Verbs

Verbs change their forms to indicate person, number, tense, mood, and voice. The various changes involved are indicated when the verb is *conjugated*. In order to conjugate a verb, its *principal parts* must be known.

Principal Parts of *to talk*

Infinite: *to talk*
Present tense: *talk*
Present participle: *talking*
Past tense: *talked*
Past participle: *talked*

When the principal parts of a verb are listed, the infinitive and the present participle are often omitted.

CONJUGATION OF THE REGULAR VERB *TO CARRY*
(principal parts: *carry, carried, carried*)

Indicative Mood—Active Voice

Present Tense

Singular	*Plural*
I carry	We carry
You carry	You carry
He, she, it carries	They carry

Past Tense

Singular	*Plural*
I carried	We carried
You carried	You carried
He, she, it carried	They carried

Future Tense

Singular	*Plural*
I shall (will) carry*	We shall (will) carry*
You will carry	You will carry
He, she, it will carry	They will carry

Present Perfect Tense

Singular	*Plural*
I have carried	We have carried
You have carried	You have carried
He, she, it has carried	They have carried

Past Perfect Tense

Singular	*Plural*
I had carried	We had carried
You had carried	You had carried
He, she, it had carried	They had carried

Future Perfect Tense

Singular	*Plural*
I shall (will) have carried*	We shall (will) have carried*
You will have carried	You will have carried
He, she, it will have carried	They will have carried

* Some traditional grammarians assert that only the auxiliary verb *shall* is correct in the first person when simple future or future perfect meaning is intended. Most modern writers and grammarians do not accept this distinction, however, and *I will* may be regarded as equally correct.

Indicative Mood—Passive Voice

Present Tense

Singular	*Plural*
I am carried	We are carried
You are carried	You are carried
He, she, it is carried	They are carried

Past Tense

Singular	*Plural*
I was carried	We were carried
You were carried	You were carried
He, she, it was carried	They were carried

Future Tense

Singular	*Plural*
I shall (will) be carried*	We shall (will) be carried*
You will be carried	You will be carried
He, she, it will be carried	They will be carried

Present Perfect Tense

Singular	*Plural*
I have been carried	We have been carried
You have been carried	You have been carried
He, she, it has been carried	They have been carried

Past Perfect Tense

Singular	*Plural*
I had been carried	We had been carried
You had been carried	You had been carried
He, she, it had been carried	They had been carried

Future Perfect Tense

Singular	*Plural*
I shall (will) have been carried*	We shall (will) have been carried*
You will have been carried	You will have been carried
He, she, it will have been carried	They will have been carried

Subjunctive Mood—Active Voice

Present Tense

Singular	*Plural*
If I, you, he carry	If we, you, they carry

Past Tense

Singular	*Plural*
If I, you, he carried	If we, you, they carried

Subjunctive Mood—Passive Voice

Present Tense

Singular	*Plural*
If I, you, he be carried	If we, you, they be carried

Past Tense

Singular	*Plural*
If I, you, he were carried	If we, you, they were carried

Imperative Mood—Present Tense

Carry!

Note that most verbs form the past and past participle forms by adding *ed* to the present tense. Verbs ending in *y* preceded by a consonant (like *carry*) change the *y* to *i* before adding *ed*. Verbs ending in *e* (like *raise*) add *d* only.

Verbs that do not follow these rules are called *irregular*. The principal parts of the most common irregular verbs follow; when two or more forms are given, the first form is preferred.

PRINCIPAL PARTS OF IRREGULAR VERBS

Present Tense	*Past Tense*	*Past Participle*
arise	arose	arisen
awake	awoke, awaked	awaked, awoke, awoken
bear	bore	borne, born
beat	beat	beaten, beat
befall	befell	befallen
begin	began	begun
bend	bent	bent
bid (command)	bade	bidden
bid (make an offer)	bid	bid
bind	bound	bound
blow	blew	blown
break	broke	broken
bring	brought	brought
broadcast	broadcast, broadcasted	broadcast, broadcasted
build	built	built
burst	burst	burst
buy	bought	bought
cast	cast	cast
catch	caught	caught
choose	chose	chosen
cling	clung	clung
come	came	come
creep	crept	crept
deal	dealt	dealt
dive	dived, dove	dived
do	did	done
draw	drew	drawn
drink	drank	drunk
drive	drove	driven
eat	ate	eaten
fall	fell	fallen
feed	fed	fed
feel	felt	felt
fight	fought	fought
find	found	found
flee	fled	fled
fling	flung	flung
fly	flew	flown
forbear	forbore	forborne
forbid	forbade, forbad	forbidden
forget	forgot	forgotten, forgot
forgive	forgave	forgiven
forsake	forsook	forsaken
freeze	froze	frozen
get	got	got, gotten
give	gave	given

Present Tense	*Past Tense*	*Past Participle*
go	went	gone
grow	grew	grown
hang (an object)	hung	hung
hang (a person)	hanged	hanged
have	had	had
hit	hit	hit
hold	held	held
kneel	knelt, kneeled	knelt, kneeled
know	knew	known
lay	laid	laid
lead	led	led
leave	left	left
lend	lent	lent
lie	lay	lain
lose	lost	lost
make	made	made
meet	met	met
put	put	put
read	read	read
ring	rang	rung
rise	rose	risen
run	ran	run
see	saw	seen
seek	sought	sought
sell	sold	sold
send	sent	sent
set	set	set
shine	shone	shone
shrink	shrank, shrunk	shrunk, shrunken
sing	sang	sung
sink	sank	sunk
slay	slew	slain
sit	sat	sat
sleep	slept	slept
slide	slid	slid
sling	slung	slung
slink	slunk	slunk
speak	spoke	spoken
spring	sprang, sprung	sprung
steal	stole	stolen
stick	stuck	stuck
sting	stung	stung
stride	strode	stridden
strike	struck	struck
swear	swore	sworn
sweat	sweat, sweated	sweated, sweat
sweep	swept	swept
swim	swam	swum
swing	swung	swung
take	took	taken
teach	taught	taught
tear	tore	torn
telecast	telecast, telecasted	telecast, telecasted

Present Tense	*Past Tense*	*Past Participle*
tell	told	told
think	thought	thought
thrive	throve, thrived	thriven, thrived
throw	threw	thrown
wake	waked, woke	waked, woken, woke
wear	wore	worn
weep	wept	wept
win	won	won
wind	wound	wound
work	worked, wrought	worked, wrought
wring	wrung	wrung
write	wrote	written

How the Verb Tenses Are Used

In addition to the six tenses listed in the typical conjugation shown before (of the verb *to carry*), there are *progressive* and *intensive* forms for some of the tenses. These will be discussed as we consider the uses of each tense.

The present tense indicates that the action or state of being defined by the verb is occurring at the time of speaking or writing.

I plan to vote for the incumbent.

The present tense is used to state a general rule.

Honesty is the best policy.

The present tense is used to refer to artistic works of the past or to artists of the past whose work is still in existence.

Michelangelo is one of Italy's most famous artists.

The present tense is used to tell the story of a fictional work.

In *Gone with the Wind*, Rhett Butler finally realizes that Scarlett O'Hara is unworthy of his love.

The progressive form of the present tense (a combination of the present tense of the verb *to be* and the present participle) indicates prolonged action or state of being.

I am thinking about the future.
You are flirting with disaster.
He is courting my sister.
We are planning a trip to Yosemite National Park.
They are being stubborn.

The intensive form of the present tense (a combination of the verb *to do* and the infinitive) creates emphasis.

He does care.
We do intend to stay.

The past tense is used to indicate that an event occurred in a specific time in the past and that the event is completed.

I lived in New York in 1979.
I lived in that house for six years. (I no longer live there.)

The progressive form of the past tense combines the past tense of *to be* and the present participle. It indicates prolonged past action or state of being.

I, he, she, it was playing.
We, you, they were going.

The intensive form of the past tense combines the past tense of *to do* and the infinitive. It creates emphasis.

I did know the answer to the question.

The future tense makes a statement about a future event. As indicated in the conjugation of the verb *to carry,* traditional grammarians distinguish between the use of *shall* and *will* in the future tense. According to this rule, the simple future uses *shall* in the first person and *will* in the second and third persons.

I, we shall go.
You, he, they will go.

To show determination, promise, or command, *will* is used in the first person and *shall* in the second and third persons.

I will pay this bill on Friday.
You, he, they shall comply with this order.

However, most contemporary grammarians accept the use of *shall* and *will* interchangeably in the future tense.

The progressive form of the future tense combines the future tense of *to be* and the present participle.

I shall be wearing a white jacket.
He will be going with my brother.

The present perfect tense combines the present tense of *to have* and the past participle.

I have gone.
He has eaten his breakfast.

Whereas the past tense refers to a definite time in the past, the present perfect tense indicates that the event is perfected or completed at the present time.

The present perfect tense is also used to indicate that the event began in the past and is continuing into the present.

He has attended Yale University for three years. (He is still attending Yale.)

The progressive form of the present perfect tense combines the present perfect tense of *to be* and the present participle.

He has been complaining about a pain in his side for some time.

The past perfect tense is formed by combining the past participle of the verb and the past tense of the verb *to have*. It describes an event which was completely perfected at a definite time in the past. Its major use is to indicate that one event occurred before another in the past.

By the time the firemen arrived, the boys had extinguished the blaze. (The fire was put out before the firemen came.)

The progressive form of the past perfect tense is formed by combining the present participle of the verb and the past perfect tense of *to be*.

I had been holding this package for you for three weeks.

The future perfect tense is formed by combining the past participle of the verb and the future tense of the verb *to have*. It indicates that a future event will be completed before a definite time in the future.

By one in the afternoon, he will have finished his lunch and will have returned to the office.

The progressive form of the future perfect tense is formed by combining the present participle of the verb and the future perfect tense of *to be*.

They will have been swimming all afternoon.

Kinds of Verbs

Transitive verbs are verbs that require an object. The object is the receiver of the action.

He hit the boy. (The object boy has been hit.)
I received a letter. (The object letter has been received.)

Intransitive verbs do not require an object.
She is walking.

Copulative verbs are intransitive verbs with the special quality of connecting the subject to a noun, pronoun, or adjective. The most common copulative verb is *to be*.
Mr. Jones is the teacher.
It is I.

(In these two sentences, teacher and I are called predicate nominatives.)
The man is rich.
The actress is beautiful.

(Rich and beautiful are predicate adjectives.)

Predicate nominatives and predicate adjectives are normally called predicate complements because they complete the thought of the copulative verb. The predicate nominative represents the same person or thing as the subject of the verb *to be* and is in the nominative case.
He is the teacher.
The teacher is he.

The predicate adjective is connected to the subject by the copulative verb. The description, the *lame horse*, becomes a statement or sentence when the copulative verb is used as follows:
The horse is lame.

The other copulative verbs are *appear, become, feel, get, grow, look, seem, smell, sound*, and *taste*. These verbs should be followed by predicate adjectives.
This tastes good.
I feel sad.
This sounds too loud.
I became ill.

Be careful to distinguish between transitive and intransitive verbs. Words like *lie* and *lay, sit* and *set, rise* and *raise* often give students trouble.

1. *Lie* is an intransitive verb, meaning "to rest or recline." Its principal parts are *lie, lay, lain.*
   Lay is transitive and means "to place down." Its principal parts are *lay, laid, laid.*
   Incorrect: I lay the book on the table.
   Correct: I laid the book on the table.
   Incorrect: Because I am tired, I am going to lay down.
   Correct: Because I am tired, I am going to lie down.

2. *Sit* is intransitive. Its principal parts are *sit, sat, sat.*
   Set may be either transitive or intransitive. Its principal parts are *set, set, set.*
   Incorrect: I am going to sit this tripod on the floor.
   Correct: I am going to set this tripod on the floor (Transitive).
   Correct: The sun is going to set at 5:42 P.M. (Intransitive).

3. *Rise*, meaning "to come up," in intransitive. Its principal parts are *rise, rose, risen.*
   Raise, meaning "to lift up," is transitive. Its principal parts are *raise, raised, raised.*
   Incorrect: The delta lowlands were in danger of being flooded when the sea raised by three feet.
   Correct: The delta lowlands were in danger of being flooded when the sea rose by three feet.

Voice and Mood

Voice is a characteristic of transitive verbs. In the **active voice**, the subject is the doer of the action stated by the verb, and the object of the verb is the receiver of the action.
John caught the ball. (John is doing the catching and the ball is being caught.)

In the **passive voice**, the receiver of the action is the subject. The doer of the action may be identified by using a phrase beginning with *by*.
The ball was caught.
The ball was caught by John.

Some writers prefer the active voice and object to the use of the passive. However, both voices have their virtues and neither should be regarded as incorrect.

It is inadvisable to switch from one voice to the other in the same sentence.

Undesirable: The outfielder raced toward the wall and the ball was caught.
Preferable: The outfielder raced toward the wall and caught the ball.

Mood is used to indicate the intentions of the writer.

The **indicative mood** makes a statement or asks a question.

I wrote you a letter.
When did you mail it?

The **imperative mood** commands, directs, or requests.

Go home!
Make a left turn at the stop light.
Please talk more slowly.

The **subjunctive mood** is used when the writer desires to express a wish or a condition contrary to fact.

I wish I were able to go with you.
(I am not able to go.)
If he were less of a bore, people would invite him to their homes more frequently.
(He is a bore.)

It is also used after a verb which expresses a command or a request.

The governor has ordered that all pay increases be deferred.
She demanded that he leave immediately.

Verbals

The infinitive, present participle, and past participle are called non-finite verbs, or **verbals**. These forms of the verb cannot function as verbs without an auxiliary word or words.

Running is not a verb.
Am running, have been running, shall be running are verbs.
Broken is not a verb.
Is broken, had been broken, may be broken are verbs.

The **infinitive** (the verb preceded by *to*) is used chiefly as a noun. Occasionally, it may serve as an adjective or an adverb.

John wants to go to the movies. (To go to the movies is the object of wants. It serves as a noun.)
I have miles to go before I sleep. (To go modifies miles. It serves as an adjective.)
To be honest, we almost lost the battle. (To be honest modifies the rest of the sentence. It serves as an adverb.)

The **present participle** usually serves as an adjective.

Flying colors
Singing waiters
Dancing waters
(In each case, the participle modifies the noun it precedes.)
Writing on the blackboard, the scientist presented his arguments in favor of his thesis.
(Writing on the blackboard is a participial phrase modifying scientist.)

The present participle may also serve as a noun. When it does so, it is called a **gerund**.

Jogging is good exercise.
Dieting to lose weight requires discipline.

A noun or pronoun preceding a gerund should be in the possessive case.

My talking to Mary annoyed the teacher.
We were frightened by Helen's fainting.

The **past participle** serves as an adjective.

Broken homes
Fallen arches
Pained expressions

ADJECTIVES

Adjectives are words that limit or describe nouns and pronouns.

Three men
The fourth quarter
(Three and fourth limit the words they precede.)
A pretty girl (Pretty describes the word it precedes.)
A daring young man (Daring is a participle used as an adjective, and describes man; young describes man.)

Adjectives usually precede the word they limit or describe. However, for emphasis the adjective may follow the word it modifies.

One nation, indivisible

Adjectives are often formed from nouns by adding suffixes such as *-al*, *-ish*, *-ly*, and *-ous*.

Noun	*Adjective*
fiction	fictional
girl	girlish
friend	friendly
joy	joyous

Predicate adjectives are adjectives that follow the copulative verbs *be, appear, become, feel, get, grow, look, seem, smell, sound,* and *taste*. These adjectives follow the verb and refer to its subject.

The man is tall. (A tall man)
The lady looks beautiful. (A beautiful lady)

Adjectives are inflected; that is, they change form to indicate degree of comparison: *positive, comparative,* or *superlative*. The *positive degree* indicates the basic form without reference to any other object. The *comparative degree* is used to compare two objects. The *superlative degree* is used to compare three or more objects. Usually, *er* or *r* is added to the positive to form the comparative degree, *est* or *st* to form the superlative. Some adjectives of two syllables and all adjectives longer than two syllables use *more* (or *less*) to form the comparative degree and *most* (or *least*) to form the superlative.

Positive	*Comparative*	*Superlative*
tall	taller	tallest
pretty	prettier	prettiest
handsome	more handsome	most handsome
expensive	less expensive	least expensive

A few adjectives have irregular comparative and superlative forms. These include:

Positive	*Comparative*	*Superlative*
good	better	best
bad	worse	worst
ill	worse	worst

ADVERBS

Adverbs are words that modify verbs, adjectives, or other adverbs.

He spoke sincerely. (Sincerely modifies spoke.)

Almost any person can afford this kind of vacation. (Almost modifies the adjective any.)

He spoke very sincerely. (Very modifies the adverb sincerely.)

Most adverbs end in *ly* (*angrily, stupidly, honestly*). However, some adjectives also end in *ly* (*manly, womanly, holy, saintly*). Some commonly used words have the same form for the adjective and the adverb. These include *early, far, fast, hard, high, late, little, loud, quick, right, slow,* and *well.*

Adjective	*Adverb*
The *early* bird	He left *early.*
A *far* cry	You have gone too *far.*
He is a *fast* worker.	Don't go so *fast.*
This is *hard* to do.	He slapped him *hard.*
A *high* voice	Put it *high* on the agenda.
A *late* bloomer	He arrived *late.*
Men of *little* faith	He is a *little* late.
A *loud* explosion	He spoke *loud.*
A *quick* step	Think *quick.*
The *right* decision	Do it *right.*
A *slow* worker	Drive *slow.*
All is *well.*	He was *well* prepared.

Adverbs, like adjectives, change form to show comparison. The comparative degree uses the word *more* (or *less*); the superlative degree, the word *most* (or *least*). *Badly* and *well* have irregular comparative forms.

Positive	*Comparative*	*Superlative*
quickly	more quickly	most quickly
rapidly	less rapidly	least rapidly
badly	worse	worst
well	better	best

PREPOSITIONS

Prepositions are words that combine with nouns, pronouns, and noun substantives to form phrases that act as adverbs, adjectives, or nouns.

I arrived at ten o'clock. (Adverbial phrase)

The man with the broken arm. (Adjective phrase)

The shout came from outside the house. (Noun phrase acting as object of *from*)

The most common prepositions are:

about	behind	during	on	to
above	below	except	out	touching
after	beneath	excepting	over	toward
against	beside	for	past	under
along	besides	from	round	underneath
amid	between	in	save	up
among	beyond	into	since	with
around	but	notwithstanding	through	within
at	by	of	throughout	without
before	down	off	till	

Some verbs call for the use of specific prepositions. See the list of Idiomatic Expressions on page 125.

CONJUNCTIONS

Conjunctions are connecting words that join words, phrases, and clauses. There are two kinds of conjunctions:

Coordinating conjunctions connect words, phrases, and clauses of equal rank. They are *and, but, or, nor, for, whereas,* and *yet.* Pairs of words like *either . . . or, neither . . . nor, both . . . and, not only . . . but also* are a special kind of coordinating conjunction called *correlative conjunctions.*

Subordinating conjunctions connect dependent clauses to independent clauses. Some of the more common subordinating conjunctions are *although, as, because, if, since, so than, though, till, unless, until, whether,* and *while.* Also, when the relative pronouns *who, which, that* introduce a dependent clause, they act as subordinating conjunctions.

Independent and dependent clauses are discussed in the section on Sentence Sense later in this chapter.

ARTICLES

The three most frequently used adjectives—*a, an,* and *the*—are called **articles**. The *definite article* is *the.* The *indefinite articles* are *a* and *an. A* is used before a word beginning with a consonant sound. *An* is used before a word beginning with a vowel sound.

A bright light
An auspicious beginning
An RCA television set
A humble beginning (the h sound is pronounced)
An hour ago (the h sound is omitted)

INTERJECTIONS

Interjections are words that express emotion and have no grammatical relation to the other words in the sentence.

Alas, I am disconsolate.
Wow! This is exciting!
Eureka! I have found it.

Sentence Sense

The ability to write complete sentences without error is characteristic of a student who has mastered standard written English. Failure to write in complete sentences is a major weakness of students whose written compositions are considered unsatisfactory.

A sentence may be defined as a group of words that contains a subject and a predicate, expresses a complete thought, and ends with a period (.), a question mark (?), or an exclamation point (!).

The sentence must contain a finite verb that makes the statement or asks the question.

The soldiers fought a battle.
Halt!
Where are you going?
The students have gone home.
I have been thinking about your offer.
Why have you been making this accusation?
Who will take your place?

(The verbs in the preceding sentences are *fought, halt, are going, have gone, have been thinking, have been making,* and *will take.*)

The forms of the verb that are not finite are the *infinitive*, the *participle*, and the *gerund*. These three forms cannot act as finite verbs.

Clauses

A clause is a group of words containing a subject and a verb. There are two kinds of clauses:

Main clauses (also called **principal** or **independent clauses**): A main clause does not modify anything; it can stand alone as a sentence.

I went to the theater.
I failed my spelling test.

A sentence containing one main clause is called a *simple sentence*.

A sentence containing two or more main clauses is called a *compound sentence*. The clauses must be connected by a coordinating conjunction or by a semicolon (;).

I went to the theater and I saw a good production of *Hamlet*.
You must pass this test, or you will be suspended from the team.
Four boys played tennis; the rest went swimming.

Subordinate clauses (also called **dependent clauses**): A subordinate clause cannot stand alone; to be a good sentence, it must always accompany a main clause. A sentence containing a main clause and one or more subordinate clauses is called a *complex sentence*. If the subordinate clause modifies a noun or pronoun, it is called an *adjective clause*. If it modifies a verb, it is an *adverb clause* or an *adverbial clause*. A clause that acts as the subject or the object of a verb or as the object of a preposition is called a *noun clause*.

The book that is on the table belongs to my sister. (The clause <u>that is on the table</u> is an adjective clause because it modifies the noun <u>book</u>.)
She quit school because she had to go to work. (The clause <u>because she had to go to work</u> is an adverbial clause because it modifies the verb <u>quit</u>.)
I asked what the teacher did. (<u>What the teacher did</u> is a noun clause because it is the object of the verb <u>asked</u>.)
Give this medal to whoever comes in first. (<u>Whoever comes in first</u> is a noun clause because it is the object of the preposition <u>to</u>.)

Phrases

A phrase is a group of words that lacks a subject and a predicate and acts as a unit. A phrase cannot serve as a complete sentence. These are the common types of phrases:

Prepositional phrases are introduced by a preposition and act as adjectives or adverbs.

This is an overt act <u>of war</u>. (<u>Of war</u> is an adjective phrase modifying <u>act</u>.)
Please come <u>at 10:00 A.M.</u> (<u>At 10:00 A.M.</u> is an adverbial phrase modifying <u>come</u>.)

Participial phrases are introduced by a participle and are used as adjectives to modify nouns and pronouns.

Fighting his way through tacklers, he crossed the goal line. (<u>Fighting his way through tacklers</u> is a present participial phrase modifying the pronoun <u>he</u>.)
Sung by this gifted artist, the words were especially stirring. (<u>Sung by this gifted artist</u> is a past participial phrase modifying the noun <u>words</u>.)

Gerund phrases are introduced by a gerund and are used as nouns.

Smoking cigarettes is harmful to one's health. (<u>Smoking cigarettes</u> is a gerund phrase used as the subject of the verb <u>is</u>.)

Infinitive phrases are introduced by the infinitive form of the verb, usually preceded by *to*. They are used as nouns, adjectives, and adverbs.

To win a decisive victory is our goal. (To win a decisive victory is an infinitive phrase used as the subject of the verb is.)
I have a dress to alter. (To alter is an infinitive modifying the noun dress.)
The ice is too soft to skate on. (To skate on is an infinitive modifying the adjective soft.)

Grammarians disagree about the interpretation of sentences like *I want him to buy a suit.* Some regard *him to buy a suit* as an infinitive clause with *him* the subject of the infinitive *to buy.* Others regard *him* as the object of the verb *want* and *to buy a suit* as an infinitive phrase acting as an objective complement. No matter how the sentence is interpreted, *him* is correct.

Common Problems in Grammar and Usage

Common Problems in Grammar

SENTENCE FRAGMENTS

A sentence fragment occurs when a phrase or a dependent clause is incorrectly used as a sentence. Examples of sentence fragments and ways of correcting them follow:

1. When he walked into the room.
2. Apologizing for his behavior.
3. To discuss the problem amicably.
4. In our discussion of the problem.
5. Or yield to their demands.

In Example 1, we have a dependent clause used as a sentence. To correct, either remove the subordinating conjunction *when* or add an independent clause.
He walked into the room.
When he walked into the room, we yelled "Surprise."

In Example 2, we have a participial or gerund phrase used as a sentence. To correct, either change the phrase to a subject and a verb or add an independent clause.
He apologized for his behavior.
Apologizing for his behavior, he tried to atone for the embarrassment he had caused.

In Example 3, we have an infinitive phrase. To change this phrase to a complete sentence, either change the infinitive to a finite verb and add a subject, or add a subject and verb that will make a complete thought.
We discussed the problem amicably.
It is advisable to discuss the problem amicably.

In Example 4, we have a prepositional phrase. To correct this fragmentary sentence, add an independent clause to which it can relate.
We failed to consider the public's reaction in our discussion of the problem.

In Example 5, we have part of a compound predicate. To correct this, combine it with the other part of the compound predicate in a single complete sentence.
We must fight this aggressive act or yield to their demands.

PRACTICE

Correct the following sentence fragments, following the methods of correction shown for Example 1.
When she gave birth to her baby.

____

____

Although I like ice cream.

____

____

Correct the following sentence fragments, following the correction patterns shown for Example 2.

Substituting for the starting pitcher.

____

____

Expecting to go to the party.

____

____

Correct the following sentence fragments, following the correction patterns shown for Example 3.

To remodel the kitchen completely.

____

____

To apologize to his father.

____

____

Correct the following sentence fragments, following the correction pattern shown for Example 4.

In our enthusiasm for the team's victory.

____

____

At the conclusion of the history lesson.

____

____

Correct the following sentence fragments, following the correction pattern shown for Example 5.

Or pay a cleaning deposit.

____

____

And save our money for a new car.

____

____

RUN-ON SENTENCES

The run-on sentence has been given many different names by grammarians, including the *comma fault* sentence or *comma splice* sentence, and the *fused* sentence.

The jurors examined the evidence, they found the defendant guilty. (Comma fault sentence)
It is very cloudy I think it is going to rain. (Fused sentence)

The *comma fault* or *comma splice* sentence may be defined as a sentence in which two independent clauses are improperly connected by a comma. The first example given is an illustration of the comma fault sentence. The *fused* sentence consists of two sentences that run together without any distinguishing punctuation. The second example illustrates this kind of error.

Any of four methods may be used to correct run-on sentences:

1. Use a period at the end of the first independent clause instead of a comma. Begin the second independent clause with a capital letter.
   The jurors examined the evidence. They found the defendant guilty.
   It is very cloudy. I think it is going to rain.

2. Connect the two independent clauses by using a coordinating conjunction.
   The jurors examined the evidence, and they found the defendant guilty.
   It is very cloudy, and I think it is going to rain.
3. Use a semicolon between two main clauses not connected by a coordinating conjunction.
   The jurors examined the evidence; they found the defendant guilty.
   It is very cloudy; I think it is going to rain.
4. Use a subordinating conjunction to make one of the independent clauses dependent on the other.
   When the jurors examined the evidence, they found the defendant guilty.
   Because it is very cloudy, I think it is going to rain.

PRACTICE

Correct each of the following run-on sentences, using all four of the methods just shown.

The organist played the wedding march, the bride came down the aisle.

1. ____________________

2. ____________________

3. ____________________

4. ____________________

It is getting very late I had better go to bed.

1. ____________________

2. ____________________

3. ____________________

4. ____________________

(It is important to master method 4; if you are able to combine independent clauses in this way, you will be able to vary sentence structure and add interest to your paragraphs.)

PROBLEMS WITH AGREEMENT

Problems with agreement generally involve a violation of one of the two basic rules governing agreement.

Rule I: A verb and its subject must agree in person and number. A singular verb must have a singular subject; a plural verb must have a plural subject.

If you examine the conjugation of the verb *to carry* on pages 156, you will observe that this rule applies only to the present and present perfect tenses. The other tenses use the same form for each of the three persons and with both singular and plural subjects. Therefore, an error in agreement cannot occur in any tense other than the present or present perfect tense, with the exception of the verb *to be*. The past tense of *to be* is:

Person	*Singular*	*Plural*
First	I was	We were
Second	You were	You were
Third	He, she, it was	They were

Rule I concerning agreement is simple and easy to remember. However, you should note the following:

1. The verb does *not* agree with the modifier of the subject or with a parenthetical expression introduced by *as well as, with, together with*, or a similar phrase.
   The father of the children is going to work. (The subject of the singular verb is going is the singular noun father. Children is part of the prepositional phrase of the children, which modifies father.)
   The pupils as well as the teacher are going to the zoo. (The subject of the plural verb are going is the plural noun pupils. Teacher is part of the parenthetical expression as well as the teacher. This parenthetical expression is not the subject.)

2. A plural verb is used with a compound subject (two or more nouns or pronouns connected by *and*).
   John and his friends are going camping.
   John and Mary are planning a party.
   However, when the compound subject can be considered as a single unit or entity, regard it as singular and follow it with a singular verb.
   "Jack and Jill" is a popular nursery rhyme.
   Bacon and eggs is one of the most popular breakfast dishes in America.

3. Collective nouns like *team, committee, jury, gang, class, army*, and so on are usually regarded as singular nouns.
   The team is practicing for the big game.
   The Revolutionary Army was at Valley Forge.
   When a collective noun is used to refer to the *individual members* of the group, it is considered a plural noun.
   The jury were unable to reach a verdict. (The individual jurors could not come to a decision.)

4. The words *billiards, economics, linguistics, mathematics, measles, mumps, news* and *physics* are considered singular nouns.
   Billiards is a game of skill.
   Mathematics is my most difficult subject.

5. The words *barracks, glasses, insignia, odds, pliers, scissors, tactics, tongs, trousers*, and *wages* are considered plural nouns.
   These barracks have been empty for some time.
   My glasses are fogged; I cannot see clearly.

6. The words *acoustics, ethics, gymnastics, politics*, and *statistics* are singular when they refer to specific fields of study or activity. They are plural at all other times.
   Ethics is part of our Humanities program.
   His ethics are questionable.

7. Names of organizations and titles of books and shows are singular.
   The Canterbury Tales was written by Chaucer.
   The United States now has a national debt that approaches a trillion dollars.

8. In a sentence beginning with *there* or *here*, the subject of the verb *follows* the verb in the sentence.
   There are many reasons for his failure. (Reasons is the subject of the plural verb are.)
   Here is my suggestion. (Suggestion is the subject of the singular verb is.)

9. The words *anybody, anyone, each, either, every, everyone, everybody, neither, nobody, no one*, and *someone* are regarded as singular and require a singular verb.
   Anyone of the students is welcome.
   Each of the songs he sang was memorable.
   Either of the two choices is satisfactory.
   Nobody in her classes likes her.

No one is going.
Someone in this group is a liar.

10. The words *few, many,* and *several* are regarded as plural and require a plural verb.
Many are called, but few are chosen.
Several have already been disqualified by the lawyers.

11. The expressions *the number* and *the variety* are regarded as singular and require a singular verb.
The number of people able to meet in this room is limited by the Fire Department.
The variety of food presented at this buffet is beyond imagination.

12. The expressions *a number* and *a variety* are regarded as plural and require a plural verb.
A number of new cases of malaria have been reported to the Health Department.
A variety of disturbances in the neighborhood have alarmed the homeowners.

13. *Either* and *neither* are regarded as singular (see item 9). However, when *either* or *neither* is coupled with *or* or *nor*, a different rule applies. In these sentences, the verb agrees with the noun or pronoun that follows the word *or* or *nor.*
Either Mary or John is eligible.
Either Mary or her sisters are mistaken.
Neither Harry nor you are eligible.
Neither you nor I was invited.

14. When using the copulative verb *to be,* be sure to make the verb agree with the subject and not with the predicate complement.
Our greatest problem is excessive taxes.
Excessive taxes are our greatest problem.

PRACTICE

Correct each of the following errors in agreement in accordance with the examples just shown.

1. The leader of the apes are swinging through the trees.

____

____

The child as well as the parents are affected by a divorce.

____

____

2. Lassie and her pups is chasing rabbits.

____

____

"Frankie and Johnny" are a love song.

____

____

3. The committee are meeting on Tuesday.

____

____

The Latin class are studying Caesar.

____

____

4. Mumps are a dangerous disease.

____

____

Economics are a complete mystery to me.

5. My trousers is wrinkled; I need the iron.

His tactics was too outmoded for modern warfare.

6. Statistics are a field worth studying.

Their statistics is incorrect.

7. *Star Wars* were directed by George Lucas.

Pacific Gas & Electricity have sent me a bill.

8. Here is my answers to the question.

9. No one of the counselors are able to advise you.

Neither of the clerks want to wait on him.

Everybody from our office are going to the party.

10. Several of the class has handed in the exercise.

Many is unemployed, but few is getting unemployment insurance.

11. The variety of grammatical errors possible are countless.

The number of students taking the test are increasing.

12. A number of bad riots has troubled the city.

A variety of attempts to remedy the situation was made.

13. Either the mayor or the city manager are in charge.

Either the teacher or his students is correct.

Neither David nor you is welcome.

Neither you nor I were elected.

14. A storekeeper's greatest worry are bad checks.

Bad checks is a storekeeper's greatest worry.

Rule II: A pronoun must agree with its antecedent in person, number, and gender. (The antecedent is the noun or pronoun to which the pronoun refers.)

The detectives arrested Mrs. Brown as she entered the building. (The antecedent Mrs. Brown is a third person singular feminine noun; she is the third person singular feminine pronoun.)

Rule II concerning agreement is also easy to remember. However, watch out for these potentially troublesome points:

1. When the antecedent is an indefinite singular pronoun (*any, anybody, anyone, each, either, every, everybody, everyone, nobody, no one, somebody,* or *someone*), the pronoun should be singular.
   Everybody on the ship went to his cabin to get his life jacket.
   Neither of the girls is writing her thesis.
2. When the antecedent is compound (two or more nouns or pronouns connected by *and*), the pronoun should be plural.
   Mary and Jane like their new school.
3. When the antecedent is part of an *either . . . or* or *neither . . . nor* statement, the pronoun should agree with the nearer antecedent.
   Either John or Henry will invite Mary to his home. (Henry is closer to his.)
   Neither the seller nor the buyers have submitted their final offers. (Buyers is closer to their.)
   Neither the buyers nor the seller has submitted his final offer. (Seller is closer to his.)

   Note: in some sentences, Rules I and II are combined.
   John is one of the boys who (is, are) trying out for the team. (In this sentence, the antecedent of who is boys, a third person plural noun. The verb should be are because are is the third person plural verb.)

PRACTICE

Correct each of the following errors in agreement in accordance with the examples just shown.

1. Everybody in the class went to their desk to get their essay.

Neither of the teachers is correcting their tests.

2. Bob and Sue remodeled her new home.

3. Either John or Tom will donate their ball to the team.

Neither the students nor the teacher has picked up their tickets to the concert.

PROBLEMS WITH CASE

Nouns and pronouns have three cases:

The **nominative case** indicates that the noun or pronoun is being used as the subject of a verb, or as a word in apposition to the subject, or as a predicate nominative.

John is the batter. (John is in the nominative case, since it is the subject of the verb is.)
Jane, my younger sister, attends elementary school. (Sister is in the nominative case because it is in apposition with Jane, the subject of the verb attends.)
Mrs. Brown is the teacher. (Teacher is the predicate nominative of the verb is.)
The culprit is he. (He is the predicate nominative of the verb is.)

The **possessive case** indicates possession.

I broke Mary's doll.
John did not do his homework.

The **objective case** indicates that the noun or pronoun is the object (receives the action) of a transitive verb, a verbal, or a preposition.

John hit her. (Her is the object of the verb hit.)
Practicing the violin can be boring at times. (Violin is the object of the participle practicing.)
Please come with me. (Me is the object of the preposition with.)

Some special rules concerning case:

1. The subject of an infinitive is in the objective case.
   I want him to go. (Him is the subject of the infinitive to go.)
   I told her to stop talking. (Her is the subject of the infinitive to stop.)
2. The predicate nominative of the infinitive *to be* is in the objective case.
   I want the leader to be him. (Him is the predicate complement of the infinitive to be.)
3. Nouns and pronouns used as parts of the compound subject of a verb are in the nominative case.
   Mary and he are going to the party. (The two parts of the compound subject, Mary and he, are both in the nominative case.)
   John and we are friends. (John and we, the two parts of the compound subject of the verb are, are both in the nominative case.)
4. Nouns and pronouns used as parts of the compound object of a verb, a verbal, or a preposition are in the objective case.
   I met Mary and him at the party. (Mary and him are the objects of the verb met.)
   Seeing Mary and him at the party was a treat. (Mary and him are the objects of the gerund seeing.)
   Take the food to him and her. (Him and her are objects of the preposition to.)

5. A noun or pronoun immediately preceding a gerund is in the possessive case.
John's talking during the lesson was rude. (John's immediately precedes the gerund talking.)
John was afraid that his speaking in class would be reported to his father. (His immediately precedes the gerund speaking.)

6. In sentences using the conjunctions *as* or *than* to make comparisons, the clause following *as* or *than* is often truncated. Such clauses are called *elliptical clauses.* In these sentences, the case of the noun or pronouns following the conjunction is based on its use in the elliptical clause.
Mary is as tall as he. (The complete sentence is Mary is as tall as he is tall. The nominative case is used because he is the subject of the verb is.)
The twins are older than I. (The complete sentence is The twins are older than I am old. The nominative case is used because I is the subject of the verb am.)

7. The case of the relative pronouns *who, whoever,* and *whosoever* is determined by their use in the clause in which they belong.
Whom are you talking to? (The objective case is used because whom is the object of the preposition to.)
Whom did you take them to be? (The objective case is used because whom is the predicate complement of the infinitive to be.)
Give this book to whomever it belongs. (The objective case is used because whomever is the object of the preposition to.)
Give this award to whoever has earned it. (The nominative case is used because whoever is the subject of the verb has earned. In this sentence, the object of the preposition to is the noun clause whoever has earned it.)

PRACTICE

Correct each of the following errors in case in accordance with the examples just shown.

1. He asked she to go dancing.

____

2. I want the leading lady to be she.

____

3. Alice and him are going to get married.

____

Judy and me are roommates.

____

4. I saw she and Stan at the restaurant.

____

Give the ice cream to Vicki and I.

____

5. Toby leaving work early left us short-handed.

____

6. John is as bright as me.

____

Susan is brighter than me.

____

7. Who is he speaking to?

____

Who did you think them to be?

____

Give this coat to whoever it fits.

____

Give this kitten to whomever wants it.

____

PROBLEMS WITH REFERENCE OF PRONOUNS

Since pronouns are words used in place of nouns, the words they refer to should be clear to the reader or speaker. Vagueness or ambiguity can be avoided by observing the following rules:

1. The pronoun should refer to only one antecedent.
Vague: The captain asked him to polish his boots. (Whose boots are to be polished?)
Clear: The captain said, "Polish your boots." The captain said, "Polish my boots."

2. The antecedent of the pronoun should be a single noun and not a general statement. The pronouns most often affected by this rule are *it, this, that,* and *which.*
Vague: The ship was pitching and tossing in the heavy seas, and it made me seasick. (It refers to the entire clause that precedes the pronoun.)
Clear: The pitching and tossing of the ship in the heavy seas made me seasick. (Combine the two clauses in order to eliminate the pronoun.)
Clear: The ship was pitching and tossing in the heavy seas, and this motion made me seasick. (Replace the vague pronoun with a noun preceded by this, that, or which.)
Vague: When the teacher walked into the room, the students were shouting, which made her very angry. (Which refers to the entire clause rather than to a single noun.)
Clear: When the teacher walked into the room, the students' shouting angered her.
Clear: When the teacher walked into the room, the students were shouting. This lack of control angered her. (A sentence has been substituted for the vague pronoun.)

3. The antecedent of the pronoun should be stated, not merely implied in the sentence.
Vague: My accountant has been taking classes at law school, but he does not intend to become one. (One what?)
Clear: My accountant has been taking classes at law school, but he does not intend to become a lawyer.

PRACTICE

Correct each of the following errors in pronoun reference in accordance with the examples just shown.

1. The hostess asked her to finish her dessert.

____

____

2. The cafeteria was filthy, and it made me lose my appetite.

____

____

3. My son has been studying the violin, but he doesn't want to be one.

____

____

PROBLEMS INVOLVING VERBS

Sequence of Tenses

In this section, we will discuss five errors in tense that can occur when two or more verbs are used in the same sentence. The following are examples of these errors:

1. When I called him, he doesn't answer the phone.

2. At the present time, I attended John Adams High School for two years.
3. Our attorney already presented our proposition to the Planning Commission by the time I arrived.
4. I hoped to have won first prize in the contest.
5. We had ought to pay our respects.

In Example 1, we have one verb in the past tense and another in the present tense. Since the actions described by both verbs have occurred or are occurring at the same time, the tenses of the two verbs should be the same:

When I called him, he didn't answer the phone. (Both verbs are in the past tense.)
When I call him, he doesn't answer the phone. (Both verbs are in the present tense.)

Example 2 confuses the use of the past and present perfect tenses. As stated in the section on Verbs in this chapter, the past tense should be used to indicate action completed in the past. The present perfect tense should be used to indicate action begun in the past and carried into the present. The phrase *At the present time* indicates that the speaker is still attending high school. Therefore, the present perfect tense is required:

At the present time, I have attended John Adams High School for two years.

Example 3 exemplifies the need for the past perfect tense. Two events are mentioned in this sentence. To differentiate between the time when the attorney spoke and the time when the speaker arrived, the past perfect tense should be used for the event that occurred first:

Our attorney had already presented our proposition to the Planning Commission by the time I arrived.

Example 4 is an example of the use of the present and the perfect infinitive. The tense of the infinitive is determined by its relation to the principal verb. At the time specified by the principal verb, *hoped,* the speaker was still expecting *to win.* Therefore, the correct form of the sentence is:

I hoped to win first prize in the contest.

Example 5 uses the expression *had ought,* which is never acceptable. *Ought* is a defective auxiliary verb. It has no other form. Thus the present and past tenses of *ought* are *ought.* The correct form of Example 5 is:

We ought to pay our respects.

PRACTICE

Correct each of the following errors in tense in accordance with the examples just shown.

1. When I asked her, she doesn't come to my party.

___

___

2. At the present time, I studied French for three years.

___

___

3. The life guard already performed artificial respiration by the time the ambulance got there.

___

___

4. I wanted to have found a new job.

___

___

5. We had ought to do our homework.

___

___

Mood

As noted earlier, verbs are conjugated in three moods: indicative, imperative, and subjunctive. Because the subjunctive mood is the least used, many students are not aware of the uses of the subjunctive:

1. The subjunctive mood is used to state a wish or a condition contrary to fact.
   I wish this party were over. (The party is not over.)
   If I were king, I would lower taxes. (I am not king.)
   If he had been elected, he would have served his full term. (He was not elected.)

2. The subjunctive mood is also used after a verb that expresses a command or a request.
   I insist that he pay me today. (Pay is in the subjunctive mood.)
   I ask that this discussion be deferred. (Be deferred is in the subjunctive mood.)

3. The most common error involving the subjunctive is the following:
   If he would have known about the side effects of this medicine, he would not have prescribed it for his patients.
   The expression *would have known* in the subordinate clause is incorrect. The subjunctive should be used:
   If he had known about the side effects of this medicine, he would not have prescribed it for his patients.

PRACTICE

Correct each of the following errors in mood in accordance with the illustrations just shown.

1. If I was President, I would end unemployment.
   ____
   ____
   I wish this Rolls Royce was inexpensive.
   ____
   ____

2. I insist that she gives up marijuana now.
   ____
   ____

3. If I would have heard about the radar trap, I would not have driven so fast on the highway.
   ____
   ____

Voice

In the active voice, the subject of the verb is the doer of the action. In the passive voice, the subject of the verb is the receiver of the action.

Active Voice: The linebacker intercepted the pass.
Passive Voice: The pass was intercepted by the linebacker.

Switching from one voice to the other within a sentence is regarded as an error in style and should be avoided.

Poor: He likes to play chess and playing bridge is also enjoyed by him.
Better: He likes to play chess and he also enjoys playing bridge.

TIP: Avoid Errors in your Essay:

1. Stick to one tense.
   (Give your opinion using the present tense.)
   (Write a summary in the past tense.)
2. Use the active voice.

PROBLEMS INVOLVING MODIFIERS

Unclear Placement of Modifiers

In general, adjectives, adverbs, adjective phrases, adverbial phrases, adjective clauses, and adverbial clauses should be placed close to the word they modify. If these modifiers are separated from the word they modify, confusion may result. Here are some specific rules to apply:

1. The adverbs *only, almost, even, ever, just, merely,* and *scarcely* should be placed next to the word they modify.
   Ambiguous: I almost ate the whole cake. (Did the speaker eat any of the cake?)
   Clear: I ate almost the whole cake.
   Ambiguous: This house only cost $42,000.
   Clear: Only this house cost $42,000. (One house was sold at this price.)
   Clear: This house cost only $42,000. (The price mentioned is considered low.)

2. Phrases should be placed close to the word they modify.
   Unclear: The advertisement stated that a table was wanted by an elderly gentleman with wooden legs. (It is obvious that the advertisement was not written to disclose the gentleman's infirmity.)
   Clear: The advertisement stated that a table with wooden legs was wanted by an elderly gentleman.

3. Adjective clauses should be placed near the words they modify.
   Misplaced: I bought groceries at the Safeway store that cost $29.47.
   Clear: I bought groceries that cost $29.47 at the Safeway store.

4. Words that may modify either a preceding or a following word are called *squinting modifiers.* In order to correct the ambiguity, move the modifier so that its relationship to only one word is clear.
   Squinting: He said that if we refused to leave in two minutes he would call the police.
   Clear: He said that he would call the police if we refused to leave in two minutes.
   Clear: He said that he would call the police in two minutes if we refused to leave.
   Squinting: We agreed on Tuesday to visit him.
   Clear: On Tuesday, we agreed to visit him.
   Clear: We agreed to visit him on Tuesday.

PRACTICE

Clear up the following ambiguous sentences, using the preceding examples as models.

1. I almost drank all the milk.

   ____

   ____

   This station wagon only seats five passengers.

   ____

   ____

2. The report mentioned that a man was wanted for murder with a wooden leg.

   ____

   ____

3. I found a roast at the supermarket that was big enough for eight.

   ____

   ____

4. We promised Mother on Sunday to go to church.

   ____

   ____

Dangling Modifiers

When modifying phrases or clauses precede the main clause of the sentence, good usage requires that they come directly before the subject of the main clause and clearly refer to the subject. Phrases and clauses that do not meet these requirements are called *dangling modifiers*. They seem to refer to a wrong word in the sentence, often with humorous or misleading results.

EXAMPLE 1:

Dangling participle: Walking through Central Park, the Metropolitan Museum of Art was seen. (Is the museum walking?)

Corrected: Walking through Central Park, the tourists saw the Metropolitan Museum of Art. (The participle walking immediately precedes the subject of the main clause tourists.)

EXAMPLE 2:

Dangling gerund phrase: Upon hearing the report that a bomb had been placed in the auditorium, the building was cleared. (Who heard the report?)

Corrected: Upon hearing the report that a bomb had been placed in the auditorium, the police cleared the building.

EXAMPLE 3:

Dangling infinitive phrase: To make a soufflé, eggs must be broken. (Do eggs make a soufflé?)

Corrected: To make a soufflé, you must break some eggs.

EXAMPLE 4:

Dangling elliptical construction: When about to graduate from elementary school, the teacher talked about the problems and joys of junior high school. (Is the teacher graduating?)

Corrected: When we were about to graduate from elementary school, the teacher talked about the problems and joys of junior high school.

PRACTICE

Correct the following dangling modifiers according to the corrections shown in the preceding examples.

1. Driving along the Monterey Peninsula, the cypress trees were beautiful.

____

____

2. On reading the report that cockroaches had been found in the school cafeteria, the kitchen was fumigated.

____

____

____

3. To repair a flat tire, the car must be jacked up.

____

____

4. When about to get married for the fourth time, the minister talked to the divorcee about the holiness of marriage.

____

____

____

PROBLEMS WITH PARALLEL STRUCTURE

Balance in a sentence is obtained when two or more similar ideas are presented in *parallel form*. A noun is matched with a noun, an active verb with an active verb, an adjective with an adjective, a phrase with a phrase. A lack of parallelism weakens the sentence.

EXAMPLE 1:

Not parallel: We are studying mathematics, French, and how to write creatively.

Parallel: We are studying mathematics, French, and creative writing. (All the objects of the verb are studying are nouns.)

EXAMPLE 2:

Not parallel: He told the students to register in his course, to study for the examination, and that they should take the test at the end of January.

Parallel: He told the students to register in his course, to study for the examination, and to take the test at the end of January. (The parallel elements are all infinitives.)

EXAMPLE 3:

Not parallel: The children ate all the candy and the birthday cake was devoured. (The use of the active voice in the first clause and the passive voice in the second clause creates a lack of parallelism.)

Parallel: The children ate all the candy and devoured the birthday cake. (The change in voice has been eliminated. The two verbs ate and devoured are both in the active voice.)

PRACTICE

Following the corrections shown in the preceding examples, correct the following unbalanced sentences to provide the parallel structure they lack.

1. The minister preached about sin, judgment, and how we needed to repent.

____

____

2. She told her husband to mow the lawn, to take out the trash, and that he should do the laundry.

____

____

3. The husband took out the trash, and the lawn was mowed.

____

____

Common Problems in Usage

WORDS OFTEN MISUSED OR CONFUSED

Errors in *diction*—that is, choice of words—often occur in student essays. Here are some of the most common diction errors to watch for.

accept/except. These two words are often confused. *Accept* means to receive; *except,* when used as a verb, means to preclude or exclude. *Except* may also be used as a preposition or a conjunction.

I will accept the award in his absence.

He was excepted from receiving the award because of his record of excessive lateness.

We all received awards except Tom.

affect/effect. *Affect* is a verb meaning (1) to act upon or influence, and (2) to feign or assume. *Effect,* as a verb, means to cause or bring about; as a noun, *effect* means result.

His poor attendance affected his grade.

To cover his embarrassment, he affected an air of nonchalance.

As he assumed office, the newly elected governor promised to effect many needed reforms in the tax structure.

What will be the effect of all this discussion?

aggravate. *Aggravate* means to worsen. It should not be used as a synonym for *annoy* or *irritate.*
You will aggravate your condition if you try to lift heavy weights so soon after your operation.
The teacher was irritated [not aggravated] by the whispering in the room.

ain't. *Ain't* is nonstandard English and should be avoided.

all the farther/all the faster. These are colloquial and regional expressions and so are considered inappropriate in standard English. Use *as far as* or *as fast as* instead.

already/all ready. These expressions are frequently confused. *Already* means previously; *all ready* means completely prepared.
I had already written to him.
The students felt that they were all ready for the examination.

alright. *All right* should be used instead of the misspelling *alright.*

altogether/all together. *All together* means as a group. *Altogether* means entirely, completely.
The teacher waited until the students were all together in the hall before she dismissed them.
There is altogether too much noise in the room.

among/between. *Among* is used when more than two persons or things are being discussed; *between,* when only two persons or things are involved.
The loot was divided among the three robbers.
This is between you and me.

amount/number. *Amount* should be used when referring to mass, bulk, or quantity. *Number* should be used when the quantity can be counted.
I have a large amount of work to do.
A large number of books were destroyed in the fire.

and etc. The *and* is unnecessary. Just write *etc.*

being as/being that. These phrases are nonstandard and should be avoided. Use *since* or *that.*

beside/besides. These words are often confused. *Beside* means alongside of; *besides* means in addition to.
Park your car beside mine.
Who will be at the party besides Mary and John?

between. See *among.*

but what. This phrase should be avoided. Use *that* instead.
Wrong: I cannot believe but what he will not come.
Better: I cannot believe that he will not come.

can't hardly. This phrase is a double negative that borders on the illiterate. Use *can hardly.*

complected. This word is nonstandard and should be avoided. Use *complexioned.*

continual/continuous. These words are used interchangeably by many writers; however, the careful stylist should make the distinction between the two words. *Continual* refers to a sequence that is steady but interrupted from time to time. A child's crying is *continual* because it does stop crying from time to time to catch its breath or to eat or sleep. *Continuous* refers to a passage of time or space that continues uninterruptedly. The roar of the surf at the beach is *continuous.*

could of. This phrase is nonstandard. Use *could have.*

different from/different than. Contemporary usage accepts both forms; however, *different from* remains the preferred choice.

effect. See *affect.*

except. See *accept.*

farther/further. *Farther* should be used when discussing physical or spatial distances; *further,* when discussing quantities.

We have six miles farther to go.

Further discussion will be futile.

fewer/less. *Fewer* should be used with things that can be counted; *less,* with things that are not counted but measured in other ways.

There are fewer pupils in this class than in the other group. (Note that you can count pupils—one pupil, two pupils, and so on.)

You should devote less attention to athletics and more to your studies.

former/latter. Use *former* and *latter* only when you are discussing a series of two. *Former* refers to the first item of the series and *latter* to the second. If you discuss a series of three or more, use *first* and *last.*

Both Judy and Charles are qualified for the position, but I will vote for the former.

Sam, Bob, and Harry invited Mary to the dance, but she decided to go with the first.

further. See *farther.*

had of. This phrase is nonstandard. Use *had.*

hanged/hung. Both words are the past participle of the verb *hang.* However, *hanged* should be used when the execution of a person is being discussed; *hung* when the suspension of an object is discussed.

The convicted murderer was scheduled to be hanged at noon.

When the abstract painting was first exhibited, very few noticed that it had been hung upside down.

healthful/healthy. These two words should not be confused. *Healthful* describes things or conditions that provide health. *Healthy* means in a state of health.

You should eat healthful foods like fresh vegetables, instead of the candy you have just bought.

To be healthy, you need good food, fresh air and sunshine, and plenty of sleep.

imply/infer. These are not synonyms. *Imply* means to suggest or indicate. *Infer* means to draw a conclusion.

Your statement implies that you are convinced of his guilt.

Do not infer from my action in this matter that I will always be this lenient.

in back of. Avoid this expression. Use *behind* in its place.

irregardless. This is nonstandard. Use *regardless* instead.

kind of/sort of. These phrases should not be used as adverbs. Use words like *quite, rather,* or *somewhat* instead.

Undesirable: I was kind of annoyed by her statement.

Preferable: I was quite annoyed by her statement.

last/latter. See *former.*

lay/lie. *Lay,* a transitive verb, means to place; *lie,* an intransitive verb, means to rest or recline. One way of determining whether to use *lay* or *lie* is to examine the sentence. If the verb has an object, use the correct form of *lay.* If the verb has no object, use *lie.*

He laid the book on the table. (Book is the object of the verb. The past tense of lay is correct.)

He has lain motionless for an hour. (The verb has no object. The present perfect tense of lie is correct.)

learn/teach. *Learn* means to get knowledge; *teach,* to impart information or knowledge.

I learned my lesson.

She taught me a valuable lesson.

leave/let. *Leave* means to depart; *let,* to permit.

Incorrect: Leave me go.

Correct: Let me go.

less. See *fewer.*

liable/likely. *Likely* is an expression of probability. *Liable* adds a sense of possible harm or misfortune.
Incorrect: He is liable to hear you.
Correct: He is likely to hear you.
Incorrect: The boy is likely to fall and hurt himself.
Correct: The boy is liable to fall and hurt himself.

lie. See *lay.*

mad/angry. These are not synonyms. Mad means *insane.*

number. See *amount.*

of. Don't substitute *of* for *have* in the expressions *could have, should have, must have,* and so on.

off of. The *of* is superfluous and should be deleted.
Incorrect: I fell off of the ladder.
Correct: I fell off the ladder.

prefer. This verb should not be followed by *than.* Use *to, before,* or *above* instead.
Incorrect: I prefer chocolate than vanilla.
Correct: I prefer chocolate to vanilla.

principal/principle. *Principal,* meaning chief, is mainly an adjective. *Principle,* meaning a rule or basic law, is a noun e.g., a Scientific Principle. In a few cases, *principal* is used as a noun because the noun it once modified has been dropped.
principal of a school (Originally, the principal teacher.)
principal in a bank (Originally, the principal sum.)
a principal in a transaction (Originally, the principal person.)

raise/rise. *Raise* is a transitive verb (takes an object); *rise* is intransitive.
Incorrect: They are rising the prices.
Correct: They are raising the prices.
Incorrect: The sun will raise at 6:22 A.M.
Correct: The sun will rise at 6:22 A.M.

real. This word is an adjective and should not be used as an adverb.
Incorrect: This is a real good story.
Correct: This is a really [or very] good story.

the reason is because. This expression is ungrammatical. The copulative verb *is* should be followed by a noun clause; *because* introduces an adverbial clause.
Incorrect: The reason I was late is because there was a traffic jam.
Correct: The reason I was late is that there was a traffic jam.

same. Do not use *same* as a pronoun. Use *it, them, this, that* in its place.
Incorrect: I have received your letter of inquiry; I will answer same as soon as possible.
Correct: I have received your letter of inquiry; I will answer it as soon as possible.

sort of. See *kind of.*

teach. See *learn.*

try and. This phrase should be avoided. Use *try to* in its place.
Incorrect: I will try and find your book.
Correct: I will try to find your book.

unique. This adjective should not be qualified by *more, most, less,* or *least.*
Incorrect: This was a most unique experience.
Correct: This was a unique experience.

IDIOMATIC EXPRESSIONS

An idiom is a form of expression peculiar to a particular language. Occasionally, idioms seem to violate grammatical rules; however, the common use of these expressions has made them acceptable. Some of the most common idioms in English involve prepositions. The following list indicates which preposition is idiomatically correct to use after each word:

accede to
accuse of
addicted to
adhere to
agreeable to
amazement at
appetite for
appreciation of
aside from
associate with
blame for
capable of
characterized by
compatible with
conversant with
desire for
desirous of
desist from
different from
disagree with
disdain for
dissent from
distaste for
enveloped in
expert in
frugal of
hint at
implicit in
negligent of
oblivious to
observant of
partial to
peculiar to
preview of
prior to
prone to
revel in
separate from
suspect of
tamper with
try to
void of
weary of
willing to

Punctuation for Sentence Sense

Errors in punctuation are noticeable: they stand out. When you write, understanding the effects of various punctuation marks on the meaning and structure of a sentence is likely to be helpful. In this section, we will review the most commonly used punctuation marks and illustrate the ways they should be used.

End Punctuation

THE PERIOD (.)

1. The period is used to indicate the end of a declarative or imperative sentence.
   I am going home.
   Go home.

2. The period is used after initials and abbreviations.
   Mr. J. C. Smith
   John Rose, M.D.

3. The period is *not* used after contractions, initials of governmental agencies, chemical symbols, or radio and television call letters.

can't	HCl	didn't	Sn
IRS	WNBC	FBI	KPIX

4. A series of three periods is used to indicate the fact that material has been omitted from a quotation.
   We, the People of the United States, In Order to form a more perfect union, . . . do ordain and establish this Constitution for the United States of America.

THE QUESTION MARK (?)

1. The question mark is used after a direct question.
   Who is going with you?

2. The question mark should *not* be used when questions appear in indirect discourse.
   He asked whether you would go with him.

3. The question mark should *not* be used when a polite or formal request is made.
   Will you please come with me.

4. The question mark should *not* be used when the question is purely rhetorical (that is, asked only for effect, with no answer expected).
   That's very good, don't you think.

Middle Punctuation

THE COMMA (,)

1. The comma is used to set off nouns in direct address.
   Mr. Smith, please answer this question.
   Tom, come here.

2. The comma is used to set off words or phrases in apposition.
   Mr. Brown, our newly elected sheriff, has promised to enforce the law vigorously.
   Dr. Alexander, my instructor, has written several authoritative books on this topic.

3. The comma is used to set off items in a series.
   I bought milk, eggs, apples, and bread at the store.
   Maine, Vermont, New Hampshire, Massachusetts, Rhode Island, and Connecticut are the states that make up New England.
   The river tumbles down lofty mountains, cuts through miles of prairie land, and finally empties into the Atlantic Ocean.

4. The comma is used to separate the clauses of a compound sentence connected by a coordinating conjunction.
   The bill to reduce taxes was introduced by Congressman Jones, and it was referred to the House Ways and Means Committee for consideration. (Note that the omission of the conjunction and would result in a run-on sentence.)

5. The comma is used to set off long introductory phrases and clauses that precede the main clause.
   In a conciliatory speech to the striking employees, Mr. Brown agreed to meet with their leaders and to consider their complaints.
   Because I was ignorant of the facts in this matter, I was unable to reach a decision.

6. The comma is used to set off unimportant (or *nonrestrictive*) phrases and clauses in a sentence.
   My brother, who is a physician, has invited me to spend Christmas week with him.

7. The comma is used to set off parenthetical words like *first, therefore, however,* and *moreover,* from the rest of the sentence.
   I am, therefore, going to sue you in small claims court.
   More than two inches of rain fell last week; however, this was not enough to fill our reservoirs.

8. The comma is used to set off contrasting, interdependent expressions.
   The bigger they are, the harder they fall.

9. The comma is used to separate adjectives that could be connected by *and.*
   He spoke in a kind, soothing voice.

10. In sentences containing direct quotations, the comma is used to separate introductory words from quoted words.
    Mary said, "I hope you will understand my reasons for doing this to you."

11. The comma may be used to indicate omitted words whose repetition is understood.
    Tall and short are antonyms; rapid and swift, synonyms.

12. The comma is used to separate items in dates, addresses, and geographical names.
    January 5, 1981
    Detroit, Michigan
    My address is 5225 East 28 Street, Brooklyn, New York.

13. The comma is used to follow the salutation in a friendly letter.
    Dear Mary,

14. The comma follows the complimentary close in business and friendly letters.
    Your sincerely,
    Truly yours,

THE SEMICOLON (;)

1. The semicolon is used as a substitute for the comma followed by *and* that connects two independent clauses in a compound sentence.
   Mary won first prize in the contest, and John came in second.
   Mary won first prize in the contest; John came in second.

2. The semicolon is used before *namely, for instance,* and *for example* when they introduce a list.
   Four students were chosen to act as a committee; namely, John, Henry, Frank, and William.

3. When the words *however, nevertheless, furthermore, moreover,* and *therefore* are used to connect two independent clauses, they should be preceded by a semicolon.
   He worked diligently for the award; however, he did not receive it.

4. The semicolon is used to separate items in a list when the items themselves contain commas.
   Among the contributors to the book were Roy O. Billett, Boston University; Lawrence D. Brennan, New York University; Allan Danzig, Lafayette College; and Mario Pei, Columbia University.

THE COLON (:)

1. The colon is used to introduce a list, especially after the words *following* and *as follows.*
   On this tour, you will visit the following countries: England, France, Spain, Italy, Greece, and Israel.

2. The colon is used after the salutation in business letters.
   Dear Sir:
   Dear Dr. Brown:
   To Whom It May Concern:

3. The colon is used when time is indicated in figures.
   Please meet me at 3:30 P.M.

4. The colon is used to indicate ratios.
   2:5 :: 6:15

QUOTATION MARKS (" ")

1. Quotation marks are used to indicate the exact words of a speaker or writer. The introductory words are separated from the quotation by a comma or commas.
   Patrick Henry said, "Give me liberty or give me death."
   "Give me liberty," Patrick Henry said, "or give me death."
   "Give me liberty or give me death," Patrick Henry said.

2. When quotation marks are used, the capitalization of the original quotation should be retained.
   "I have always wanted," John said, "to ride a ten-speed bike." (And small t is used because to was not capitalized in the statement being quoted.)

3. If the quotation is a question, the question mark should appear inside the quotation marks.
   John asked, "When does the party start?"
   "When does the party start?" John asked.

PRACTICE WRITING SAMPLES

This section provides sample topics for practice essays. Allow yourself 30 minutes for each essay. Have an honest critic read and respond to each practice essay you complete.

WRITING SAMPLE TOPIC 1

SAMPLE TOPIC: Your school of education advisor, although he realizes that your primary interest is teaching, wants to know what you would pursue instead of teaching, if choosing an alternative goal becomes necessary. Describe your "alternative interest," and give reasons for your interest.

WRITING SAMPLE TOPIC 2

SAMPLE TOPIC: As state-supported community colleges feel the effects of budget cuts, they are asking students who are state residents to pay tuition, just as out-of-state residents do. These resident students, for whom a college education was once free, are now complaining that even minimal tuition is an unfair burden. Write an article for the college newspaper in which you develop an argument for or against tuition for all community college students.

WRITING SAMPLE TOPIC 3

SAMPLE TOPIC: Faced with budget cuts, your local high school has decided to eliminate competitive sports from its curriculum. The school officials argue that competitive sports have always fostered unhealthy aggression in team members, and they welcome ideas for inexpensive recreational activities in which there are no winners or losers. Write a letter to the school officials responding to their position.

SAMPLE TOPIC: Imagine that your application to a student teaching program has been rejected, and that the only criterion was your CBEST score. Compose a letter to the school explaining strengths of yours that are relevant to success in teaching, but are *not* measured by the CBEST.

WRITING SAMPLE TOPIC 5

SAMPLE TOPIC: Life and literature are filled with examples of men and women who were self-educated. Self-education may be possible today, but schools provide experiences that individuals cannot get on their own. Assume that a fellow student, claiming that schools interfere with education instead of educating, plans to drop out of school. Write an essay that would convince the fellow student to change his or her mind. If you can think of examples from life or literature to support your arguments, use them. Otherwise, write from the standpoint of your own experience.

WRITING SAMPLE TOPIC 6

SAMPLE TOPIC: The high school you attended has invited you to its annual College Conference as a speaker. The school would like you to talk about the pros and cons of your college experience because several seniors are thinking of applying to your college and majoring in education. Since you can't make it to the conference, you've decided to send a statement to be read there. Write the remarks that you'd like those high school seniors to hear.

WRITING SAMPLE TOPIC 7

SAMPLE TOPIC: In recent years a common complaint about education has been that America's schools are in bad shape because the best and brightest college students choose professions other than teaching. It wasn't always that way. In the old days, people say, teachers were as highly regarded as the clergy—and somewhat higher than the local mayor. Although you can't be expected to know how to change the status of the country's teachers, write an essay that proposes feasible steps for making teaching more attractive and thereby enticing better students into the field.

WRITING SAMPLE TOPIC 8

SAMPLE TOPIC: Reading books is one of the vital occupations of an educated person. Choose a book you've read in the last 12 months—not one assigned in a course but one you chose on your own. Ask yourself why the book deserves to be read. In what ways did the book touch your intellect or emotions? Did it alter the way you think or feel? Was it valuable as a commentary on important issues or as an insight into life? Write an essay in which you discuss the effect of the book on your life. Think of your reader as someone who hasn't read the book. Your intent is to persuade that reader to rush home and read the book tonight!

SAMPLE TOPIC: Some people learn best by reading, others by seeing, still others by hearing or touching or any combination of ways. What about you? How do you learn best? Write an essay that analyzes your learning style. Cite specific instances from your history as a learner to support your analysis.

WRITING SAMPLE TOPIC 10

SAMPLE TOPIC: A question that you may face in your search for a job goes something like this: "What kind of teacher will you be in the classroom?" Or, in other words: "After a year in your class, what will students say about you as a teacher?" Suppose one of these questions appeared on a job application. Write your answer.

ANSWER SHEET— MODEL TEST ONE

Reading

1. Ⓐ Ⓑ Ⓒ Ⓓ Ⓔ	11. Ⓐ Ⓑ Ⓒ Ⓓ Ⓔ	21. Ⓐ Ⓑ Ⓒ Ⓓ Ⓔ
2. Ⓐ Ⓑ Ⓒ Ⓓ Ⓔ	12. Ⓐ Ⓑ Ⓒ Ⓓ Ⓔ	22. Ⓐ Ⓑ Ⓒ Ⓓ Ⓔ
3. Ⓐ Ⓑ Ⓒ Ⓓ Ⓔ	13. Ⓐ Ⓑ Ⓒ Ⓓ Ⓔ	23. Ⓐ Ⓑ Ⓒ Ⓓ Ⓔ
4. Ⓐ Ⓑ Ⓒ Ⓓ Ⓔ	14. Ⓐ Ⓑ Ⓒ Ⓓ Ⓔ	24. Ⓐ Ⓑ Ⓒ Ⓓ Ⓔ
5. Ⓐ Ⓑ Ⓒ Ⓓ Ⓔ	15. Ⓐ Ⓑ Ⓒ Ⓓ Ⓔ	25. Ⓐ Ⓑ Ⓒ Ⓓ Ⓔ
6. Ⓐ Ⓑ Ⓒ Ⓓ Ⓔ	16. Ⓐ Ⓑ Ⓒ Ⓓ Ⓔ	26. Ⓐ Ⓑ Ⓒ Ⓓ Ⓔ
7. Ⓐ Ⓑ Ⓒ Ⓓ Ⓔ	17. Ⓐ Ⓑ Ⓒ Ⓓ Ⓔ	27. Ⓐ Ⓑ Ⓒ Ⓓ Ⓔ
8. Ⓐ Ⓑ Ⓒ Ⓓ Ⓔ	18. Ⓐ Ⓑ Ⓒ Ⓓ Ⓔ	28. Ⓐ Ⓑ Ⓒ Ⓓ Ⓔ
9. Ⓐ Ⓑ Ⓒ Ⓓ Ⓔ	19. Ⓐ Ⓑ Ⓒ Ⓓ Ⓔ	29. Ⓐ Ⓑ Ⓒ Ⓓ Ⓔ
10. Ⓐ Ⓑ Ⓒ Ⓓ Ⓔ	20. Ⓐ Ⓑ Ⓒ Ⓓ Ⓔ	30. Ⓐ Ⓑ Ⓒ Ⓓ Ⓔ

31. Ⓐ Ⓑ Ⓒ Ⓓ Ⓔ	41. Ⓐ Ⓑ Ⓒ Ⓓ Ⓔ
32. Ⓐ Ⓑ Ⓒ Ⓓ Ⓔ	42. Ⓐ Ⓑ Ⓒ Ⓓ Ⓔ
33. Ⓐ Ⓑ Ⓒ Ⓓ Ⓔ	43. Ⓐ Ⓑ Ⓒ Ⓓ Ⓔ
34. Ⓐ Ⓑ Ⓒ Ⓓ Ⓔ	44. Ⓐ Ⓑ Ⓒ Ⓓ Ⓔ
35. Ⓐ Ⓑ Ⓒ Ⓓ Ⓔ	45. Ⓐ Ⓑ Ⓒ Ⓓ Ⓔ
36. Ⓐ Ⓑ Ⓒ Ⓓ Ⓔ	46. Ⓐ Ⓑ Ⓒ Ⓓ Ⓔ
37. Ⓐ Ⓑ Ⓒ Ⓓ Ⓔ	47. Ⓐ Ⓑ Ⓒ Ⓓ Ⓔ
38. Ⓐ Ⓑ Ⓒ Ⓓ Ⓔ	48. Ⓐ Ⓑ Ⓒ Ⓓ Ⓔ
39. Ⓐ Ⓑ Ⓒ Ⓓ Ⓔ	49. Ⓐ Ⓑ Ⓒ Ⓓ Ⓔ
40. Ⓐ Ⓑ Ⓒ Ⓓ Ⓔ	50. Ⓐ Ⓑ Ⓒ Ⓓ Ⓔ

Mathematics

1. Ⓐ Ⓑ Ⓒ Ⓓ Ⓔ	11. Ⓐ Ⓑ Ⓒ Ⓓ Ⓔ	21. Ⓐ Ⓑ Ⓒ Ⓓ Ⓔ
2. Ⓐ Ⓑ Ⓒ Ⓓ Ⓔ	12. Ⓐ Ⓑ Ⓒ Ⓓ Ⓔ	22. Ⓐ Ⓑ Ⓒ Ⓓ Ⓔ
3. Ⓐ Ⓑ Ⓒ Ⓓ Ⓔ	13. Ⓐ Ⓑ Ⓒ Ⓓ Ⓔ	23. Ⓐ Ⓑ Ⓒ Ⓓ Ⓔ
4. Ⓐ Ⓑ Ⓒ Ⓓ Ⓔ	14. Ⓐ Ⓑ Ⓒ Ⓓ Ⓔ	24. Ⓐ Ⓑ Ⓒ Ⓓ Ⓔ
5. Ⓐ Ⓑ Ⓒ Ⓓ Ⓔ	15. Ⓐ Ⓑ Ⓒ Ⓓ Ⓔ	25. Ⓐ Ⓑ Ⓒ Ⓓ Ⓔ
6. Ⓐ Ⓑ Ⓒ Ⓓ Ⓔ	16. Ⓐ Ⓑ Ⓒ Ⓓ Ⓔ	26. Ⓐ Ⓑ Ⓒ Ⓓ Ⓔ
7. Ⓐ Ⓑ Ⓒ Ⓓ Ⓔ	17. Ⓐ Ⓑ Ⓒ Ⓓ Ⓔ	27. Ⓐ Ⓑ Ⓒ Ⓓ Ⓔ
8. Ⓐ Ⓑ Ⓒ Ⓓ Ⓔ	18. Ⓐ Ⓑ Ⓒ Ⓓ Ⓔ	28. Ⓐ Ⓑ Ⓒ Ⓓ Ⓔ
9. Ⓐ Ⓑ Ⓒ Ⓓ Ⓔ	19. Ⓐ Ⓑ Ⓒ Ⓓ Ⓔ	29. Ⓐ Ⓑ Ⓒ Ⓓ Ⓔ
10. Ⓐ Ⓑ Ⓒ Ⓓ Ⓔ	20. Ⓐ Ⓑ Ⓒ Ⓓ Ⓔ	30. Ⓐ Ⓑ Ⓒ Ⓓ Ⓔ

31. Ⓐ Ⓑ Ⓒ Ⓓ Ⓔ
32. Ⓐ Ⓑ Ⓒ Ⓓ Ⓔ
33. Ⓐ Ⓑ Ⓒ Ⓓ Ⓔ
34. Ⓐ Ⓑ Ⓒ Ⓓ Ⓔ
35. Ⓐ Ⓑ Ⓒ Ⓓ Ⓔ
36. Ⓐ Ⓑ Ⓒ Ⓓ Ⓔ
37. Ⓐ Ⓑ Ⓒ Ⓓ Ⓔ
38. Ⓐ Ⓑ Ⓒ Ⓓ Ⓔ
39. Ⓐ Ⓑ Ⓒ Ⓓ Ⓔ
40. Ⓐ Ⓑ Ⓒ Ⓓ Ⓔ
41. Ⓐ Ⓑ Ⓒ Ⓓ Ⓔ
42. Ⓐ Ⓑ Ⓒ Ⓓ Ⓔ
43. Ⓐ Ⓑ Ⓒ Ⓓ Ⓔ
44. Ⓐ Ⓑ Ⓒ Ⓓ Ⓔ
45. Ⓐ Ⓑ Ⓒ Ⓓ Ⓔ
46. Ⓐ Ⓑ Ⓒ Ⓓ Ⓔ
47. Ⓐ Ⓑ Ⓒ Ⓓ Ⓔ
48. Ⓐ Ⓑ Ⓒ Ⓓ Ⓔ
49. Ⓐ Ⓑ Ⓒ Ⓓ Ⓔ
50. Ⓐ Ⓑ Ⓒ Ⓓ Ⓔ

PRACTICE YOUR SKILLS

CHAPTER 6

MODEL TEST ONE

EXAMINATION

Reading

Directions: Each passage in this section is followed by a question or questions about its content. Select the best answer to each question based on what is stated or implied in the selection. You may spend up to 60 minutes on this section.

1. Throughout America, on campuses and in the streets, people express their opinions on everything from foreign policy to meteorological forecasting to drug addiction. Americans have invented many techniques of expression. Although speechmaking remains the most common, newer forms, such as silent sit-ins, passive non-violence, and sign-carrying marches, are also used.

The author would probably agree that

(A) techniques for expressing one's opinion in public have been developed in America only because of the constitutional right to freedom of speech.
(B) the proliferation of techniques for expressing opinions in America has probably clouded many issues.
(C) speechmaking is still commonly used as a persuasive technique, but it has become largely ineffective.
(D) people choose topics on which to voice their opinions without careful consideration or research.
(E) the use of newer techniques of expression for the purpose of swaying public opinion is perhaps more common in the United States than elsewhere.

Questions 2–3

TABLE

MEDIAN PERCENTAGE OF SUCCESS BY THEMES FOR FOUR AGE GROUPS

	9-YEAR OLDS		13-YEAR OLDS		17-YEAR OLDS		ADULTS	
THEME	POSITION	NATIONAL MEDIAN	POSITION	NATIONAL MEDIAN	POSITION	NATIONAL MEDIAN	POSITION	NATIONAL MEDIAN
1. Word Meanings	1	87 %	2	76 %	6	68 %	6	72 %
2. Visual Aids	2	85 %	4	72 %	2	84 %	4	80 %
3. Written Directions	3	81 %	1	83 %	3	84 %	3	86 %
4. Reference Materials	5	64 %	3	74 %	1	84 %	1	93 %
5. Facts from Passages	6	60 %	5	71 %	4	84 %	2	88 %
6. Main Ideas from Passages	8	45 %	8	51 %	7	68 %	5	75 %
7. Drawing Inferences from Passages	4	78 %	7	59 %	8	68 %	8	50 %
8. Critical Reading	7	58 %	6	60 %	5	72 %	7	70 %
Range of Medians		45–87 (42)		51–83 (32)		68–84 (16)		50–93 (43)

SOURCE: National Assessment of Educational Progress

2. According to this table, 9-year olds and 13-year olds

(A) did better than 17-year olds in "Written Directions."
(B) both did least well in "Main Ideas from Passages."
(C) did best in "Word Meanings."
(D) did better than adults in all but one category.
(E) did better in the skill area (theme) of "Reference Materials" than older groups.

3. The range of median scores is smallest for

(A) 9-year olds.
(B) 9-year olds and adults.
(C) 13-year olds and adults.
(D) 17-year olds.
(E) adults.

Questions 4–5

Almost unnoticed, scientists are reconstructing the world of plants. A new technique using colchicine, a poisonous drug, has allowed scientists to remodel many kinds of flowers, fruits, vegetables, and trees, creating new varieties with unexpected frequency. Even plants native to other countries are used to obtain the desired effects.

4. One can conclude from this passage that

(A) the reconstruction of so many plants will be detrimental to the environment.
(B) the new strains of plants that are produced are often better in some way.
(C) the remodelling of plants is a controversial activity.
(D) the creation of new varieties of plants rarely happens.
(E) scientists must satisfy rigid requirements in order to experiment with plant varieties.

5. The title that best fits this passage is

(A) Concern for Plant Life.
(B) Dangers in Plant Drugs.
(C) Reconstructing Plant Life.
(D) Plant Growth and Heredity.
(E) Renewing the Earth.

Questions 6–7

Conserving natural resources can be a formidable task in our national community. The preservation of small bits of irreplaceable biotic communities is so entangled with economic and social considerations that in the time spent resolving jurisdictional questions, some specimens may be permanently lost.

6. The author's attitude is one of

(A) unhappy remorse.
(B) uninformed naivete.
(C) overzealous devotion.
(D) detached disregard.
(E) concerned interest.

7. As used in this passage, the best definition of "biotic" is

(A) neighboring.
(B) animal.
(C) life.
(D) growth.
(E) environment.

8. In response to the student's request for clarification of the theory, he wrote a paper couched in such formal circumlocutions that the student was as perplexed as he had been before. The best meaning for "circumlocutions" as used in this passage is

(A) judgments.
(B) indirect language.
(C) uninhibited expressions.
(D) assumptions.
(E) references.

Questions 9–10

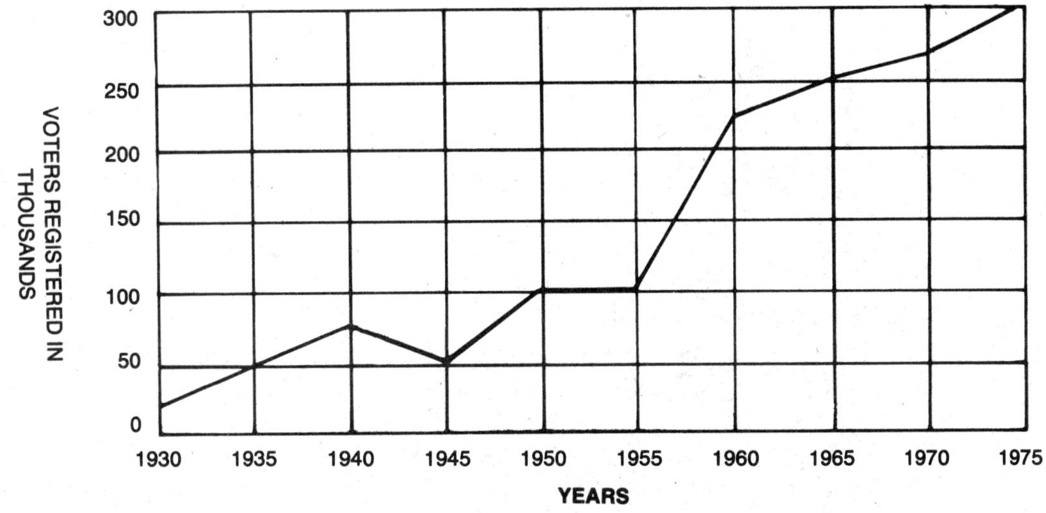

The graph shows the number of voters registered in one state between 1930 and 1975. Refer to the graph to answer the following questions.

9. Between what two periods was the increase in voter registration the greatest?

(A) 1930 and 1940
(B) 1955 and 1960
(C) 1945 and 1950
(D) 1960 and 1975
(E) 1930 and 1950

10. How much of a difference was there between voter registration in 1950 and 1975?

(A) 50,000 voters
(B) 225,000 voters
(C) 15,000 voters
(D) 150,000 voters
(E) 200,000 voters

Questions 11–13

A debate has gone on for centuries that focuses on the question of how much financial or other assistance should be given to the poor. The argument on one side emphasizes the misfortunes and deprivations those of low income must endure and appeals to the moral instincts of those in policy-making positions to use compassion in their judgments. On the other side, people speak about the role that indolence has played in engendering poverty and how public assistance programs vitiate incentives to work and to save.

11. A word that could meaningfully replace "vitiate" as used in this passage is

(A) support.
(B) impair.
(C) outline.
(D) manifest.
(E) implicate.

12. According to this passage, providing assistance for the poor is

(A) a debatable question.
(B) a poor choice.
(C) not up to those in policy-making positions.
(D) merely perpetuating poverty.
(E) an essential ingredient of a democracy.

13. Which of the following would be a good title for the ideas in this passage?

(A) Human Rights
(B) When Is Enough Too Much?
(C) Compassion in Government
(D) How Much Should Be Given to the Poor?
(E) Poverty and the Poor

Questions 14–16

Psychologists often refer to a certain phenomenon, one that has existed in every society and in every period of history, as an expression of the "evil eye syndrome". It is reflected in and referred to as the fear of success, or, in some instances, as the need to fail. It may be thought of as the general fear that calamity waits in the wings in the hour of success and rejoicing. It is interesting to consider how this ancient heritage actively influences us today.

14. The "evil eye syndrome" can be equated with

(A) witchcraft.
(B) a fear of failure.
(C) a fear of success.
(D) paranoia.
(E) the need for success.

15. One example of a class of behaviors that might be manifested over the years as a reaction to the "evil eye syndrome" would be

(A) superstitions.
(B) celebrations.
(C) funeral rites.
(D) reunions.
(E) legal actions.

16. Which one of the following statements best expresses an idea found in this passage?

(A) Success and failure are one and the same.
(B) Misfortune has ever existed.
(C) The future determines the present.
(D) Joy and sadness work hand in hand.
(E) Disaster often follows triumph.

Questions 17–18

The presence in most higher-order land animals of prehensile organs for grasping and exploring the environment creates the impression that intelligence is the sole province of animals with this characteristic. This generalization, then, makes it seem surprising that an animal with as superior a brain as the porpoise is not accompanied by any type of manipulative organ.

17. In a continuation of this paragraph, it would be reasonable for the writer to discuss

(A) the intelligent echo-sounding ability of porpoises.
(B) the uniqueness of the thumb as a prehensile organ.
(C) the differences between higher-order land animals.
(D) the intelligence levels of animals with manipulative characteristics.
(E) the mating habits of porpoises.

18. The author's main point is that

(A) porpoises exhibit the same characteristics as many land animals.
(B) people assume incorrectly that because the more intelligent animals have a prehensile organ that only animals with this characteristic manifest a high degree of intelligence.
(C) superior brains reside only in animals with prehensile organs.
(D) the presence of a prehensile tail or other organ is an essential attribute for animals with higher levels of intelligence.
(E) no one characteristic can be identified as the criterion for rating the level of intelligence in animals.

Questions 19–20

One is so helpless in the face of propaganda. The possibility of manipulating the minds of the public by withholding or distorting the facts is appalling. How can one think or speak intelligently without a clear understanding of the facts?

19. The author of this passage indicates that propaganda

(A) can be used most effectively only if the facts are manipulated in subtle ways.
(B) is a tool that can be used in a frightening manner.
(C) is only effective with those who are uninformed, who have no understanding of the facts.
(D) manipulates the public's mind by presenting issues that detract from the main issue of interest.
(E) makes one helpless by inundating the public with pieces that present contradictory information.

20. Which of the following could be the next sentence in this paragraph?

(A) One needs to elicit from propaganda the facts which are most accurate.
(B) Distorting facts to suit one's purpose is contrary to the fundamental beliefs of all systems of government.
(C) How can one participate in the development of propaganda without knowing the facts?
(D) Withholding information from the public is illegal.
(E) The control of information is ruinous in a democracy, and it becomes a farce.

Questions 21–22

Writers have often been told that the vitality of literary expression rests on authentic experience. It is likely that this demand does nag fitfully at writers' consciences, but creativity, at its most mysterious, is profound and unexplainable. Can anyone seriously believe that it is necessary to become a soldier of fortune or sail on the high seas in order to feel the pain, the bewilderment or the joy of the human predicament?

21. One idea presented in the passage is that

(A) creative instincts do not come easily to a writer.
(B) the creativity required in writing is responsible for great mysteries.
(C) the creative ability of a writer compensates for any supposed lack of actual experience.
(D) all creative writers have a depth that is not the result of a writing experience.
(E) the conscience of a creative writer is not bothered by his critics.

22. The author of this passage does NOT feel that

(A) writers are concerned with the need to base their writing on experience.
(B) the only worthwhile writing is based on real experience.
(C) it is necessary to know something about being a soldier in order to write about being a soldier.
(D) the human predicament can be written about without suffering.
(E) writers should dwell on personal experience in their writing.

Questions 23–25

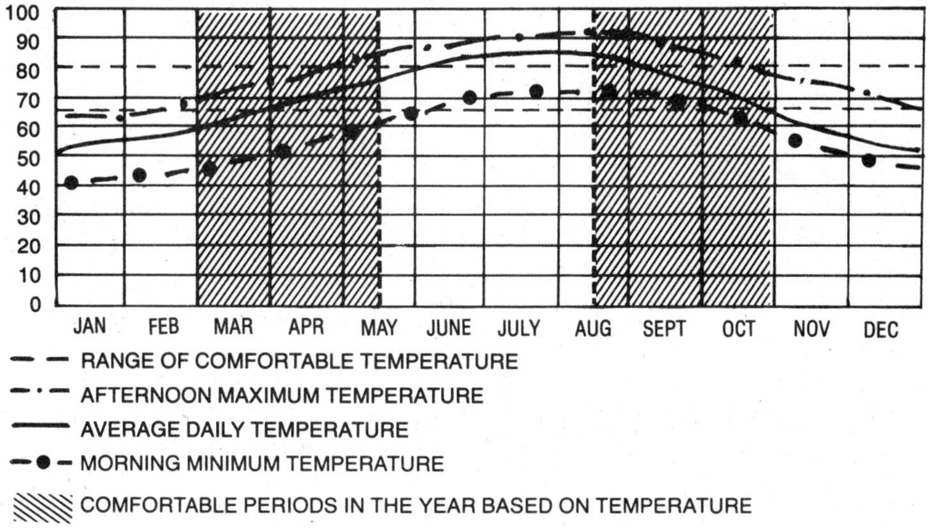

The graph represents average temperature conditions in Tampa, Florida. Refer to the graph to answer the following questions.

23. According to the graph, in Tampa,

(A) the highest temperatures occur in the afternoon in September and May.
(B) periods of comfortable temperatures occur in March and September.
(C) average daily temperatures are lowest in February.
(D) May and June are the warmest months.
(E) morning temperatures range from 30° to 60°.

24. The range of year-round temperatures for Tampa is approximately

(A) 50°–85°
(B) 70°–90°
(C) 40°–90°
(D) 38°–95°
(E) 40°–65°

25. This graph could reasonably be used to

(A) determine the appropriateness of solar applications to a building.
(B) determine the potential for use of a windmill in this area.
(C) identify risk of hurricane damage in this area.
(D) plot barometric ratings for different times of the year.
(E) find out how temperatures vary during storm activity.

26. In the absence of any empirical evidence of how people reacted to seeing the war on television, it is just as plausible to suggest that television promoted support for the war as to say it promoted opposition.

As used in this passage, the most appropriate definition for "empirical" is

(A) clearly incorrect.
(B) foreboding.
(C) taken from unfamiliar material.
(D) based on research.
(E) original.

27. There is much pent-up frustration in this country, and the opposing frustrations which inflict religion and politics are expressed in feelings of nostalgia as well as jeremiads of the one against the other.

From the context of this passage, it is possible to conclude that the best definition of "jeremiad" is

(A) great journey.
(B) embellishment.
(C) tale of woe.
(D) donation.
(E) sigh of relief.

Questions 28–30

Conformity is not considered desirable in many areas of life, so why do we think that it is necessary to eliminate the variations of language that are provided by dialects? Does equality come by eliminating those that are different or by removing the differences? In recent years, black people have rejected hair straighteners and other applications only because they are asking for the basic human right of respecting themselves. It would sometimes seem as if the inability of children to learn grammatical rules is the result of a subconscious refusal to deny their own identity, to deny a part of themselves. If we tell them that the way they use language is wrong, are we not asking them to do just that? Freedom is not real if it is simply the freedom to conform to everyone else.

28. The author's main point is that

(A) the right of a person to speak like himself may be violated by teaching him that there is only one correct way to speak.
(B) children have difficulty learning grammar because the rules are difficult to apply.
(C) equality can be achieved more easily by establishing better lines of communication.
(D) teaching the grammar of one dialect is an essential aspect of providing education for all.
(E) one must express some conformity if effective communication is the goal.

29. The author's attitude in this passage reflects

(A) generosity.
(B) some confusion.
(C) a clear bias.
(D) disgust.
(E) ambivalence.

30. In order to make his point, the writer uses the technique of

(A) contrast.
(B) examples.
(C) logical exclusion.
(D) comparison.
(E) detailed analysis.

Questions 31–32

Nature evidently expected us to take a daily dose of radiation in much the same way that we experience the cuts and bruises of ordinary living. There was never any intention for man to experiment with radioactive elements as concentrated extracts. As a result of this experimentation, man has had to develop various devices to extend his perception and detect untoward situations involving radiation.

31. The "devices" mentioned in this passage refer to

(A) radioactive elements.
(B) optical equipment.
(C) "sixth sense."
(D) tools used to detect radioactivity.
(E) equipment used in nuclear reactors.

32. According to the author, we are exposed to radiation daily

(A) only if we live in industrialized areas.
(B) as a result of man's experimentation.
(C) in concentrated extracts.
(D) more frequently than we get cuts and bruises.
(E) in very small doses.

Questions 33–35

God how I envy the artist! When he sees or feels or senses something that is worthy to remember, he need only turn to his easel and, with colors and texture and even a minimum of talent, in some way interpret and thus capture what he has experienced. A later glimpse will still make him clearly mindful of what he had observed, and it will also give to the outsider an idea of what he is displaying, varying in depth and intensity according to the degree of the artist's talent.

The lonely writer, however, sees, feels, or senses, and then is forced to search deep and longingly for those special words that are the exact ones to convey or interpret what he has experienced. If words are not chosen with extreme care, a later glimpse will not enable him to recall exactly what the feeling or emotion was, and moreover, will not give the outsider the all-important idea or understanding of the experience the writer wished to share with him.

33. The writer of this passage would probably agree that

(A) the artist has difficulty creating an impression because of his many choices of medium and color.
(B) capturing the essence of a feeling in words or in colors is equally difficult.
(C) less competent artists may present an impression that is far from accurate.
(D) returning to a piece of written or artistic work after it has been completed never arouses the same impression.
(E) writing is a very special and demanding talent.

34. The tone of this passage could be identified as

(A) ambivalent.
(B) flippant.
(C) despairing.
(D) indifferent.
(E) determined.

35. The author makes his point by the use of

(A) comparison and contrast.
(B) logical explanation.
(C) examples and details.
(D) generalization.
(E) fact and opinion.

Questions 36–38

It is estimated that for the expert mastery of a specialized field, about 50,000 pieces of information, an amount about equivalent to the recognition vocabulary of college-educated readers, may be required. In order to gain literacy in many demanding endeavors, it is essential that abstract groups of items be ''chunked'' to make it possible to process them efficiently. This skill is the greatest advantage for the expert and, conversely, the greatest problem for the beginner.

36. According to the author, ''chunking'' information

(A) is only required in specialized fields.
(B) prevents the clear discrimination of details.
(C) enables one to gain a basic level of literacy.
(D) makes it possible to learn more.
(E) is a skill learned in college.

37. One reason that the skill described in this passage might be a problem for the beginner is that

(A) the beginner has not yet developed a command of the skill of estimating.
(B) the unfamiliarity of the material makes it difficult to ''chunk'' information in meaningful ways, and there are, therefore, too many isolated bits to remember.
(C) beginners in this field are often not college-educated.
(D) even readers with a large recognition vocabulary have difficulty with this type of material.
(E) information essential to understanding the demands of a task must be acquired from other sources.

38. By ''chunking,'' the author means

(A) putting of literary works into specialized groups.
(B) developing abridged versions of work manuals.
(C) cutting down the size of written passages.
(D) transforming abstract information into more concrete terms.
(E) grouping pieces of information in meaningful patterns.

Questions 39–41

As an alternative to the experimental approach, one that offers the opportunity for a radically different view of things, the ethnographic approach is being used more and more frequently. No ''variables'' or ''controls'' are part of such an approach, since all of the elements which make up the context of situation, including the experimenter, are integral parts of the process and of the phenomena one wishes to explain.

39. One can conclude from this passage that

(A) the experimental approach is more productive than the ethnographic approach.
(B) variables and controls are associated with the experimental approach.
(C) an opportunity to use the ethnographic approach is not often found.
(D) elements which make up the situational context are extraneous in the ethnographic approach.
(E) the phenomena observed in the experimental approach are of little interest.

40. Which of the following statements could have preceded this passage?

(A) The ethnographic approach was often used in conjunction with the experimental approach.
(B) The experimental approach offers the only viable possibility for studying unexplained phenomena.
(C) When one wishes to change or control variables, the ethnographic approach is more appropriate.
(D) One assumption underlying the experimental approach is that variables can be broken down and studied in isolation.

(E) Methodological differences between the two approaches result in very different findings.

41. In the ethnographic approach, the experimenter

(A) is considered part of the situational context.
(B) is removed.
(C) creates the phenomena.
(D) can be ignored because he is not part of the process.
(E) controls variables by distorting relationships.

Questions 42–44

The leap of a grasshopper is so prodigious—150 times its one-inch length—that an equivalent feat for a man would be a casual jump, from a standing position, over the Washington Monument. Its skeleton, worn on the outside like all insects, is composed of a chemical compound called chitin. This sheath is extremely tough and resistant to alkali and acid compounds that would eat the clothing, flesh, and bones of man. Muscles are attached to this outside armor and arranged around catapult-like hind legs so as to permit their astonishing jumps.

42. The best meaning for "prodigious" as used in this passage is

(A) immense.
(B) innocuous.
(C) original.
(D) fluid.
(E) intense.

43. Chitin is

(A) a sheath consisting of an acid and an alkali.
(B) a substance in the outside coating of a grasshopper.
(C) part of the muscle of a grasshopper.
(D) a catapult structure.
(E) a chemical in all insects.

44. According to the author, the grasshopper is

(A) a lowly insect.
(B) a troublesome nuisance.
(C) inclined to damage clothing and other goods.
(D) made up of chemicals.
(E) a small creature of amazing strength.

Questions 45–48

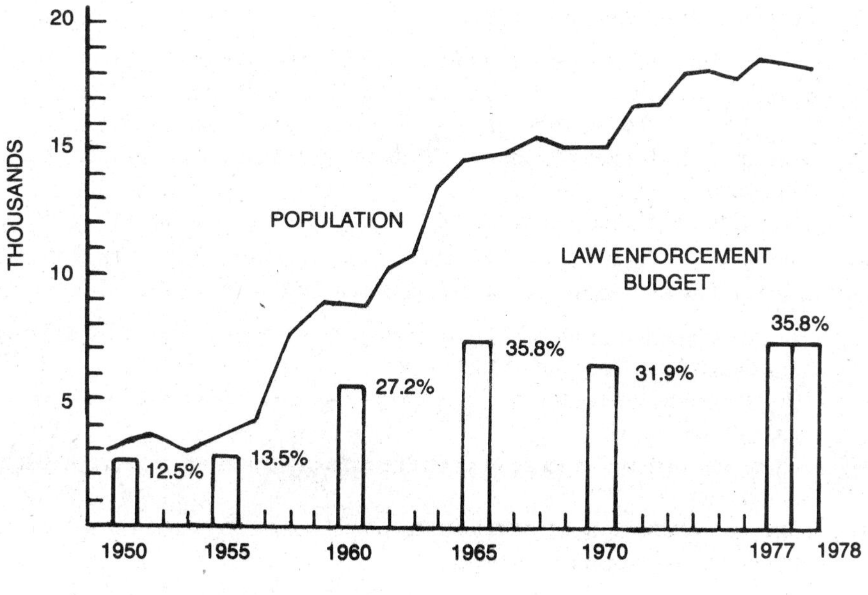

The graph represents the growth in population in one U.S. city and the percent of the budget of that city allocated to law enforcement. Refer to the graph to answer the following questions.

45. For the period between 1950 and 1978 in this city,

(A) the increase in the population was not matched by a similar increase in money spent on law enforcement.
(B) the growth in the population outstripped the increase in law enforcement monies by 3 to 1.
(C) the law enforcement budget showed a consistent increase while the population showed a dramatic increase.
(D) the population doubled while the law enforcement budget only increased by about 10%.
(E) the population and the law enforcement budget rose in about equal increments.

46. In the period covered by the graph, the population in the city grew by approximately

(A) 10,000.
(B) 15,000.
(C) 25,000.
(D) 30,000.
(E) 35,000.

47. According to the graph, it may be concluded that the amount of the budget reserved for law enforcement

(A) rose sharply between 1950 and 1955.
(B) decreased between 1960 and 1965.
(C) almost tripled between the first and last years shown.
(D) doubled since 1965.
(E) remained stable between 1955 and 1965.

48. The greatest increase in the city's population occurred during the period

(A) 1950–1955.
(B) 1956–1960.
(C) 1960–1963.
(D) 1966–1970.
(E) 1974–1978.

Questions 49–50

Two, then, appears to be the magic number. At every level of biological organization, the significance of pairs is evident. There is a pairing of chemical substances in DNA, a pairing of chromosomes in the nucleus of a cell, and the pairing of individuals in sexual reproduction. Part of the theory holds that simple characters, ones which separate in an all-or-none fashion, are regulated by two particles (genes), one from each parent organism. When the particles are different, the offspring will show one or the other character, but not a mixture of both.

49. One can conclude that the topic of this paragraph is

(A) numerology.
(B) DNA.
(C) genetics.
(D) living organisms.
(E) biology.

50. From the information presented in this passage, one could determine that an example of a "simple" character would be

(A) height.
(B) eye color.
(C) sex.
(D) intelligence.
(E) build.

Mathematics

Directions: Select the best answer to each of the following questions. Any figures provided are there as reference; they are approximations and are not drawn to scale except when stated.

You may refer to the following information during this section of the test:

$=$ is equal to	$\sqrt{\ }$ square root of
$\neq$ is unequal to	$^\circ$ degrees
$<$ is less than	$\parallel$ is parallel to
$>$ is greater than	$\perp$ is perpendicular to
$\leq$ is less than or equal to	π pi, approximately 3.14
$\geq$ is greater than or equal to	

Circle: Radius $= r$; Circumference $= 2\pi r$; Area $= \pi r^2$; a circle contains 360°

Triangle: In triangle ABC, if $\angle BDA$ is a right angle, Area of $\triangle ABC = \dfrac{AC \times BD}{2}$;

Perimeter of $\triangle ABC = AB + BC + CA$

Sum of the measures of the degrees of the angles is 180.

Rectangle: Area $= L \times W$; Perimeter $= 2 \times (L + W)$

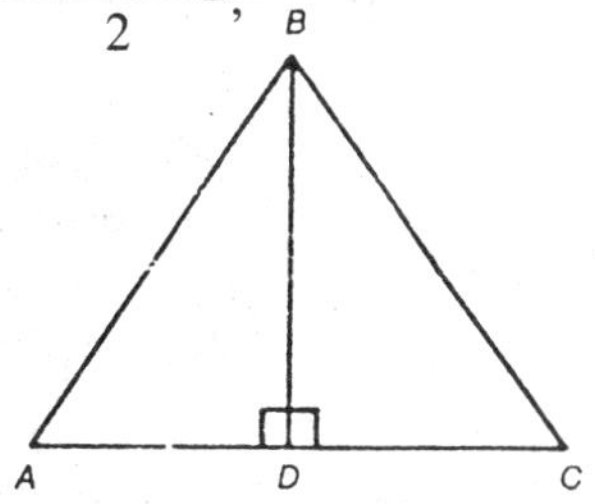

Rectangle: Area $= L \times W$; Perimeter $= 2 \times (L + W)$

1. Which of the following numbers is closest to 27?

(A) 26¼
(B) 26.3
(C) 26.74
(D) 27.28
(E) 27¼

2. 7 ☐ (4 ☐ 2) = 14

What operations go in the boxes?

(A) ×, +
(B) +, +
(C) +, ×
(D) −, +
(E) ×, −

3. Which of the following is the numerical form for "fourteen thousand fourteen"?

(A) 14,000,14
(B) 14,014
(C) 1414
(D) 140,014
(E) 1,400,014

4. In which of the following numerals does 7 have the greatest value?

(A) 74.03
(B) 237.46
(C) 3347.98
(D) 9.9997
(E) 1709.46

5. What is the cube root of $(2^2 \times 2)$?

(A) 2
(B) 4
(C) 8
(D) 2×2
(E) 512

6. The sum of 3 numbers, A, B, and C is 100. Also, a 4th number, D, is greater than A. Which of the following statements can you be certain is true?

(A) $D + B + C < 100$
(B) $D + B + C > 100$
(C) $A + D + B > 100$
(D) $A + D + C > 100$
(E) $D + B + C = 100$

7. If there are C cats and D dogs in a pet store, what is the ratio of the number of cats to the total number of dogs and cats in the pet store?

(A) $\frac{C - D}{C + D}$

(B) $\frac{C}{C + D}$

(C) $\frac{C}{D}$

(D) $\frac{D}{C}$

(E) $\frac{C + D}{C}$

8. If the average of six x's is 6, what is the average of twelve x's?

(A) $\frac{1}{6}$
(B) $\frac{1}{2}$
(C) 1
(D) 6
(E) 12

9. $150 is 75% of what amount?

(A) $11.25
(B) $2000.00
(C) $112.50
(D) $200.00
(E) None of the above

10. Which of the following numbers are primes?

I. 9 III. 113

II. 13 IV. 121

(A) I and II only
(B) II and III only
(C) II, III, and IV only
(D) III and IV only
(E) All are prime.

11. If $x = -5 - (-6)$, what is the additive inverse (opposite) of x?

(A) 0
(B) 1
(C) -1
(D) 11
(E) -11

12. An ice cream parlor has 6 different flavors of ice cream and 3 different toppings. A sundae is defined as: two scoops of ice cream of different flavors and one topping. How many different sundaes can be made?

(A) 18
(B) 36
(C) 108
(D) 90
(E) 200

13. This tank holds 16 gallons and the car averages 22 miles per gallon.

How much farther can the car travel?

(A) 264 miles
(B) 88 miles
(C) 22 miles
(D) 64 miles
(E) None of the above

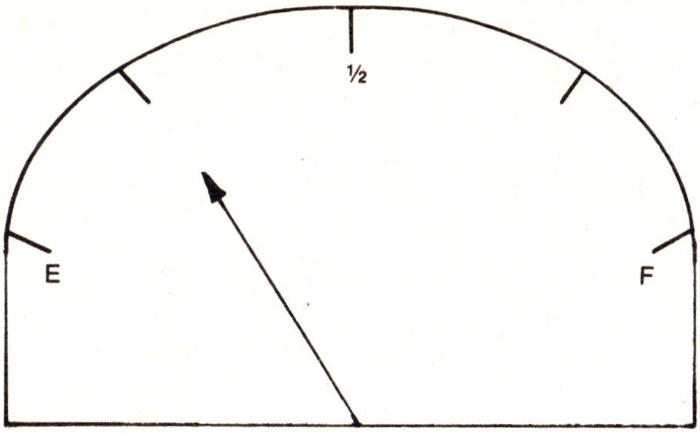

14. In a game of darts, Marie threw 3 darts. If each one landed in a different ring, which score would have been impossible for her to have gotten?

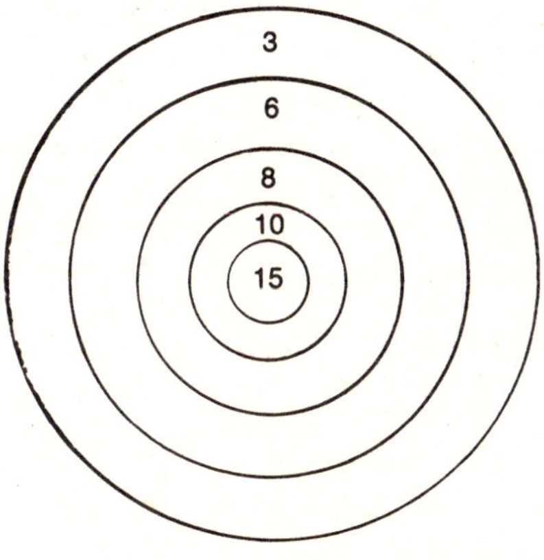

(A) An odd score greater than 30.
(B) An even score greater than 30.
(C) An odd score less than 20.
(D) A score of 19.
(E) A score of 24.

15. A rubber ball is dropped from the top of a tree 16 feet high. Sam is keeping track of how many times the ball hits the ground. He knows that every time it hits the ground it bounces back up half as high as the distance it fell. Also, it is caught when it bounces to a high point of 1 foot. How many times will Sam record it having hit the ground?

(A) 6 times
(B) 5 times
(C) 4 times
(D) 2 times
(E) 1 time

16. Scuba divers are concerned about the water temperatures because the water gets colder the deeper they go. This drop in temperature averages 4.5 degrees for every 1000 feet down.
If the temperature at 6000 feet under water is 37 degrees, what is the temperature at sea level?

(A) 10 degrees
(B) 27 degrees
(C) 64 degrees
(D) 75 degrees
(E) None of the above

17. Which of the following graphs represents the taxi rates for a company that charges $.50 for the first quarter mile and $.25 for each additional quarter of a mile?

A.

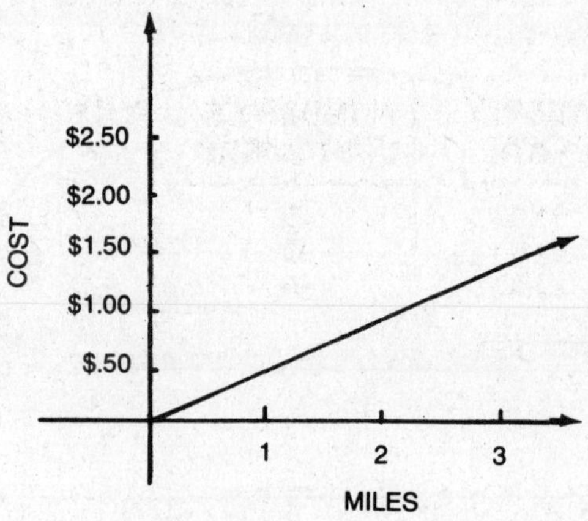

B.

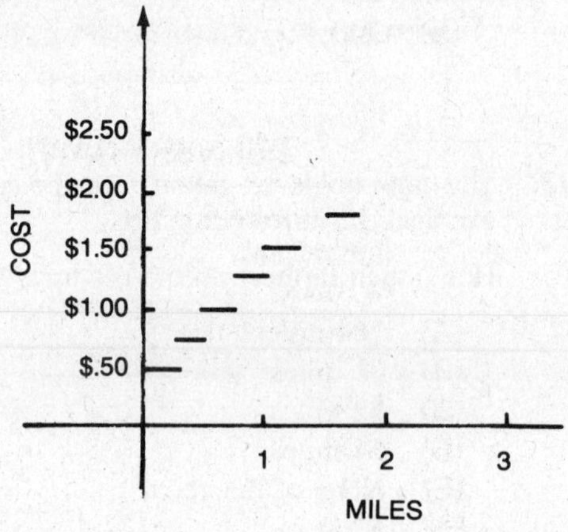

C.

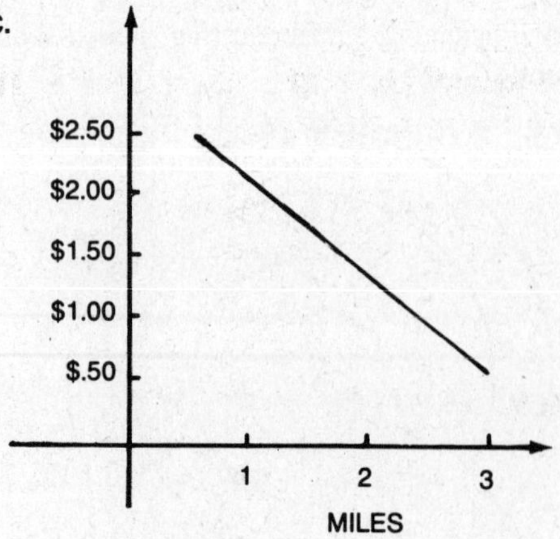

D.

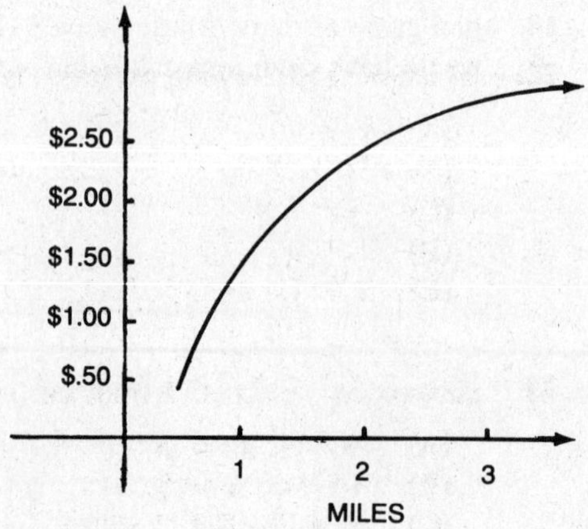

E. NONE OF THE ABOVE

18. If ⅔ of the capacity of a tank is 60 gallons, what is the total capacity of the tank?

(A) 30 gallons
(B) 40 gallons
(C) 90 gallons
(D) 120 gallons
(E) None of the above

19. We need to divide $2100.00 among 3 people, Shelley, Mario, and Pat, so that Mario receives double what Shelley receives and Pat receives double what Mario receives. How much will Pat receive?

(A) $300.00
(B) $600.00
(C) $900.00
(D) $1200.00
(E) None of the above

20. Ms. White spent $5.04 on dinner. This included 5% tax. How much of the bill was for tax?

(A) $.25
(B) $.26
(C) $.20
(D) $.21
(E) None of the above

21. Harold decided to keep a record of the money he collects from his newspaper route. Using the information given, how much money does Harold collect in the month of February? (Note: Assume February has 28 days and that February 1 was on a Sunday.)

DELIVERY DAYS	WEEKLY RATE	NUMBER OF CUSTOMERS
Daily except Sunday	$1.75	20
Sunday only	$1.00	30
All week (daily & Sunday)	$2.50	50

(A) $190
(B) $525
(C) $21
(D) $760
(E) None of the above

22. Which of the following expressions is a simplified form of $(3x + 5) - [3x - (-x + 1) - 3]$?

(A) $x - 7$
(B) $3x + 7$
(C) $-x + 9$
(D) $x + 9$
(E) $x + 1$

23. Subtract $3x^2 - 2x + 3$ from $2x^2 - 2$. The result is:

(A) $-x^2 + 2x - 5$
(B) $-x^2 - 2x - 5$
(C) $x^2 + 2x + 1$
(D) $-x^2 + 2x + 1$
(E) $x^2 - 2x + 5$

24. Lemon drops come in packs of 8 for 72¢. Chocolate mints come in packs of 6 for 45¢. Ruth bought 48 pieces of candy. How many of each kind of candy did she buy, if she spent $3.96? (Choose the *best* answer.)

(A) 6 packs of lemon drops, no chocolate mints
(B) 8 packs of chocolate mints, no lemon drops
(C) 3 packs of lemon drops, 4 packs of chocolate mints
(D) Choices A, B, and C are possibilities.
(E) None of the above is a possibility.

25. A factor of $3x^2 + 2x - 5$ is:

(A) $x + 1$
(B) $x + 5$
(C) $3x + 1$
(D) $3x - 1$
(E) $3x + 5$

26. What is the value of $x^2y - xy^2$ when $x = 4$ and $y = 2$?

(A) 24
(B) 16
(C) 0
(D) −8
(E) −32

27. If $\sqrt{x - 5} - 3 = 0$, then x is:

(A) 4
(B) 11
(C) 8
(D) 14
(E) There is no solution for x.

28. The formula given by $F = (9/5)C + 32°$ gives the relationship between Celsius (C) and Fahrenheit (F) temperature. If the temperature is 68 degrees Fahrenheit, what is the corresponding Celsius temperature?

(A) 64.8
(B) 20
(C) 154.4
(D) 198
(E) None of the above

29. If a function is defined by the set of ordered pairs (1, 2), (2, 4), (3, 8), (4, 16), (5, y), then the value of y is:

(A) 20
(B) 24
(C) 28
(D) 32
(E) 36

30. If $.5x - 3 = 7$ then $x = ?$

(A) 20
(B) 8
(C) 2
(D) .8
(E) .2

31. If $m > 0$ and $n < 0$, which of the following is true?

(A) $\frac{m}{n} > 0$

(B) $m \cdot n > 0$

(C) $\frac{1}{m} > \frac{1}{n}$

(D) $\frac{1}{n} > \frac{1}{m}$

(E) $m \cdot n = 0$

32. Mr. Jones wants to make a rectangular garden in his backyard. He has determined that the garden will measure 21 feet by 27 feet. In order to increase the fertility of the soil he will add 4 inches of top soil. How many cubic yards of soil will he add?

(A) 252
(B) 2268
(C) 189
(D) 63
(E) None of the above

33. In the figure, angle y is more than 90 degrees and less than 180 degrees. Side x is between which 2 numbers?

(A) 0, 10
(B) 0, $10\sqrt{2}$
(C) 10, $10\sqrt{2}$
(D) $10\sqrt{2}$, 20
(E) Both B and C

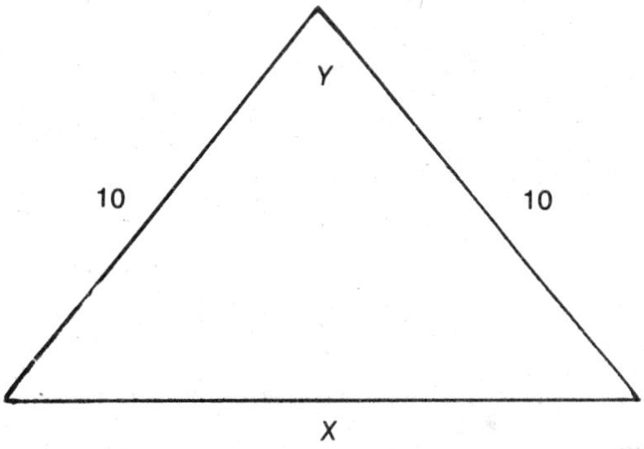

34. In the graph, if a straight line passes through point P (6, 2) and point Q (9, 0) it should also pass through what point on the y axis?

(A) (0, 2)
(B) (0, 4)
(C) (0, 5)
(D) (0, 6)
(E) (0, 9)

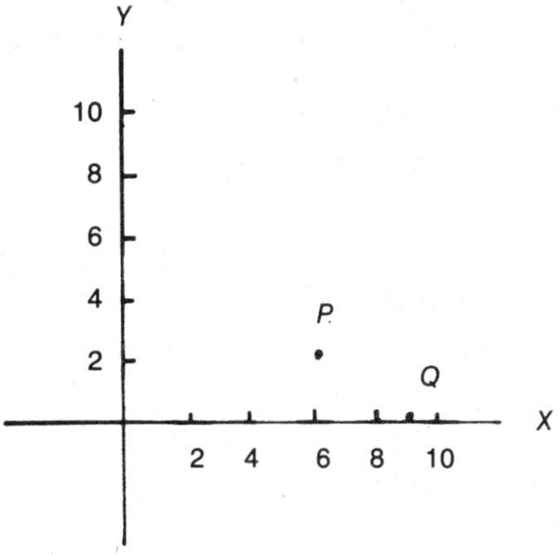

35. How many degrees are there in the angle formed by the hands of a clock at 5:00 p.m.?

(A) 100
(B) 114
(C) 120
(D) 150
(E) 175

36. Suppose a flagpole has a 25-foot shadow and a yardstick next to the flagpole has a 5-foot shadow at the same time. How tall is the flagpole?

(A) 10 feet
(B) 15 feet
(C) 20 feet
(D) Not enough information given
(E) None of the above

37. In the figure, triangle *ABC* is a right triangle with right angle at *B*. What is the area of triangle *ABC*?

(A) 12 square units
(B) 20 square units
(C) 10 square units
(D) 6 square units
(E) 15 square units

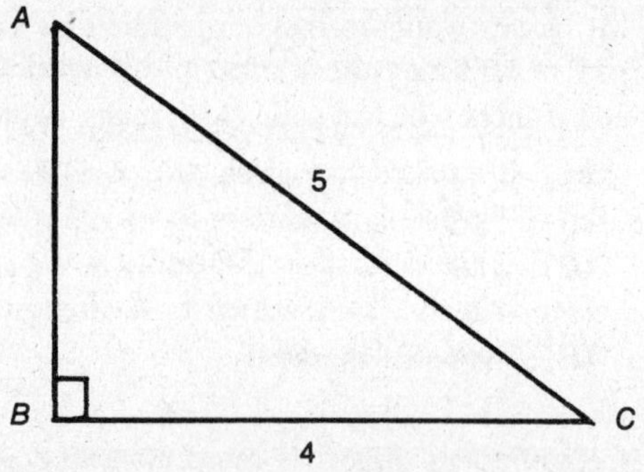

38. Which of the following triples of numbers could *not* be the lengths of the sides of a triangle?

I. (1, 2, 3) III. (5, 12, 13)
II. (3, 4, 5) IV. (2, 4, 10)

(A) I only
(B) I and III only
(C) II and III only
(D) I and IV only
(E) IV only

39. A square and an equilateral triangle have equal perimeters. What is the length of a side of the triangle if the area of the square is 9 square units?

(A) 3 units
(B) 4 units
(C) 6 units
(D) 9 units
(E) 12 units

40. For which of the following lengths of a side of a square would the perimeter be divisible by both 3 and 4?

(A) ¼
(B) 2
(C) 4
(D) 7
(E) None of the above

Use the problem stated below to answer item 41.
Problem: Suppose you bought a side of beef weighing 500 pounds at a cost of $1.25 per pound. At no additional cost the butcher removed the waste and packaged the meat. If the waste was 33% of the total weight, how much did you pay for a pound of packaged beef?

41. Which statement is another way of asking what you are trying to find out in this problem?

(A) What is 33% of 500 pounds?
(B) How many pounds of waste are in a 500-pound side of beef?
(C) How much does one pound of edible meat cost if you know the total cost for all of the meat?
(D) How much does it cost to buy one pound of packaged meat at $1.25 per pound?
(E) None of the above

Use the problem stated below to answer item 42.
Problem: Last week the student bus took two hours to travel to a school 100 miles away for a football game. How long can we expect the bus to take to travel to a school 80 miles away?

42. What is another way of stating the problem?

(A) If it takes two hours to travel 100 miles, how long will it take to travel 80 miles?
(B) If it takes two hours to travel 80 miles, how long will it take to travel 100 miles?
(C) If it takes two hours to travel 100 miles, how long will the entire trip take?
(D) If one school is 100 miles away and another is 80 miles away, how much longer does it take to travel to the school 100 miles away?
(E) None of the above

Use the information stated below to answer items 43 and 44.
Information: During Elmhurst High School's annual candy sale, Bert sold the most boxes of candy. Joan sold one box less than Bert, and Rhonda sold half as many boxes as Bert. Together the three sold 89 boxes.

43. Let B be the number of boxes sold by Bert. Which expression best represents the number sold by Joan?

(A) $B/1$
(B) $B - 1$
(C) $1 - B$
(D) $B \times 1$
(E) None of the above

44. What equation would you use to find the number of boxes sold by Bert?

(A) $B/1 + (\frac{1}{2})B + B = 89$
(B) $(B - 1) + (\frac{1}{2})B + B = 89$
(C) $(1 - B) + (\frac{1}{2})B + B = 89$
(D) $(B - 1) + 2B + B = 89$
(E) None of the above

Use the problem stated below to answer items 45 and 46.
Problem: The 8th grade Outdoors Skills class took a bike trip to the county park. They averaged nine miles an hour on the way to the park and, because of a downhill grade, averaged 10 miles per hour on the return trip. They spent some time at the park hiking and eating lunch before returning to school. How long did it take to bike from the park back to school?

45. What additional information is needed to determine how long it took to bike from the park back to school?

(A) How many miles per hour the students averaged going to the park.
(B) How many hours the students spent at the park.
(C) How many miles per hour the students averaged on the trip back to school.
(D) How long they spent hiking and eating lunch.
(E) How many miles it is from the school to the park.

46. What information included in the problem is needed to find the answer?

(A) How many miles per hour the students averaged going to the park.
(B) How many hours the students spent at the park.
(C) How many miles per hour the students averaged on the trip back to school.
(D) How many miles it is from the school to the park.
(E) All of the above information is needed.

Use the following problem stated below to answer item 47.
Problem: A farmer has 6 more hens than dogs. The total number of dogs and hens is 132. To find the number of each, guess that there are as many hens as dogs—66 of each. Then add 3 to the number of hens and subtract 3 from the number of dogs. So, 66 + 3 = 69 hens and 66 − 3 = 63 dogs.

47. Which problem below could be solved using exactly the same steps?

(A) Bill earns $6 more per week than Lou. If Bill earns $132 per week, how much does Lou earn?
(B) Bill earns $6 more per week than Lou. If Lou earns $132 per week, how much does Bill earn?
(C) Bill earns $6 more per week than Lou. Together they earn $132. How much does each earn per week?
(D) Bill earns $6 more per week than Lou. Together they earn $132. How much less does Lou earn than Bill?
(E) None of the above

Use the problem stated below to answer item 48.
Problem: Clara and Herb, 2 young parents, took their 3 children to Disneyland. Adult tickets cost $12 each and child tickets cost $8 each. Senior citizens can get tickets for ½ the adult ticket price and groups of 4 or more persons get a 20% discount on the total ticket cost. How much did they pay for tickets altogether?

48. Which information is needed to solve this problem?

(A) All you need are the prices of the tickets for adults and children.
(B) All you need is the total number of people who bought tickets.
(C) All you need are the total prices for the tickets, the number of adults, and the discount for groups of 4 or more.
(D) All you need are the number of adults, the number of children, the price of senior citizen tickets, and the price of adult and child tickets.
(E) All you need are the number of adults, the number of children, the price of adult and children tickets, and the discount for groups of 4 or more.

Use the problem stated below to answer item 49.
Problem: In a recent survey of 250 people, 130 preferred *Softie* paper towels to *Kleenup* paper towels, 100 people had no preference, and the remainder preferred *Kleenup*. What percent of those surveyed preferred *Kleenup* paper towels? Answer: 40%

49. Which statement best describes why the answer given is *not* reasonable?

(A) Only 20% of those surveyed preferred *Kleenup*.
(B) 130 is 52% of 250.
(C) 100 people had no preference and 100 is 40% of 250.
(D) Only 20 people preferred *Kleenup* and 20 is 8% of 250.
(E) There is not enough information to determine what percent preferred *Kleenup*.

Use the problem stated below to answer item 50.
Problem: Harvey started a savings account. At the beginning of the year he put \$284 in the account and left it for one year. At the end of the year he had earned 10¼% interest. How much money did he have in his savings account at the end of the year? Answer: \$313.11

50. Which statement best describes why the answer given for this problem is reasonable?

(A) The answer must be greater than \$284.
(B) \$313.11 is almost \$30 greater than \$284.
(C) \$313.11 rounds to \$310 and \$310 − \$284 = \$26; to the nearest ten \$26 rounds to \$30.
(D) 10% of \$284 is \$28.40; \$284 + \$28.40 = \$312.40; the answer will be a little more than \$312.40.
(E) Because he should get at least \$313 if he leaves his money in a savings account for an entire year.

Writing

Directions: You will have 60 minutes to write an essay on each of the following two topics. Try to spend approximately 30 minutes on each topic, as they are of equal value in the evaluation. While quantity is not as important as quality, the topics selected will probably require an essay rather than just a paragraph or two. Organization is an integral part of effective writing, so you may want to use some of the allotted time to plan your work. Support your ideas with clear, specific examples or explanations. Write legibly, and do not skip lines.

First Topic:

A lack of discipline in the schools, from unruliness in the classroom to vandalism on school property, is a constant topic of discussion among parents and educators. Discuss what you feel are the reasons for discipline problems.

Second Topic:

Describe one person you have known well who has significantly influenced your life.

ANSWER KEY

Reading

1. E	11. B	21. C	31. D	41. A
2. B	12. A	22. B	32. E	42. A
3. D	13. D	23. B	33. E	43. B
4. B	14. C	24. C	34. C	44. E
5. C	15. A	25. A	35. A	45. A
6. E	16. E	26. D	36. D	46. B
7. C	17. A	27. C	37. B	47. C
8. B	18. B	28. A	38. E	48. B
9. B	19. B	29. C	39. B	49. C
10. E	20. E	30. D	40. D	50. C

Mathematics

1. E	11. C	21. D	31. C	41. C
2. E	12. D	22. C	32. E	42. A
3. B	13. B	23. A	33. D	43. B
4. E	14. B	24. C	34. D	44. B
5. A	15. C	25. E	35. D	45. E
6. B	16. C	26. B	36. B	46. C
7. B	17. B	27. D	37. D	47. C
8. D	18. C	28. B	38. D	48. E
9. D	19. D	29. D	39. B	49. D
10. B	20. E	30. A	40. E	50. D

ANALYSIS OF ERRORS

The following table lists the subject matter covered in each question of the Reading and Mathematics sections of the test. Find the question numbers that you got wrong and review the subject matter covered in those questions again.

SECTION	QUESTION NUMBERS	SUBJECT AREA
READING		
	5, 13, 16, 18, 28, 49	Finding the Main Idea
	12, 14, 19, 21, 31, 32, 36, 37, 41, 43, 50	Finding Specific Details
	1, 4, 6, 15, 17, 20, 22, 29, 33, 34, 39, 40, 44	Finding Implications
	7, 8, 11, 26, 27, 31, 38, 42	Determining the Meaning of Strange Words
	30, 35	Determining Special Techniques
	2, 3, 9, 10, 23, 24, 25, 45, 46, 47, 48	Interpreting Tables and Graphs

SECTION	QUESTION NUMBERS	SUBJECT AREA
MATHEMATICS		
Arithmetic	2, 3, 10, 13, 14, 15, 16	Whole Numbers (IA)
	13, 18	Fractions (IB)
	4, 16, 21	Decimals (IC)
	9, 20	Percentage (ID)
	1	Rounding Off Numbers (IE)
	11	Signed Numbers (IF)
	8	Averages, Medians, Ranges, and Modes (IG)
	5	Powers, Exponents, and Roots (IH)
Algebra	22, 23, 25, 26, 43, 47, 48, 49, 50	Algebraic Expressions (IIA)
	27, 30, 44	Equations (IIB)
	19, 24, 41, 42, 45, 46	Verbal Problems (IIC)
	12	Counting Problems (IID)
	7, 36	Ratio and Proportion (IIE)
		Sequence and Progression (IIF)
	6, 14, 31	Inequalities (IIG)
Geometry	35	Angles (IIIA)
		Lines (IIIB)
		Polygons (IIIC)
	33, 38	Triangles (IIID)
		Quadrilaterals (IIIE)
		Circles (IIIF)
	32, 37, 39, 40	Area, Perimeter, and Volume (IIIG)
	29, 34	Coordinate Geometry (IIIH)
Formulas	28	Formulas
Other	17	Interpreting Graphs (see Reading Section)

ANSWER EXPLANATIONS

Reading

1. E It is implied that the freedom to protest creatively is uniquely American. Answer A limits the reasons for protest and B, C and D are not mentioned in the passage.

2. B The table shows that the median percentage for 9-year olds in "Main Ideas from Passages" was 45% (8th position) and for 13-year olds, it was 51% (8th position).

3. D The last line of the table must be used, which shows the range of medians for each age group. The range for 17-year olds is 68–84, a range of only 16 points, the smallest of all the ranges.

4. B The passage implies that the scientists' goal in creating new varieties of plants is to improve upon them. Answers A, C and E are not mentioned in the passage. D is inaccurate.

5. C The other titles are too specific or too general. The passage is mainly about the reconstruction process.

6. E The author apparently is concerned that debates over jurisdiction may delay the taking of action to prevent the loss of living specimens. Answer A is too strong, and B, C and D are inaccurate.

7. C It is safe to conclude that biotic refers to a more general classification, i.e., pertaining to life.

8. B The idea that the student asked for a clarification and was still confused suggests that the language was unclear or indirect.

9. B In 1955, voter registration was 100,000. This increased to approximately 225,000 in 1960, the greatest increase for any one period.

10. E In 1950, voter registration was 100,000, and in 1975, it was 300,000, an increase of 200,000 voters.

11. B In discussing the "other side," the author indicates that providing assistance may get in the way of (impair) the development of a motivation to work and save.

12. A The author does not support either side but presents the issue as a debatable question, with two sides.

13. D The issue discussed is whether it is helpful to provide assistance to the poor, i.e., how much should they be given and how much should they be encouraged to work for themselves? Answers A, C and E are too general; answer B is too specific.

14. C The writer states in the second sentence that the syndrome is sometimes referred to as a fear of success or as the need to fail. Paranoia (D) is too strong a statement.

15. A It is not stated, but one could easily conclude that it is the best answer because people always have believed in superstitious acts to ward off evil spirits or to keep from being jinxed.

16. E A paraphrase of the statement, "calamity waits in the wings in the hour of success," would be the idea that disaster often follows triumph.

17. A The last sentence in the passage allows one to assume that the author will go on to talk about the behavior of porpoises as an indication of their superior brains. The earlier references to prehensile organs are used to emphasize how surprising it is that porpoises are so intelligent.

18. B The author wishes to make the point that the correlation in animals between a high level of intelligence and the presence of a prehensile organ does not necessarily mean that the absence of such an organ is an indication of the absence of intelligence. Answer C states the opposite.

19. B The author states that using propaganda to manipulate minds is appalling.

20. E The author could most appropriately go on to talk about the adverse effect of propaganda in a democracy. It is unlikely that he would say it was contrary to *all* systems of government.

21. C It is implied that, although some people suggest that writers must base their writing on actual experience, their amazing creativity can compensate for any lack of experience.

22. B The writer seems to feel that personal experience is important but that writing which is worthwhile can be based on other, probably more important, creative instincts as well. The author does not advocate writing about subjects about which one is totally ignorant, so C is a poor choice.

23. B The shaded area of the graph, including the months of March and September, show the comfortable periods of the year. The other answers are not supported by the graph.

24. C The lowest temperature shown on the graph is 40° and the highest is about 90°.

25. A No wind, storm, or barometric pressure information is provided on the graph. It can be assumed, however, that the warm temperatures are a result of sunshine, so answer A is a viable use for this graph.

26. D Since the writer says it is plausible to suggest either of two sides of a question, one can conclude that there is no research evidence to support either side.

27. C The writer indicates that feelings of frustration have led to looking back with a fondness for the past and relating tales of woe that tend to blame the other side.

28. A The author feels that insisting that people conform to a dialect different from their own may be a violation of their rights.

29. C It is clear in the passage that the writer is biased against the attempt to eliminate variations in language.

30. D To make his point, the writer compares children's resistance to denying their own dialect to the rejection by black people of processes which deny their identity.

31. D The author's lament that man's experimentation has led to the exposure to greater dangers from radioactivity includes a reference to the need for tools to detect radioactivity.

32. E We are exposed to small doses of radiation that are part of our natural environment. Answer A is never mentioned, and answers B and C are clearly not daily occurrences for most people. Answer D is inaccurate.

33. E The author reflects his bias that it is much more difficult and demanding to create an image with words.

34. C The author feels his work is difficult to the point where it is nearly impossible to achieve the goals a writer sets out to accomplish.

35. A The writer compares and contrasts his task with that of the artist.

36. D It is emphasized that the only way one can master all of the information in a specialized field is to "chunk," or group it, into meaningful units, thus to process and learn more.

37. B Beginners, by definition, are unfamiliar with new material and, therefore, they cannot group bits of information, making it very difficult for them to remember so many pieces.

38. E The meaning of "chunking" is quite clearly implied in the passage as the grouping of pieces of information in order to make them more manageable.

39. B Since the writer is comparing the two approaches and states that variables and controls are not part of the ethnographic approach, one can assume that they belong to the other.

40. D One can assume that the writer discussed the experimental approach preceding this passage, but he introduces the ethnographic approach here, so he would not have written about it before.

41. A The writer is clear that the unique aspect of the ethnographic approach is that all elements are seen as part of the process.

42. A In explaining how much of a jump this would represent for man, the writer is indicating that the grasshopper's leap is immense.

43. B In lines 4 and 5, the writer specifies that chitin is a chemical compound found in the outside skeleton of the grasshopper.

44. E The writer is clearly respectful of the grasshopper's strong qualities.

45. A The population of the city increased by almost five times while the law enforcement budget only increased by about three times for the period shown.

46. B In 1950, the population was 3,000, and in 1978, it was about 18,000, an increase of 15,000 citizens.

47. C The amount of the budget for law enforcement was 12.5% in 1950, and 35.8% in 1978. This is an increase of almost three times.

48. B A careful reading of the graph shows that the population increased from 4,000 to 9,000 during these years.

49. C Enough information is presented and specific terms used that, even if it is not stated, one could conclude that the passage is about genetics.

50. C The writer states that *simple* characters are ones that are acquired in their entirety or not at all. The would be true of maleness or femaleness. The genes determine that one is either a male or a female. The other answers all could encompass a range of possible characteristics.

Mathematics

1. E $27\frac{1}{4} = 27.25$ which is .25 greater than 27. All other choices are further from 27 than .25.

2. E $7 \boxed{\times} (4 \boxed{-} 2)$
$= 7 \times 2$
$= 14$

3. B Answer A is not written as a number (has only 2 digits after the last comma).
Answer C is one thousand four hundred fourteen.
Answer D is one hundred forty thousand fourteen.
Answer E is one million four hundred thousand fourteen.

4. E The value of the 7 in each of the numerals is:
(A) 70
(B) 7
(C) 7
(D) 0.0007 (7/10000)
(E) 700

5. A The cube root r of a number n is that number such that $r^3 = n$ (i.e., $r \times r \times r = n$). Clearly $2 \times 2 \times 2 = (2^2 \times 2)$ or 8. So the cube root of $(2^2 \times 2)$ is 2.

6. B We are given that $A + B + C = 100$. If we replace A with D, which is greater than A, then the sum will be greater than 100 (i.e., $D + B + C > 100$).

7. B $C =$ number of cats
$C + D =$ total number of cats and dogs
$\frac{C}{C + D} =$ ratio of cats to total number of cats and dogs.

8. D Whenever a group of identical numbers, x, are averaged, the average will equal x. Thus, in this problem, no matter how many x's are averaged, the average must be 6.

9. D Let A be the amount we need to know:
$150 = {}^{75}\!/\!_{100} \times A$
${}^{100}\!/\!_{75} \times 150 = {}^{100}\!/\!_{75} \times {}^{75}\!/\!_{100} \times A$
$200 = A$

10. B A prime is a whole number that is divisible only by itself and 1.
I. $9 = 3 \times 3$ (not prime)
II. 13 has only 1 and 13 as factors, thus is prime.
III. 113 has only 1 and 113 as factors, thus is prime.
IV. $121 = 11 \times 11$ (not prime)

11. C $x = -5 - (-6)$
$x = -5 + 6$
$x = 1$
The additive inverse (opposite) of a number n is the number m such that $n + m = 0$. So the opposite of 1 is -1.

12. D Number of choices for first ice cream scoop = 6, for second scoop = 5, and for the topping = 3. Number of different sundaes
$= 6 \times 5 \times 3$
$= 90$

13. B The tank is ¼ full, so it has 4 gallons ($\frac{1}{4} \times 16 = 4$). Since the car averages 22 miles per gallon, it can go $4 \times 22 = 88$ miles.

14. B Try to create a score for each choice.

A. $15 + 10 + 8 > 30$ and is odd.

B. It is impossible to get a score greater than 30 without using 15, but if you use 15 and want an even score, you must also use 3. However, the largest score possible using 15 and 3 is $15 + 3 + 10 = 28$, which is smaller than 30.

C. $8 + 6 + 3 < 20$ and is odd.

D. $10 + 6 + 3 = 19$

E. $10 + 8 + 6 = 24$

15. C Draw a sketch and count the bounces.

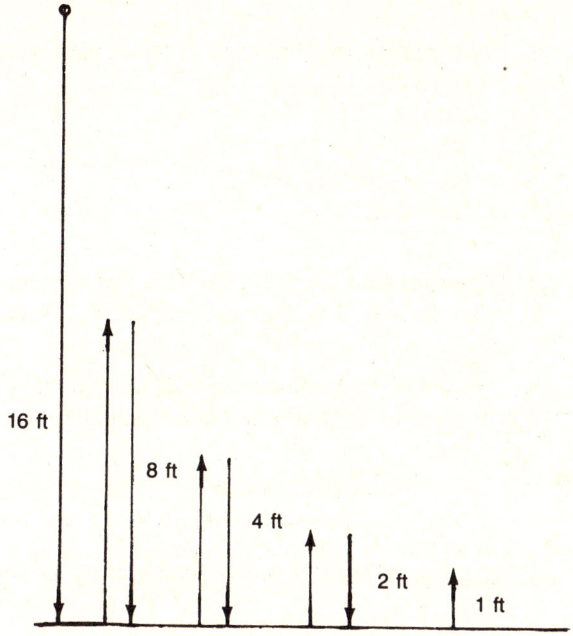

16. C If the temperature drops 4.5° for every 1000 feet, for 6000 feet it will have dropped $6 \times 4.5° = 27°$. If the underwater temperature is 37° and is 27° lower than at the surface, then the surface temperature is $37° + 27° = 64°$.

17. B Only graph B is constantly $.50 from 0 to ¼ mile and then rises at a rate of $.25 for each quarter mile thereafter.

18. C If ⅔ of the capacity is 60 gallons, then ⅓ of the capacity is 30 gallons ($60 \div 2$). So the total capacity (3/3) must be 3×30 or 90 gallons.

19. D Think of each person's share in terms of Shelley's share, S. Shelley gets S, Mario gets $2S$, and Pat gets $2 \times (2S)$ or $4S$. Since the total amount of money is $2100, we have

$$S + 2S + 4S = 2100$$
$$7S = 2100$$
$$S = 2100/7$$
$$S = 300$$

So Shelley gets $300. Since Pat gets $4S$, then Pat gets $4 \times 300 = \$1200$.

20. E Suppose x represents the cost of the dinner (not including tax). Then the tax is $.05x$. Ms. White paid $5.04 which included the cost of the dinner (x) and the tax ($.05x$).

$$\text{So, } x + .05x = 5.04$$
$$1.05x = 5.04$$
$$x = 5.04/1.05$$
$$x = 4.80$$

The dinner cost $4.80. So the tax was $.24.
($5.04 − 4.80 = $.24 or .05 × $4.80 = $.24)

21. D If February 1 is a Sunday and there are 28 days in the month, there are four Sundays and four full weeks in the month. Daily except Sunday, Harold gets $\$1.75 \times 20 \times 4 = \$140.00$. Sunday only, Harold gets $\$1.00 \times 30 \times 4 = \$120.00$. All week, Harold gets $\$2.50 \times 50 \times 4 = \$500.00$. Adding these 3 amounts gives a total for the month of \$760.

22. C $(3x + 5) - [3x - (-x + 1) - 3]$
$= (3x + 5) - [3x + x - 1 - 3]$
$= (3x + 5) - [4x - 4]$
$= 3x + 5 - 4x + 4$
$= -x + 9$

23. A $2x^2 - 2 - (3x^3 - 2x + 3)$
$= 2x^2 - 2 - 3x^2 + 2x - 3$
$= -x^2 + 2x - 5$

24. C Try each of the choices.
A. $6 \times 8 = 48$ candies (OK)
and $6 \times \$.72 = \$4.32$ (not OK)
B. $8 \times 6 = 48$ candies (OK)
and $8 \times \$.45 = \$3.60$ (not OK)
C. $(3 \times 8) + (4 \times 6) = 48$ candies (OK)
and $(3 \times \$.72) + (4 \times \$.45) = \$3.96$ (OK)

25. E Try to match each choice with another linear factor to give the product $3x^2 + 2x - 5$. In each case, except E, whenever a factor gives the correct first and last terms, the middle term is incorrect.
(A) $(x + 1)(3x - 5) = 3x^2 - 2x - 5$
(B) $(x + 5)(3x - 1) = 3x^2 + 14x - 5$
(C) $(3x + 1)(x - 5) = 3x^2 - 14x - 5$
(D) $(3x - 1)(x + 5) = 3x^2 + 14x - 5$
(E) $(3x + 5)(x - 1) = 3x^2 + 2x - 5$

26. B Given: $x = 4,\ y = 2$
Substituting into: $x^2\, y - xy^2$
We obtain: $(4)^2\, 2 - 4\,(2)^2$
$= 16 \cdot 2 - 4 \cdot 4$
$= 32 - 16 = 16$

27. D $\sqrt{x - 5} - 3 = 0$
$\sqrt{x - 5} = 3$
$(\sqrt{x - 5})^2 = (3)^2$
$x - 5 = 9$
$x = 9 + 5$
$x = 14$

28. B Given: $F = (9/5)C + 32°$
$F = 68°$
Substituting: $68° = (9/5)C + 32°$
$(9/5)C = 68° - 32°$
$(9/5)C = 36°$
$(5/9)(9/5)C = (5/9)(36°/1)$
$(1)C = (180°/9)$
$C = 20°$

29. D The pattern is such that each pair (x, y) is determined by $y = 2^x$. So $y = 2^5$, $y = 32$.

30. A $.5x - 3 = 7$

$$.5x = 7 + 3$$
$$.5x = 10$$
$$x = (10/.5)$$
$$x = 20$$

31. C Given: $m > 0$ and $n < 0$
In other words, m is positive and n is negative. $1/m$ is positive, $1/n$ is negative so $1/m > 1/n$. (Any positive number is greater than any negative number.)

32. E In order to determine the number of cubic yards (i.e. volume) we must transform all the measurements into the same units.
Since 3 feet = 1 yard we have: 21 feet = 7 yards
27 feet = 9 yards
and since 36 inches = 1 yard
4 inches = $1/9$ yard
The volume is the product of all the measurements of the garden: Volume = $1/9 \times 7 \times 9 = 7$ cubic yards

33. D Examine the extreme cases for y. If y were exactly 90 the Pythagorean Theorem could be used to find x:

$$x^2 = 10^2 + 10^2$$
$$x = 2 \cdot 10^2$$
$$x = 10\sqrt{2}$$

If y were exactly 180, the side would form a straight line of length 20.
So, in order to form a triangle according to the restrictions of the problem, side x must be between $10\sqrt{2}$ and 20.

34. D The straight line PQ and the x and y axes form similar triangles, for all points on PQ. So the triangle PQR is similar to triangle SOQ, where S is the point on the y axis. The coordinates of point S can be determined by the following proportion:

$$\frac{3}{9} = \frac{2}{y}$$
$$3y = 18$$
$$y = 6$$

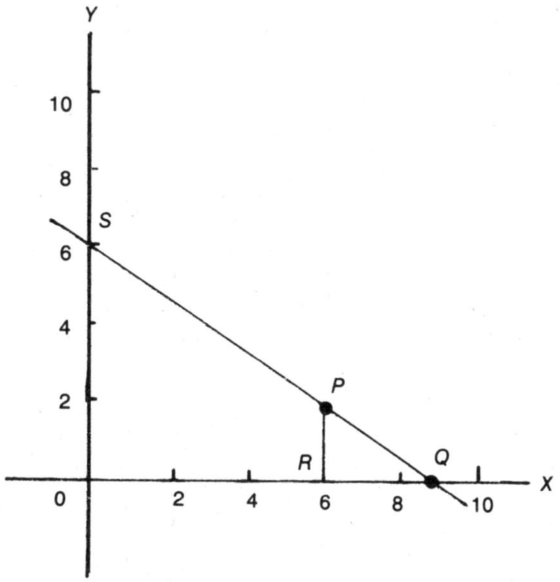

35. D The face of the clock (total of 360°) is subdivided into 12 equal parts (30° each). Each hour the hour hand moves exactly 30°. So at 5 o'clock the hands of the clock form an angle of:

$$5 \times 30° = 150°$$

36. B The figures above represent the flagpole and yardstick and the shadows they cast, respectively. The situation involves similar triangles for which the following proportions can be written:

$$\frac{x}{25} = \frac{3}{5}$$
$$5x = 3 \times 25$$
$$5x = 75$$
$$x = 15$$

So, the flagpole is 15 feet high.

37. D Triangle *ABC* is a right triangle. In order to find the measure of side *AB* we can use the Pythagorean Theorem:

$$(AB)^2 + 4^2 = 5^2$$
$$(AB)^2 + 16 = 25$$
$$(AB)^2 = 25 - 16$$
$$(AB)^2 = 9$$
$$(AB) = 3$$

The area of a right triangle is:

$$\text{Area} = \tfrac{1}{2} \times \text{base} \times \text{height}$$
$$\text{Area} = \tfrac{1}{2} \times 3 \times 4 = \tfrac{12}{2}$$
$$\text{Area} = 6 \text{ square units}$$

38. D In order for a triple of numbers to qualify as sides of a triangle the sum of any two of the numbers must be greater than the third. Only choices II and III satisfy this condition. So choices I and IV could not be the lengths of the sides of a triangle.

39. B Ps: Perimeter of square $= 4 \times s$
As: Area of square $= s \times s$
Pt: Perimeter of an equilateral triangle $= 3 \times t$

$$\text{As} = s \times s = 9 \text{ units}$$
$$s = 3 \text{ units}$$
$$\text{Ps} = 4 \times s = 12 \text{ units}$$
$$\text{Pt} = 3 \times t = 12 \text{ units}$$
$$t = 4 \text{ units}$$

So, the side of the triangle measures 4 units.

40. E If the side of the square is s, the perimeter will be $4s$. Because it has a factor of 4, the perimeter will always be divisible by 4. But, if the perimeter is also to be divisible by 3 it must have a factor of 3 as well. So s must be a multiple of 3 (e.g., 3, 6, 9, 12, etc.) None of choices A–D is a multiple of 3.

41. C The problem asks us to find the price per pound of beef which has had the waste removed, given that we know the price per pound of the beef including the waste. Choice C is the only one that asks this same question.

42. A We are told that it takes two hours to travel 100 miles, and asked how long it would take to travel 80 miles. Only choice A rephrases this same question.

43. B Bert sold B boxes. Joan sold one box less than Bert. So, the number of boxes sold by Joan is $B - 1$.

44. B Bert sold B boxes. Joan sold $B - 1$ boxes (one box less than Bert). Rhonda sold $(\frac{1}{2})B$ boxes (half as many boxes as Bert). Altogether they sold 89 boxes. Thus, $B + B - 1 + (\frac{1}{2})B = 89$.

45. E (Recall: Distance = Rate × Time or Time = Distance/Rate) To determine how long it took to bike from the park to school, we would need to divide the distance by the rate (10 m.p.h.). However, the distance between the park and the school is not given. This additional information is necessary to answer the question.

46. C Refer to the explanation of problem 45. It is necessary to know both the distance and the rate to find the time. The rate (10 miles per hour) is included in the problem.

47. C Choice C can be solved as follows:

Begin by guessing that Bill and Lou make the same amount, $66 each. Then (since Bill actually earns $6 more) add $3 to Bill's salary and subtract $3 from Lou's salary. So $66 + 3 = 69$ is Bill's salary and $66 - 3 = 63$ is Lou's salary. These steps are exactly the same as those used in the farmer problem.

48. E The answer would be found by first multiplying the number of adults (2) times the price per adult (12), next multiplying the number of children (3) times the price per child ($8) and then adding the two results ($24 + 24 = 48$). Since the family has more than 5 persons, we would then subtract the 20% discount ($.20 \times 48$) from the total ticket price to obtain the final total price. Choice E includes all the information necessary for this solution.

49. D If, in a survey of 250 people, 130 people preferred Softie and 100 people had no preference then 20 people preferred Kleenup ($250 - 130 - 100$). Twenty people of a total of 250 people is less than 10% (10% of 250 is 25), so 40% is clearly not a reasonable answer. Choice D outlines this line of reasoning.

50. D Harvey earned 10¼% interest—just slightly more than 10%. It is easy to figure 10% of 284—multiply $.10 \times 284 = 28.4$ (just move the decimal point in 284 one place to the left). So Harvey will have slightly more than $284 + $28.40 ($312.40) at the end of one year. Choice D explains this line of reasoning.

Writing

The following essay outlines have been written to demonstrate the planning of well-written answers to the topics given. Use these only as guidelines to evaluating your own organization. Many different organization patterns and plans could work equally well for the topics given.

First Topic:

A lack of discipline in the schools, from unruliness in the classroom to vandalism on school property, is a constant topic of discussion among parents and educators. Discuss what you feel are the reasons for discipline problems.

Essay Outline:

A. Introduction
   1. General description of background information; presentation of setting for thesis.
   2. Presentation of thesis or point of view.

B. Reasons
   1. State reason in clear, concise terms.
      (Ex.: "A lack of discipline in the schools, whether it is manifested as distracting behavior in the classroom or violent aggressiveness on school grounds, can be attributed to specific situations in the home.")
      a. Elaborate idea presented by giving more information, stating the position another way, or explaining more.
      b. Support thesis with examples.
   2. Present additional reasons in same manner as above.

C. Summary and conclusions
   1. Restate in brief terms the reasons stated in the body of the paper.
   2. Give conclusions in the form of implications, prognosis, or recommendations.

Second Topic:

Describe one person you have known well who has significantly influenced your life.

Essay Outline:

A. Introduction
   1. Introduce person by giving a personal anecdote or unique characteristic of the person.
   2. Give an indication of how your life was changed by this person.

B. Description in more extensive detail
   1. Special qualities
   2. Context of acquaintance
   3. Nature of relationship

C. Influence—positive or negative
   1. Direction and nature of influence
   2. Personal reaction to person's influence
   3. Specific examples

D. Conclusions
   1. Summarize what has been said about person's influence.
   2. Conclude with general feelings currently about person's influence.

ANSWER SHEET— MODEL TEST TWO

Reading

1. Ⓐ Ⓑ Ⓒ Ⓓ Ⓔ
2. Ⓐ Ⓑ Ⓒ Ⓓ Ⓔ
3. Ⓐ Ⓑ Ⓒ Ⓓ Ⓔ
4. Ⓐ Ⓑ Ⓒ Ⓓ Ⓔ
5. Ⓐ Ⓑ Ⓒ Ⓓ Ⓔ
6. Ⓐ Ⓑ Ⓒ Ⓓ Ⓔ
7. Ⓐ Ⓑ Ⓒ Ⓓ Ⓔ
8. Ⓐ Ⓑ Ⓒ Ⓓ Ⓔ
9. Ⓐ Ⓑ Ⓒ Ⓓ Ⓔ
10. Ⓐ Ⓑ Ⓒ Ⓓ Ⓔ
11. Ⓐ Ⓑ Ⓒ Ⓓ Ⓔ
12. Ⓐ Ⓑ Ⓒ Ⓓ Ⓔ
13. Ⓐ Ⓑ Ⓒ Ⓓ Ⓔ
14. Ⓐ Ⓑ Ⓒ Ⓓ Ⓔ
15. Ⓐ Ⓑ Ⓒ Ⓓ Ⓔ
16. Ⓐ Ⓑ Ⓒ Ⓓ Ⓔ
17. Ⓐ Ⓑ Ⓒ Ⓓ Ⓔ
18. Ⓐ Ⓑ Ⓒ Ⓓ Ⓔ
19. Ⓐ Ⓑ Ⓒ Ⓓ Ⓔ
20. Ⓐ Ⓑ Ⓒ Ⓓ Ⓔ
21. Ⓐ Ⓑ Ⓒ Ⓓ Ⓔ
22. Ⓐ Ⓑ Ⓒ Ⓓ Ⓔ
23. Ⓐ Ⓑ Ⓒ Ⓓ Ⓔ
24. Ⓐ Ⓑ Ⓒ Ⓓ Ⓔ
25. Ⓐ Ⓑ Ⓒ Ⓓ Ⓔ
26. Ⓐ Ⓑ Ⓒ Ⓓ Ⓔ
27. Ⓐ Ⓑ Ⓒ Ⓓ Ⓔ
28. Ⓐ Ⓑ Ⓒ Ⓓ Ⓔ
29. Ⓐ Ⓑ Ⓒ Ⓓ Ⓔ
30. Ⓐ Ⓑ Ⓒ Ⓓ Ⓔ
31. Ⓐ Ⓑ Ⓒ Ⓓ Ⓔ
32. Ⓐ Ⓑ Ⓒ Ⓓ Ⓔ
33. Ⓐ Ⓑ Ⓒ Ⓓ Ⓔ
34. Ⓐ Ⓑ Ⓒ Ⓓ Ⓔ
35. Ⓐ Ⓑ Ⓒ Ⓓ Ⓔ
36. Ⓐ Ⓑ Ⓒ Ⓓ Ⓔ
37. Ⓐ Ⓑ Ⓒ Ⓓ Ⓔ
38. Ⓐ Ⓑ Ⓒ Ⓓ Ⓔ
39. Ⓐ Ⓑ Ⓒ Ⓓ Ⓔ
40. Ⓐ Ⓑ Ⓒ Ⓓ Ⓔ
41. Ⓐ Ⓑ Ⓒ Ⓓ Ⓔ
42. Ⓐ Ⓑ Ⓒ Ⓓ Ⓔ
43. Ⓐ Ⓑ Ⓒ Ⓓ Ⓔ
44. Ⓐ Ⓑ Ⓒ Ⓓ Ⓔ
45. Ⓐ Ⓑ Ⓒ Ⓓ Ⓔ
46. Ⓐ Ⓑ Ⓒ Ⓓ Ⓔ
47. Ⓐ Ⓑ Ⓒ Ⓓ Ⓔ
48. Ⓐ Ⓑ Ⓒ Ⓓ Ⓔ
49. Ⓐ Ⓑ Ⓒ Ⓓ Ⓔ
50. Ⓐ Ⓑ Ⓒ Ⓓ Ⓔ

Mathematics

1. Ⓐ Ⓑ Ⓒ Ⓓ Ⓔ
2. Ⓐ Ⓑ Ⓒ Ⓓ Ⓔ
3. Ⓐ Ⓑ Ⓒ Ⓓ Ⓔ
4. Ⓐ Ⓑ Ⓒ Ⓓ Ⓔ
5. Ⓐ Ⓑ Ⓒ Ⓓ Ⓔ
6. Ⓐ Ⓑ Ⓒ Ⓓ Ⓔ
7. Ⓐ Ⓑ Ⓒ Ⓓ Ⓔ
8. Ⓐ Ⓑ Ⓒ Ⓓ Ⓔ
9. Ⓐ Ⓑ Ⓒ Ⓓ Ⓔ
10. Ⓐ Ⓑ Ⓒ Ⓓ Ⓔ
11. Ⓐ Ⓑ Ⓒ Ⓓ Ⓔ
12. Ⓐ Ⓑ Ⓒ Ⓓ Ⓔ
13. Ⓐ Ⓑ Ⓒ Ⓓ Ⓔ
14. Ⓐ Ⓑ Ⓒ Ⓓ Ⓔ
15. Ⓐ Ⓑ Ⓒ Ⓓ Ⓔ
16. Ⓐ Ⓑ Ⓒ Ⓓ Ⓔ
17. Ⓐ Ⓑ Ⓒ Ⓓ Ⓔ
18. Ⓐ Ⓑ Ⓒ Ⓓ Ⓔ
19. Ⓐ Ⓑ Ⓒ Ⓓ Ⓔ
20. Ⓐ Ⓑ Ⓒ Ⓓ Ⓔ
21. Ⓐ Ⓑ Ⓒ Ⓓ Ⓔ
22. Ⓐ Ⓑ Ⓒ Ⓓ Ⓔ
23. Ⓐ Ⓑ Ⓒ Ⓓ Ⓔ
24. Ⓐ Ⓑ Ⓒ Ⓓ Ⓔ
25. Ⓐ Ⓑ Ⓒ Ⓓ Ⓔ
26. Ⓐ Ⓑ Ⓒ Ⓓ Ⓔ
27. Ⓐ Ⓑ Ⓒ Ⓓ Ⓔ
28. Ⓐ Ⓑ Ⓒ Ⓓ Ⓔ
29. Ⓐ Ⓑ Ⓒ Ⓓ Ⓔ
30. Ⓐ Ⓑ Ⓒ Ⓓ Ⓔ
31. Ⓐ Ⓑ Ⓒ Ⓓ Ⓔ
32. Ⓐ Ⓑ Ⓒ Ⓓ Ⓔ
33. Ⓐ Ⓑ Ⓒ Ⓓ Ⓔ
34. Ⓐ Ⓑ Ⓒ Ⓓ Ⓔ
35. Ⓐ Ⓑ Ⓒ Ⓓ Ⓔ
36. Ⓐ Ⓑ Ⓒ Ⓓ Ⓔ
37. Ⓐ Ⓑ Ⓒ Ⓓ Ⓔ
38. Ⓐ Ⓑ Ⓒ Ⓓ Ⓔ
39. Ⓐ Ⓑ Ⓒ Ⓓ Ⓔ
40. Ⓐ Ⓑ Ⓒ Ⓓ Ⓔ
41. Ⓐ Ⓑ Ⓒ Ⓓ Ⓔ
42. Ⓐ Ⓑ Ⓒ Ⓓ Ⓔ
43. Ⓐ Ⓑ Ⓒ Ⓓ Ⓔ
44. Ⓐ Ⓑ Ⓒ Ⓓ Ⓔ
45. Ⓐ Ⓑ Ⓒ Ⓓ Ⓔ
46. Ⓐ Ⓑ Ⓒ Ⓓ Ⓔ
47. Ⓐ Ⓑ Ⓒ Ⓓ Ⓔ
48. Ⓐ Ⓑ Ⓒ Ⓓ Ⓔ
49. Ⓐ Ⓑ Ⓒ Ⓓ Ⓔ
50. Ⓐ Ⓑ Ⓒ Ⓓ Ⓔ

CHAPTER 7

MODEL TEST TWO

EXAMINATION

Reading

Directions: Each passage in this section is followed by a question or questions about its content. Select the best answer to each question based on what is stated or implied in the selection. You may spend up to 60 minutes on this section.

Questions 1–2

A new form of painting developed by a group of former illustrators in 1909 was called the ''Ashcan School.'' The name was derived from the fact that these artists portrayed distinctly unglamorous subjects. Their works often depicted the harsh reality of life faced by those who live in large urban areas—especially New York City.

1. The nickname borne by the group of artists mentioned in the passage

(A) was not the one adopted by the artists themselves.
(B) was given to them by a teacher from the original school.
(C) identified them as former newspaper men.
(D) resulted from their unpleasant subjects.
(E) reflected the opinion of the artistic community.

2. Any of the following might be included in works by artists of the ''Ashcan School'' EXCEPT

(A) slum dwellings.
(B) city beautification projects.
(C) littered sidewalks.
(D) subway entrances.
(E) crowded downtown sidewalks.

Questions 3–4

Recent archeological findings have suggested the fact that humans and the apes have a common ancestor which is less simian than creatures previously considered to be the human ancestor. The discovery of a 17 million-year-old fossil in Africa brings into question the long-held idea that humans evolved from the apes. Since it predates the time when the two species are supposed to have branched apart, it suggests a common ancestor which is more humanlike than apelike.

3. According to the passage, it is possible that

(A) more fossils which support the theory will soon be found.
(B) apes evolved from humans.
(C) the discovered fossil predates all other findings.
(D) the human species evolved from simians.
(E) the fossil is not really 17 million years old.

4. Which of the following statements is most appropriate as a continuation of this passage?

(A) Fossil jawbones and molars provide dental evidence to support this suggestion.
(B) It calls into question the use of anatomical traits to determine ancestry.
(C) Scanning primal remains with electron microscopes reveals its simian characteristics.
(D) Both species, then, can be considered to be the likely progenitor.
(E) The new family tree will show orangutans, rather than chimps, to be the closest relative.

Questions 5–7

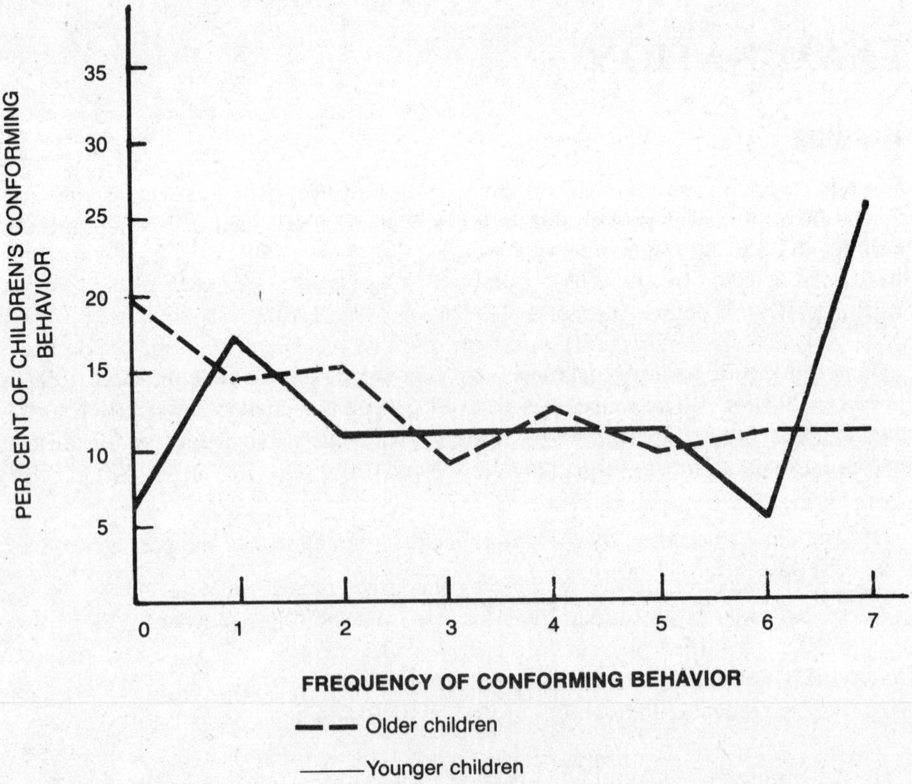

The graph shows the results of an experiment that studied the effects on a child's judgment o[f] being in a group which unanimously gives wrong answers. The experimenter's purpose was t[o] find out how often younger and older children yield to group influences. Refer to the graph t[o] answer the questions.

5. From the graph, one could say that

(A) four percent of the older children exhibit conforming behavior.
(B) about 18% of the younger children conformed to the group in one instance.
(C) 20% of the younger children and about 6% of the older children never followed th[e] group.
(D) there was no evidence that either younger or older children changed their judgment in order to conform to the group.
(E) the younger children were influenced by the older children.

6. The findings show that, in general,

(A) the experiment was too complicated to reveal anything.
(B) the effect of peer pressure is much more evident in the older children.
(C) the influence of the group was more pronounced on the younger than on the olde[r] children.

(D) children cannot make accurate judgments when they are in a group of their peers.
(E) children will stick with an answer if they are sure they are right.

7. The experimenter found that when a child had given what was obviously a correct response and the group (as instructed) gave an incorrect response, the child would show signs of discomfort: fidget in his seat, rub his eyes, etc. From this, and the findings as shown on the graph, the experimenter could conclude that

(A) the effect of a group's judgment on a child is not very strong.
(B) a willingness to change judgments to conform to a group is not evident in children.
(C) incorrect responses make a child feel uncomfortable.
(D) there is a strong tendency of children to conform to a group, but it is not easy for them to do so.
(E) pressuring a child to respond when he is uncertain of an answer is an unfair tactic.

Questions 8–11

The possibility of the existence of black holes in space has generated a vast amount of speculation, debate, and research since it was first suggested in the 1930's. Signals from deep in space have been detected by an orbiting satellite that indicate the presence of an object smaller than the earth, but with a degree of energy 1,000 times greater than the sun. Having named it Cygmus X-1, scientists generally agree that forces being exerted to slacken the pace of disintegrating galaxies probably originate in black holes such as this one. When thermonuclear fires that power very large stars are extinguished, the star's atoms compress with such a tremendous force that only the nuclei remain, nuclei with the same amount of matter and the same gravitational force. The force, however, is so intensely focused that no light can escape, and the star literally turns itself inside out, becoming a black hole.

8. Cygmus X-1 is

(A) an orbiting satellite.
(B) a black hole.
(C) a force.
(D) an object floating in space.
(E) a disintegrating galaxy.

9. From this passage, one could conclude that

(A) the presence of such an object in space is a great danger to space travellers.
(B) information about black holes is based on speculation, and there is little agreement among scientists about their origin.
(C) the nucleus of an extinguished star eventually breaks apart.
(D) black holes are referred to in this way because no light from them reaches our eyes.
(E) all stars eventually burn out.

10. The writer implies that

(A) galaxies are disintegrating at a decreasing rate.
(B) signals in space are often unidentified.
(C) objects entering a black hole move only in one direction.
(D) as a star shrinks, its gravitational force abates.
(E) time and space are extended within a black hole.

11. Which of the following statements is most appropriate as a continuation of the passage?

(A) Thermonuclear fires are extinguished, and the star's gravitational force begins to increase.

(B) While the gravitational force exerted outside the hole is a ''pulling'' one, inside it becomes a ''pushing'' force, and an object pulled in is lost forever in space.
(C) The force created by this action is so tremendous that the star may be drawn into this vacuum in space.
(D) This black hole no longer exhibits any gravitational force or any form of energy.
(E) The gravitational radius is the point where the star's compacting action is at its limit, and the creation of a black hole is no longer possible.

Questions 12–13

Why children everywhere throughout history have invariably exhibited the unconscious inclination, at some specific point in learning to draw, to draw a circle with an X or cross in it, known as a *mandala,* is unknown. Art can be an expression of feeling or ideas, and it is often an index of a time and a culture. People have always drawn mandalas in association with very intense experiences.

12. An idea that is expressed in this passage is that

(A) art is an unconscious expression of hostility.
(B) art transcends all time.
(C) children's art provides keys to the history of a culture.
(D) children draw mandalas without thinking or learning about them.
(E) symbols represent intense feelings.

13. According to the author, all of the following are true about mandalas EXCEPT

(A) they are commonly drawn by children.
(B) they can be used to study cultures.
(C) they can be circular or elliptical.
(D) they have been used throughout history.
(E) no one knows why children draw them.

Questions 14–15

When two lions made a raid on the village, three English officers and several natives were off in pursuit the very next day. After a very few hours, one of the pair had been killed, but the other escaped into the jungle. When one of the officers caught a glimpse of the lion, he instantly fired, enraging the beast so that it rushed toward him at full speed. The captain saw its movement and knew that if he tried to get into a better position for firing, he would be directly in the way of the charge. He decided to stand transfixed, trusting that when the lion passed by him unaware, he could shoot to advantage. He was, however, deceived.

14. Which of the following sentences would be most appropriate as a continuation of this passage?

(A) Unlike his adversary, his efforts were thwarted.
(B) The animal saw him and flew at him in a dreadful rage.
(C) The villagers suddenly appeared shouting their objections.
(D) The other officer turned and fired at him.
(E) The lion cowered and fell to the ground.

15. The best title for this selection is

(A) The Captain's Misjudgment.
(B) Hunting.
(C) Revenge by a Lion.
(D) Raid on a Village.
(E) Escape to the Jungle.

Questions 16–18

It is sometimes lost sight of that the importance of educational endeavors, of studying and pushing the mind not only to remember, but to grasp and calculate, is not in the number of facts retained, since most are not, but in the development of a better and more powerful instrument. The mind, like the body, is a thing whereof the powers are developed by effort.

16. The author makes the point that many of the facts acquired through study

(A) are of dubious value.
(B) are too changeable to be considered important.
(C) will be forgotten.
(D) will be of more use later in life.
(E) will contribute to a broader understanding of life.

17. The ''instrument'' referred to by the author is

(A) the body.
(B) a calculator.
(C) something which processes information, such as a computer.
(D) something used to solve simple problems, such as a ruler.
(E) the mind.

18. The ''powers'' in line 5 could be referred to as

(A) the powers that be.
(B) the powers at large.
(C) the powers generated.
(D) the powers of the mind.
(E) muscle power.

Questions 19–20

The majority of the population of the Near East lives in the villages. The villager is rooted to the land, land which is not owned by the villagers but by landlords or the government. The vagaries of the seasons, along with high rentals and taxes, have made village farming difficult. When difficulties arise, nomads can move to escape those difficulties, but, tied as they are to the land, villagers find it almost impossible, making them more exploitable.

19. A good title for this selection would be

(A) Plight of the Villagers in the Near East.
(B) Land Exploitation in the Near East.
(C) Village Life in the Third World.
(D) Farming and the Nomads.
(E) Agricultural Progress in the Near East.

20. A word that could be used in place of ''vagaries'' as used in this passage is

(A) temperatures.
(B) precipitation.
(C) significance.
(D) changeableness.
(E) conditions.

Questions 21–22

The elements found in plant and animal cells—oxygen, hydrogen, nitrogen, carbon, phosphorus, sulfur, and trace elements—are, in themselves, nonliving or inorganic. Combined in the right proportions, however, they become part of a living system. The nucleus of the cell, which contains the vital chromosomal material, determines, indirectly, the biochemical activity and specific characteristics of all cellular organisms.

21. Substances in the nuclei of cells are

(A) combined with chromosomal material.
(B) in different proportions depending on their activity.
(C) essential to life.
(D) biochemical.
(E) all organic when found in isolation.

22. The author stresses

(A) the unique composition of the nucleus of a plant or animal cell.
(B) the interaction of substances in living cells.
(C) the effect of chromosomal activity in cellular organisms.
(D) the contrast between organic and inorganic substances in cells.
(E) the characteristics determined by chromosomes.

Questions 23–25

The upsurge of interest in reading comprehension has been so dramatic in recent years that i is difficult to review pertinent information from related disciplines, analyze it for commonalitie and interrelationships, and make generalizations or draw any conclusions. Current references b educators to relevant information from the varying disciplines of psycholinguistics, sociolinguis tics, and cognitive psychology do not seem to be amenable to any language of coherence. Re searchers in the related disciplines are either looking at language processing in very general term or are analyzing small bits and pieces, or they are only beginning to consider certain aspects o language. Psycholinguists, for example, spent a considerable amount of time investigating th psychological reality of various linguistic units and the processing of these units and, only recently have begun to consider the role of semantics.

23. According to the writer, information from related disciplines

(A) has provided the most important facts about reading comprehension.
(B) has no bearing at all on the study of reading comprehension.
(C) has been largely unproductive thus far.
(D) is based on poorly done research.
(E) allows researchers to form a specific model of comprehension.

24. By "language of coherence," the author means

(A) colloquial expressions.
(B) mutually intelligible languages.
(C) terms for putting divergent ideas together.
(D) specialized jargons.
(E) a related language and its derivatives.

25. The writer implies that

(A) knowing if a linguistic element, such as a phoneme, is psychologically real con tributes little to an overall understanding of comprehension.

(B) it is difficult to understand the research of unrelated disciplines.
(C) researchers do not apply what they learn from research in any practical way.
(D) as with other information from related fields, semantics will not be a productive area.
(E) sociolinguists and psycholinguists cannot speak the same language.

Questions 26–27

One of the most powerful forces in the human psyche, phobias are enigmatic because they also will loosen their grip on a person quite readily. This fact accounts for their common identification as a set of symptoms, rather than as a neurosis with a ponderous label. Therapists, in fact, have taken the position that, in most cases, the symptoms are, themselves, the disease. As such, they can be treated and often with relatively quick results. The woman who has withdrawn into the shell of her house for a period of thirty years because she is terrified of going out may, with a very short period of treatment, be back on the streets.

26. The main point of this passage is that

(A) phobias afflict a large proportion of people in modern society.
(B) while a phobia may handicap a person for a long time, it can be alleviated easily.
(C) the cause for phobias has not been determined.
(D) like alcoholism, a phobia is a disease that resists treatment.
(E) a phobia is a neurosis that mainly afflicts women.

27. The author makes his point by use of

(A) example.
(B) allusion.
(C) exaggeration.
(D) logic.
(E) analogy.

Questions 28–30

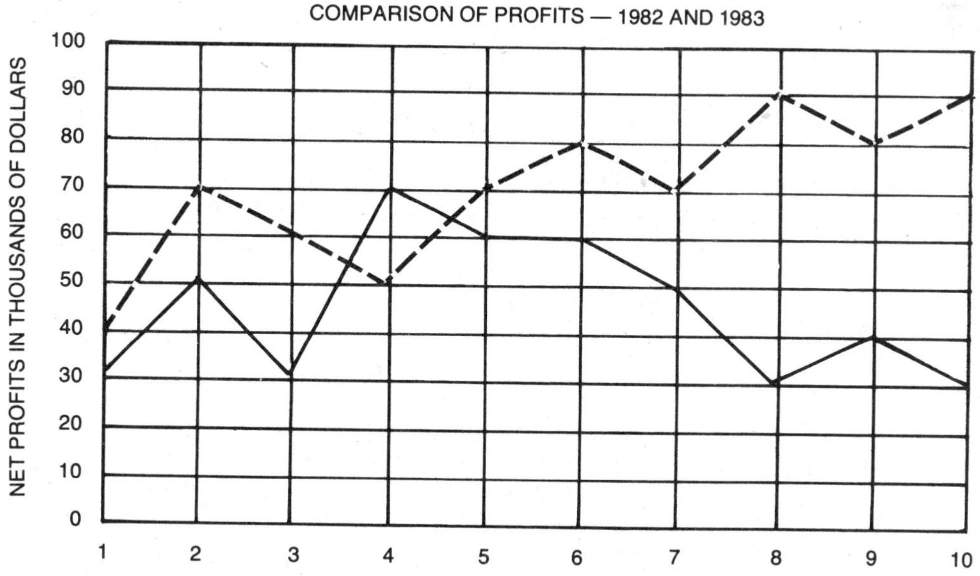

28. A small company wants to compare profits for two different years of operation. The solid line on the graph represents its profits in 1982. The broken line represents profits for 1983.

According to the graph, profits for 1982 were lower than 1983 for every month except the month numbered

(A) 3
(B) 8
(C) 4
(D) 7
(E) 5

29. How much more were the profits for the best month in 1983 over the best month in 1982?

(A) $20,000
(B) $10,000
(C) $40,000
(D) $15,000
(E) $30,000

30. Which pair of figures below represents the comparison of average monthly profits for 1982 and 1983?

(A) $45,000–$70,000
(B) $35,000–$65,000
(C) $10,000–$30,000
(D) $30,000–$90,000
(E) $50,000–$85,000

Questions 31–33

Without constant and active participation, not necessarily in an official capacity, in the details of politics on the part of the most intelligent citizens, there is the danger that the conduct of public affairs will fall under the control of selfish and ignorant or crafty and venal men. The duties and services which, when selfishly and ignorantly performed, stigmatize a man as a mere politician, ensure the success of democracy when performed with honor and vigilance.

31. In this passage, the term "politician" is used with

(A) respect.
(B) the best intentions.
(C) disdain.
(D) amusement.
(E) some degree of compassion.

32. It is clear in this passage that the author is in favor of

(A) control of services by politicians.
(B) vigilant monitoring of committees.
(C) less involvement in public affairs by those who are uninformed.
(D) democratic participation by interested citizens.
(E) more emphasis on the needs of the community at large.

33. A word that could be used in place of "venal" in this passage is

(A) vengeful.
(B) rebellious.
(C) corrupt.
(D) progressive.
(E) naive.

Questions 34–36

Students who are considered gifted need to be concerned with the structure and form of literature, and they are able to deal with the poet's technique in a way that is not possible with less able students. Yet they are not different from other students so far as interests and rewards sought in reading are concerned. It is possible for bright students to present glib technical analyses of literary selections without really developing a mature understanding of literature as a reconstruction of experience. Depth should be the goal.

34. Which of the following sentences is most appropriate as a continuation of the paragraph?

(A) Literature study for gifted students should be planned to avoid this pitfall.
(B) If instead, the goal is merely to cover the most material, many important works will be given a surface reading, without any real understanding or appreciation as the result.
(C) It is better for these students to study a wide range of selections in the interest of forming many bases of comparison than to attempt to develop a thorough understanding of one piece.
(D) In literature, the needs of gifted students can be met by using procedures for differentiating instruction.
(E) At the same time, comparative study of similar genres will provide additional information.

35. The author's purpose is to

(A) convince the reader that technical analyses of literary selections do not enhance one's understanding of them.
(B) direct the teacher to help students to develop their ability to analyze literary form and structure.
(C) explain the difference in literary interests between gifted and less able students.
(D) encourage the teacher to explore literature with gifted students in ways that will ensure their understanding.
(E) provide specific ideas for differentiating instruction.

36. The statements made in this passage seem most to represent

(A) facts based on specific examples.
(B) facts gathered from different sources.
(C) both fact and opinion.
(D) opinions based on experience.
(E) opinions based on stated research.

Questions 37–38

There was, perhaps, some degree of association between the perfecting of symmetry as art form and the discovery of perspective, both of them contributions from the Arab world. The Arabs were captivated by calculations and played with ingenious symmetrical design, as evidenced in their architecture. Perspective was a concept that vitalized both art and mathematics, and it provided a new tool for the artist to capture on canvas a particular view of reality.

37. The writer indicates that

(A) the Arabs had no mathematical ability.
(B) symmetry and perspective were borrowed from other cultures.
(C) perspective was discovered by the Arabs.
(D) Arab architecture was all advanced.
(E) symmetry is evident in nature.

38. Which of the following statements represents an idea that could be part of this paragraph?

(A) Calculus, the mathematics of change, captures the changing character of nature.
(B) There is unity and harmony in nature that can be described through numbers.
(C) The Arab world preserved the mathematical knowledge of ancient civilizations.
(D) The eye of the artist and the mind of the mathematician bridged the gap from a static to a dynamic concept of nature.
(E) The scientist needed a new mathematics to capture instantaneous motion.

Questions 39–40

An interesting distinction existed in the language of the ancient Greeks, having to do with the study of mathematics. They differentiated something called *arithmetic* from something called *logistic*. Arithmetic was more of an investigation of the world of numbers, while logistic was merely a set of rules to memorize and use for doing rote operations. Arithmetic then, was seen as a science, open to endless investigation. Logistic was more of a dull craft, needed for book-keeping and other such practices.

39. Based on the information in the passage, which of the following points could the writer support?

(A) There is little difference between the way mathematics was taught in ancient Greece and the way it is taught today.
(B) The world of numbers was not accessible to the ancient Greeks.
(C) What is commonly taught in the early years of schools today is mainly logistic and as such, it does not promote inquiry.
(D) Rote operations can be performed without learning rules considered by the ancient Greeks to be part of logistic.
(E) The science of logistic could not be taught in the public schools with the curriculum as it is today.

40. The writer implies that, in the distinction the Greeks made in the study of mathematics,

(A) information was lost.
(B) arithmetic was more interesting.
(C) mathematical rules were clarified.
(D) logistic was too difficult for small children to deal with.
(E) arithmetic was more elementary than logistic.

Questions 41–43

Theater reviewers, often unjustly stigmatized as baleful and destructive fiends, should really be allowed their occasional verbal irruptions when one considers that they must scrutinize everything offered up for public inspection. The column space that might yesterday have seemed wholly inadequate to contain a reviewer's comments on *Long Day's Journey into Night* is about the same as that which, today, must tax the reader's patience with the verdict on the latest scrap that has chanced to find for itself a backer with a hundred thousand dollars to lose.

41. The author's attitude toward the "fiends" is

(A) argumentative.
(B) antagonistic.
(C) resentful.
(D) sympathetic.
(E) contemptuous.

42. The passage suggests that the drama critic is

(A) affected adversely by the requirements of his job.
(B) aware of the value of public opinion.
(C) suspicious of criticism directed at him.
(D) captivated by most of what he sees.
(E) interested in obliging the backers of plays.

43. The writer implies that the play, *Long Day's Journey into Night,* was

(A) poorly written.
(B) too long.
(C) inconsequential.
(D) momentous.
(E) pleasant.

Questions 44–46

PRIORITIES OF SCHOOL BOARDS AND THE PUBLIC

SCHOOL BOARD MEMBERS CONCERNS	PERCENT	PUBLIC OPINION POLL CONCERNS	PERCENT
Declining enrollment	39.0	Discipline	24.0
Collective bargaining	29.7	Drug abuse	13.0
Curriculum reform	23.2	Declining tax base	12.0
Discipline	22.8	Curriculum reform	11.0
Federal interference	19.3	Poor teachers	10.0
Declining tax base	18.8	Crime/vandalism	4.0
Outmoded facilities	15.3	Overcrowded schools/ classes	4.0
Drug abuse	9.6	Alcoholism	2.0
Teacher militancy	7.2	Mismanagement	2.0
Student legal rights	2.9	Outmoded facilities	2.0
Desegregation	2.4	Federal interference	2.0
		Declining enrollment	1.0

44. In general, the table shows that

(A) "discipline" in the schools is a high-priority concern both of school boards and of the public.
(B) the public is more concerned about schools than are school boards.
(C) the priority of school board concerns is completely different from that of the public.
(D) a "declining tax base" and "declining enrollment" are, as would be expected, high-priority concerns, both for school boards and for the public.
(E) the public needs to be more involved with and concerned about school needs.

45. According to the table, "drug abuse"

(A) is a greater concern to the public than to school boards.
(B) is a low-priority concern, both for school boards and for the public.
(C) is, for the public, a less significant concern than the curriculum or the quality of teachers.
(D) is a concern for 13% of the school board members surveyed in the poll.
(E) is the greatest problem in schools today.

46. From the table, one can determine that

(A) "federal interference" is a concern of 19.3% of the people responding to the poll.
(B) 10% of board members are concerned about "poor teachers."
(C) because of "declining enrollment," "overcrowded schools" is not a concern of either the public or of school boards.
(D) "declining enrollment" is a concern for 39% of school board members who responded to the poll.
(E) the percentage of board members and of the public concerned about "outmoded facilities" is about the same.

Questions 47–50

Many researchers have become increasingly aware of the fact that early experiences of many kinds can have permanent effects on an animal's behavior. The idea of imprinting as an early experience during which a young animal forms a strong social attachment to a mother-object has aroused a great deal of interest and research. Although the effort to formulate laws of learning has demonstrated that behaviors which were once thought to be instinctive are modifiable by learning, behaviors such as imprinting are so persistent in character and resistant to alteration by reinforcement that they cannot be explained by conventional laws of learning. Other explanatory devices must be constructed.

In a broad sense, imprinting refers to an early experience that has a profound influence on the later adult social behavior of an animal. Although imprinting has been studied mainly in birds, it also has been observed in other animals. It seems that processes very much like imprinting exist in every social species, particularly those in which there are parent-young relationships.

47. The title that best expresses the ideas of this selection is

(A) Effects of Early Experiences on Animals.
(B) Research Results on Imprinting.
(C) Instinctive Behaviors in Animals.
(D) The Process of Imprinting.
(E) Social Behaviors of Animals.

48. From the style of this selection, one would assume that it was taken from

(A) a research report on reinforcement techniques.
(B) a psychology textbook.
(C) an informal essay.
(D) a book on the care of animals.
(E) a treatise on the validity of behavioral techniques.

49. The author indicates that

(A) all animal behaviors can be easily explained.
(B) the adult social behavior of animals is mostly conditioned behavior.
(C) imprinting provides valuable information about learning.
(D) imprinting never occurs in bird species.
(E) strong social attachments between different species are never formed.

50. Which of the following could be considered to be an example of imprinting?

(A) Recognition of parents by their young even when separated at birth.
(B) Kittens which are not handled by adults just after their eyes are open remain wil and fearful of people for their whole life.
(C) Ducks making associations between adults similar in appearance.
(D) A young animal's preference for one food over another, even when it has not eve tasted the ones offered.
(E) A mother gull's tendency to stop laying eggs if all eggs are removed from her nes

Mathematics

Directions: Select the best answer to each of the following questions. Any figures provided are there as reference; they are approximations and are not drawn to scale except when stated.

You may refer to the following information during this section of the test:

$=$ is equal to	$\sqrt{\ }$ square root of
$\neq$ is unequal to	$^\circ$ degrees
$<$ is less than	$\parallel$ is parallel to
$>$ is greater than	$\perp$ is perpendicular to
$\leq$ is less than or equal to	π pi, approximately 3.14
$\geq$ is greater than or equal to	

Circle: Radius $= r$; Circumference $= 2\pi r$; Area $= \pi r^2$; a circle contains 360°

Triangle: In triangle *ABC*, if $\angle BDA$ is a right angle, Area of $\triangle ABC = \dfrac{AC \times BD}{2}$,

Perimeter of $\triangle ABC = AB + BC + CA$

Sum of the measures of the degrees of the angles is 180.

Rectangle: Area $= L \times W$; Perimeter $= 2 \times (L + W)$

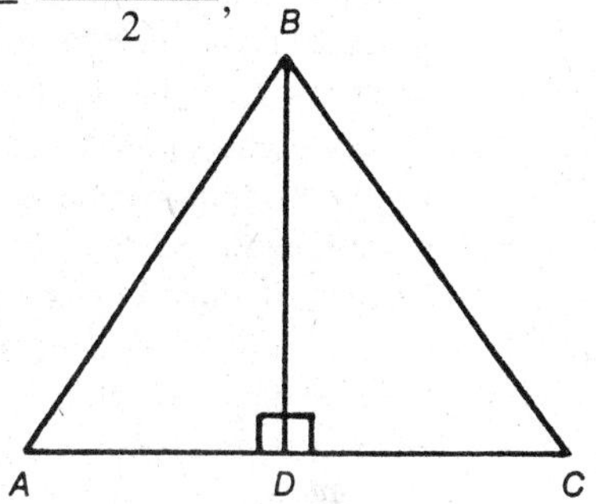

Rectangle: Area $= L \times W$; Perimeter $= 2 \times (L + W)$

1. Which of these fractional parts is the largest?

(A) $3/8$
(B) $4/7$
(C) $4/9$
(D) $3/5$
(E) $1/3$

2. Last week the lowest temperature was 15°F. This week it was 21 degrees colder. What was the lowest temperature this week?

(A) 6°F
(B) −6°F
(C) 36°F
(D) −36°F
(E) None of the above

3. How would this numeral be read: 6,004,005?

(A) Six hundred thousand four hundred five
(B) Six thousand four thousand five
(C) Six million four thousand five
(D) Six thousand four and five thousandths
(E) None of the above

4. 42,578.1502

In the numeral above, the value of the *2* to the left of the decimal point is how many times greater than the value of the *2* to the right of the decimal point?

(A) 10^3 times greater
(B) 10^6 times greater
(C) 10^7 times greater
(D) 10^{-6} times greater
(E) None of the above

5. What number is the square of 16?

(A) 256
(B) 4
(C) 32
(D) 4 or -4
(E) None of the above

6. Put in order (least to greatest):

$-\frac{5}{3}, -.3, \frac{1}{3}, \frac{1}{5}, .5$
(A) $-\frac{5}{3}, -.3, \frac{1}{5}, \frac{1}{3}, .5$
(B) $-\frac{5}{3}, -.3, .5, \frac{1}{3}, \frac{1}{5}$
(C) $-.3, -\frac{5}{3}, \frac{1}{5}, \frac{1}{3}, .5$
(D) $-\frac{5}{3}, -.3, \frac{1}{5}, .5, \frac{1}{3}$
(E) None of the above

7. In a glass we have 180 grams of milk with sugar. If there are 20 grams of sugar in the solution, what is the ratio of pure milk to milk and sugar?

(A) $\frac{180}{180 + 20}$
(B) $\frac{180}{20}$
(C) $\frac{20}{180}$
(D) $\frac{20}{180 + 20}$
(E) $\frac{180 - 20}{180}$

8. After 3 swimming tests, Mark's times were 78 seconds, 81 seconds, and 73 seconds. What must be his time on the fourth test to have an average of 76 seconds?

(A) 66
(B) 70
(C) 74
(D) 76
(E) None of the above

9. In an election with three candidates, Tom received 240 votes, Donna received 100 votes, and Gregory received 60 votes. What percent of the total number did Tom receive?

(A) 6%
(B) 30%
(C) 50%
(D) 60%
(E) 120%

10. If x, y, and z are all numbers which are divisible by 5, which of the following must be divisible by 5?

I. $x + y$
II. $x \cdot y$
III. $x + y + z$

(A) I only
(B) II only
(C) III only
(D) II and III only
(E) I, II, and III

11. $-2 \cdot \left[\dfrac{-63}{-7} - (6 - 12)\right] =$

(A) 18
(B) -30
(C) 6
(D) -12
(E) None of the above

12. How many different 2 letter "words" can be made with the letters "a," "b," and "c"? (Example: bc is a "word.")

(A) 6
(B) 3
(C) 4
(D) 9
(E) None of the above

13. A wading pool holds 100 gallons of water. The pool is three-fourths empty. If a hose can fill the pool at a rate of 20 gallons per hour, how long will it take to fill the pool?

(A) 2 hours 30 minutes
(B) 3 hours
(C) 3 hours 30 minutes
(D) 3 hours 45 minutes
(E) None of the above

14. If the digits of a two digit number are reversed, the new number is greater by 54. Which choice could have been the original number?

(A) 64
(B) 49
(C) 37
(D) 28
(E) 82

15. There are eight basketball teams in a tournament. Each team will play each of the other teams only once. How many games will be played?

(A) 28
(B) 56
(C) 64
(D) Impossible to determine
(E) None of the above

16. John owes Jerry \$126.50. If John is going to pay it back at a rate of \$5.50 a month, how many months will it take?

(A) 23 months
(B) 18 months
(C) 30 months
(D) Not enough information
(E) None of the above

17. Which of the following graphs represents a postage rate schedule where letters of ½ ounce or less cost 20¢ and each additional ½ ounce costs 15¢ more?

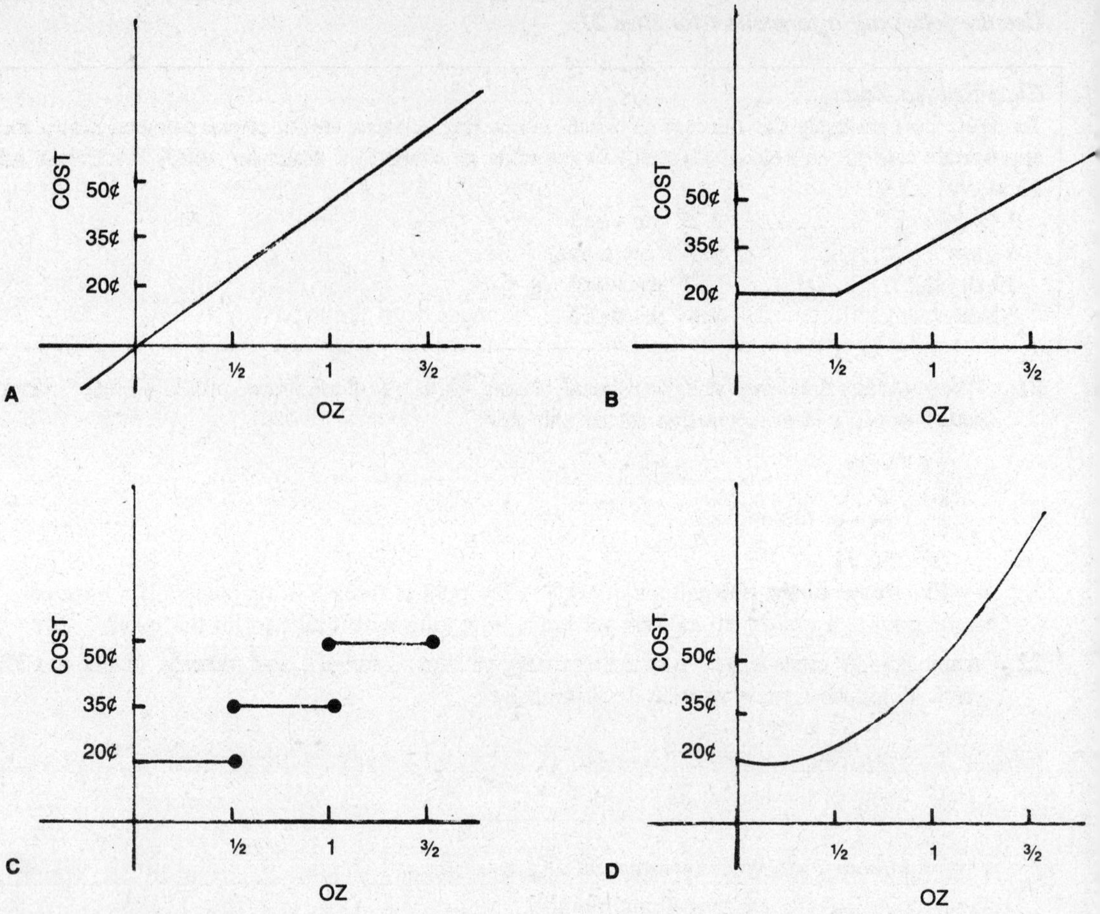

(A) A
(B) B
(C) C
(D) D
(E) None of the above

18. A government owed ¾ billion dollars and has paid ⅙ billion. How much does it still owe?

(A) 7/12 billion dollars
(B) ½ billion dollars
(C) 4/10 billion dollars
(D) 11/12 billion dollars
(E) None of the above

19. Separate 56 into two parts such that three times the smaller is 7 more than one half of the larger number. The two numbers are:

(A) 45 and 11
(B) 33 and 23
(C) 36 and 20
(D) 46 and 10
(E) None of the above

20. The telephone company gave a 0.9% discount on all bills which were paid on time. What would be the discount on a $23.75 telephone bill?

(A) $.25
(B) $23.54
(C) $.21
(D) $26.39
(E) $2.14

Use the following information for item 21.

Classified Ad Rates
To figure cost multiply the number of words (including address and/or phone number) times the appropriate rate given below. Cost equals (number of words) × (rate per word). Minimum ad 10 words, \$2.80.

1–3 days	\$.28 per word
5 days	\$.315 per word
10 days	\$.40 per word
30 days	\$.84 per word

21. "Boy's black Schwinn bike, five speed, basket, light, good condition, call 338-1462." How much would it cost to run this ad for one day?

(A) \$.56
(B) \$3.36
(C) \$3.78
(D) \$6.72
(E) None of the above

22. Annie has 79 cents in her pocket consisting of dimes, nickels, and pennies. If she has 13 coins in all, how many nickels does she have?

(A) 1
(B) 2
(C) 3
(D) 1 or 3
(E) Cannot tell with the information provided

23. $r = mn - 2pq$
$s = 10pq - 5mn$
$r = (?) \times s$

(A) -5
(B) $-\frac{1}{5}$
(C) $\frac{1}{5}$
(D) 5
(E) None of the above

24. Which of the following equals $\frac{x}{y} - \frac{x}{z}$?

(A) $\frac{1}{y - z}$

(B) $\frac{1}{yz}$

(C) $\frac{xz - xy}{yz}$

(D) $\frac{x}{y - z}$

(E) $\frac{xy - xz}{yz}$

25. $(x - 7)(2x - 3) = ?$

(A) $2x^2 - 17x + 21$
(B) $2x^2 + 21$
(C) $2x^2 - 17x - 21$
(D) $2x^2 + 21$
(E) None of the above

26. If $x = \frac{2}{3}$ and $y = 5$, then $\frac{x + y}{x} = ?$

(A) 5
(B) $\frac{34}{9}$
(C) $8\frac{1}{2}$
(D) $17\frac{1}{2}$
(E) None of the above

27. If $3.5x = 70$, then $x = ?$

(A) 2
(B) 20
(C) 245
(D) 200
(E) None of the above

28. We wish to write a formula which will reflect the total cost of operating a motorcycle. If gasoline costs x cents per mile and other expenses total y cents per mile, how many *dollars* will it cost to run the motorcycle 200 miles?

(A) $2(x + y)$
(B) $(100)(200)(x + y)$
(C) $200x + 200y$
(D) $\frac{x + y}{100}$
(E) None of the above

29. If $y = 2x + 3$ what is $3y$?

(A) $6x + 6$
(B) $6x + 9$
(C) $2x + 9$
(D) $6x + 3$
(E) None of the above

30. If $\frac{5t}{2} = \frac{3}{2}$, then $t = ?$

(A) $-\frac{3}{5}$
(B) $\frac{3}{5}$
(C) 4
(D) -4
(E) None of the above

31. If x^3 is odd which of the following is (are) true?
I. $(x - 1)$ is even.
II. x is odd.
III. x is even.

(A) I only
(B) II only
(C) III only
(D) I and II only
(E) I and III only

32. If the volume of a cone is given by $V = \frac{1}{3}\pi \cdot r^2 \cdot h$ (where r is the radius of the base and h is the height), what is the height of a cone with volume = 24 cubic centimeters and radius of base = 3 centimeters?

(A) 24 centimeters
(B) 8π centimeters
(C) $\frac{8}{\pi}$ centimeters
(D) 8 centimeters
(E) None of the above

33. If the radius of a circle is tripled, how many times larger will the area of the circle be?

(A) 3
(B) 6
(C) 9
(D) 12
(E) None of the above

34. Point P, with coordinates (6, 8) is on a circle with center at the origin (0, 0). If point Q is on the circle and has coordinates $(x, 0)$, what is x?

(A) 6
(B) 10
(C) 8
(D) $\sqrt{10}$
(E) $\sqrt{14}$

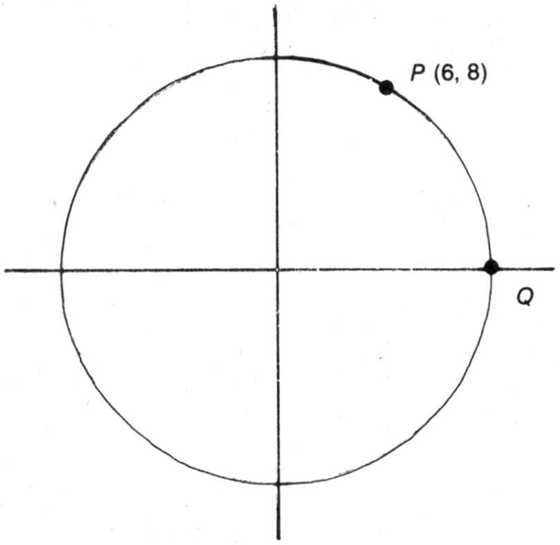

35. A regular hexagon (six-sided figure with all sides the same length) can be divided into 6 triangles as shown. What is the measure, x, of the angle formed by 2 sides of the hexagon?

(A) 120°
(B) 60°
(C) 90°
(D) 150
(E) Cannot be determined from information given

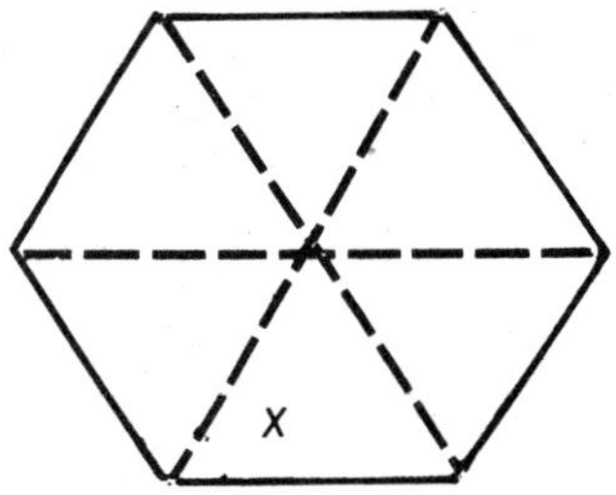

36. On Frank's map 1 inch represents 10 miles. If the distance from Bloomingdale to Watersedge on the map is 3½ inches, what is the real distance between the towns?

(A) 3½ miles
(B) 155 miles
(C) 35 miles
(D) 350 miles
(E) None of the above

37. A rectangle has a perimeter of 56 meters. If one of its sides measures 12 meters, then its area is equal to:

(A) 112 square meters
(B) 114 square meters
(C) 168 square meters
(D) 192 square meters
(E) None of the above

38. Which of the following triples of numbers could be the sides of a right triangle?

I. 10, 24, 26
II. 6, 6, 6
III. 9, 12, 15
IV. 5, 5, $5\sqrt{2}$

(A) I only
(B) II and III only
(C) I and III only
(D) I, II, and III only
(E) I, III, and IV only

39. A dangerous watch dog is tied to a stake by a chain that is 15 meters long. How many square meters of area does the dog have to walk around in?

(A) 225π
(B) 225
(C) 30π
(D) 112.5
(E) None of the above

40. Rectangle *PQRS* has the same area as rectangle *TUVW*. The areas of the small shaded rectangles are *J* and *K*, as shown. $K = J \times$?

(A) ½
(B) ⅔
(C) ¾
(D) 1
(E) 3/2

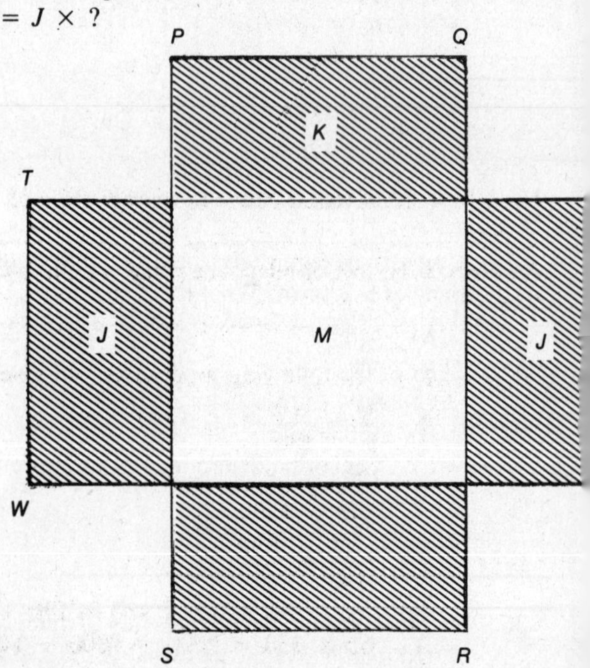

Use the problem stated below to answer item 41.

Problem: Ms. Rodriquez gave a math test of 25 items. She gave three points for each correct answer and subtracted two points for each wrong answer. Hal answered all the questions and got a score of zero. How many items did Hal answer wrong?

41. In solving this problem, Rhonda guesses that Hal had 15 right and 10 wrong. Why is Rhonda's guess wrong?

(A) It gives more than 25 items.
(B) It gives less than 25 items.
(C) The test score would be more than 0.
(D) The test score would be less than 0.
(E) None of the above is a valid reason.

42. Which of the following statements can be represented by the equation $\frac{1}{3} \times n = 2\frac{1}{2}$?

(A) Only $2\frac{1}{2}$ sticks of gum were left after $\frac{1}{3}$ of a pack was chewed. How many sticks were in the pack originally?
(B) A cookbook recommends that a turkey be roasted $\frac{1}{3}$ hour for each pound of turkey. How large a turkey could be cooked in $2\frac{1}{2}$ hours?
(C) A cookbook recommends that a $2\frac{1}{2}$ kg turkey be roasted $\frac{1}{3}$ hour for each kg. How long must the turkey be roasted?
(D) A certain number is $\frac{1}{3}$ of $2\frac{1}{2}$. What is the number?
(E) If a certain number is divided by $\frac{1}{3}$, the result is $2\frac{1}{2}$. What is the number?

Use the information below to answer item 43.

Statement: At Elm Ridge High School the number of students is 40 more than 16 times the number of teachers.

43. Which number sentence is a correct expression of this information?

(A) $16s = t + 40$
(B) $16s + 40 = t$
(C) $16s - 40 = t$
(D) $s = 16t + 40$
(E) $16t = s + 40$

Use the problem stated below to answer item 44.

Problem: If 60 feet of telephone cable weighs 140 pounds, what is the weight of 150 feet of this wire?

44. Which of the following procedures will give a correct solution?

I. $\frac{60}{n} = \frac{140}{150}$
II. $\frac{60}{140} = \frac{n}{150}$
III. $\frac{60}{140} = \frac{150}{n}$
IV. $60 + 60 + 30 = 150 \rightarrow 140 + 140 + 70 = \text{weight}$
V. $60 \times 150 = 9000 \rightarrow 9000 + 140 = \text{weight}$

(A) I only
(B) II only
(C) I and II only
(D) III and IV only
(E) I, II, and V only

45. Arthur is able to save \$125 per month from his paycheck. He needs \$425 more to buy a microcomputer that costs \$1800. He has forgotten how many months he has been saving, but he would like to know. Arthur could find out if he did which of the following?

(A) Subtract \$425 from \$1800 and divide \$125 into the answer.
(B) Divide \$125 into \$1800 and add \$425 to the answer.
(C) Divide \$125 into \$425 and subtract the answer from \$1800.
(D) Multiply \$125 times \$425 and divide the answer into \$1800.
(E) Multiply \$125 times \$425 and subtract the answer from \$1800.

Use the problem stated below to answer item 46.

Problem: Ivan saved money from his monthly paycheck for 7 consecutive months to buy a new television. At the end of the 7 months he had saved \$315. The total cost of the television he wanted, including tax, was \$289.49. How much money did Ivan have after he bought the television? Answer: \$604.49

46. Which statement describes best why the answer given for this problem is *not* reasonable?

(A) The television cost \$289.49.
(B) If he had \$315, he spent \$289.49.
(C) If he had \$315 and spent \$289.49, the amount left must be less than \$315.
(D) If the television cost \$289.49, he saved more money than the television actually cost.
(E) Because there is not enough information to answer the question.

Use the problem below to answer item 47.

Problem: Harriet was washing her car when she noticed that George was washing his car also. It happens that Harriet washes her car every 9 days and George washes his every 12 days. How many days will pass before they next wash their cars on the same day?

47. Which of the following solution methods is most likely to give a correct solution?

(A)

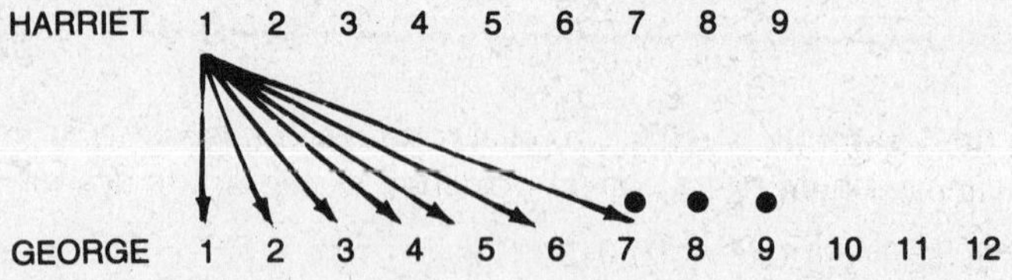

(B) $9 + 12 = 21$

(C)

HARRIET	9	18	27	36	45		
GEORGE	12	24	36	48	60		

(D)

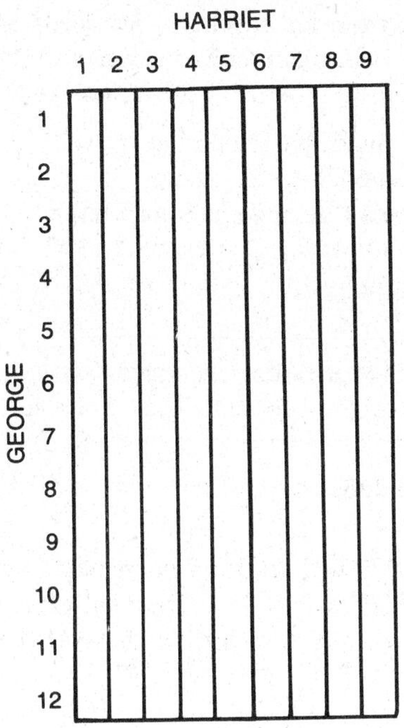

(E) $9 \times 12 = 108$

Use the information given below to answer item 48.

CALIFORNIA ELECTRIC COMPANY

FOR OCT. 4 THROUGH NOV. 5

PREVIOUS BILL - - - - - - -	$132.56
CREDITS- - - - - - - - - - - -	$132.56
BALANCE - - - - - - - - - - -	$ 0.00

AMOUNT DUE:	
IF PAID BY DEC. 1- - - -	$175.18
AFTER DEC. 1- - - - - - -	$180.18

PRESENT READING (KW-H)	PREVIOUS READING (KW-H)	KW-H USED	AMOUNT
9682	11526	1844	$175.18

48. What does the California Electric Co. charge for each kilowatt-hour used? Which statement indicates a correct operation to perform to answer this question?

(A) $175.18 ÷ 11526 = $0.015
(B) $175.18 ÷ 1844 = $0.095
(C) $175.18 ÷ 9682 = $0.018
(D) $175.18 − $132.56 = $42.62
(E) 1844 ÷ 9682 = 0.19

Use the problem stated below to answer item 49.

Problem: It takes Lisa 28 minutes to get to and from school each day. She wondered how many minutes she spends going to and from school in an entire school year.

49. Lisa could solve this problem if she also knew . . .

(A) There are 60 minutes in an hour.
(B) There are 180 school days in a year.
(C) The school is half a mile from Lisa's house.
(D) There are 5 school days in a week.
(E) How many days she goes to school in an entire school year.

Use the problem stated below to answer item 50.

Problem: The following problem statement has insufficient information. From a piece of cardboard in the shape of a square the largest possible circle is cut out. What is the area of the circle?

50. This problem can be solved if you also know;

I. The thickness of the cardboard.
II. The length of a side of the cardboard.
III. The area of the piece of cardboard.

(A) I and II
(B) I and III
(C) II and III
(D) Only I is needed.
(E) Either II or III is needed.

Writing

Directions: You will have 60 minutes to write an essay on each of the following two topics. Try to spend approximately 30 minutes on each topic, as they are of equal value in the evaluation. While quantity is not as important as quality, the topics selected will probably require an essay rather than just a paragraph or two. Organization is an integral part of effective writing, so you may want to use some of the allotted time to plan your work. Support your ideas with clear, specific examples or explanations. Write legibly, and do not skip lines.

First Topic:

Some educators feel that declaring a moratorium on testing, or halting the use of tests in schools for a period of time, would be helpful to give people time to consider their uses and misuses and their value. Discuss whether you agree or disagree with this position.

Second Topic:

Everyone has, at one time or another, suffered from a fear of some sort. Describe one situation in which you experienced this emotion.

ANSWER KEY

Reading

1. D	11. B	21. C	31. C	41. D
2. B	12. D	22. A	32. D	42. A
3. B	13. C	23. C	33. C	43. D
4. A	14. B	24. C	34. B	44. C
5. B	15. A	25. A	35. D	45. A
6. C	16. C	26. B	36. D	46. D
7. D	17. E	27. A	37. C	47. D
8. B	18. D	28. C	38. D	48. B
9. D	19. A	29. A	39. C	49. C
10. A	20. D	30. A	40. B	50. B

Mathematics

1. D	11. B	21. B	31. D	41. C
2. B	12. D	22. C	32. C	42. B
3. C	13. D	23. B	33. C	43. D
4. C	14. D	24. C	34. B	44. D
5. A	15. A	25. A	35. A	45. A
6. A	16. A	26. C	36. C	46. C
7. E	17. C	27. B	37. D	47. C
8. E	18. A	28. A	38. E	48. B
9. D	19. D	29. B	39. A	49. E
10. E	20. C	30. B	40. D	50. E

ANALYSIS OF ERRORS

The following table lists the subject matter covered in each question of the Reading and Mathematics sections of the test. Find the question numbers that you got wrong and review the subject matter covered in those questions again.

SECTION	QUESTION NUMBERS	SUBJECT AREA
READING	12, 15, 19, 26, 35, 47	Finding the Main Idea
	1, 8, 13, 16, 21, 37, 49	Finding Specific Details
	2, 3, 4, 9, 10, 11, 14, 23, 25, 31, 32, 34, 38, 39, 40, 41, 42, 43, 48, 50	Finding Implications
	17, 18, 20, 24, 33	Determining the Meaning of Strange Words
	27, 36	Determining Special Techniques
	5, 6, 7, 28, 29, 30, 44, 45, 46	Interpreting Tables and Graphs

ANALYSIS OF ERRORS

MATHEMATICS Arithmetic	3, 5, 10	Whole Numbers (IA)
	1, 6, 13, 18	Fractions (IB)
	4, 6, 16, 21	Decimals (IC)
	9, 20	Percentage (ID)
		Rounding Off Numbers (IE)
	2, 6, 11	Signed Numbers (IF)
	8	Averages, Medians, Ranges, and Modes (IG)
	4, 31	Powers, Exponents, and Roots (IH)
Algebra	23, 24, 25, 26, 28, 29	Algebraic Expressions (IIA)
	27	Equations (IIB)
	14, 19, 22, 41, 42, 43, 45, 46, 47, 48, 49, 50	Verbal Problems (IIC)
	12, 15	Counting Problems (IID)
	7, 30, 36, 44	Ratio and Proportion (IIE)
		Sequence and Progression (IIF)
		Inequalities (IIG)
Geometry		Angles (IIIA)
		Lines (IIIB)
	35	Polygons (IIIC)
	38	Triangles (IIID)
		Quadrilaterals (IIIE)
	34	Circles (IIIF)
	32, 33, 37, 39, 40	Area, Perimeter, and Volume (IIIG)
	34	Coordinate Geometry (IIIH)
Formulas		Formulas
Other	17, 48	Interpreting Graphs and Tables (see Reading Section)

ANSWER EXPLANATIONS

Reading

1. D It is stated in the passage that the name came from the fact that they painted unpleasant subjects.

2. B One could conclude that the artists' works portrayed only the unpleasant side of urban living and not anything as optimistic as a beautification project.

3. B The most significant point here is that the discovery of the fossil, which is more humanlike than apelike, suggests the possibility that the common ancestor of apes and humans was human.

4. A It is likely that the writer will suggest supporting evidence, and also refers back to the "suggestion" of the previous sentence.

5. B Reading the graph carefully, one can see that the solid line representing the younger children indicates that 18% of them conformed to the group only once (frequency of one on the bottom line).

6. C The line representing the younger children shows that a larger percent of them (25%) conformed to the group influences the greatest number of times (7).

7. D The results of the study, as given on the graph, show that there is, in fact, evidence that children are influenced by a group, but the observations stated indicate that it is not an easy thing for them to do.

8. B "Having named *it*" (line 6), the author states, this object detected in space is a black hole, "such as this one." (line 8)

9. D Since no light escapes from this extinguished star, it is safe to conclude that that is why they are so named.

10. A None of the other implications is supported by the passage, and the author does say that the forces of black holes are "slackening the pace of disintegrating galaxies."

11. B The gravitational force remains the same, so A is wrong; a great deal of energy is given off from black holes, 1,000 times more than from the sun, so D is wrong. The black hole already has been created at this point in the description, so E is inappropriate. The author could very well discuss the type of gravitational force that is exerted once the black hole is created.

12. D The author states this (lines 2–3). The other statements are not accurate based on the passage or are merely implied.

13. C While all of the other statements represent references made in the passage, no reference is made to any variation in shape.

14. B This is the only response that represents how he was deceived, that is, how his plan did not work.

15. A B and E are too general; D is inaccurate; revenge by the lion (C) is never mentioned.

16. C The author states (lines 3–4) that most facts are not retained.

17. E The author's main point is that studying helps to develop the powers of the mind, here referred to as an instrument.

18. D The author discusses the need for study to develop the powers of the mind. A, B and C do not refer to powers. Muscle power (E) is used as comparison.

19. A The passage describes the problems faced by the village farmers in the Near East. Answers B, D and E are too general; the Third World (C) is not mentioned.

20. D Answers A and B are too specific. Inconsistent weather conditions are a serious problem for farmers.

21. C The writer mentions that the substances in the nuclei of cells are, in some way, responsible for biochemical activity and characteristics; hence, they are essential to life.

22. A The passage focuses on the unique way in which the substances are combined and how they contribute to life.

23. C Although the writer indicates that the information has not been integrated thus far and has, therefore, been largely unproductive, he does imply that it is important to know about.

24. C The need, the author points out, is to find means to put divergent ideas together and determine what they all say about the process.

25. A The writer states that psycholinguists have been investigating small units and their reality and have not considered the larger picture.

26. B All of the ideas presented by the writer—that a phobia is considered a set of symptoms, that it is enigmatic, and that it can be treated with quick results—focus on this point.

27. A The last sentence in the passage provides an example of the point the author is making.

28. C In only one case, month number 4, is the solid line representing 1982 above the broken line representing 1983.

29. A The best profits for one month in 1983 were $90,000, and in 1982, the best profits for one month were $70,000, so the difference is $20,000.

30. A It is necessary to average the monthly profits for each year, but the sum is easily divided by 10.

31. C In suggesting that concerned citizens must participate in government, the writer implies a general distrust of the stereotyped politician by use of the word ''mere.'' (line 6)

32. D The author's point is that if concerned and intelligent citizens do not participate in government affairs, they leave them in the hands of those who may be less than honest.

33. C The terms used in reference to the individuals who might gain control of public affairs if honest people do nothing include ''selfish, ignorant, and crafty,'' a category into which ''corrupt'' fits well.

34. B The author wants to make the point that developing a real appreciation and understanding of literature is more important than covering a large number or wide range of selections. Answers A and D are too general; answer E is bringing up a new subject; answer C conflicts with the author's main point.

35. D The author wants the teacher to go beyond technical analyses of literature with gifted students.

36. D The author's statement are all opinions based apparently on some teaching experience. No facts or research results are presented.

37. C The writer states that both the perfecting of symmetry and the ''discovery of perspective'' came from the Arab world.

38. D Since the passage focuses on the discovery and use of both symmetry and perspective, it is reasonable to make a generalization about how these two concepts changed man's perception of the world.

39. C The author's purpose in writing this passage could easily be to make the point that the way math is taught in the schools today is limited and limiting. Answers A, B and D conflict with statements in the passage. E conflicts with what is implied.

40. B The writer speaks of *logistic* in dull terms and seems to imply that *arithmetic* was much more interesting.

41. D The writer is sympathetic to drama critics because he understands the problems they confront.

42. A It is indicated that the drama critic is occasionally vicious only because he must review so much that is of no value.

43. D The writer's statement that the column space allocated in the past would have been wholly inadequate indicates that the drama critic was reviewing a very worthwhile play.

44. C It seems the most noteworthy finding of the poll is that the concerns of school boards and of the public do not match at all.

45. A Since it is a concern of 13% of the people polled from the public sector, and only 9.6% of school board members listed it as a concern, one could conclude that it is a greater concern for the public.

46. D The table shows that 39% of school board members (left-hand column) are concerned about ''declining enrollment''; it is their greatest concern.

47. D Although social behavior is discussed and early experiences are mentioned, the passage in general, is about imprinting.

48. B The information is presented in a general way to give background facts. It is not limited to reinforcement or behavioral techniques (A and E), and does not deal with the care of animals (D); nor is the tone casual enough for answer (C).

49. C The author indicated that there is much interest in imprinting because it is a unique process and reveals a great deal about learning.

50. B Although the author does not mention an example of a negative experience of imprinting he does specify that imprinting is an early experience that affects the social behavior of an animal, even into adulthood. The other answers do not deal directly with the early learning from parent-offspring attachments.

Mathematics

1. D Choices A, C, and E are smaller than ½, and choices B and D are greater than ½. So we need only decide which is the larger of B and D.

$\frac{4}{7} \times \frac{5}{5} = \frac{20}{35} \qquad \frac{3}{5} \times \frac{7}{7} = \frac{21}{35}$

Since, $\frac{21}{35} > \frac{20}{35}, \qquad \frac{3}{5} > \frac{4}{7}$

2. B $15° - 21° = 15° + -21° = -6°$

3. C A is 600,405.
B is not a standard way of expressing any number.
D is 6,004.005.

4. C The value of each place in a decimal numeral is 10 times greater than the place to its immediate right. Therefore, we need only count how many places apart the twos are to obtain the answer. 42 578. 1502 The answer is $10 \times 10 \times 10 \times 10 \times 10 \times 10 \times 10$ or 10^7.

5. A The square of a number n is the number $n \times n$ or n^2.

$$16^2 = 256$$

6. A First write all of the numerals in decimal form (divide top by bottom).

$$-5/3 = -1.66 \quad 1/3 = .33 \quad 1/5 = .2$$

Arrange on a number line. Negatives go to the left of zero, and the larger in absolute value (ignoring sign) the further from zero.

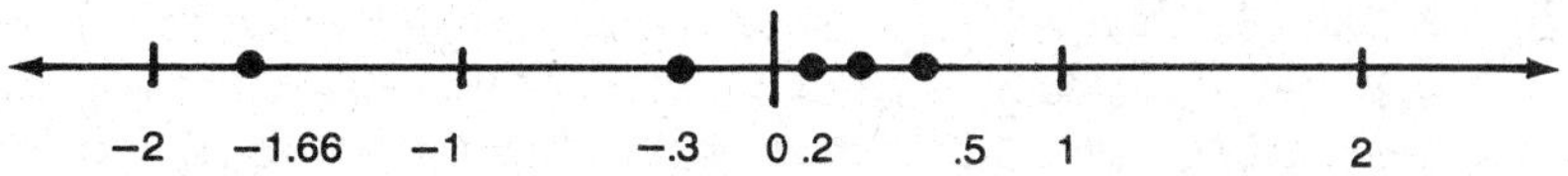

7. E Total weight (of milk and sugar) is 180 grams (milk and sugar). Sugar weighs 20 grams. Thus pure milk weighs 180 − 20 (or 160 grams). Ratio of pure milk to milk and sugar is

$$\frac{180 - 20}{180}$$

8. E Let t = Mark's time on the fourth test.

$$(78 + 81 + 73 + t)/4 = 76$$
$$78 + 81 + 73 + t = 4(76)$$
$$232 + t = 304$$
$$t = 304 - 232$$
$$t = 72$$

9. D Total votes = 240 + 100 + 60 = 400
Tom's percentage = $240/400 = 240/400 \div 4/4 = 60/100 = 60\%$

10. E If a whole number n is divisible by 5, then it can be written $n = 5 \times m$ for some whole number m.
So, x, y, and z can be written as $x = 5 \cdot a$

$$y = 5 \cdot b$$
$$z = 5 \cdot c$$

Then I. $x + y = 5a + 5b = 5(a + b)$
So, $x + y$ is divisible by 5.

II. $x \cdot y = 5a \cdot 5b = 5 \cdot 5 \cdot a \cdot b$
So, $x \cdot y$ is divisible by 5.

III. $x + y + z = 5a + 5b + 5c = 5(a + b + c)$
So, $x + y + z$ is divisible by 5.

11. B $-2\,[-63/-7 - (6 - 12)]$
$= -2\,[9 - (-6)]$
$= -2\,[9 + 6]$
$= -2 \times 15$
$= -30$

12. D In forming the two letter "words" we have three choices for the first letter, and three choices for the second letter. Thus we have 3 × 3 different two letter "words" possible.

13. D 100 gallons to start. $\frac{3}{4} \times 100 = 75$ gallons missing.
The hose pumps 20 gallons per hour.
$\frac{75}{20} = 3\frac{15}{20} = 3\frac{3}{4}$ hours to fill the 75 gallons.
(3 hours 45 minutes)

14. D Although this problem can be solved by setting up equations and using algebra, it is easier and quicker to just test each of the choices. The original number is 28, since $82 - 28 = 54$.

15. A Each team will play each of the 7 other teams. Thus each of the 8 teams has 7 games on its schedule. So there are $7 \times 8 = 56$ games listed on the schedules. But, of course a game between teams A and B is the same as a game between teams B and A (i.e every game is listed on 2 schedules). So there are actually only $\frac{56}{2} = 28$ differen games.

16. A $126.50 ÷ $5.50 = 23
It will take 23 months.

17. C Only graph C is 20¢ for letters up to ½ ounce, 35¢ for letters between ½ ounce an 1 ounce, 50¢ for letters between 1 ounce and 1½ ounce, etc.

18. A We need to figure ¾ billion − ⅙ billion.
The answer will clearly be in billions of dollars. We need only to figure $\frac{3}{4} - \frac{1}{6}$.

$$\frac{3}{4} - \frac{1}{6} = \frac{9}{12} - \frac{2}{12} = \frac{7}{12}$$

19. D Rather than using algebra, it is easiest to examine each of the choices. Notice that eac pair presented does total 56 as required. Only choice D satisfies the condition that times the smaller is 7 more than ½ the larger. ($3 \times 10 = \frac{1}{2} \times 4 + 7$)

20. C The discount is only slightly less than 1%, so we expect it to be a little less than 24 (.01 × $23.75 = .2375; just move the decimal point two places to the left). Thu choice C seems most likely (more precisely, .9% × 23.75 = .009 × 23.75 = .21375 so the discount is about 21¢).

21. B The ad contains 12 "words." The cost per word (for 1 day) is 28¢. So the ad cost i 12 × .28 = $3.36.

22. C By a process of systematic elimination, you can determine that Annie must have nickels. None of the other choices satisfies all 3 conditions (79¢, dimes, nickels, an pennies, and 13 coins in all).

23. B The question asks, what can we multiply times s to get r? Notice that both r and contain terms involving mn and pq. In fact if we multiply r by -5 we get s. In othe words, $-5 \times r = s$. So, $r = (-\frac{1}{5}) \times s$.

24. C This problem involves 2 fractions to be subtracted. Their common denominator is yz

$$\frac{x}{y} - \frac{x}{z} = \left(\frac{x}{y} \cdot \frac{z}{z}\right) - \left(\frac{x}{z} \cdot \frac{y}{y}\right)$$
$$= \frac{xz}{yz} - \frac{xy}{yz}$$
$$= yz$$

25. A

$$\begin{aligned}(x - 7)(2x - 3) &= x(2x) - 3(x) - 7(2x) - 7(-3)\\ &= 2x^2 - 3x - 14x + 21\\ &= 2x^2 - 17x + 21\end{aligned}$$

26. C $x = 2/3$ and $y = 5$

Substituting into the given formula $\frac{x + y}{x}$ we obtain:

$$\begin{aligned}&\frac{2/3 + 5}{2/3}\\ &= (2/3 + 5) \times 3/2 =\\ &= 17/3 \times 3/2\\ &= 17/2\\ &= 8\tfrac{1}{2}\end{aligned}$$

27. B Given: $3.5x = 70$

Solving for x: $x = 70/3.5$

$x = 20$

28. A

$$\begin{aligned}\text{gasoline} &= x \text{ cents per mile}\\ \text{total expenses} &= y \text{ cents per mile}\\ \text{dollars to run the motorcycle 200 miles} &= ?\\ x + y &= \text{total cents per mile}\\ (x + y)/100 &= \text{total dollars per mile}\\ 200 \times (x + y)/100 &= \text{total dollars for 200 miles}\\ \text{Simplifying: } 2(x + y) &= \text{total dollars to run 200 miles}\end{aligned}$$

29. B

$$\begin{aligned}\text{Given: } y &= 2x + 3\\ \text{Question: } 3y &= ?\\ \text{Substituting: } 3y &= 3(2x + 3)\\ &= 6x + 9\end{aligned}$$

30. B Given: $\frac{5t}{2} = \frac{3}{2}$

$$\begin{aligned}2 \times 5t &= 2 \times 3\\ 10t &= 6\\ t &= 6/10 = 3/5\end{aligned}$$

31. D Given: x^3 is odd

This implies that x is odd.

If x is odd then: I. "$(x - 1)$" is even is a true statement.

II. "x is odd" is a true statement.

III. "x is even" is a false statement.

32. C Volume of cone: $V = \frac{1}{3}\pi \cdot r^2 \cdot h$

$$\begin{aligned}h &= ?\\ V &= 24 \text{ cm}^3\\ r &= 3 \text{ cm}\end{aligned}$$

Substituting: $24 = \frac{1}{3}\pi \cdot 3^2 \cdot h$

$$h = \frac{24 \cdot 3}{9 \cdot \pi} = \frac{8}{\pi} \text{ cm}$$

33. C Area of circle $= a = \pi \cdot r^2$
If the radius is tripled, then the new radius R is:
$R = 3r$
so the new area will be:
$A = \pi \cdot R^2$
substituting: $A = \pi \cdot (3r)^2$
$A = \pi \cdot 9r^2$
$A = 9 \cdot \pi \cdot r^2 = 9a$
so the new area is 9 times larger than the previous area.

34. B From Point P with coordinates (6, 8) we determine the radius of the circle, using the Pythagorean theorem.
$r^2 = 6^2 + 8^2$
$r^2 = 36 + 64$
$r^2 = 100$
$r = 10$
So the x coordinate at point Q is 10.

35. A The triangles formed are equilateral triangles. (Triangles with equal angles and equal sides.) Since the angles of a triangle always add up to 180°, each angle in these triangles must measure 60°. Angle x is the angle formed by two adjacent, equal angles of 60° each. Hence, angle x measures $2 \times 60° = 120°$.

36. C 1 inch represents 10 miles.
So, 3½ inches represents (3½) × 10 miles = 7⁄2 × 10 miles = 35 miles.

37. D The perimeter of this rectangle is:
$$2a + 2b = 56$$
If $a = 12$ then $b = 16$.

The area of this rectangle is $a \times b$.
So area $= 12 \times 16$
$= 192 \text{ m}^2$

38. E To be the sides of a right triangle the numbers must satisfy the Pythagorean theorem, or be multiples of the sides of a triangle that satisfies the Pythagorean theorem. We must examine each triple:

I. (10, 24, 26) is a multiple of (5, 12, 13)
$5^2 + 12^2 = 13^2$
$25 + 144 = 169$
$169 = 169$
So, (10, 24, 26) can be a right triangle.

II. (6, 6, 6) is an equilateral triangle (triangle with 3 equal sides). Each angle in any equilateral triangle measures 60°. So an equilateral triangle can never be a right triangle.

III. (9, 12, 15) is a multiple of (3, 4, 5) for which
$3^2 + 4^2 = 5^2$
$9 + 16 = 25$
So, (9, 12, 15) can be a right triangle.

IV. $(5, 5, 5\sqrt{2})$ is a multiple of $(1, 1, \sqrt{2})$ for which
$1^2 + 1^2 = (\sqrt{2})^2$
$1 + 1 = 2$
So, $(5, 5, 5\sqrt{2})$ can be a right triangle.

39. A The watch dog will have access to the region within the circle of radius $r = 15$.
The area of this region is: $A = \pi \cdot r^2$
$A = \pi \cdot (15)^2$
$A = 225 \cdot \pi$

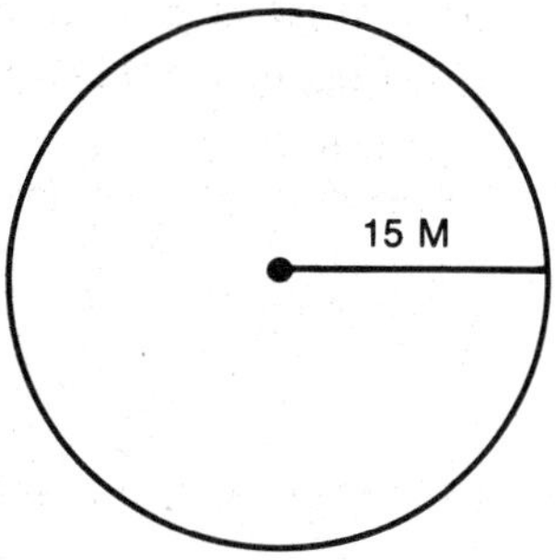

40. D The areas of the large rectangles are the same.
A $(PQRS)$ = A $(TUVW)$
A $(PQRS) = M + 2K$
A $(TUVW) = M + 2J$
Since the areas are the same: $M + 2J = M + 2K$
So, $2J = 2K$
$J = K$
or $K = J \times 1$

41. C There are two conditions that must be checked for in this item.
I. The total number of items must be exactly 25.
II. Score for right answers = 3 × the number of right answers (r) and score for wrong answers = −2 × the number of wrong answers (w).

Since Hal got a score of zero, the equation $3r + (-2)w = 0$ represents Hal's performances.
Rhonda guessed that Hal had 15 right and 10 wrong answers.
Let's check the above conditions:
I. $10 + 15 = 25$ (condition satisfied)
II. $3 \times 15 + (-2) \times 10 = 45 - 20 = 25$
Hal would get a score of 25, not 0.

So answer C is correct, Hal's score would be more than 0.

42. B $\frac{1}{3} \times n = 2\frac{1}{2}$
1 pound of turkey takes ⅓ × 1 hours to cook
2 pounds of turkey takes ⅓ × 2 hours to cook
n pounds of turkey takes ⅓ × n to cook
Since we know that it takes 2½ hours to cook a turkey, we set up the equation:
$\frac{1}{3} \times n = 2\frac{1}{2}$

43. D Number of students = 16 × number of teachers + 40
$s = 16t + 40$

44. D 60 feet of cable weigh 140 pounds.
150 feet of cable weigh?
This can be set up as a ratio in the following way:
$$\frac{60}{140} = \frac{150}{n}$$
or 150 feet = 60 feet + 60 feet + 30 feet and in weight this is equivalent to:
150 feet weighs 140 pounds + 140 pounds + 70 pounds
(Since 30 feet is ½ of 60 feet, the weight of 30 feet should be ½ of 140 pounds or 70 pounds.) So answers III and IV are correct.

45. A To find how much he has saved Arthur should subtract \$425 from \$1800. Since he saves \$125 a month, to find out how many months he has been saving he should divide the answer above by \$125.

46. C Once you spend some of the money that you've saved, the amount left must be less than what you had saved. Since Ivan had saved $315 and spent part of that, the amount left must be less than $315.

47. C Since Harriet washes her car every 9 days, she washes it on days 9, 18, 27, 36, 45, etc. Since George washes his car every 12 days he washes it on days 12, 24, 36, 48, etc. The only suggested solution that shows these two patterns is choice C.

48. B There were 1844 kilowatt-hour used and the company charged a total of $175.18. The amount paid for each kilowatt-hour is $175.18 ÷ 1844 = $0.095.

49. E Lisa can solve the problem by multiplying 28 times the number of days she goes to school in a year. To solve this problem Lisa must know the number of days she goes to school in an entire year. (Note: Choice B does not consider the possibility that she may be absent on some days.)

50. E In order to find the area of the circle, all we need to know is the radius of the circle to be cut. The radius is ½ the side of the square. If we knew the side of the square we would have the solution. It would also be enough to know the area of the cardboard (since we know it is a square, and thus we can figure the length of each side of the square).

Writing

The following essay outlines have been written to demonstrate the planning of well-written answers to the topics given. Use these only as guidelines to evaluating your own organization. Many different organization patterns and plans could work equally well for the topics given.

First Topic:

Some educators feel that declaring a moratorium on testing, or halting the use of tests in school for a period of time, would be helpful to give people time to consider their uses and misuses and their value. Discuss whether you agree or disagree with this position.

Essay Outline:

A. Introduction
   1. General statements on testing in the schools, background, i.e., give a general context for the thesis being presented.
   2. Presentation of thesis statement or point of view—a moratorium on testing would would not be helpful.

B. Reasons: pro or con
   1. State each reason in clear, specific terms. (Ex.: "Tests are misused when they are used to place students in reading groups.")
      a. Elaborate or explain more about how the reason supports your point of view
      b. Support with specific examples.
   2. Present additional reasons in same manner as above.

C. Summary and conclusions
   1. Restate your point of view in brief terms.
   2. Conclude with statement about likelihood of such a moratorium, future of schools with or without tests, or recommendations for alternative solutions.

Second Topic:

Everyone has, at one time or another, suffered from a fear of some sort. Describe one situation in which you experienced this emotion.

Essay Outline

A. Introduction
   1. Describe, in general terms, the type of situation in which you have found yourself when you experienced this particular fear.
   2. Discuss, in general terms, the nature and quality of the fear.
   3. Give the reader a strong impression of the fear you have felt and interest him in reading further.

B. Elaboration
   1. Extend explanation of situation and fear which attended it.
   2. Give additional information to support description.
   3. Use comparison/contrast to give reader a more exact sense of how you felt.
   4. Discuss how this experience influenced your behavior or other aspects of your life.

C. Summary and conclusions
   1. Restate your experience in very brief terms.
   2. Conclude by indicating how you have assimilated this experience.

ANSWER SHEET—MODEL TEST THREE

Reading

1. Ⓐ Ⓑ Ⓒ Ⓓ Ⓔ	11. Ⓐ Ⓑ Ⓒ Ⓓ Ⓔ	21. Ⓐ Ⓑ Ⓒ Ⓓ Ⓔ
2. Ⓐ Ⓑ Ⓒ Ⓓ Ⓔ	12. Ⓐ Ⓑ Ⓒ Ⓓ Ⓔ	22. Ⓐ Ⓑ Ⓒ Ⓓ Ⓔ
3. Ⓐ Ⓑ Ⓒ Ⓓ Ⓔ	13. Ⓐ Ⓑ Ⓒ Ⓓ Ⓔ	23. Ⓐ Ⓑ Ⓒ Ⓓ Ⓔ
4. Ⓐ Ⓑ Ⓒ Ⓓ Ⓔ	14. Ⓐ Ⓑ Ⓒ Ⓓ Ⓔ	24. Ⓐ Ⓑ Ⓒ Ⓓ Ⓔ
5. Ⓐ Ⓑ Ⓒ Ⓓ Ⓔ	15. Ⓐ Ⓑ Ⓒ Ⓓ Ⓔ	25. Ⓐ Ⓑ Ⓒ Ⓓ Ⓔ
6. Ⓐ Ⓑ Ⓒ Ⓓ Ⓔ	16. Ⓐ Ⓑ Ⓒ Ⓓ Ⓔ	26. Ⓐ Ⓑ Ⓒ Ⓓ Ⓔ
7. Ⓐ Ⓑ Ⓒ Ⓓ Ⓔ	17. Ⓐ Ⓑ Ⓒ Ⓓ Ⓔ	27. Ⓐ Ⓑ Ⓒ Ⓓ Ⓔ
8. Ⓐ Ⓑ Ⓒ Ⓓ Ⓔ	18. Ⓐ Ⓑ Ⓒ Ⓓ Ⓔ	28. Ⓐ Ⓑ Ⓒ Ⓓ Ⓔ
9. Ⓐ Ⓑ Ⓒ Ⓓ Ⓔ	19. Ⓐ Ⓑ Ⓒ Ⓓ Ⓔ	29. Ⓐ Ⓑ Ⓒ Ⓓ Ⓔ
10. Ⓐ Ⓑ Ⓒ Ⓓ Ⓔ	20. Ⓐ Ⓑ Ⓒ Ⓓ Ⓔ	30. Ⓐ Ⓑ Ⓒ Ⓓ Ⓔ

31. Ⓐ Ⓑ Ⓒ Ⓓ Ⓔ	41. Ⓐ Ⓑ Ⓒ Ⓓ Ⓔ
32. Ⓐ Ⓑ Ⓒ Ⓓ Ⓔ	42. Ⓐ Ⓑ Ⓒ Ⓓ Ⓔ
33. Ⓐ Ⓑ Ⓒ Ⓓ Ⓔ	43. Ⓐ Ⓑ Ⓒ Ⓓ Ⓔ
34. Ⓐ Ⓑ Ⓒ Ⓓ Ⓔ	44. Ⓐ Ⓑ Ⓒ Ⓓ Ⓔ
35. Ⓐ Ⓑ Ⓒ Ⓓ Ⓔ	45. Ⓐ Ⓑ Ⓒ Ⓓ Ⓔ
36. Ⓐ Ⓑ Ⓒ Ⓓ Ⓔ	46. Ⓐ Ⓑ Ⓒ Ⓓ Ⓔ
37. Ⓐ Ⓑ Ⓒ Ⓓ Ⓔ	47. Ⓐ Ⓑ Ⓒ Ⓓ Ⓔ
38. Ⓐ Ⓑ Ⓒ Ⓓ Ⓔ	48. Ⓐ Ⓑ Ⓒ Ⓓ Ⓔ
39. Ⓐ Ⓑ Ⓒ Ⓓ Ⓔ	49. Ⓐ Ⓑ Ⓒ Ⓓ Ⓔ
40. Ⓐ Ⓑ Ⓒ Ⓓ Ⓔ	50. Ⓐ Ⓑ Ⓒ Ⓓ Ⓔ

Mathematics

1. Ⓐ Ⓑ Ⓒ Ⓓ Ⓔ
2. Ⓐ Ⓑ Ⓒ Ⓓ Ⓔ
3. Ⓐ Ⓑ Ⓒ Ⓓ Ⓔ
4. Ⓐ Ⓑ Ⓒ Ⓓ Ⓔ
5. Ⓐ Ⓑ Ⓒ Ⓓ Ⓔ
6. Ⓐ Ⓑ Ⓒ Ⓓ Ⓔ
7. Ⓐ Ⓑ Ⓒ Ⓓ Ⓔ
8. Ⓐ Ⓑ Ⓒ Ⓓ Ⓔ
9. Ⓐ Ⓑ Ⓒ Ⓓ Ⓔ
10. Ⓐ Ⓑ Ⓒ Ⓓ Ⓔ
11. Ⓐ Ⓑ Ⓒ Ⓓ Ⓔ
12. Ⓐ Ⓑ Ⓒ Ⓓ Ⓔ
13. Ⓐ Ⓑ Ⓒ Ⓓ Ⓔ
14. Ⓐ Ⓑ Ⓒ Ⓓ Ⓔ
15. Ⓐ Ⓑ Ⓒ Ⓓ Ⓔ
16. Ⓐ Ⓑ Ⓒ Ⓓ Ⓔ
17. Ⓐ Ⓑ Ⓒ Ⓓ Ⓔ
18. Ⓐ Ⓑ Ⓒ Ⓓ Ⓔ
19. Ⓐ Ⓑ Ⓒ Ⓓ Ⓔ
20. Ⓐ Ⓑ Ⓒ Ⓓ Ⓔ
21. Ⓐ Ⓑ Ⓒ Ⓓ Ⓔ
22. Ⓐ Ⓑ Ⓒ Ⓓ Ⓔ
23. Ⓐ Ⓑ Ⓒ Ⓓ Ⓔ
24. Ⓐ Ⓑ Ⓒ Ⓓ Ⓔ
25. Ⓐ Ⓑ Ⓒ Ⓓ Ⓔ
26. Ⓐ Ⓑ Ⓒ Ⓓ Ⓔ
27. Ⓐ Ⓑ Ⓒ Ⓓ Ⓔ
28. Ⓐ Ⓑ Ⓒ Ⓓ Ⓔ
29. Ⓐ Ⓑ Ⓒ Ⓓ Ⓔ
30. Ⓐ Ⓑ Ⓒ Ⓓ Ⓔ
31. Ⓐ Ⓑ Ⓒ Ⓓ Ⓔ
32. Ⓐ Ⓑ Ⓒ Ⓓ Ⓔ
33. Ⓐ Ⓑ Ⓒ Ⓓ Ⓔ
34. Ⓐ Ⓑ Ⓒ Ⓓ Ⓔ
35. Ⓐ Ⓑ Ⓒ Ⓓ Ⓔ
36. Ⓐ Ⓑ Ⓒ Ⓓ Ⓔ
37. Ⓐ Ⓑ Ⓒ Ⓓ Ⓔ
38. Ⓐ Ⓑ Ⓒ Ⓓ Ⓔ
39. Ⓐ Ⓑ Ⓒ Ⓓ Ⓔ
40. Ⓐ Ⓑ Ⓒ Ⓓ Ⓔ
41. Ⓐ Ⓑ Ⓒ Ⓓ Ⓔ
42. Ⓐ Ⓑ Ⓒ Ⓓ Ⓔ
43. Ⓐ Ⓑ Ⓒ Ⓓ Ⓔ
44. Ⓐ Ⓑ Ⓒ Ⓓ Ⓔ
45. Ⓐ Ⓑ Ⓒ Ⓓ Ⓔ
46. Ⓐ Ⓑ Ⓒ Ⓓ Ⓔ
47. Ⓐ Ⓑ Ⓒ Ⓓ Ⓔ
48. Ⓐ Ⓑ Ⓒ Ⓓ Ⓔ
49. Ⓐ Ⓑ Ⓒ Ⓓ Ⓔ
50. Ⓐ Ⓑ Ⓒ Ⓓ Ⓔ

CHAPTER **8**

MODEL TEST THREE

EXAMINATION

Reading

Directions: Each passage in this section is followed by a question or questions about its content. Select the best answer to each question based on what is stated or implied in the selection. You may spend up to 60 minutes on this section.

Questions 1–2

The development of the scientific attitude in an ever-increasing number of people resulted from achievements of science and invention. Marked by a spirit of open-mindedness and critical-mindedness, the scientific attitude emphasizes the need to review an issue carefully, to understand the relationship between cause and effect, and to refrain from drawing conclusions until all facts have been presented and weighed carefully. Such an attitude is vital in a democratic government, since the choice between principles and policies demands a careful and open-minded consideration of issues and the ultimate choice rests with the majority of the people.

1. The author's attitude toward the scientific attitude and democratic government could best be described as

(A) pessimistic.
(B) confused.
(C) ambivalent.
(D) positive.
(E) critical.

2. The author would probably agree with all of the following statements EXCEPT which one of the following?

(A) The use of the scientific method has had a favorable influence on the establishment of democratic government.
(B) In a democracy, the opportunity to consider issues carefully is actually precluded by the need for expediency.
(C) The practice of democracy and the development of a new scientific invention require a similar approach.
(D) The open-mindedness and painstaking research demanded by the scientific method can be used by people participating in a democratic government.
(E) Since decisions in a democracy are made by a majority of the people, many points of view need to be considered.

Questions 3–4

Linguists who study the development of language in children note that child speech deviates from adult speech in systematic fashion. These deviations are constructed by the child on the basis of his or her own partial analysis of language and the cognitive tendencies of the child's mind. The occurrence of overregularizations, instances when irregular verbs are inflected for past tense as if they were regular, demonstrates that this systematic process is going on as children learn language.

3. An example of an "overregularization" in a child's speech would be

(A) "broke."
(B) "comed."
(C) "no I go."
(D) "walked."
(E) "coat on."

4. The main point of this passage is that

(A) children make many errors when learning language.
(B) children's overcorrections reveal that they are figuring out the rules of language.
(C) child speech is similar to adult speech and is really an imitation.
(D) a child's mind is overburdened by the volume of rules he must learn to master language.
(E) no one can teach a child language as well as he can learn it by himself.

Questions 5–6

Television is often cited as a dominant force in changing our political structure. At its worst, it turns a system of parties into a contest of personalities, exchanging a concern with ideas and policies for a preoccupation with images and styles.

5. This passage primarily discusses

(A) public policies and television polls.
(B) general reactions to the force of television.
(C) the system of political parties in the U.S.
(D) political dominance as portrayed in television programs.
(E) the negative effect television can have on politics.

6. An idea presented in this passage is that

(A) political parties do not benefit from television coverage of campaigns.
(B) television coverage of politics focuses attention on physical images rather than mental concepts.
(C) the need for an alteration of political structure is more evident when television reviews politics.
(D) the interest in political images has made television a natural medium for politics
(E) television and politics do not mix.

Questions 7–8

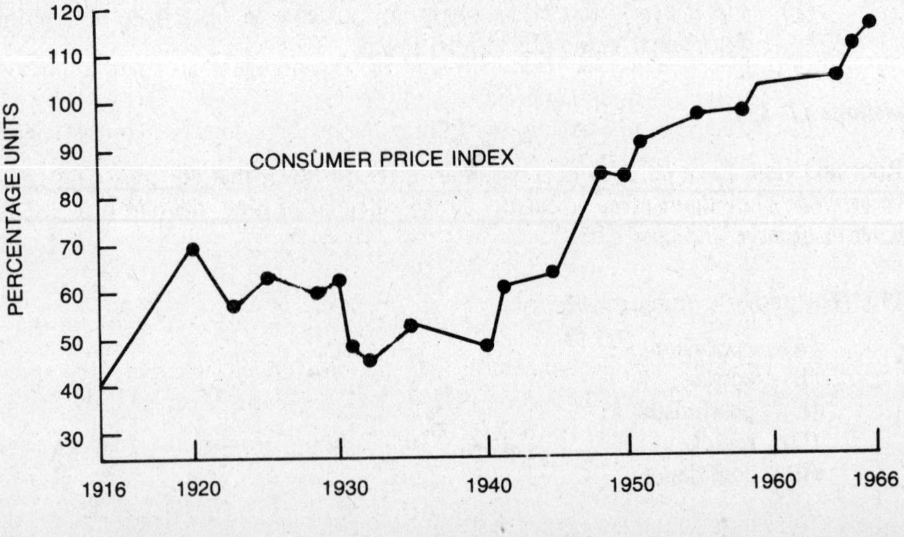

The graph represents the Consumer Price Index for the period 1916 to 1966. Refer to the graph to answer the following questions.

7. If the dots represent specific points when the Consumer Price Index was "read," then the number of times (one dot to another) that the index went down was

(A) one.
(B) three.
(C) four.
(D) six.
(E) eight.

8. In 1950, the Consumer Price Index was approximately

(A) 93%.
(B) 82%.
(C) 100%.
(D) 65%.
(E) 74%.

Questions 9–10

Impulsive, unconventional, boundlessly energetic, Alice Roosevelt pursued pleasure with the same abandon that Roosevelt demonstrated in his activities. She kept the newspaper-reading public captivated. Alice lived by her own law. She smoked, a habit considered most unladylike at that time. She was often reported to be involved in the sort of adventures not commonly associated with a president's daughter.

9. The author's attitude toward Alice Roosevelt could best be identified as

(A) reserved.
(B) uncanny.
(C) respectful.
(D) naive.
(E) conservative.

10. One conclusion that could be drawn from this passage is that

(A) Alice Roosevelt was not very well thought of because of her outrageous behavior.
(B) President Roosevelt and his daughter were not on good terms for the term of his presidency.
(C) Alice Roosevelt's activities provoked the antagonism of law enforcement officials.
(D) journalists found Alice Roosevelt to be a rich topic for newspaper copy.
(E) a president's family members are not free to participate in activities that are detrimental to the presidential image.

Questions 11–12

Root and stem have no need of a calendar to inform them that the calm days of midsummer have arrived. They themselves are marks on the calendar of time, there in field and meadow for anyone to observe and take note.

11. The author's attitude is one of

(A) confusion.
(B) ecstasy.
(C) pessimism.
(D) regret.
(E) confidence.

12. The author compares the parts of a plant to

(A) midsummer days.
(B) numbers on a calendar.
(C) the parts of a day.
(D) seasons of the year.
(E) flowers in a field.

Questions 13–14

If a group is to get on with its work, whether it is working out a new budget or learning about physics, indirect processes may require special attention. Difficulties often emerge which have no direct relation to the budget or to physics. Problems in communication often develop when a group assembles to do a particular job, even though the language is clear.

13. According to the author, ''indirect processes'' are

(A) only apparent to people working in a group.
(B) ones which can interfere with group communications.
(C) sometimes attributable to the work of the group.
(D) those that can be carried out best in a group.
(E) the tasks undertaken by a specific group.

14. In writing this passage, the author's purpose seems to be

(A) to argue the point that the work of a group, such as a committee, cannot be effective because of inhibiting factors.
(B) to discuss the pros and cons of studying physics in a group.
(C) to report the results of an experiment in group dynamics.
(D) to provide information about group dynamics or factors that influence communication in a group.
(E) to entertain the reader with a sarcastic comment on group dynamics.

Questions 15–18

The laser is a fairly recent technological discovery, but it is proving to be a revolutionary alternative in a great many fields. To understand why, it is important to understand the nature of the laser beam. It is an extremely narrow beam of light, but it is significantly different in quality from ordinary light, which consists of waves referred to as ''incoherent'' light. The ''coherent'' light waves produced by the laser are parallel and of the same size and frequency, each wave fitting closely to the contiguous one. While the waves of ordinary light fly off in every direction, the laser can travel long distances without scattering. The waves of a laser also have extremely short wavelengths, allowing a much greater amount of information to be carried.

The laser serves as a carrier of information, capable of transmitting the messages carried by telephone, radio, and television combined. In the medical field, the laser is being used to perform bloodless, painless surgery. Hard substances, such as diamonds, can be cut with a laser, and enormous distances can be measured to within a few feet. It is evident that only the surface of this gem has been scratched in finding new and beneficial uses.

15. Laser is different from ordinary light in

(A) shape and sensation.
(B) type and nature.
(C) hue and color.
(D) order and influx.
(E) repetition and regularity.

16. Each of the following terms could be used to describe ordinary light EXCEPT

(A) scattered.
(B) not parallel.
(C) coherent.
(D) restricted substance.
(E) dispersed.

17. From this passage, it can reasonably be concluded that laser beams could be used to do all of the following EXCEPT

(A) calculate the distance from the moon to the earth.
(B) remove a wart.
(C) transmit television programs.
(D) guide a spaceship.
(E) convert sea water into drinking water.

18. The writer most likely used the figurative expression in the last sentence of the passage to

(A) refer to the use of the laser in surgery.
(B) allude to the ability of the laser to cut diamonds.
(C) emphasize the need to find additional uses for the laser.
(D) identify characteristics of the laser beam.
(E) clarify specific uses of the laser not mentioned previously in the passage.

Questions 19–21

Tax shelters with real economic value may eventually begin to show profits. In this case, the investor will gain, not only from the tax deductions, but from the profits as well. As a rule, when the profits start to accrue, it is time to look for another investment to shelter those profits.

19. Which one of the following statements best expresses an idea found in this selection?

(A) Sheltering the profits from another tax shelter is not a recommended action.
(B) Profits and deductions both constitute gains from tax shelters.
(C) Profits will increase when deductions decrease.
(D) Investing in tax shelters is no longer beneficial if the shelters show profits.
(E) The real value of tax shelters is negligible.

20. The author would agree that most tax shelters

(A) produce profits.
(B) are sources for reinvestment.
(C) permit tax deductions.
(D) are illegal.
(E) result in financial gains but not significant ones.

21. The word "accrue" in line 4 could be replaced most accurately by

(A) combine.
(B) operate.
(C) hold.
(D) dissipate.
(E) accumulate.

Questions 22–23

The civilization of the 20th century, highly technical as it is, is like an airplane in flight, supported by its forward motion. It cannot stop without falling.

22. To extend the simile in this passage, one might say which of the following?

(A) As the airplane becomes larger and travels longer distances, flight technology must improve to keep pace with the increased demands.
(B) The need for man to "spread his wings" will be satisfied only by longer and more productive airplane flights.
(C) Falling without a parachute available to rescue him from certain death, man will find ways to improve the state of civilization.
(D) The technology needed to keep an airplane aloft is not adequate to meet the demands of modern technological society.
(E) Referring to basic laws of motion, one can see that the airplane is headed toward disaster.

23. The author would agree that

(A) the world's use of natural resources will decline as techniques are improved.
(B) the curve of scientific progress will ultimately lead to the world's destruction.
(C) to stop science would create more problems than solutions.
(D) twentieth century civilization has not really progressed as much as the degree of technology would indicate.
(E) present techniques used in science are so undependable that they cannot possibly effect improvements in society.

Questions 24–26

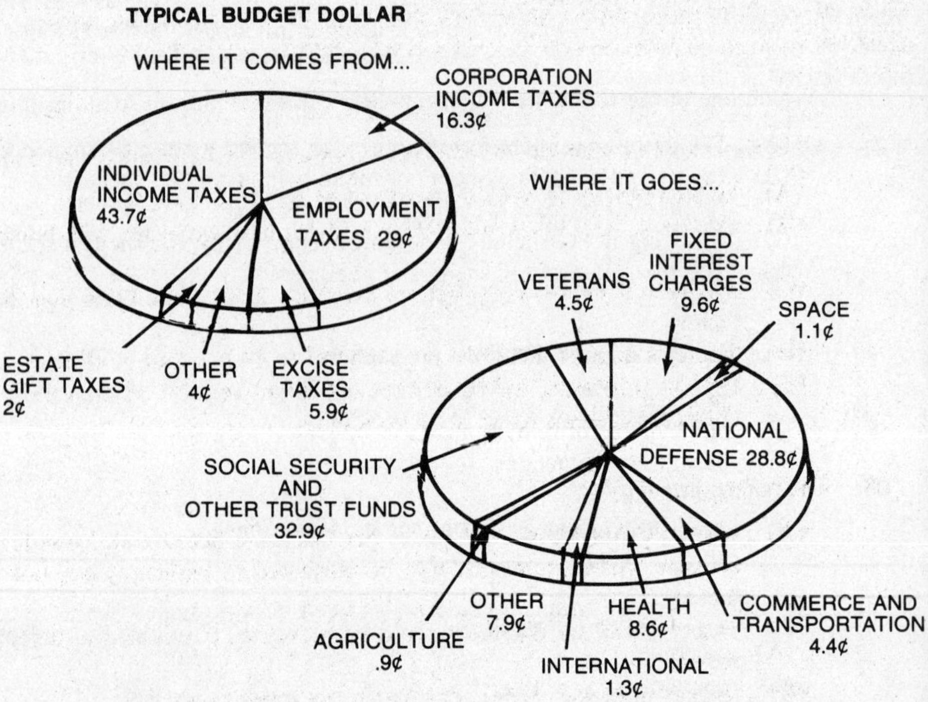

Refer to the diagram to answer the next three questions.

24. Next to individual income taxes, the greatest amount of money to run the government comes from

(A) employment taxes.
(B) social security.
(C) corporation income taxes.
(D) fixed interest charges.
(E) excise taxes.

25. If National Defense spending were reduced by 8.0¢, and this 8.0¢ were added to the health budget, the budget amount for health would then be

(A) 17.6¢.
(B) 37.4¢.
(C) 8.6¢.
(D) 18.4¢.
(E) 16.6¢.

26. In the budget of the U.S. government, income from employment taxes is about equal to

(A) individual income taxes.
(B) national defense spending.
(C) all other taxes combined.
(D) social security costs.
(E) health and agriculture spending.

Questions 27–28

It is important to remember that almost all accidents are psychological in origin, not mechanical. Eighty-four percent of all vehicles involved in fatal accidents are found to be in good condition. The fact that, in the other 16 percent, the defects are usually in brakes, lights, or tires, most of which the driver probably knows about, and that he or she goes on driving anyhow, makes these accidents seem to be appropriately characterized as ones in which there is also a strong psychological factor.

27. All of the following facts are included in the passage EXCEPT which one of the following?

(A) Sixteen percent of vehicles involved in accidents have defects.
(B) Drivers usually know when their vehicles have problems with brakes, lights, or tires.
(C) Mechanical factors contribute to accidents much more often than psychological factors.
(D) Vehicles in good condition are involved in 84 per cent of all fatal accidents.
(E) Defects in brakes, lights, or tires are found in most of the cars in which mechanical problems result in an accident.

28. The author implies that

(A) when a driver knows that his or her car has a defect and drives it anyway, the accident that may result could be attributed to psychological, not mechanical, factors.
(B) 84 percent of all accidents could be prevented if mechanical defects were corrected.
(C) failures in brakes, lights, or tires do not result in accidents.
(D) drivers cannot be held responsible for accidents caused by mechanical failure.
(E) accidents are caused by psychological factors 16 percent of the time.

Questions 29–30

After seemingly endless hours of practice, after years of planning and hoping, he stood in a daze, awaiting the judges' decision. The moment of trial had finally come. Suddenly, it was over. The results were read, carefully and deliberately. I've actually won, he repeated incredulously to himself.

29. Which of the following sentences best completes the paragraph?

(A) Like a defendant awaiting a verdict, he slowly rose to his feet and turned to face his judges.
(B) Suddenly, he was overwhelmed with a sense of timidity and turned and fled from the scene.
(C) As if he were a victorious warrior from times past, he raised his arms to embrace the applause from the crowd.
(D) Like a child in need of approval, he jumped to his feet and ran to his teammates, expecting their congratulations.
(E) Filled with a quiet sense of exaltation, unmatched by anything he had ever known, he turned and approached the judges' platform.

30. The passage describes how a person feels who

(A) has to endure a trial.
(B) has to spend hours waiting.
(C) is required to serve as a judge.
(D) has won a competition.
(E) has completed years of work on a project.

Questions 31–32

The dramatic increase in the earth's population—since 1750, it has more than tripled—has no been a biologically-caused evolutionary phenomenon. The evolution has occurred in the world's economic organization. That the human population has tripled in seven generations can be attrib-uted to the amelioration in economic unification. A cooperating world society moves goods across the earth's surface with great ease and, thereby, supports its inhabitants.

31. The main point of this passage is that

(A) the earth's population is three times what it was in 1750.
(B) the world's economic system has unified the world.
(C) the improvement in the economic organization of the world has been the primary cause of the increase in population since 1750.
(D) cooperation among the countries of the world has been erratic, but there is nonetheless, greater economic unification.
(E) achieving world unification is an evolutionary process.

32. In the writer's opinion, trade is necessary for

(A) democracy.
(B) self-preservation.
(C) political unity.
(D) economic growth.
(E) open communication.

Questions 33–34

Writers must be held in some part accountable for the deplorable state of criticism. For the most part, writers are contemplative and retiring individuals, withdrawing to their ivory towers to reflect on the absurdities of a foolish world, requesting only to be left alone with their work. In this way, the writer lays himself open to criticism. He does not see this enemy who has stolen into the shadows at the back gate and is slowly scaling the walls.

33. In the last sentence of this passage, the image created by the author is used to

(A) explain the effects of a writer's personality on his works.
(B) emphasize the need for monitoring the works of writers more closely.
(C) describe how critics assault writers while they are unaware or unprepared.
(D) highlight the contribution of constructive criticism to the literary world.
(E) create the impression that writers are isolated from the world and have no understanding of it.

34. From the passage, one could conclude that the author would identify critics as

(A) ivory tower dwellers.
(B) retirees.
(C) absurdities of a foolish world.
(D) the "enemy."
(E) a necessary evil.

Questions 35–38

It is not in the interest of that general cultural background, used so often as a cloak for the snob or the pedant, that I argue for the experience of a liberal education. I speak for an introduction to the thoughts and actions of those who have gone before, to the inhabitants of countries other than their own with different struggles and needs, and to concepts divorced from their primary interests.

35. A writer with an opposing point of view to that of the author of this passage might argue for

(A) the inclusion of courses in a broad, rather than narrow or specific, range of curricular areas.
(B) a course of education which leads to something of immediate practical use.
(C) a college curriculum that allows students to structure their program to meet their own needs.
(D) a traditional course of study often reserved only for those who become known as snobs or egg-heads.
(E) a program focused on great books, the classics, history, or the humanities.

36. In this passage, the word "pedant" is used to refer to

(A) a respected scholar.
(B) one who is pretentious about his learning.
(C) an educator.
(D) someone who does not work for a living.
(E) an educated patent medicine peddler.

37. Which of the following would be an accurate paraphrase of the first sentence in this passage?

(A) It is not that I am indifferent to the need for a cultural background, but rather that I don't think it can be equated with a liberal education.
(B) I am not in favor of an education that pursues the past in the interest only of creating the impression of being educated.
(C) A liberal education can lead to a derogatory classification of those suffering from a cultured background.
(D) The pedant is one who pursues a liberal education for the purpose of appearing cultured.
(E) I am in favor of a liberal education, but not in the interest of providing a cause for snobbery.

38. In a word, the author's purpose in writing this passage is to

(A) persuade.
(B) entertain.
(C) report.
(D) describe.
(E) quibble.

Questions 39–40

There are at least two quite different kinds of things we learn when we learn our language. We learn the language itself, which includes the sound system, the syntax, and the vocabulary. We also learn something which is, perhaps, not as apparent. We learn how to manipulate our language so that we can communicate effectively and efficiently with others. That is not quite the same thing as having learned the language.

39. The writer of the passage implies that

(A) one does not "know" a language until he knows how to use the language in social situations.
(B) once you have mastered the basic structures of a language, the ability to use it effectively follows naturally.
(C) learning a language is one of the most difficult things an individual can do.
(D) communicating effectively requires a mastery of all the basic elements of a language.
(E) a person who knows more than one language gains a greater ability to use any language effectively.

40. This passage is most likely taken from

(A) a textbook for English grammar instruction.
(B) an article on linguistics and language development.
(C) a paper on topics for speech-making.
(D) a review of a communications textbook.
(E) a manual for ham radio operators.

Questions 41–42

There seems to be a tendency to induce all children to write with their right hands. Both parents and teachers have evidenced an antipathy to a child using his or her left hand. Some psychologists however, believe that to compel a left-handed child to write with his or her right hand may result in emotional damage.

41. The author of this passage would agree with all of the following statements EXCEPT which one of the following?

(A) Children should be allowed to use their left hand if they have a tendency to do so.
(B) The parents of left-handed children often exhibit a negative reaction to their using their left hand.
(C) Psychologists do not support the contention that encouraging a child to switch from a natural use of his left hand to the use of his right hand presents any problems.
(D) The tendency to encourage children to switch to the use of their right hand has been exhibited by both parents and teachers.
(E) To compel a child to use his right instead of his left hand may not be a good idea.

42. As used in line 2, the best synonym for the word, "antipathy," is

(A) aversion.
(B) indifference.
(C) gentleness.
(D) prejudice.
(E) recurrence.

Questions 43–44

In the interest of making test results for a group more meaningful, information other than the raw scores are often provided. The median or midpoint, which indicates the central tendency of a distribution, may be given, along with so-called measures of dispersion, statistics which indicate whether the scores cluster close to the center or are dispersed at some distance from the center.

43. One group of statistical indicators which tells how test scores are distributed in a group is called

(A) the median.
(B) the test score midpoint.
(C) measures of dispersion.
(D) distribution markers.
(E) measures of central tendency.

44. According to this passage,

(A) tests are useful for measuring academic growth.
(B) test scores have more meaning when the range of scores for the group is known.
(C) test developers need to increase the reliability of tests.
(D) test scores are meaningless without other information about classroom performance.
(E) cluster scores provide more valuable information than individual test scores.

Questions 45–46

When the desire to write overwhelms you, never deny it. What you are able to put into words may not be worthy of a prize, but at least you have succeeded in doing something few people ever attempt—capturing forever something that may only be experienced once—a feeling, a sensation, an emotion, an idea.

45. In this passage, the writer's tone is one of

(A) indifference.
(B) delight.
(C) scorn.
(D) encouragement.
(E) pessimism.

46. Which of the following statements is most appropriate as a continuation of the paragraph?

(A) The rewards are few, but the need to accomplish something new can be met.
(B) What one accomplishes as a result of this work will be duplicated.
(C) These are far more precious than anything tangible as they attribute life to the mind.
(D) No one of these goals can be worth more effort than the others.
(E) At such a time, the only appropriate response may be to silence one's longings.

Questions 47–49

It is generally acknowledged that the United States, although it remains powerful, no longer stands at the top of various status rankings that measure a country's position in the world. Whether the nation is judged on political, economic, or military criteria, it is evident that it has lost its number one status. National attention has turned to a search for ways to halt the decline. Reasons for the decline are offered in every sector. Businessmen point to government interference in the free market; religious leaders focus on declining moral standards; parents complain about an inadequate public education system; the party out of power blames the party in power, and the party in power blames everyone else. Some few realists—or defeatists, as the case may be—suggest that the dominance enjoyed by this country was purely an accident of history and not the result of some special quality of the American people or of some unique destiny.

47. The title that best expresses the ideas of this selection is

(A) National Priorities.
(B) Historical Accident.
(C) U.S. Decline in Position.
(D) World Status for Nations.
(E) Democratic Flaws.

48. Reasons for the current U.S. status in the world are

(A) not given.
(B) easily specified.
(C) abundant.
(D) offered by other nations.
(E) found primarily in the military.

49. In this selection, the author does NOT mention

(A) statistics supporting the U.S. position.
(B) education as a factor affecting the U.S. position.
(C) the opinion of politicians.
(D) the factors on which a national ranking is based.
(E) any attempts to explain how the U.S. achieved its current ranking.

50. Education has been, from the beginning, a sort of American obsession. Even the first colonists brought with them a respect for education. Americans were among the first to assert that all children would be educated in elementary schools.

Which of the following sentences is most appropriate as a continuation of the paragraph?

(A) Although these schools were public, they were not "free," except to those students who could not pay.
(B) Book learning for girls was almost totally neglected in the colonial period.
(C) It took a long time, but today the majority of Americans receives at least an elementary education.
(D) As registration increased, the high school changed.
(E) Education is a process by which the individual is influenced by informal and formal means.

Mathematics

Directions: Select the best answer to each of the following questions. Any figures provided are there as reference; they are approximations and are not drawn to scale except when stated.

You may refer to the following information during this section of the test:

$=$ is equal to	$\sqrt{\ }$ square root of
$\neq$ is unequal to	$^\circ$ degrees
$<$ is less than	$\parallel$ is parallel to
$>$ is greater than	$\perp$ is perpendicular to
$\leq$ is less than or equal to	π pi, approximately 3.14
$\geq$ is greater than or equal to	

Circle: Radius $= r$; Circumference $= 2\pi r$; Area $= \pi r^2$; a circle contains 360°

Triangle: In triangle ABC, if $\angle BDA$ is a right angle,

$$\text{Area of } \triangle ABC = \frac{AC \times BD}{2};$$

$$\text{Perimeter of } \triangle ABC = AB + BC + CA$$

Sum of the measures of the degrees of the angles is 180.

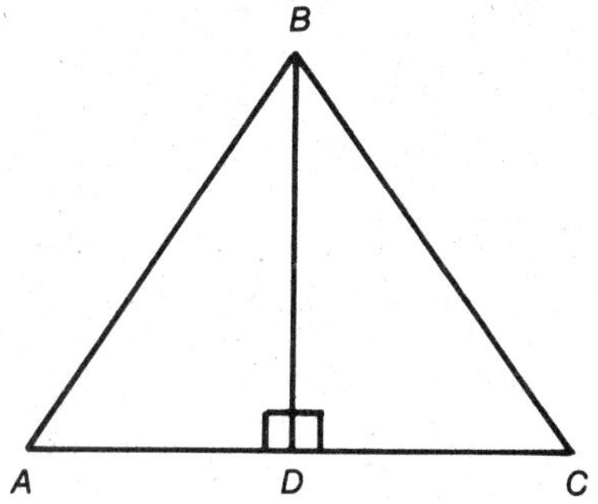

Rectangle: Area $= L \times W$; Perimeter $= 2 \times (L + W)$

1. Which of the following is less than N, if N is any number?

(A) $1 \times N$
(B) $1\frac{1}{4} \times N$
(C) $\frac{3}{2} \times N$
(D) $\frac{3}{4} \times N$
(E) $N \div \frac{3}{4}$

2. $3 + 5 \times 6 - 4 \div 2 = ?$

(A) 22
(B) 46
(C) 31
(D) 14.5
(E) None of the above

3. Which of the following is the numeral for "five thousand two hundred and eight tenths?"

(A) 5,280
(B) 5,000.208
(C) 5,200.08
(D) 5,200.8
(E) None of the above

4. In the numeral below, which digit is in the hundredths place?

3457.682

(A) 2
(B) 4
(C) 6
(D) 8
(E) None of the above

5. What is the square root of 324?

(A) (324)
(B) 162
(C) 18
(D) 648
(E) None of the above

6. Which of the following is smaller than and closest to ½?

(A) $\frac{2}{7}$
(B) $\frac{3}{7}$
(C) $\frac{4}{7}$
(D) $\frac{1}{3}$
(E) $\frac{2}{3}$

7. A factory has 320 daytime workers and the number of night workers is one-fourth the number of daytime workers. What is the ratio of day workers to total workers?

(A) $\frac{320}{400}$
(B) $\frac{80}{320}$
(C) $\frac{320}{80}$
(D) $\frac{320}{480}$
(E) None of the above

8. In which of the following sequences does the average of the sequence equal one of the terms of the sequence?

I. $x, x + 1, x + 2$
II. $x, x + 2, x + 4$
III. $x, x + 1, x + 3$
IV. $x, x + 2, x + 4, x + 6$

(A) I only
(B) II only
(C) I and II only
(D) I, II, and III only
(E) II and IV only

9. The school football team lost 25% of the games it played. If it won 18 games, how many games did it lose?

(A) 4
(B) 24
(C) 6
(D) 7
(E) None of the above

10. In which of the following is 360 written as a product of prime numbers?

(A) 10×36
(B) $2 \times 2 \times 2 \times 5 \times 9$
(C) $5 \times 8 \times 9$
(D) $2 \times 2 \times 2 \times 3 \times 3 \times 5$
(E) None of the above

11. $(\frac{1}{3} - 1) \times \square = 1$

Which number goes in the box to make a true statement?

(A) $\frac{2}{3}$
(B) $-\frac{3}{2}$
(C) $-\frac{2}{3}$
(D) 2
(E) None of the above

12. Sally has 2 skirts, 5 blouses, and 3 dresses. If Sally wears either a dress or a skirt and blouse, how many different outfits does she have?

(A) 10
(B) 30
(C) 13
(D) 17
(E) None of the above

13. Our backyard is 225 square meters in area. We have mowed $\frac{2}{3}$ of it. If it takes us 5 minutes to mow 25 square meters, how long will we need to mow to finish the job?

(A) 10 minutes
(B) 15 minutes
(C) 30 minutes
(D) 45 minutes
(E) None of the above

14. A number, X, is more than 30, but less than 50. The sum of its digits is 8. X is even. What number is X?

(A) 53
(B) 62
(C) 71
(D) 44
(E) None of the above

15. Mary's 5th grade class is planning a chess tournament. If there are 4 people who signed up to play, how many games must be played so that every person plays every other person just once?

(A) 12
(B) 5
(C) 16
(D) 8
(E) None of the above

16. A car that has a 16 gallon tank was filled with 12.5 gallons of gas at $1.08 a gallon. How much was spent on gas?

(A) $17.28
(B) $3.78
(C) $13.50
(D) $22.50
(E) None of the above

17. Which of the following is the graph of $y = x^2 + 2$?

A
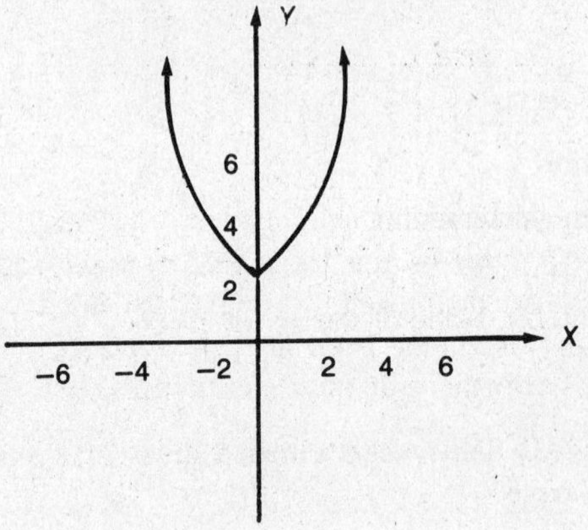

B
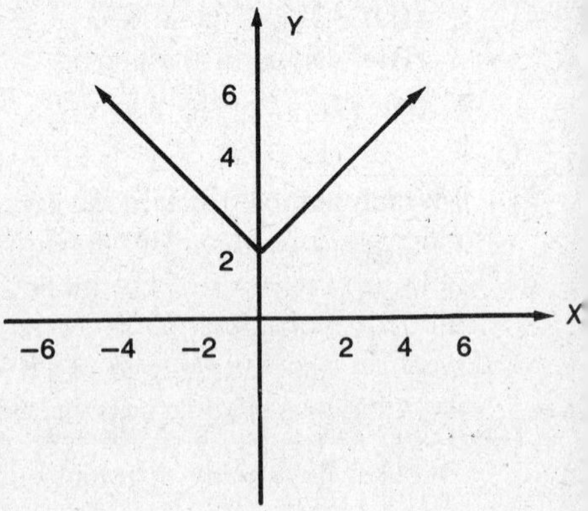

C
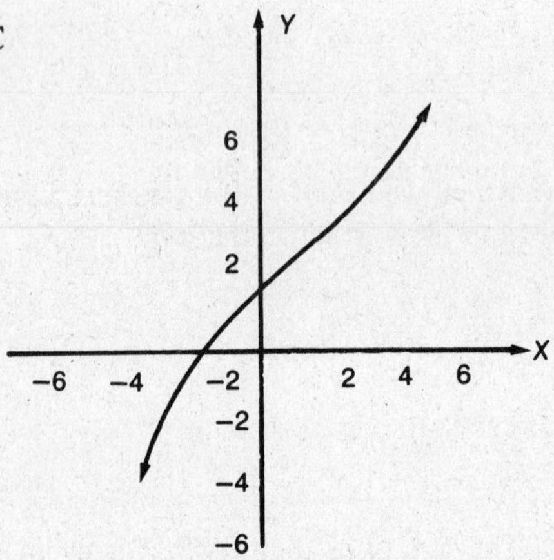

D
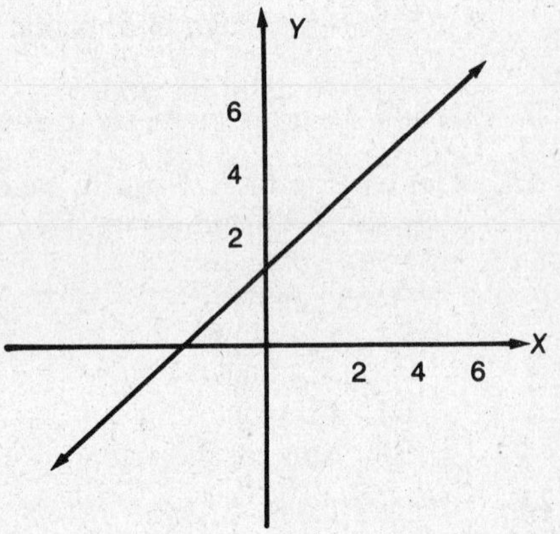

(A) Graph A
(B) Graph B
(C) Graph C
(D) Graph D
(E) None of the above

18. ⅕ of a keg of beer was used at a party last Saturday. Yesterday, ½ of what was left wa drunk. How much of the keg still remains?

(A) ⅖
(B) ⅗
(C) ½
(D) $\frac{3}{10}$
(E) $\frac{7}{10}$

19. Three times the lesser of two consecutive whole numbers is less than twice the greater. Which of these is the only possibility for the greater?

(A) 3
(B) 6
(C) 4
(D) 2
(E) 1

20. A suit which is regularly $105.00 is on sale for 20% off. How much do you save on the suit?

(A) $2.10
(B) $5.25
(C) $84.00
(D) $20.00
(E) None of the above

21. Martha worked in a fast food restaurant for ten weeks during her summer vacation. She was paid $4.25 per hour and made from $10 to $15 a day on tips. She lived at home and was able to save most of her money to buy a used car that cost $1800 (taxes included). After all deductions, Martha averaged $3.50 per hour take home pay. She also averaged $54 per week in tips. By the end of the ten weeks, what is the minimum number of hours Martha must have worked to buy the car?

(A) 360 hours
(B) 297 hours
(C) 515 hours
(D) 400 hours
(E) Not enough information is given.

22. George went to the drugstore and bought gumballs and stickers. The gumballs cost 5¢ each and the stickers cost 8¢ each. He spent 60¢. How many gumballs did he buy?

(A) 3 gumballs
(B) 4 gumballs
(C) 5 gumballs
(D) 7 gumballs
(E) 1 gumball

23. $\frac{x}{y} = y$, so $y = ?$

(A) x
(B) $2x$
(C) $\frac{x}{6}$
(D) $\sqrt{x}$
(E) $\frac{x}{2}$

24. If $1/x = 14$ and $y = 7$, what is x in terms of y?

(A) $2y$
(B) $\frac{1}{2}y$
(C) $-2y$
(D) $y/2$
(E) None of the above

25. $x^2 - 16 = ?$

(A) $(x - 4)^2$
(B) $(x + 4)^2$
(C) $(x - 4)(x + 4)$
(D) $(x + 8)(x - 2)$
(E) None of the above

26. If $x = 3$, then $5x - 2x^2 = ?$

(A) 117
(B) 24
(C) −21
(D) −3
(E) None of the above

27. If $3x - 5 = 2$, then $x - \frac{1}{3} = ?$

(A) 2
(B) $2\frac{1}{3}$
(C) 3
(D) $7\frac{1}{3}$
(E) 7

28. The circumference of a circle of radius, R, is given by $C = 2 \cdot \pi \cdot R$. Which expression gives the value of the radius if you know the circumference?

(A) $R = \frac{C}{\pi}$

(B) $R = \frac{\pi C}{2R}$

(C) $R = \frac{C}{2 \cdot \pi}$

(D) $R = C + 2$
(E) $R = C - 2$

29. Which of the following equations gives the relationship shown in the table below?

(A) $y = 2x + 1$
(B) $y = x^2 - 1$
(C) $y = (x + 1)^2$
(D) $y = x^2 + 1$
(E) None of the above

X	0	1	2	3	4	5
Y	1	2	5	10	17	2

30. If $\frac{15}{45} = \frac{50}{x}$, then $x = ?$

(A) 30
(B) 70
(C) 200
(D) 110
(E) 150

31. If $m < 0$ and $n > 0$ and n is even, which of the following is (are) definitely a negative even number?

I. $m \cdot n$
II. $m - n$
III. $2m$

(A) I only
(B) II only
(C) III only
(D) I and II only
(E) I and III only

32. If the volume of a cylinder is found by multiplying the area of its base times its height, what is the volume of the cylinder pictured?

(A) 25×20
(B) $25 \times 20 \times \pi$
(C) $10 \times 20 \times \pi$
(D) $5 \times 20 \times \pi$
(E) None of the above

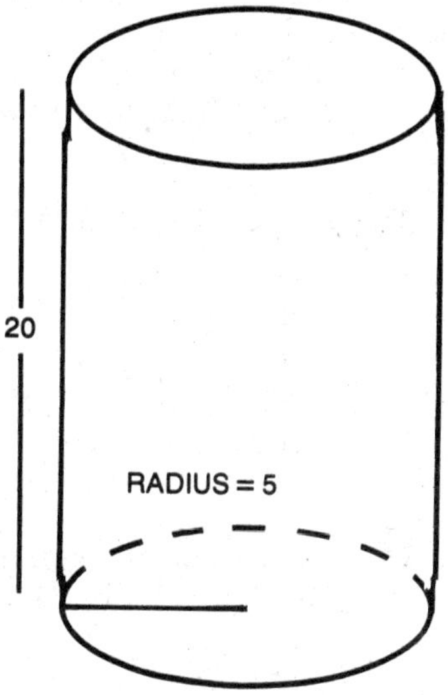

33. A and B are two regular pentagons (five sided figures with all angles and sides equal). If pentagon B is twice as large as pentagon A, and the angles of A measure 108° each, what is the measure of each angle in pentagon B?

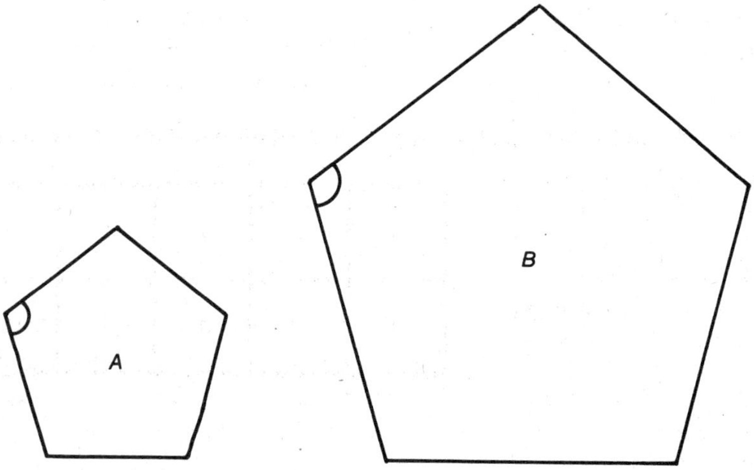

(A) 216°
(B) 54°
(C) 108°
(D) 72°
(E) None of the above

34. Suppose the line *PQ* is parallel to the line *MN*. If the coordinates of *N* are (5, *y*), then *y* must be equal to ?

(A) 5
(B) 4
(C) 3
(D) 2
(E) None of the above

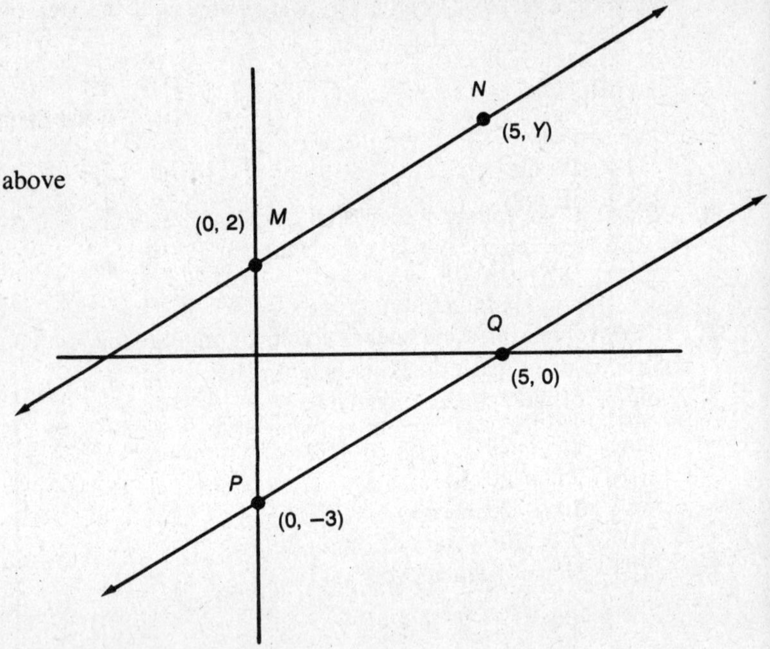

35. In the figure you see triangle *ABC* and the measures of two of its angles. What is *x* (the measure of angle *BCD*)?

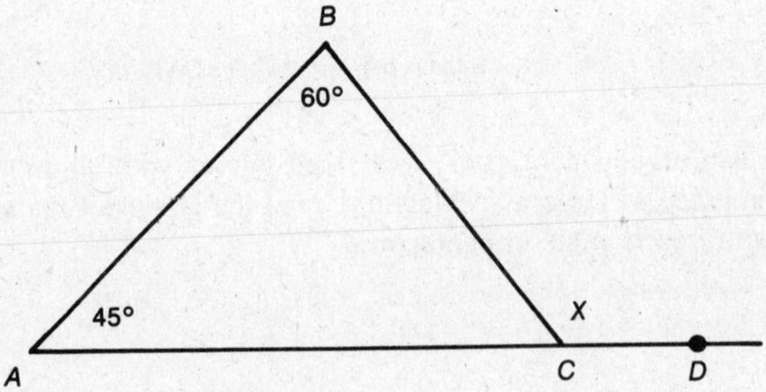

(A) 75
(B) 60
(C) 135
(D) 105
(E) Cannot be determined from information given

36. Sam is going to make a scale drawing of his rectangular garden. The graph paper he wi use is 8½ inches by 11 inches and has squares that are ¼ inch on each side. He decide that he will let each square represent 1 square foot. If he can use only 1 sheet of grap paper, which of the following sizes of gardens can he draw to scale?

I. 30 feet × 42 feet
II. 35 feet × 40 feet
III. 21 feet × 43 feet

(A) I only
(B) II only
(C) III only
(D) I and II only
(E) I and III only

37. A rectangular painting which measures 12 centimeters by 30 centimeters needs framing. If we want a frame 2 centimeters wide, what will the area of the frame itself be in square centimeters?

(A) 448
(B) 360
(C) 184
(D) 88
(E) None of the above

38. Which of the following could be lengths of the sides of a parallelogram (that is, a 4-sided figure in which the opposite sides are parallel)?

I. 5, 10, 5, 10
II. 5, 10, 5, 15
III. 5, 6, 5, 6

(A) I only
(B) II only
(C) III only
(D) I and III only
(E) I and II only

39. The area of a small square in the figure is 16. The perimeter of the figure is:

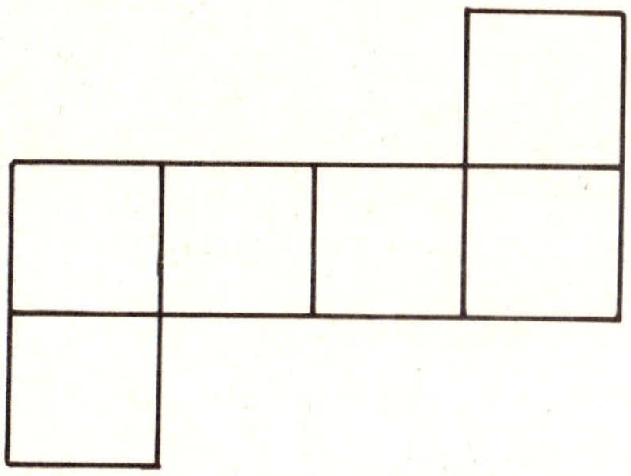

(A) 24
(B) 40
(C) 44
(D) 48
(E) 56

40. A square has a side of $3 \cdot \sqrt{\pi}$ centimeters. Find the radius of a circle that would have area equal to that of the square.

(A) 9 centimeters
(B) 3 centimeters
(C) $3 \cdot \pi$ centimeters
(D) $3\sqrt{\pi}$ centimeters
(E) None of the above

41. Harry has only quarters and dimes. Some kids made guesses about how much money Harry could have. Which guess does not belong?

(A) Lisa guessed 55¢.
(B) Laura guessed 35¢.
(C) Kim guessed 75¢.
(D) Heather guessed 45¢.
(E) Carrie guessed 30¢.

42. Which problem statement can be solved using the number sentence

$$3n + 2 = 35?$$

(A) Mario's father's age is 2 years more than 3 times Mario's age. Mario's father is 35 years old. How old is Mario?
(B) Mario's father is 35 years old. Two years from now Mario's father will be 3 times as old as Mario. How old is Mario?
(C) There are 35 cats and dogs in a pet store. There are 2 dogs and 3 times as many cats. How many cats are there?
(D) There are n cats in a pet store. If you add 2 to this number and multiply by 3, you get 35. How many cats are there?
(E) Two more than 35 is 3 times a number.

Use the problem stated below to answer item 43.

> ***Problem:*** There are 152 students who study French, Spanish, or German at Lincoln High School. Of these, 37 take only French, 60 take only Spanish, and 22 take only German. Also, 17 take both French and Spanish but not German, 3 take both Spanish and German but not French, and 9 take French and German but not Spanish. How many students study all 3 languages?

43. Which diagram(s) correctly represent(s) the information stated in this problem?

I.

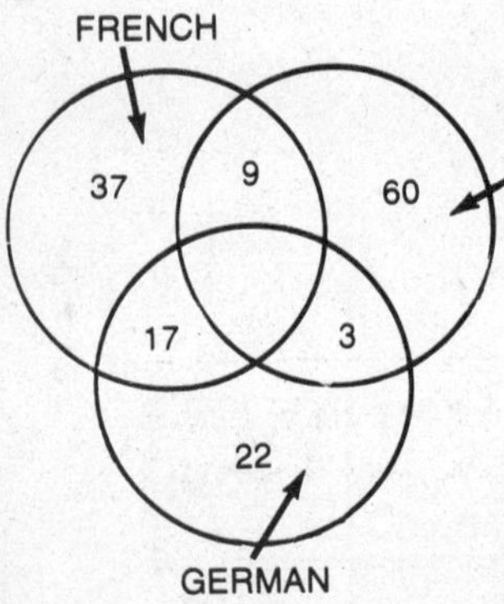

II.

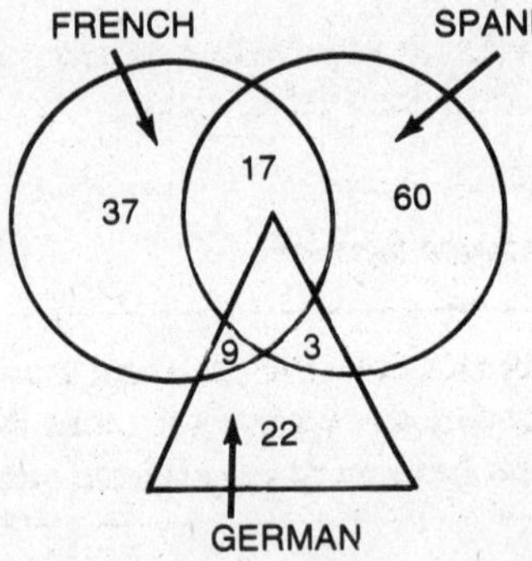

III.

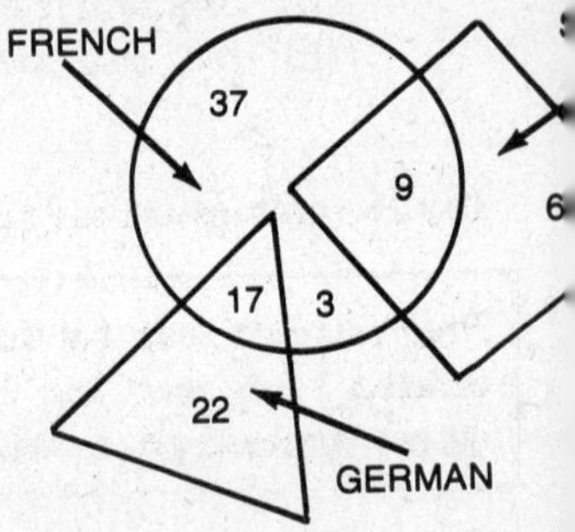

(A) I only
(B) II only
(C) III only
(D) I and II only
(E) II and III only

Use the problem stated below to answer item 44.

> ***Problem:*** Ooey Gooey Gum is on sale at 8 pieces for \$.59. At this rate, how many pieces could Terry buy for \$1.00?

44. Which of the following equations could be used to solve this problem?

(A) $\frac{8}{59} = \frac{100}{n}$

(B) $\frac{n}{8} = \frac{59}{100}$

(C) $\frac{8}{59} = \frac{n}{100}$

(D) $\frac{8}{100} = \frac{n}{59}$

(E) None of the above

45. The farmer could find the length of one side of a farm if he also knew:

(A) Two sides of the farm have the same length.
(B) 1 acre = 4840 square yards.
(C) The farm has an area of 50 acres.
(D) The farm is triangular in shape.
(E) The farm is rectangular in shape.

Use the problem stated below to answer item 46.

Problem: Jim, Ruth, and Peter took turns driving home from the lake. Ruth drove 40 miles more than Jim. Jim drove twice as far as Peter. Peter drove 86 miles. How far was the total drive? Answer: 126

46. Which statement best describes why the answer given for this problem is *not* reasonable?

(A) Jim drove more than Peter.
(B) Ruth drove 40 miles more than Jim.
(C) Peter drove 86 miles himself.
(D) Because there is not enough information to answer the question.
(E) Because you want to find the total distance.

Use the problem stated below to answer item 47.

Problem: Box seats for the World Series cost \$40 each and grandstand seats cost \$18 each. Luis ordered 3 box seats and 7 grandstand seats. Orders for more than \$150 received 10% discount on the purchase price. What did Luis have to pay for all the seats he ordered?

47. Which is an appropriate first step in solving the problem?

(A) Find the total number of seats.
(B) Find 10% of \$150.
(C) Find 10% of the total cost of the seats.
(D) Find the total cost for 3 box seats.
(E) Subtract \$150 from the total cost of the 10 seats.

Use the problem stated below to answer item 48.

Problem: Carla bought all of the available bell trim fabric and 2⅓ yard of the lace at a remnant sale. She paid for the items with a \$5 bill. How much change should she get?

REMNANT SALE

Bell trim	5½ yards	40¢ per yard
Ribbon	4¼ yards	25¢ per yard
Lace	2¾ yards	60¢ per yard

48. Which solution method is correct for this problem?

(A) 40¢ + 60¢ = \$1.00 → \$5 − \$1 = \$4
(B) 5½ + 2⅓ = 7⅚
(C) 5½ × 40¢ = \$2.20; 2⅓ × 60¢ = \$1.40 } → \$2.20 + \$1.40 = \$3.60 → \$5 − \$3.60 = \$1.40
(D) 5½ + 2⅓ = 7⅚ → \$1 + 7⅚ = \$7.83
40¢ + 60¢ = \$1
(E) 5½ × 40¢ = \$2.20; 2¾ × 60¢ = \$1.65 } → \$2.20 + \$1.65 = \$3.85 → \$5 − \$3.85 = \$1.15

Use the problem stated below to answer item 49.

Problem: Two of the cash registers in a grocery store contain a total of \$740. If you shift \$45 from the first register to the second, the two registers then contain equal amounts.

49. Which question(s) could be answered using this information?

I. How much money is in each register before the money is shifted?
II. How much money is in each register after the money is shifted?
III. How many cash registers are there in the grocery store?

(A) I only
(B) I and II only
(C) II only
(D) III only
(E) I, II and III

Use the problem stated below to answer item 50.

Problem: Julie's Juice Joint is open 7 days per week and sells an average of 1400 glasses of freshly squeezed orange juice per week. Each week, 1050 pounds of oranges and 9500 pounds of grapefruits are used. Julie bought 750 pounds of oranges on Wednesday. How many days supply is this?

50. To solve this problem, you need to know:

I. Julie's Juice Joint is open 7 days a week.
II. 1400 glasses of orange juice are sold each week.
III. 1050 pounds of oranges are used each week.
IV. 950 pounds of grapefruit are used each week.
V. 750 pounds of oranges were bought one day.

(A) I, II, and III only
(B) I, II, III, and IV only
(C) I, III, and V only.
(D) I, II, III, and V only.
(E) I, II, III, IV, and V.

Writing

Directions: You will have 60 minutes to write an essay on each of the following two topics. Try to spend approximately 30 minutes on each topic, as they are of equal value in the evaluation. While quantity is not as important as quality, the topics selected will probably require an essay rather than just a paragraph or two. Organization is an integral part of effective writing, so you may want to use some of the allotted time to plan your work. Support your ideas with clear, specific examples or explanations. Write legibly, and do not skip lines.

First Topic:

Research studies on effective teaching usually demonstrate that it is the teacher that "makes the difference," but it has been difficult to identify specific qualities that are evident in a "good" teacher. Discuss qualities which you think an effective teacher should have.

Second Topic:

At one time or another, everyone has an experience that did not turn out as expected. Describe one such experience you have had and how it affected you.

ANSWER KEY

Reading

1. D	11. E	21. E	31. C	41. C
2. B	12. B	22. A	32. B	42. A
3. B	13. B	23. C	33. C	43. C
4. B	14. D	24. A	34. D	44. B
5. E	15. B	25. E	35. B	45. D
6. B	16. C	26. B	36. B	46. C
7. D	17. E	27. C	37. E	47. C
8. B	18. B	28. A	38. A	48. C
9. C	19. B	29. E	39. A	49. A
10. D	20. C	30. D	40. B	50. C

Mathematics

1. D	11. B	21. A	31. E	41. E
2. C	12. C	22. B	32. B	42. A
3. D	13. B	23. D	33. C	43. B
4. D	14. D	24. B	34. A	44. C
5. C	15. E	25. C	35. D	45. E
6. B	16. C	26. D	36. E	46. E
7. A	17. A	27. A	37. C	47. D
8. C	18. A	28. C	38. D	48. C
9. C	19. D	29. D	39. E	49. B
10. D	20. E	30. E	40. B	50. C

ANALYSIS OF ERRORS

The following table lists the subject matter covered in each question of the Reading and Mathematics sections of the test. Find the question numbers that you got wrong and review the subject matter covered in those questions again.

SECTION	QUESTION NUMBERS	SUBJECT AREA
READING	4, 5, 14, 31, 37, 39, 44, 47	Finding the Main Idea
	3, 6, 12, 15, 16, 19, 27, 41, 43, 44, 48, 49	Finding Specific Details
	1, 2, 9, 10, 11, 13, 17, 20, 23, 28, 29, 30, 32, 34, 35, 38, 39, 40, 45, 46, 50	Finding Implications
	13, 21, 36, 42	Determining the Meaning of Strange Words
	18, 22, 33	Determining Special Techniques
	7, 8, 24, 25, 26	Interpreting Tables and Graphs

SECTION	QUESTION NUMBERS	SUBJECT AREA
MATHEMATICS	2, 5, 10	Whole Numbers (IA)
Arithmetic	1, 6, 13, 18	Fractions (IB)
	3, 4, 16	Decimals (IC)
	9, 20	Percentage (ID)
		Rounding Off Numbers (IE)
	11, 31	Signed Numbers (IF)
	8	Averages, Medians, Ranges, and Modes (IG)
		Powers, Exponents, and Roots (IH)
Algebra	23, 24, 25, 26	Algebraic Expressions (IIA)
	27, 29, 42	Equations (IIB)
	14, 19, 21, 22, 23, 41, 45, 46, 47, 48, 49, 50	Verbal Problems (IIC)
	12, 15	Counting Problems (IID)
	7, 30	Ratio and Proportion (IIE)
		Sequence and Progression (IIF)
	19	Inequalities (IIG)
Geometry		Angles (IIIA)
		Lines (IIIB)
	33	Polygons (IIIC)
	35	Triangles (IIID)
	38	Quadrilaterals (IIIE)
	28	Circles (IIIF)
	32, 37, 39, 40	Area, Perimeter, and Volume (IIIG)
	17, 34	Coordinate Geometry (IIIH)
Formulas		Formulas

ANSWER EXPLANATIONS

Reading

1. D The author suggests that the development of the scientific attitude works well in a democratic government.

2. B In this passage, the author does not acknowledge that the need for expediency may prevent the idealistic use of procedures guided by a scientific attitude.

3. B The writer defines an overregularization as the inflection of an irregular verb ("come") with a regular verb ending ("-ed") (instead of saying "came").

4. B The author wishes to make the point that children are analyzing the language they hear and figuring out the rules, as evidenced by their over-application of the rules. The author infers no judgment on teaching techniques, so E would be a wrong answer. A is true but is not a main point. C and D are inaccurate.

5. E The author suggests that television can focus on personality factors and divert attention away from the real issues. Polls (A) are never mentioned; B and C are too general, and D introduces a new aspect.
6. B The nature of the medium, focusing attention on appearance, style, voice, and manner, leads the viewer away from the contemplation of ideas. A is inaccurate.
7. D Counting carefully, from dot to dot, the times the line goes down, one should get six.
8. B It is necessary to follow very carefully up from 1950 and straight across. It is about 82%.
9. C The author writes with admiration of Alice Roosevelt's free-spirited attitude.
10. D Since the author speaks of the "newspaper-reading public," and her activities are clearly ones that would draw attention, reporters would enjoy writing about her. B, C, and E are not mentioned in the passage, and A is portrayed as secondary to how interesting she was.
11. E The author expresses the confidence that the growth of plants has gone on and will continue on nature's schedule. B is an exaggeration of the feelings the author displays.
12. B The growth of plants occurs with such regularity over time that it is compared to marks on a calendar.
13. B The writer implies in line 4 that communication problems are factors outside of the immediate task, an example of "indirect processes."
14. D The purpose is merely to discuss group dynamics and how factors interact to affect the workings of a group.
15. B The passage explains the differences in terms of quality, using terms like coherence, frequency, size, etc.
16. C The writer distinguishes laser from ordinary light on the basis of "coherence," a quality of the former.
17. E All of the other possibilities could be predicted from the uses mentioned in the passage.
18. B The use of the terms, "scratch" and "gem," bring to mind the laser's use in cutting diamonds.
19. B The principal advantage of tax shelters is in tax deductions, but the author points out that profits also can be made. The other answers contradict points made by the author.
20. C The author refers to tax shelters in a way that implies that they all permit tax deductions.
21. E From the context, as the author suggests that profits accrued should be reinvested, it is clear that "accumulate" is the best definition.
22. A The comparison suggests that technology must "fly on"; as the needs of society increase, so must technology's answers to the questions that arise with society's increasing complexity.
23. C The author implies that science must go forward to find ever-new technologies so that civilization is not left without resources.
24. A As displayed in the symbolic dollar on the left, Employment Taxes, at 29¢ per dollar, is second only to Individual Income Taxes.
25. E If 8.0¢ from the defense budget is added to the 8.6¢ allocated to the health budget, the result is 16.6¢.
26. B Income from employment taxes is 29¢ and national defense spending is 28.8¢, the closest of all the answers given.
27. C The author states in the first sentence that the reverse is the case.
28. A The author implies that even those accidents where mechanical failure is involved could be attributed to psychological factors since the driver often knows about the car's defects.
29. E This sentence fits the style and situation of the passage best. A is incorrect from the description of his position; B and C do not fit the style nor one's predictions of what might happen; the passage does not convey the impression that he would act (D) like this or, in fact, that there are teammates.
30. D Since the passage describes practice, planning, and judges' decision, it seems clear that it is a competition. While a competition may be a "trial" to some extent, D is the clearer answer.
31. C The *main* point is that the large population increase is due to economic factors.

32. B The writer is suggesting that, without an efficient exchange of goods, preserving the human race is difficult, if not impossible. Political considerations (A and C) and communication (E) are not mentioned. Economic growth is part of trade in this passage, so (D) is not the best answer.

33. C The author's main point is that writers largely try to remain aloof from the world and, therefore, allow critics to sneak in while they're not watching.

34. D The author describes literary critics as the villains who attack the poor unsuspecting writer. A and B would best fit the author's description of writers; C his view of writers' subject matter; and E is not appropriate.

35. B The writer is in favor of a liberal education, while an opponent would favor a more practical course of study in business, science, law, or the like. Answers A, D and E advocate courses of study more or less consistent with the author's view. Answer C is irrelevant.

36. B By definition, a "pedant" is one who is pretentious about his learning. In addition, paired as it is with "snob," answers A and C would be inconsistent with its meaning. D and E are inaccurate.

37. E The author supports a liberal education because of the knowledge that it provides, not because of the air of snobbery which some may use it to create.

38. A The passage could be part of a written debate, and the author is arguing his case.

39. A The writer's main point is that one must and does learn more than just the basic structures of a language; he must know how to use the language. It must be learned, so B is wrong. C and D are too general, and E may be true but is not mentioned in the passage.

40. B The topic is primarily language, how and why it is developed in people.

41. C The writer does, in fact, report that psychologists suggest the possibility of emotional damage.

42. A Antipathy means aversion, and the passage suggests that parents and teachers have a strong negative reaction.

43. C Measures of dispersion are mentioned in the passage as ones which indicate where the scores are grouped, near or far away from the center.

44. B The passage emphasizes the need to know more than raw scores in order to understand a group's performance.

45. D The author is trying to encourage others to respond to their penchants for writing.

46. C "These" refers to "feeling, sensation, emotion, idea," and the sentence explains the value of and reward for putting words on paper.

47. C Although the passage mentions world status, the primary focus is on the decline of the U.S. position and reasons for it.

48. C As the writer indicates in lines 7-12, there is no shortage of explanations offered for the decline in U.S. status.

49. A The author describes the U.S. status and reasons for it, but does not include any statistics supporting it.

50. C The author is presenting background facts on the general progress and history of American education. Subjects B and D are not directly on the subject; E is too general; A is defeating the author's purpose by showing limits to public education.

Mathematics

1. D Multiplying N by a number smaller than 1 will always give a product smaller than N whereas multiplying by a number larger than 1 will give a product larger than N.

In choices A, B, and C, N is multiplied by 1 or by a number larger than 1. In choice E, $N \div \frac{3}{4} = N \times \frac{4}{3}$, so the product is larger than N. Only in choice D is N multiplied by a number smaller than 1.

2. C The standard order of operations is (from left to right)

1. Multiplications and divisions
2. Additions and subtractions

Therefore,

$$\begin{aligned} 3 + 5 \times 6 - 4 \div 2 &= 3 + (5 \times 6) - (4 \div 2) \\ &= 3 + 30 - 2 \\ &= 33 - 2 \\ &= 31 \end{aligned}$$

3. D A is five thousand two hundred eighty.
B is five thousand and two hundred eight thousandths.
C is five thousand two hundred and eight hundredths.

4. D The places are:

thousands	(3)
hundreds	(4)
tens	(5)
ones	(7)
tenths	(6)
hundredths	(8)
thousandths	(2)

5. C Clearly, A, B, and D are all too large to give 324 when multiplied by themselves. The only possible correct answer listed is 18. And, in fact $18 \times 18 = 324$.

6. B C ($\frac{4}{7}$) and E ($\frac{2}{3}$) are both larger than $\frac{1}{2}$. B ($\frac{3}{7}$) is larger than A ($\frac{2}{7}$), thus closer than $\frac{1}{2}$. Thus, we need only to compare B ($\frac{3}{7}$) and D ($\frac{1}{3}$) and to choose the larger. A common denominator for these two is 21.

$$\frac{3}{7} \times \frac{3}{3} = \frac{9}{21} \qquad \frac{1}{3} \times \frac{7}{7} = \frac{7}{21}$$

$$\frac{9}{21} > \frac{7}{21}, \text{ so } \frac{3}{7} > \frac{1}{3}$$

7. A Let N = number of night workers
$N = (\frac{1}{4})(320) = 80$
Thus, the total number of workers is: $320 + 80 = 400$
The ratio of day workers to total workers $= \frac{320}{400}$

8. C (yes) I. $\dfrac{x + (x + 1) + (x + 2)}{3}$

$$= \frac{3x + 3}{3} = \frac{3(x + 1)}{3} = x + 1$$

(yes) II. $\dfrac{x + (x + 2) + (x + 4)}{3}$

$$= \frac{3x + 6}{3} = \frac{3(x + 2)}{3} = x + 2$$

(no) III. $\dfrac{x + (x + 1) + (x + 3)}{3}$

$$= \frac{3x + 4}{3} = \frac{3(x + \frac{4}{3})}{3} = x + \frac{4}{3}$$

(no) IV. $\dfrac{x + (x + 2) + (x + 4) + (x + 6)}{4}$

$$= \frac{4x + 12}{4} = \frac{4(x + 3)}{4} = x + 3$$

9. C The team lost 25% or $\frac{1}{4}$ of its games ($25\% = \frac{25}{100} = \frac{1}{4}$). So they must have won $\frac{3}{4}$ of their games. In other words, they won three times as many games as they lost. They won 18 games. So $\frac{18}{3} =$ the number of games lost. They lost 6 games.

10. D Each of the choices has product 360. We need to find the one which consists entirely of prime numbers (numbers whose only factors are themselves and 1).

In A neither 10 nor 36 is prime.

$(10 = 2 \times 5), (36 = 6 \times 6)$

In B 9 is not prime. $(9 = 3 \times 3)$

In C neither 8 nor 9 is prime.

$(8 = 2 \times 4), (9 = 3 \times 3)$

In D all the factors are prime.

11. B $(\frac{1}{3} - 1) \times \square = 1$

$-\frac{2}{3} \times \square = 1$

$-\frac{2}{3} \times -\frac{3}{2} = \frac{6}{6} = 1$

12. C Sally has $2 \times 5 = 10$ blouse-skirt combinations, and 3 dresses. So she has $10 + 3 = 13$ different outfits.

13. B Since $\frac{2}{3}$ of the yard is mowed, $\frac{1}{3}$ remains to be done. So, $\frac{1}{3} \times 225 = 75$ square meters remains to be done. If 25 square meters can be done in 5 minutes, then 75 square meters can be done in $15(3 \times 5)$ minutes.

14. D It is easiest here to simply examine the choices. None of A, B, or C is less than 50. Choice D (44) satisfies all the given criteria (more than 30, less than 50, sum of digits $(4 + 4)$ is 8).

15. E The answer is $3 + 2 + 1 = 6$. Imagine telling children what order they will play in. The first child must be assigned a time to play each of the other 3 children. The second child needs only 2 assignments (because she already has an assignment for child number 1). The third child already is scheduled to play children #1 and #2, so needs only 1 assignment. The fourth child's schedule is fully determined by the arrangements already made.

16. C $\$1.08 \times 12.5 = \$13.50$

17. A Make a table containing several ordered pairs which satisfy the equation $y = x^2 + 2$.

x	y
-2	6
-1	3
0	2
1	3
2	6

Check which of the graphs contain all the points in your table.

18. A $\frac{1}{5}$ was used Saturday. (So, $1 - \frac{1}{5} = \frac{4}{5}$ remained.) Half of the remainder was drunk, so the other half of the remainder still remains. In other words, $\frac{1}{2} \times \frac{4}{5} = \frac{4}{10} = \frac{2}{5}$ still remains.

19. D Rather than using algebra, it is easiest to examine the choices here.

(A) If 3 is the greater, then 2 is the lesser.
Is $3 \times 2 < 2 \times 3$? NO $(6 = 6)$

(B) If 6 is the greater, then 5 is the lesser.
Is $3 \times 5 < 2 \times 6$? NO $(15 > 12)$

(C) If 4 is the greater, then 3 is the lesser.
Is $3 \times 3 < 2 \times 4$? NO $(9 > 8)$

(D) If 2 is the greater, then 1 is the lesser.
Is $3 \times 1 < 2 \times 2$? YES $(3 < 4)$

20. E You save 20% of \$105.
$105 × 20% = $21

21. A Martha needed \$1800. In ten weeks she made $10 \times 54 =$ \$540 in tips. Since \$1800 − \$540 = \$1260, she needed to make \$1260 in wages. She was paid \$3.50 per hour (take-home pay). So she needed to work \$1260 ÷ 3.50 = 360 hours to have enough money for the car.

22. B Given: gumballs are 5¢ each (g)
stickers are 8¢ each (s)
Total George spent was 60¢
$5 \times g + 8 \times s = 60$

Analyzing this equation we realize that if we substitute an odd number of gumballs in the equation, $5 \times g$ will be odd, so $8 \times s$ will have to be odd. But this is impossible since 8 is even. This means the number of gumballs will necessarily have to be even. The only choice is, thus, choice B.

23. D

$$y \cdot \frac{x}{y} = y + y$$
$$x = y^2$$
$$\sqrt{x} = y$$

24. B

$$y/x = 14$$
$$x/1 = 1/14$$

Since $y = y$, then

$$x/1 = 1/2y$$
$$x = 1/2y$$

25. C If you recognize this expression as the "difference of squares" $x^2 - a^2$, you may recall that $x^2 - a^2 = (x - a)(x + a)$. Thus $x^2 - 16 = (x - 4)(x + 4)$. If you do not recall this relationship multiply out each choice.

26. D Given: $x = 3$

Substituting: $5(3) - 2(3)$
$= 15 - 2(9)$
$= 15 - 18$
$= -3$

27. A

$$3x - 5 = 2$$
$$3x = 7$$
$$x = 7/3$$

Then $x - 1/3 = 7/3 - 1/3 = 6/3 = 2$

28. C $C = 2 \cdot \pi \cdot R$

$$\frac{C}{2 \cdot \pi} = \frac{2 \cdot \pi \cdot R}{2 \cdot \pi}$$

$$R = \frac{C}{2 \cdot \pi}$$

29. D Substitute the value of x and y given in the table into each of the equations given. Choice D is the only equation which is true when each pair of values is substituted for x and y.

30. E $\frac{15}{45} = \frac{50}{x}$

Cross multiply: $15x = 45 \cdot 50$

and solve $x = \frac{45 \cdot 50}{15}$

$x = 150$

31. E m is negative.

n is positive and even.

I. $m \cdot n$ is negative and even.

II. $m - n$ is negative but not necessarily even.

III. $2 \cdot m$ is negative and even.

So, I and III are negative even numbers.

32. B The area of the base is the area of the circle of radius 5.

$A = \pi \cdot r^2$

$A = \pi \cdot (5)^2 = 25 \cdot \pi$

height $= 20$

volume $=$ area of base $\times$ height

volume $= 25 \cdot \pi \times 20 = 25 \times 20 \times \pi$

33. C Each angle of any regular pentagon measures 108°. The reason for this is that the pentagon can be divided into 3 triangles (180° each) totaling 540° (3 × 180°). Since the regular pentagon has 5 equal angles each one is 540 ÷ 5 = 108°.

34. A Since the lines MN and PQ are parallel their slopes are equal. So we set up the following proportions:

$$\frac{0 - (-3)}{5 - 0} = \frac{y - 2}{5 - 0}$$

Hence, $\frac{3}{5} = \frac{y - 2}{5}$

$5y - 10 = 15$

$5y = 25$

so $y = 5$

35. D The sum of the interior angles of the triangle is 180° ($A + B + C = 180°$). So angle BCA is $180° - (60° + 45°) = 75°$. So x, which is the supplement of angle BCA (together they form a straight angle of 180°) is $180° - 75° = 105°$.

36. E To determine the measures of the largest possible garden we imagine it taking up th entire page. In this case 8½ inches is equivalent to:

$(8\frac{1}{2}) \div \frac{1}{4} = \frac{17}{2} \times \frac{4}{1} = 34$ feet

11″ is equivalent to: $11 \div \frac{1}{4} = 11 \times \frac{4}{1} = 44$ feet. So the largest possible dimensions are 34 feet × 44 feet. I and III represent gardens with dimensions that fit on this paper, using the scale given.

37. C The area of the frame will be equal to the difference between the areas of the two rectangles indicated in the figure.
$(34 \times 16) - (30 \times 12) = 544 - 360 = 184$

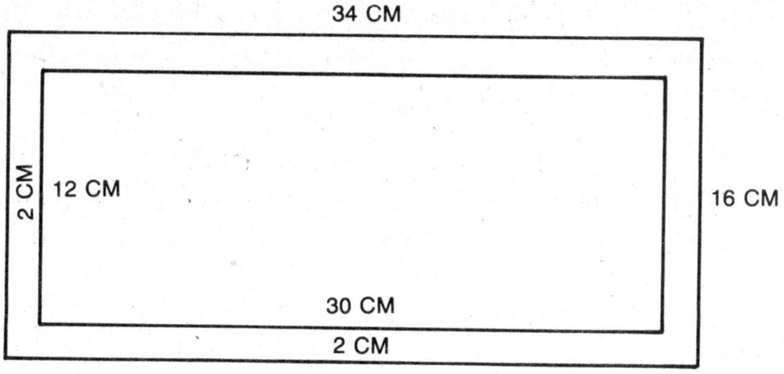

Area of the frame is 184 square centimeters.

38. D If both pairs of opposite sides are parallel then the measures of opposite sides must be the same. I and III are the only possibilities.

39. E The area of each small square is 16. This implies that the side of each small square is 4. Since the perimeter is the distance all the way around the figure,
perimeter $= 14 \times 4$
$= 56$

40. B Area of the square $= (\text{side})^2 = (3 \cdot \sqrt{\pi})^2 = 9 \cdot \pi$
Area of the circle $= \pi \cdot r^2 = 9 \cdot \pi$
$r^2 = 9 \cdot \pi/\pi$
$r^2 = 9$
$r = 3$

41. E Since Harry has only quarters and dimes the least he could have is one of each, which is equal to 35¢. Carrie's guess is unreasonable because it is less than the minimum Harry could have.

42. A Problem statement A is the only one that could be solved using the number sentence given. Suppose n is Mario's age. Three times Mario's age plus 2 years is equal to 35, which is his father's age, as indicated by the number sentence $3n + 2 = 35$.

43. B Diagram I is incorrect because it represents 17 students taking French and German but not Spanish.
Diagram II is correct.
Diagram III is incorrect because it represents the intersection of all three languages to be 0. If this is the case then we don't have enough students represented in the diagram. Since $37 + 9 + 17 + 60 + 3 + 22 < 152$.

44. C Determine an equation which represents the proportion: 8 is to \$.59 as an unknown amount is to \$1.00. The equation would be: $\frac{8}{59} = \frac{n}{100}$, which is choice C.

45. E The farmer needs to know the shape of the farm. However, if it were a triangle he would also need to know how the sides of the triangle were related. If it is a rectangle by knowing one side he can determine the other.

46. E Ruth drove 40 miles more than Jim. Jim drove twice as far as Peter. Peter drove 86 miles. The total distance is the sum of everyone's driving. The answer given of 126 miles is only Peter's and part of Ruth's distances driven. So answer E explains this error.

47. D The first thing you want to determine is how much would be paid for either the box seats or the grandstand seats.

48. C First, find the amount paid for the bell trim fabric:

$5\frac{1}{2} \times 40¢ = \frac{11}{2} \times 40¢ = \$2.20$

Second, find the amount paid for the lace:

$2\frac{1}{3} \times 60¢ = \frac{7}{3} \times 60¢ = \$1.40$

Finally, add the amount spent on both the lace and bell trim fabric and subtract from \$5.00.

$\$2.20 + \$1.40 = \$3.60$

$\$5.00 - \$3.60 = \$1.40$

Answer C has all these steps.

49. B There is no way to determine how many cash registers there are in the store, so choice III can be eliminated. Both I and II can be determined. (Let A and B be the amounts in the 2 registers at first. A + B = \$740 and A = B + \$45. Solving these 2 equations gives A = \$392.50, B = \$347.50.)

50. C She uses 1050 pounds of oranges in 1 week (7 days). This information will allow us to find the number of pounds used per day. Once this information is obtained, divide it into 750 pounds of oranges bought and determine how many days that is equivalent to. Answer C includes these 3 pieces of information.

Writing

The following essay outlines have been written to demonstrate the planning of well-written answers to the topics given. Use these only as guidelines to evaluating your own organization. Many different organization patterns and plans could work equally well for the topics given.

First Topic:

Research studies on effective teaching usually demonstrate that it is the teacher that "makes the difference," but it has been difficult to identify specific qualities that are evident in a "good" teacher. Discuss qualities which you think an effective teacher should have.

Essay Outline:

A. Introduction
   1. Give background information to lead in to the thesis, perhaps reiterating the point others have made that the teacher "makes the difference."
   2. Present thesis or point of view to be given in paper.

B. Effective qualities
   1. State each quality in clear, concise terms.
   2. Support each quality you suggest with a rationale and supporting details or examples from your own experience or that of others.

C. Summary and conclusions
   1. Restate in brief terms the main point made in the body of the paper.
   2. Suggest conclusions to draw, implications, or recommendations.

Second Topic:

At one time or another, everyone has an experience that did not turn out as expected. Describe one such experience you have had and how it affected you.

Essay Outline:

A. Introduction
   1. Give background information to provide setting for theme of paper.
   2. State theme of paper, i.e., the main idea or gist of the experience to be described.
B. Description of the experience
   1. Lead in to the description by setting the scene, giving the context.
   2. Continue the description with supporting details.
   3. Describe the effects on you produced by the experience.
C. Summary and conclusions
   1. Restate experience and effects in brief terms.
   2. State conclusions in the form of comparisons to other experiences, lessons learned, resolutions made, or recommendations.